LAW, LIBERTY, ANI

Law, Liberty, and Justice

The Legal Foundations of British Constitutionalism

T. R. S. ALLAN

CLARENDON PRESS · OXFORD

Oxford University Press, Walton Street, Oxford OX2 6DP
Oxford New York
Athens Auckland Bangkok Bombay
Calcutta Cape Town Dar es Salaam Delhi
Florence Hong Kong Istanbul Karachi
Kuala Lumpur Madras Madrid Melbourne
Mexico City Nairobi Paris Singapore
Taipei Tokyo Toronto
and associated companies in
Berlin Ibadan

Oxford is a trade mark of Oxford University Press

Published in the United States
by Oxford University Press Inc., New York

First published 1993
First issued new as paperback 1994

British Library Cataloguing in Publication Data
Data available

Library of Congress Cataloging in Publication Data
Allan, T. R. S. (Trevor R. S.)
Law, liberty, and justice: legal foundations of British constitutionalism / T. R. S. Allan.
p. cm.
Includes bibliographical references and index.
1. Great Britain—Constitutional law. 2. Rule of law—Great Britain. 3. Legislative power—Great Britain. I. Title.
KD3989 A75 1993 342.41—dc20 [344.102] 93–16308

ISBN 0–19–825253–6
ISBN 0–19–825991–3 (Pbk)

Printed in Great Britain
on acid-free paper by
Biddles Ltd, Guildford and Kings Lynn

To my parents
R. W. A. and P. D. A.

. . . even constitutions are based on, or presuppose, an underlying agreement on more fundamental principles—principles which may never have been explicitly expressed, yet which make possible and precede the consent and the written fundamental laws . . . Constitutionalism means that all power rests on the understanding that it will be exercised according to commonly accepted principles, that the persons on whom power is conferred are selected because it is thought that they are most likely to do what is right, not in order that whatever they do should be right.

F. A. Hayek, *The Constitution of Liberty* (London, 1960), 181.

Preface

I have attempted in this book to offer a more systematic account of some ideas about public law, developing the themes of previous essays. Its purpose is to challenge a number of traditional views and orthodox doctrines, by reflecting on interesting contemporary contributions to legal and political theory. In particular, the book seeks to alleviate the stranglehold which legal positivism has placed on modern constitutional law. In contesting the value of rigid distinctions between law and politics, or between legal doctrine and political principle, I hope also to narrow the customary gulf between public law and legal theory.

From a broader, more philosophical perspective, our familiar distinctions between constitutional and administrative law, or between 'high' constitutional law and the law relating to civil liberties, also come to seem unhelpful and even arbitrary—as do a number of other well-worn distinctions, like that between 'written' and 'unwritten' constitutions. By making the theoretical and ideological premisses of public law more explicit, we can understand the relevant connections more clearly. If the book thereby provokes opposition and controversy, it will serve its principal task of stimulating renewed debate in Britain about constitutional fundamentals.

In the spirit of my endeavour to fuse legal doctrine and legal theory, I have not allowed more abstract speculation to deflect me from detailed analysis of case-law, when that seemed appropriate and helpful. Nor have I sought to disguise my own critical standpoint, insisting that legal interpretation entails evaluation quite as much as description. The book unashamedly attempts a defence of the 'liberal variant of normativism' (see Martin Loughlin, *Public Law and Political Theory* (Oxford, 1992), 206–10).

Although I have drawn on previously published work, where that seemed most convenient, none of the chapters of the book has appeared elsewhere in its present form; and much of the argument is entirely new. I have, however, incorporated or adapted material from the following articles: 'The Limits of Parliamentary Sovereignty' [1985] *Public Law* 614; 'Law, Convention, Prerogative: Reflections Prompted by the Canadian Constitutional Case' [1986] *Cambridge Law Journal* 305; 'Pragmatism and Theory in Public Law' 104 *Law Quarterly Review* 422 (1988); 'Disclosure of Journalists' Sources, Civil Disobedience and the Rule of Law' [1991] *Cambridge Law Journal* 131; 'Constitutional Rights and Common Law' 11 *Oxford Journal of Legal Studies* 453 (1991); 'Justice and Fairness in Law's Empire' [1993] *Cambridge Law Journal* 64.

I gratefully acknowledge the useful advice and constructive criticism of friends and colleagues over a number of years; and Neil MacCormick, Michael Detmold, Robert McCorquodale, Susan Owens, Nicola Padfield, Nigel Simmonds, Tony Smith, and Sir David Williams have in particular provided recent help and encouragement, as has Richard Hart at Oxford University Press.

Completion of the book was made possible by the award of a British Academy/Leverhulme Trust Senior Research Fellowship, which relieved me of normal College and University duties in 1991–2.

T. R. S. ALLAN

Pembroke College, Cambridge
October 1992

Contents

Table of Cases

Australia

Canada

European Court of Human Rights

European Court of Justice

New Zealand

South Africa

United Kingdom (Including Privy Council Cases)

United States

Zimbabwe (Rhodesia)

1
British Constitutionalism

> Political . . . or civil, liberty, which is that of a member of society, is no other than natural liberty so far restrained by human laws (and no farther) as is necessary and expedient for the general advantage of the publick. Hence we may collect that . . . every wanton and causeless restraint of the will of the subject, whether practiced by a monarch, a nobility, or a popular assembly, is a degree of tyranny . . . But then . . . that constitution or frame of government, that system of laws, is alone calculated to maintain civil liberty, which leaves the subject entire master of his own conduct, except in those points wherein the public good requires some direction or restraint.
>
> Sir William Blackstone, *Commentaries on the Laws of England*, i, ch. 1.

> In accordance with British jurisprudence no member of the executive can interfere with the liberty or property of a British subject except on the condition that he can support the legality of his action before a court of justice. And it is the tradition of British justice that judges should not shrink from deciding such issues in the face of the executive.
>
> *Eshugbayi Eleko* v. *Government of Nigeria* [1931] AC 662, 670 (Lord Atkin).

Contemporary public law is rife with strange notions. And many of these result from taking Blackstone and Dicey rather too literally, overlooking the core of good sense in their writings beneath some more questionable dogmas. Potentially the most serious of these dogmas—and the most awesome—is that of parliamentary sovereignty. Notwithstanding his reflections on the nature of tyranny, Blackstone followed Coke in asserting the 'transcendent and absolute' power of Parliament, relegating any idea of a breach of the legislative 'trust', reposed in the legislature by the people, to the realm of political theory, devoid of practical legal significance.[1] A. V. Dicey, of course, followed suit and established the modern orthodoxy.[2]

As if the idea of unbounded legislative supremacy—unlimited not merely as a matter of practical politics but even as a matter of legal principle—were not bad enough, British constitutional lawyers have also generally repudiated the doctrine of the separation of powers. It

[1] *Commentaries*, 15th edn. (London, 1809), i. 160–2.
[2] *The Law of the Constitution*, 10th edn. (London, 1959; first published in 1885), Part 1.

has never been made clear quite how their hostility to this (arguably) fundamental feature of constitutional government is consistent with the claim that the executive, if not the legislature, is subject to legal control.[3] Perhaps, as has been recently suggested, some form of the separation of powers is only a matter of convention, rather than law. But then the confusion is surely compounded. Dicey's dogmatic distinction between law and convention, for all its continuing influence on public lawyers, is only another manifestation of the positivist outlook responsible for the rule of parliamentary omnipotence.[4]

The stark separation of legal rule from political principle, which the law–convention dichotomy reflects, is ultimately incoherent. It is certainly not compatible with a developing system of administrative law, which involves the courts in making judgments about the fairness and reasonableness of the actions of public authorities. What is fair and reasonable—or what is *unfair* and *unreasonable*—can hardly be determined in deliberate disregard of political practice, and the settled expectations which may have arisen on the basis of it.[5] Nor can such judgments be made in abstraction from the wider constitutional landscape within which public agency and individual citizen interact. Legal rule, that is to say, cannot be isolated from political principle, even if it would suit positivist legal theory.

This book will attempt to defend a different Dicey—the constitutional theorist struggling to escape the shackles of the Hobbesian authoritarianism he learned from Austin.[6] Dicey's doctrine of the rule of law, with its emphasis on equality and civil liberties, seems a better starting point than parliamentary sovereignty.[7] We shall seek to understand the constitutional doctrine as a reflection of, and intimately associated with, the underlying political ideal of the rule of law. No doubt, the great complexity of that ideal, as well as continuing philosophical controversy about both its nature and importance, explain the relative neglect of Dicey's doctrine, by comparison with his other principles. The practical lawyer's distrust of theory and desire for clear-cut rules is understandable. If, then, Dicey's work laid the foundations of a theory of British constitutionalism, little work has yet been done to build a viable structure by developing his conception of the rule of law. It may

[3] See further Ch. 3, below.
[4] This distinction is considered in Ch. 10.
[5] For the doctrine of legitimate expectation and principle of fairness, see Ch. 8.
[6] Dicey discusses John Austin's work in *Law of the Constitution*, 71–6, distinguishing legal from political sovereignty. For a similar analysis, showing conflicting influences on Dicey's thought, see Martin Loughlin, *Public Law and Political Theory* (Oxford, 1992), 140–59.
[7] *Law of the Constitution*, Part 2.

now be necessary, however, to cloud the purity of 'legal science' by rather more abstract speculation.[8]

In striving to explain the meaning of the rule of law as a constitutional principle, and to explore its implications for British public law, this book is inevitably something of a mixture of public law and legal and political theory. Since public law involves fundamental questions about the distribution of power and the relations between citizen and state, it is hard to see how else it could be written. It is certainly my view that there is no useful division between constitutional law and constitutional theory. That view explains the ubiquity of such magisterial figures as F. A. Hayek and Ronald Dworkin, amongst other writers more briefly noticed.[9] There are, of course, many differences between the conceptions of liberalism such writers espouse, and none can be accepted uncritically. If a constitutional lawyer is not bound slavishly to follow a single theorist, however, or embrace one set of ideas to the exclusion of every other, he must nevertheless acknowledge the profound influence which Dicey's writings still exert on contemporary perceptions of the subject. Hayek and Dworkin each assist us, in different ways, to extract the core of good sense in Dicey's discussion, and to adapt his insights to the demands of modern constitutionalism.

Hayek's work is of value to the legal theorist because it clarifies so much of the philosophical basis of liberal constitutionalism. In particular, it provides an account of the separation of powers which, although only an ideal to which we might aspire, is none the less unrivalled in elegance and clarity. I shall invoke Hayek's thought in defence of my view of the central importance of the separation of powers to the political ideal of the rule of law. Dicey neglected the separation of powers largely, it seems, because he associated it with French *droit administratif*, and the exemption of officials from the jurisdiction of the ordinary courts which that implied. The resuscitation of his rule of law doctrine, however, requires us to make good that deficiency.

A system of government which depends on the close co-operation of executive and legislature, and even permits the former to dominate the latter, as a matter of practical politics, seems superficially to flout the separation of powers. It certainly violates any 'pure' model of that doctrine, as it might be conceived by a political scientist for the purpose of describing or classifying constitutional forms. Dicey, however, was

[8] Dicey followed Austin's 'scientific' approach to legal analysis: see Loughlin, *Public Law and Political Theory*, 13–23.

[9] See esp. F. A. Hayek, *The Constitution of Liberty* (Chicago, 1960), and *Law, Legislation and Liberty* (London, 1982); Ronald Dworkin, *Taking Rights Seriously* (London, 1977), *A Matter of Principle* (Oxford, 1985), and *Law's Empire* (London, 1986). For discussion of the role of theory in public law, see also P. P. Craig, *Public Law and Democracy in the United Kingdom and the United States of America* (Oxford, 1990), ch. 1.

intent on expounding the constitution as a matter of law, expressly distinguishing his task from both history and political science.[10] And as a matter of legal theory, his principle of the rule of law is hardly comprehensible without some appropriate conception of separation of powers. If the executive were not subordinate to the existing law in some sense in which the legislature is not, Dicey's account of the equality of all before the law, including public officials, could make no sense.

The common law constitution

In the absence of a higher 'constitutional' law, proclaimed in a written Constitution and venerated as a source of unique legal authority, the rule of law serves in Britain as a form of constitution. It is in this fundamental sense that Britain has a *common law constitution*: the ideas and values of which the rule of law consists are reflected and embedded in the ordinary common law. If important liberties are given protection, and standards of justice and fairness accepted and upheld, it is ultimately because—and largely to the extent that—they find expression in the common law. The great influence of Dicey's *Law of the Constitution* rested mainly on his firm grasp of this fundamental idea. He was careful to juxtapose the principle of parliamentary sovereignty with that of the rule of law, even if his attempt to reconcile the two has hardly met with universal acclaim. The rule of law meant essentially the rule of common law, supplemented by statutes, which 'being passed to meet special grievances, bear a close resemblance to judicial decisions, and are in effect judgments pronounced by the High Court of Parliament'.[11]

The central role of the common law in the constitutional scheme placed unique responsibility on the shoulders of the judges of the ordinary courts. If in those Continental countries which possessed written constitutions, individual rights were 'deductions drawn from the principles of the constitution', in England by contrast the principles of the constitution were 'inductions or generalisations based upon particular decisions pronounced by the courts as to the rights of given individuals'.[12] Dicey avoided the mistake of supposing that individual liberties could not be as well (or perhaps better) protected with a constitutional declaration of rights: he noted that the rule of law was as marked a feature of the United States as of England. But he was right to emphasize the inherent strength of common law adjudication as a

[10] *Law of the Constitution*, 1–35, 'The True Nature of Constitutional Law'.
[11] Ibid. 197. [12] Ibid. 197–8.

basis of protection: a common law right is intrinsically related to the means of its enforcement.

Dicey's account of the plainly subordinate role played by statute in the constitutional order now looks strange. We are accustomed to the use of legislation to achieve major programmes of social reform, and to the modern practice of granting extensive powers to government ministers to implement their policies by issuing rules, orders, and directions. Indeed, Dicey's other generalizations about the rule of law have had to be qualified in consequence. We can no longer accept, without reservation, his assertion that the rule of law excluded 'the existence of arbitrariness, of prerogative, or even of wide discretionary authority on the part of the government'.[13] If arbitrariness is excluded, and prerogative controlled, it is only because English law has belatedly developed a body of 'administrative law', which seems superficially to contradict Dicey's emphasis on 'legal equality' between official and ordinary citizen—the 'universal subjection of all classes to one law administered by the ordinary courts'.[14]

However, this familiar criticism can be overdone. Dicey's rejection of 'administrative law' has been misunderstood. What he opposed was the *exemption* of officials from the constraints of the ordinary law, which he took to be the chief characteristic of *droit administratif*. His claim that every official was amenable to the jurisdiction of the ordinary courts accurately asserted the basic constitutional position. The modern law of judicial review testifies to the truth of his observation that disputes involving the government were not in England beyond the jurisdiction of the ordinary civil courts: that (French) idea was 'fundamentally inconsistent with our traditions and customs'.[15]

Dicey's insistence on equality before the law, and the universal role of the ordinary courts, was consistent with his view that the constitution was the result of the ordinary law of the land—of private law, as it applied to the activities of public officials as well as private citizens. The underlying conception of constitutionalism here is precisely the one Hayek's work exemplifies. The rule of law entails the subjection of government to the law—rule by law as opposed to politicians or public officials—in the sense of its being bound to comply with 'rules of just conduct', which regulate the ordinary relations between citizens, and which are independent of any particular purpose or policy, public or private.[16] Individual liberty is secured, and political oppression prevented, by denying government the power to violate these universal rules of just conduct in its relations with the governed.

The rule of law, in Hayek's account, requires a thoroughgoing

[13] Ibid. 202. [14] Ibid. 193. [15] Ibid. 203.
[16] Hayek, *Law, Legislation and Liberty*, i and ii.

separation of powers, which denies even the legislature the right to alter the law as it sees fit. A legislative assembly should exist to improve and supplement the existing corpus of rules of just conduct: it should not act, in the manner of a *governmental* body, to direct the performance of particular tasks or authorize, by changes in the general law, the pursuit of specific policies. Hayek distinguished between *nomos*—those rules of just conduct which have come to be accepted (by long usage) as the framework of social co-operation—and *theseis*, or those instructions which command the execution of particular tasks.[17] He considered that the principle of separation of powers had been subverted by confusing these different senses of 'law'. Instead of institutions charged with the function of enacting general rules of just conduct—changing the law, in the primary sense of that expression—modern legislatures had become merely representative assemblies chiefly occupied with directing or controlling *government*.[18]

The distinction between *nomos* and *theseis*, or between rules of just conduct and administrative 'measures', illuminates the distinction between law and policy which (I argue below[19]) is fundamental to an understanding of modern public law. In the sense of 'administrative powers over persons and property', administrative law entails the kinds of discriminations and discretion which the rule of law is supposed to inhibit.[20] It is only to the extent that public authorities are subject to the ordinary private law, in their dealings with the citizen, that the rule of law, in Hayek's illuminating conception of that ideal, truly exists as a safeguard against the suppression of liberty. It does little harm to the public lawyer's pride—and probably much good for his humility—to be reminded that a constitution 'is essentially a superstructure erected over a pre-existing system of law to organise the enforcement of that law'.[21] It is possible to exaggerate the 'particular dignity and fundamental character'[22] of constitutional law. As Hayek reminds us, and the doctrine of the primacy of European Community law perhaps affirms, even when the structure of government changes—or the location of 'sovereignty' alters—'most of the rules of just conduct, the civil and criminal law, will remain in force'.[23]

Nevertheless, we must acknowledge the peculiar inadequacies of Dicey's theory of the rule of law to the circumstances of the modern administrative state; and here Hayek—whose principal concern, of course, was to limit that state in the interests of liberty—will offer us little assistance. It is therefore part of the present project to offer an account of the separation of powers which accommodates the exercise of government power beyond the ordinary realm of private law. For

[17] Ibid. i. 126–8. [18] Ibid. 129–31. [19] Chs. 8–9.
[20] *Law, Legislation and Liberty*, i. 137–40.
[21] Ibid. 134. [22] Ibid. [23] Ibid. 135.

this purpose, we will take up the distinction between law and policy, suggested by Hayek's distinction between *nomos* and *theseis*, and argue that it explains the legitimacy of judicial review. Modern administrative law has recognized the need for general principles of law which, while they apply only to the 'public sphere', serve to constrain the exercise of administrative powers in the interests of justice or fairness to those most directly affected.[24]

I shall argue that Ronald Dworkin's account of the distinction between principle and policy makes a helpful contribution to the task of defining the nature and limits of public law.[25] Questions of principle are those which concern the scope and content of individual rights, as opposed to the general welfare or the public interest. Matters of public interest or public policy should be determined by the 'political' branches of government—executive or legislature. Questions of right, by contrast, are peculiarly the province of the courts. As counter-majoritarian entitlements, or 'trumps' over general utility or the public interest, the relative insulation of the judges from the ordinary political process ought to be especially conducive to their protection and enforcement.[26] I shall suggest that administrative law may be helpfully interpreted as a system of public law rights; and that the legitimate boundaries of judicial review may be found in the process of defining and enforcing those rights.[27] Issues of standing and justiciability may usefully be considered in the light of a rights-based approach to public law.

It will not be suggested, however, that Dworkin's distinction may be applied in any mechanical way, or that the division between principle and policy is always self-evident or uncontroversial.[28] Although the doctrine of legitimate expectation plainly amounts to the recognition of rights against the state, in the manner Dworkin's analysis would appear to commend, it may involve the court in detailed review of the general merits of an application for relief—a review which can scarcely escape an appraisal of the reasons given in justification of the administrative action in question. The doctrine expresses a principle of justice or fairness, which is ultimately dependent (I argue below[29]) on all the circumstances of the particular case. That seems an embarrassing

[24] For the different senses of 'administrative law' see Hayek, *Law, Legislation and Liberty*, i. 137–8. Cf. D. J. Galligan, 'Judicial Review and the Textbook Writers' (1982) 2 OJLS 257 at 258. Definition of the 'public sphere' is subject to change in response to novel modes of exercising governmental (or quasi-governmental) power: see *Datafin* case [1987] QB 815.

[25] *Taking Rights Seriously*, ch. 4. See Ch. 3, below.

[26] Cf. Dworkin, *A Matter of Principle*, ch. 1.

[27] For analysis of the nature of legal interpretation, see Dworkin, *Law's Empire*, esp. ch. 2.

[28] For discussion, see *Taking Rights Seriously*, Appendix (Reply to Critics), and Marshall Cohen (ed.) *Ronald Dworkin and Contemporary Jurisprudence* (London, 1984), Part 2.

[29] Ch. 8.

conclusion, if it is correct, for the traditional theory of judicial review, which distinguishes sharply between the merits of a public agency's action or decision, on the one hand, and its legality, on the other.

Admittedly, the distinction between the merits of an action and its legality roughly reflects Dworkin's distinction between policy and principle—a correspondence which confirms the appropriateness of a Dworkinian analysis. While fundamental to the constitutional legitimacy of judicial review, however, the merits–legality dichotomy must be applied with sensitivity to particular cases. In particular, the traditional distinction between appeal and review—corresponding to that between the merits of an action and its legal validity—will in practice sometimes be only one of degree.[30]

If it were possible to identify and isolate a finite set of discrete public law rights, whose satisfaction ensured the legality of administrative action, the principle–policy dichotomy could perhaps be applied with greater precision. (Of course, controversy over the exact nature and scope of such rights would inevitably remain.) Reflection on the role of the courts as defenders of the ordinary citizen against abuse of executive power, however, indicates that no such set of rights could ever be exhaustive, even in principle. The circumstances of practical politics, and the infinite variety of (generally legitimate) public projects and purposes, suggest the need to acknowledge a more general, open-ended right to fair treatment at the hands of the state.

Many readers will instinctively recoil from a doctrine which places so much trust in the judges, apparently so dependent on the wise exercise of judicial power. It seems necessary, however, to match executive discretion with judicial discretion. The discretions are complementary, rather than opposed; and exercise of the latter, if not the former, must be fully reasoned and open to public scrutiny.[31] Modern government cannot be entirely conducted within the constraints of purpose-independent general rules. And the scope and style of judicial review—if it is to constitute a genuine protection from abuse of executive power—must reflect the discretionary nature of contemporary government.

It is also true that many legal commentators have doubted whether it is accurate, even if desirable, to ascribe to the courts a primary concern with rights in the public law field. In an interesting essay, for example, it was recently suggested that the dominant political theory in the House of Lords is a form of 'democratic élitism', coupled with an

[30] Ibid.

[31] Cf. Galligan, 'Judicial Review', 269–76; id., *Discretionary Powers* (Oxford, 1986), ch. 6. There is no general rule at common law requiring reasons to be given by public authorities, but see Ch. 8, below.

exaggerated deference to professional expertise.[32] This may be accompanied by a similar élitism in respect of judgments about the requirements of the law itself, as I argue in Chapter 5. In seeking to indicate a coherent theoretical grounding for administrative law, however, it is necessary to look beyond the idiosyncrasies and predilections of particular judges, even those in the highest court. As an interpretative exercise in political theory, our task must be one of evaluation, as much as description.[33] Moreover, we should recognize that theoretical analysis may contribute to constitutional change by affecting the style and categories of legal thought. It has been aptly observed that 'there can be no value-free facts about the British constitution'.[34] Legal analysis, then, must necessarily be creative: to analyse is to reinterpret and therefore—within reasonable limits—to re-create.

Nor should we expect the most persuasive account of the judicial function always to be readily apparent on the face of court judgments. If Lord Bridge's speech in the *Gillick* case[35] illustrates his adherence to 'democratic élitism', it may also be consistent with a broadly coherent conception of rights. It is hard to know whether Lord Scarman's contrasting speech comes closer to the 'ideal of accountability under law', enabling the application of 'legal principles of good administration',[36] unless we can make more explicit our theory of 'law'. Without an explanation of the legitimacy of judicial review, within a democratic polity, we cannot assess the respective merits of judicial 'activism' or passivity. A rights-based view may indeed reveal that Lord Scarman's approach serves only 'to substitute the view of a legal élite for that of a politically accountable political élite'.[37]

In the same way, one cannot defend an elastic conception of *locus standi*, on the basis of the public interest in keeping public agencies within the law, without further analysis of the rule of law. The problem of legitimacy in judicial review concerns precisely the nature of the courts' superior claim to determine the law. A conception of public law as protecting rights—individual entitlements which fetter the exercise of government power—may explain the court's ability to substitute its view of the applicable law for that of the public agency. We cannot escape the need for an explicit conception of the rule of law. In the absence of a normative theory of law—evaluative as well as descriptive—one can give no account of the real nature of judicial

[32] David Feldman, 'Public Law Values in the House of Lords' (1990) 106 LQR 246.
[33] Cf. Loughlin, *Public Law and Political Theory*, ch. 3.
[34] Ibid. 50.
[35] *Gillick* v. *W. Norfolk AHA* [1986] AC 112.
[36] Feldman, 'Public Law Values', 249–50.
[37] Ibid. 251.

review. Appeal to the 'rule of law' is empty rhetoric in the absence of further elaboration.

Chapters 6 to 9 below are devoted to a discussion of public law rights, in an attempt to give more substance to Dicey's doctrine of the rule of law. No doubt, the attempt marks only the start of an enterprise whose validity many will question. It none the less forms part of a broader endeavour to elicit the merits and advantages of traditional common law reasoning, and to demonstrate its potential for the renewal of British constitutionalism. Although the courts have been rightly condemned by many commentators and critics for failing to develop a public law which is adequate to contemporary needs, we should guard against the danger of identifying such failure with inherent weakness in the common law. As a constitutional framework for securing justice and fairness, the common law is self-evidently adaptable to new insights and fresh demands. In the absence of a radical 'new constitutional settlement',[38] but while absorbing the full implications of European Community membership, the common law must be developed with imagination to meet the needs of modern constitutionalism.

Common law and statute

The primacy Dicey accorded the common law reflects our basic constitutional arrangements much more closely than is usually understood. First, legislation obtains its force from the doctrine of parliamentary sovereignty, which is itself a creature of the common law and whose detailed content and limits are therefore matters of judicial law-making. (It could hardly, without circularity, be a doctrine based on statutory authority.) Parliament is sovereign because the judges acknowledge its legal and political supremacy; and the rule of implied repeal, whereby a later statute always abrogates an earlier one to the extent of any conflict, is a doctrine developed by the courts to preserve the supremacy of the contemporary legislature.

Secondly, for all its intrusive impact on the detailed content of the modern law—in almost all fields of government and public affairs—legislation is in one important sense inferior to judicial precedent as a source of constitutional law. (It is usually asserted that statute is the superior source because common law rules may be abrogated by statute.) The point here is not simply that a statute is always necessarily subject to judicial interpretation—a process inevitably dependent on common law standards and traditions. Dicey's attempted reconciliation of fundamental principles rested largely on this claim: 'Powers, however

[38] Cf. Sir Leslie Scarman, *English Law—The New Dimension*, Hamlyn Lectures, 26th series (London, 1974), 75.

extraordinary, which are conferred or sanctioned by statute, are never really unlimited, for they are confined by the words of the Act itself, and what is more, by the interpretation put upon the statute by the judges.'[39]

It is also the case that while the common law embodies many of the values traditionally associated with the rule of law, statute is necessarily more piecemeal and technical. It may supplement common law principles in specified classes of cases, or operate to overturn and defeat them (usually within fairly narrow boundaries). What it cannot do is displace the common law by providing a rival vision of the constitutional order. For that, if it is desired, we are largely dependent on developing the common law. Sir Owen Dixon's tribute to the common law as 'an ultimate constitutional foundation' rested primarily on that perception.[40] The form and method of modern legislation imposed real limitations on its content and scope: 'A rhetorical question may be enough to make this clear. Would it be within the capacity of a parliamentary draftsman to frame, for example, a provision replacing a deep-rooted legal doctrine with a new one?'[41]

Dicey's account is not as dated as it superficially appears. Statutes may, of course, be *interpreted* with the aim of achieving consistency of principle across a wide range of public affairs. But the criteria of interpretation can hardly be supplied wholly by statute. (Which principles are to be taken as fundamental when statutes seem to conflict?) Sir Owen Dixon's rhetorical question points us towards important limitations on legislation as a source of legal principle. The relationship between statute and common law has not generally been well understood, and we shall need to explore it in some detail.[42] It is of central importance to the account of British constitutionalism which I wish to advance.

The nature of the rule of law as a political ideal is illuminated by reflection on the theory of law defended by Ronald Dworkin in *Law's Empire*.[43] Dworkin's proposal that a judge should follow the guide of 'integrity' in his decisions echoes Dicey's emphasis on the role of general principles of law applied by the ordinary courts. Dicey, like Dworkin, was concerned with the overall coherence and unity of the legal order.[44] I shall argue, however, that Dworkin fails to distinguish sufficiently between the nature of the principal sources of law. Although his insistence on the close interdependence of law and morality is persuasive, his attempt to reconcile the conflicting requirements of

[39] *Law of the Constitution*, 413.
[40] 'The Common Law as an Ultimate Constitutional Foundation' (1957) 31 ALJ 240.
[41] Ibid. 241. [42] Ch. 4, below. [43] London, 1986.
[44] Cf. T. R. S. Allan, 'Dworkin and Dicey: The Rule of Law as Integrity' (1988) 8 OJLS 266.

political morality gives exaggerated weight to 'fairness' at the expense of 'justice'. I shall suggest that fairness—meaning here the appropriate distribution of political power—finds its constitutional expression in the enactment and application of statute. It has no relevance to adjudication at common law.[45]

None the less, Dworkin's vision of the legal order as an integrated whole, in which both common law and statute may be viewed as harmonious aspirations of a 'community of principle', makes an important contribution to an understanding of modern constitutionalism. In particular, we should accept his invitation to treat legislation as 'flowing from the community's present commitment to a background scheme of political morality'.[46] It would be mistaken, however, to understand this idea as a proposal to give equal weight to the requirements of legislation and common law, taken at face value and without regard to the nature of those requirements in the circumstances of particular cases. I shall argue instead that the common law embodies principles of equality and reasonableness, and traditional conceptions of individual rights, which—within appropriate limits—must govern the interpretation of statute.

P. S. Atiyah's study of the relation between common law and statute helps to identify the necessary qualifications to Dworkin's account of law as integrity.[47] Doubting the notion that legislation might be invoked as a source of analogy, where it was not directly applicable, he pointed out that, 'if statute law and common law really constituted one integral body of law, there seems no reason why our sovereign Parliament should not be able to declare the common law to be something different from what the judges say it is'.[48] He was inclined to think that 'most lawyers and even most parliamentarians would today think this improper, if not indeed in some sense conceptually impossible'. I shall seek to support those conclusions, contending that legislation is inherently incapable of displacing the common law as a body of legal principle, and defending the interpretative role of the courts as essential to the separation of powers and, therefore, to the rule of law.

At the heart of the rule of law ideal is a conception of adjudication which treats legislation as the outcome of a democratic process whose legitimacy is ultimately dependent on its respecting minimum standards of justice. A judge defers to the popular will, as represented by statutes duly enacted, because his conception of political morality includes (we may reasonably suppose) a commitment to democracy. But it is necessarily a qualified commitment. He would be unlikely, for example, to accept that the (existing) legal rights of individual litigants could be

[45] Ch. 4, below. [46] *Law's Empire*, 346.
[47] P. S. Atiyah, 'Common Law and Statute Law' (1985) 48 MLR 1.
[48] Ibid. 19.

determined, in cases of dispute, by popular opinion.[49] And the virtues of democracy will not persuade a judge—if he is rational—of the necessity to give automatic and unqualified allegiance to every parliamentary enactment, whatever its content. A wise judge will be reluctant to accept at face value legislation which violates important civil rights, and will strive to interpret it consistently with traditional (common law) values of individual liberty and autonomy.

Dworkin's ideal of integrity should therefore be placed in the context of well-established presumptions of legislative intent, which impose necessary, if limited, constraints on majoritarian government in the interests of liberty and equality, and in defence of individual rights and expectations. The requirements of those rights and interests are not immutable, and their content always vulnerable to fresh appraisal, but they are none the less fundamental to liberal democracy. The 'community of principle' which the legal order should seek to reflect is essentially dependent—in the British context—on the principles of justice embedded in the common law.

David Dyzenhaus has shown how the resources of the common law have provided certain, bolder judges in South Africa with the means of administering justice in the teeth of laws enforcing apartheid.[50] He ably defends the 'common law approach' of judges who, embracing an ideal of law akin to Dworkin's, have refused to co-operate with legislative policies which violate fundamental standards of justice and equality—except in so far as the clear terms of unambiguous legislation have left them no choice. Their stance is contrasted with that of 'plain fact judges'—an outlook bolstered by legal positivism[51]—who have given largely uncritical allegiance to the goals of repression and inequality which have undeniably informed the legislative process.

Dyzenhaus shows how some judges have sought to preserve the separation of powers by attributing to the legislature an underlying commitment to fundamental principles of justice consonant with common law values—a fiction fully justified by their conception of the legal order. Legislation is then viewed, not as a simple expression of the wishes of a majority of legislators—unrepresentative of the population as a whole—but as something to be reconciled, so far as possible, with

[49] For criticism of *Law's Empire* in this respect, see Ch. 4 below.

[50] *Hard Cases in Wicked Legal Systems: South African Law in the Perspective of Legal Philosophy* (Oxford, 1991).

[51] 'Plain fact judges hold that the judicial role is not to make law in accordance with their convictions about what morality requires, but to apply the law as it, on a particular conception of fact, exists . . . If it is obvious from the public record . . . how legislators responsible for enacting the statute would have wanted it interpreted, the judges' doctrine of judicial responsibility compels them—a matter of legal duty—to decide the case in accordance with that want' (ibid. 57–8). Dyzenhaus argues that, notwithstanding its notion of judicial 'discretion' in the absence of unambiguous law, positivism encourages the plain fact approach.

the values which underpin the rule of law. In refusing to relinquish the court's jurisdiction to protect detainees from illegal detention, or to acknowledge any greater deprivation of legal rights than is explicitly enacted, such judges work to 'make statutes cohere with the fundamental purposes or ideals of their legal system, which are expressed in the common law'.[52]

The study of administrative law in modern South Africa is complemented by an instructive analysis of *Liversidge* v. *Anderson*.[53] Dyzenhaus explains how, as in the decisions of the South African Appellate Division, divergent styles of interpretation produced very different reactions to radical departures from common law principles. For the majority in *Liversidge* the extraordinary nature of the powers of detention conferred on the Home Secretary, and the perceived requirements of national security in time of war, weakened the relevance of traditional modes of interpretation. Echoing Lord Finlay LC's refusal, in 1917, to apply a presumption in favour of liberty to an executive measure intended to avert a 'public danger',[54] the majority thought that the immediate context of the Emergency Powers (Defence) Act 1939 justified a purposive construction of Defence Regulation 18B in the interests of national security.[55] It followed that the minister's decision to detain a man without trial, on the basis of his 'hostile origin or association', was not subject to judicial control. There could 'plainly be no presumption applicable to a regulation made under this extraordinary power that the liberty of the person in question will not be interfered with, and equally no presumption that the detention must not be made to depend . . . on the unchallengeable opinion of the Secretary of State'.[56]

When, in his forceful dissent, Lord Atkin insisted that the regulation's requirement of 'reasonable cause' for the minister's order invited judicial scrutiny, he took the unusual nature of the legislation as justification for especial vigilance in defence of individual liberty. His famous restatement of common law orthodoxy—that 'the judges are no respecters of persons and stand between the subject and any attempted encroachment on his liberty by the executive, alert to see that any coercive action is justified in law'[57]—was grounded in an understanding of the moral complexity of the interpretative process. Drastic invasions of liberty call for more urgent appraisal as a necessary check on the operation of legislation which is clearly capable of producing great injustice and suffering. And if that is a political judgment, it is also

[52] Ibid. 119. [53] [1942] AC 206.

[54] *R.* v. *Halliday, ex p. Zadig* [1917] AC 260, 270.

[55] Reg. 18B provided: 'If the Secretary of State has reasonable cause to believe any person to be of hostile origin or associations . . . and that by reason thereof it is necessary to exercise control over him, he may make an order against that person directing that he be detained.'

[56] [1942] AC 206, 219 (Lord Maugham). [57] Ibid. 244.

a legal one—entailed by judicial responsibility under an adequate conception of the rule of law.

Lord Atkin's outspoken rebuke to the majority for being 'more executive minded than the executive'—a rebuke vindicated by subsequent cases[58]—obtained its authority from his grasp of the fundamental nature of ordinary common law reasoning from established principle. Where legislative intention is too readily identified with the immediate purposes of government or parliamentary majorities—even broadly representative majorities—judicial co-operation with the statutory purpose can undermine rather than uphold the rule of law. As Dyzenhaus explains the point, on Lord Atkin's approach, 'Parliament's intentions are best seen as a construct of reasoning in accordance with common law principles'.[59] For Lord Atkin, then, 'the common law interpretative context is the master over legal meaning'.[60]

In the result, the dissenting speech in *Liversidge* v. *Anderson* is a fine illustration of adjudication in the common law tradition, which enables judges to control the executive by interpreting statutes in accordance with the 'rule and reason of the common law'.[61] They employ the 'principles of critical morality protective of . . . liberty already embedded in the law'.[62] Sir Edward Coke's maxim was rightly applauded by C. K. Allen as an 'essential guiding rule', which ensured the continuity of legal development, adjusting the impact of new measures to fit the broader constitutional scheme. In Allen's view, it was a 'dominant principle' that 'the common law is wider and more fundamental than statute' and that 'wherever possible, legislative enactments should be construed in harmony with established common law principles rather than in antagonism to them'.[63]

It is, of course, often suggested that the traditional precedence given to common law values is inconsistent with a modern, progressive legal order, in which legislation deserves enhanced respect. I shall argue, none the less, that the common law is a constantly evolving apparatus for protecting basic values. It is inherently open to changing perceptions of the requirements of justice and the demands of basic principle. It follows that the content of the common law is ultimately a matter of reason. If the common law is primarily constituted by general principles, moreover, it follows that lawyers' perceptions of justice have no unique authority.[64] Principles cannot be imposed by authority but must be

[58] See *Ridge* v. *Baldwin* [1963] 2 All ER 66, 76; *R.* v. *IRC, ex p. Rossminster* [1980] AC 952, 1011, 1024–5.

[59] *Hard Cases*, 95.

[60] Ibid.

[61] Sir Edward Coke: 'The surest construction of a statute is by the rule and reason of the common law' (cited by C. K. Allen, *Law in the Making* (Oxford, 1978), 456).

[62] Dyzenhaus, *Hard Cases*, 94.

[63] *Law in the Making* (Oxford, 1978), 456.

[64] Here I part company with Coke's conception of the common law as 'artificial reason': see *Prohibitions del Roy* (1607) 12 Co. Rep. 63.

argued for and *understood*. The common law constitution therefore enshrines a 'protestant' conception of the rule of law, which might usefully be understood as a continuing process of argument about the requirements of justice and reason—a process in which every citizen should be encouraged to participate as an integral part of conscientious citizenship.[65]

The legacy of legal positivism

Dicey's failure to provide a consistent and coherent theory of the constitution was mainly attributable to his adherence to Austinian legal positivism. It was ultimately impossible to reconcile his emphasis on the rule of law with the unlimited sovereignty of Parliament. If there are truly no limits to legislative supremacy, common law rights and liberties can always be overridden. An insistence on there being a source of ultimate political authority, which is free from all legal restraint and from which every legal rule derives its validity, is incompatible with constitutionalism. It envisages the legitimate exercise of absolute power, albeit according to constitutional forms, regardless of its consequences for established rights or settled expectations. According to F. A. Hayek, 'the whole history of constitutionalism, at least since John Locke . . . is that of a struggle against the positivist conception of sovereignty and the allied conception of the omnipotent state'.[66]

Dicey's conception of legislative supremacy has become so ingrained amongst English lawyers—Scots lawyers have wisely been more cautious—that it is hard to question his doctrine without appearing to lose touch with practical reality. Until very recently, it was almost unthinkable that the courts would ever refuse to apply an Act of Parliament; and attempts to indicate necessary exceptions to the doctrine were understandably thought to be somewhat unreal, addressing 'improbable extremes'.[67] But Dicey's positivist assumptions—and those of his adherents—have skewed our wider constitutional vision, and the confused condition of contemporary theory seems to be the consequence.

It is a question of the nature of public law and the legitimacy of the judicial function. If all authority ultimately derives from Parliament, on the ground of its connections to the electorate, even the interpretative function must be seriously constrained. If judicial review must be

[65] This theme is taken up in Ch. 5. Dworkin defends a 'protestant' conception: *Law's Empire*, 413. Cf. Dyzenhaus, *Hard Cases*, 267: 'The conception of the common law advanced . . . is a conception of a process. The process is one such that the law remains an arena for participation in a public debate about what law is after the primary legislative decisions in the arena of parliamentary politics have been made.'

[66] *Law, Legislation and Liberty*, ii. 61.

[67] Simon Lee, Comment on Allan, 'Limits of Parliamentary Sovereignty' [1985] PL 632.

understood—as standard explanations would have it—as essentially a means of ensuring compliance with the legislative will, the traditional role of the courts in defence of individual rights is undermined. Inevitably, it comes to appear an illegitimate usurpation of political power, because individual rights—if they are genuine—necessarily inhibit the freedom of majorities or governments to enforce their will.

The truth seems to be that there is no straightforward or objective distinction between the *application* of statutes and their *interpretation*. A restrictive interpretation of statute, in defence of individual rights, necessarily limits the field of its operation; and the *most* restrictive construction may reduce it to practical impotence. The *legitimacy* of such interpretative approaches to duly enacted legislation is obviously a question of great importance and lively controversy. The point remains, however, that the traditional role of the common law in defence of justice and liberty—as those ideals have been understood—is radically inconsistent with a notion of unlimited legislative supremacy. The interpretative function itself denies that the only source of legal authority is Parliament, even in respect of statute; or at least entails that, in the course of applying statutory injunctions to particular cases, the legislative will must be tempered with (judicial) reason.[68]

Other writers have drawn attention to the 'pragmatic contradiction' in the work of Dicey and his contemporary disciples.[69] It is particularly plain in Sir William Wade's critique of the judicial attitude to privative clauses, which seek to oust the court's jurisdiction in obvious violation of the rule of law doctrine. On the one hand, the judges are described as 'disobeying' Parliament in service of a higher constitutional mandate; on the other, unlimited legislative supremacy is not denied. Wade therefore seems to claim that 'judges act in violation of legal norms both when they disobey Parliament's will, as he conceives it, and when they do not'.[70] What is missing here is an account of the constitutional basis of judicial 'disobedience'.

D. J. Galligan has sought to distinguish between two judicial functions.[71] The courts must both settle jurisdictional, or 'demarcation', disputes, keeping public authorities within their allotted spheres of action, and ensure the observance of principles of good administration by such authorities in exercising their powers. While the former function may be dependent on dutiful adherence to the legislative mandate, the latter must be independently justified: 'the primary source of principles

[68] For interesting analysis of this dichotomy, see M. J. Detmold, 'Law as Practical Reason' [1989] CLJ 436; id., *The Australian Commonwealth* (Sydney, 1985), ch. 13.

[69] Cf. Dyzenhaus, *Hard Cases*, 236–8. See also Geoffrey de Q. Walker, *The Rule of Law, Foundation of Constitutional Democracy* (Melbourne, 1988), ch. 4.

[70] Dyzenhaus, *Hard Cases*, 238.

[71] 'Judicial Review and the Textbook Writers' (1982) 2 OJLS 257 at 261–3.

of good administration lies beyond Parliament, and their justification depends on values in the constitutional order that precede the doctrine of sovereignty'.[72] In practice, these different functions are likely to be closely related and intertwined. If principles of good administration are ultimately dependent, as I shall suggest, on underlying convictions about justice and fairness, their application will be sensitive to the nature of official action and its impact on individual interests. Those considerations will inevitably affect the court's view of the legitimate scope of an agency's jurisdiction, and the appropriate construction of its statutory grant of power.[73]

It follows that the court's adherence to legislative supremacy must, if rational, be a qualified one. On some questions Parliament must have full authority. It is not the courts' function to formulate conceptions of the public interest in opposition to legislative requirements. In supervising the execution of public policy in particular cases, however, the judicial function must rely on constitutional principles which are accepted for their intrinsic value, and not because they have legislative approval—unless such approval is purely notional, and therefore mainly fictitious. It is therefore worth contesting the scope of parliamentary sovereignty, not merely on account of the ultimate contradiction between unlimited legislative supremacy and constitutional government, but also because by taking Dicey's doctrine literally public lawyers have confused the nature of public law.[74]

Lon Fuller repudiated the notion of parliamentary omnicompetence in the course of his critique of legal positivism.[75] Like the conception of the legal order as a hierarchical system of rules or commands, which positivism assumed, Dicey's theory mistook the structure of legal authority for the nature of law itself. Dicey's observation that retrospective laws—Acts of Indemnity—'being as it were the legalisation of illegality', were the 'highest exertion and crowning proof of sovereign power',[76] demonstrated a strange detachment from the realities of constitutional government. His doctrine of sovereignty derived from theories of law which displayed a 'fatal abstraction from the enterprise of creating and administering a system of rules for the control of human conduct'.[77]

[72] Ibid. 262.

[73] Galligan accepts that the two functions are related, noting the 'blurring' of the distinction in cases like *Anisminic* [1969] 2 AC 147: ibid. 262–3.

[74] Cf. Geoffrey de Q. Walker, 'Dicey's Dubious Dogma of Parliamentary Sovereignty: A Recent Fray with Freedom of Religion' (1985) 59 ALJ 276 at 283–4: 'It seems that Dicey's theory is like some huge, ugly Victorian monument that dominates the legal and constitutional landscape and exerts a hypnotic effect on legal perception.' See further id., *The Rule of Law*, ch. 5.

[75] *The Morality of Law*, revised edn. (New Haven, Conn. and London, 1969), 113–17.

[76] *Law of the Constitution*, 50.

[77] *The Morality of Law*, 115.

F. A. Hayek made a similar point in contesting the positivist thesis that both validity and content of law derive ultimately from the will of a legislator.[78] Hayek considered that legal positivism, which denied any necessary connection between law and justice, and emphasized the dependence of the content of law on the choice of the law-giver, was founded on a 'constructivist fallacy'. Ignoring the possibilities of spontaneous social order, positivism wrongly assumed that all law was the deliberate product of somebody's will.[79] A legislator who wishes to maintain a functioning legal order cannot pick and choose any rules he likes, and thereby confer validity on them: 'His power is not unlimited because it rests on the fact that some of the rules which he makes enforceable are regarded as right by the citizens, and the acceptance by him of these rules necessarily limits his powers of making other rules enforceable.'[80]

Fuller adds to his analysis an appropriate contribution to the tradition of testing assertions of legislative supremacy which are 'extreme to the point of absurdity' by 'illustrations that are equally absurd'.[81] The best justification for that tradition, however, is that such illustrations may help to bring more familiar and mundane uncertainties and tensions into high relief. It is the philosophic unity of the practical problems of the interpretation and application of statutes, and of legal and political theory, which precludes analysis which eschews the worst eventualities. The thesis is that the deference due to the parliamentary will is necessarily a qualified one, and its interpretation in particular cases rightly sensitive to the requirements of justice and fairness. The 'practical lawyer's' objection to testing the limits of sovereignty—that the content of law is always subject in the last resort to the exercise of political power—assumes the unqualified, uncritical deference to statutes which better political theory condemns.

[78] *Law, Legislation and Liberty*, ii. 61.

[79] Ibid. i. 28–9.

[80] Ibid. ii. 61.

[81] *The Morality of Law*, 117. Fuller denies that Parliament could enact secret laws, or assign its powers to a dictator, and provides a colourful example of an 'invalid' statute: 'At some point we take leave of the gravitational field within which the distinction between law and not-law makes sense.' That point would be reached, he thought, 'far short' of his illustrations of invalidity.

2
The Rule of Law

> For all the power the government has, being only for the good of the society, as it ought not to be arbitrary and at pleasure, so it ought to be exercised by established and promulgated laws, that both the people may know their duty, and be safe and secure within the limits of the law, and the rulers, too, kept within their due bounds . . .
>
> John Locke, *Two Treatises of Government*, ii, para. 137.

Contrary to orthodox opinion, A. V. Dicey was wise to seek an interpretation of the rule of law which reflected the traditions and peculiarities of English common law.[1] Whatever its faults, Dicey's work recognized the importance of expounding a constitutional philosophy, which could serve as a basis for the systematic exposition and consistent development of legal principle. More recent efforts to give analytical precision to the concept of the rule of law have not always been wholly successful; and constitutional law—at least in Britain—has perhaps been weakened in consequence, because its foundations have come to seem uncertain and insecure. Many public lawyers have apparently abandoned even the attempt to understand and restate the rule of law doctrine, thinking it futile and unrewarding.[2]

At the heart of the problem lies the difficulty of articulating a coherent doctrine which resists a purely formal conception of legality—according to which even brutal decrees of a dictator, if formally 'valid', meet the requirements of the rule of law—without instead propounding a complete political and social philosophy.[3] The formal conception, which serves only to distinguish the commands of the government in power (whatever their content) from those of anyone else, offers little of value to the constitutional theorist. And the richer seams of political theory—ideal versions of justice in the liberal, constitutional state—are inevitably

[1] *The Law of the Constitution*, 10th edn. (London, 1959).

[2] Cf. R. W. Blackburn, 'Dicey and the Teaching of Public Law' [1985] PL 679 at 692–3.

[3] Cf. Joseph Raz, 'The Rule of Law and its Virtue' (1977) 93 LQR 195 at 195–6. The final resolution of the Delhi Congress of the International Commission of Jurists (1959) declared the rule of law to be a dynamic concept 'which should be employed not only to safeguard and advance the civil and political rights of the individual in a free society, but also to establish social, economic, educational and cultural conditions under which his legitimate aspirations and dignity may be realised'. See generally Norman S. Marsh, 'The Rule of Law as a Supra-National Concept', in A. G. Guest (ed.), *Oxford Essays in Jurisprudence*, first series (Oxford, 1961), 223.

too ambitious (because too controversial) to provide a secure basis for practical analysis. The constitutional theorist who wishes to offer an interpretation of legal and political practice must necessarily focus on existing institutions; and the contribution of ideal theory, which may recommend quite different arrangements, is therefore likely to be limited.[4]

It seems very doubtful whether it is possible to formulate a theory of the rule of law of universal validity—which might serve as a model for all legal systems (or even all the Western democracies) and at the same time escape the opposite extremes of formal legality and substantive interpretations of justice.[5] But it does not follow that we cannot seek to elaborate the meaning and content of the rule of law within the context of the British polity—exploring the legal foundations of constitutionalism in the setting of contingent political institutions.[6] That was, of course, Dicey's purpose in *The Law of the Constitution*; and—though on a grander, more abstract scale—also Ronald Dworkin's, whose work largely eschews ideal theory in favour of analysis based on existing legal institutions and grounded in established political principle.[7]

In the mouth of a British constitutional lawyer, the term 'rule of law' seems to mean primarily a corpus of basic principles and values, which together lend some stability and coherence to the legal order. It expresses his commitment to a scheme of ideas regarded as legally fundamental. They help to define the nature of the constitution, reflecting constitutional history and generating expectations about the conduct and character of modern government. The rule of law is an amalgam of standards, expectations, and aspirations: it encompasses traditional ideas about individual liberty and natural justice, and, more generally, ideas about the requirements of justice and fairness in the relations between government and governed. Nor can substantive and procedural fairness be easily distinguished: each is premissed on respect for the dignity of the individual person; and the content of justice or fairness (procedure and substance) is inevitably dependent—to a degree—on the circumstances of the particular case. Allegiance to the rule of law is not, therefore, a technical (or even 'lawyerly') commitment: it is necess-

[4] But see discussion of the general concept of the rule of law below.

[5] See, however, the instructive discussion by Geoffrey de Q. Walker, *The Rule of Law, Foundation of Constitutional Democracy* (Melbourne, 1988), esp. ch. 1.

[6] For a useful discussion, see Jeffrey Jowell, 'The Rule of Law Today', in Jeffrey Jowell and Dawn Oliver (eds.), *The Changing Constitution*, 2nd edn. (Oxford, 1989), 3. See also Ian Harden and Norman Lewis, *The Noble Lie: The British Constitution and the Rule of Law* (London, 1986).

[7] Ronald Dworkin, *Taking Rights Seriously* (London, 1977); *A Matter of Principle* (Oxford, 1985); *Law's Empire* (London, 1986). For previous comparison between Dworkin and Dicey, see Neil MacCormick, 'Jurisprudence and the Constitution' [1983] *Current Legal Problems* 13; T. R. S. Allan, 'Dworkin and Dicey: The Rule of Law as Integrity' (1988) 8 OJLS 266.

arily allegiance to a political philosophy—albeit a practical philosophy grounded in existing constitutional tradition.

The idea of the rule of law is also inextricably linked with certain basic institutional arrangements. The fundamental notion of equality, which lies close to the heart of our convictions about justice and fairness, demands an equal voice for all adult citizens in the legislative process: universal suffrage may today be taken to be a central strand of the rule of law. There is also a commitment implied to some form of the principle of separation of powers. A legal order constructed on British constitutional lines necessitates a division of institutional competence between legislature, executive, and judiciary. A government which could make laws at its own pleasure, and determine the extent of its own infractions of the laws, would not be a government under the rule of law.[8]

Political ideal and juridical principle

We shall, then, seek an interpretation of the rule of law which reflects the idea of constitutional government as it pertains (primarily) to the British polity. However, we can learn much about its content by examining the concept in its more abstract guise—as a general political ideal—and noticing some of the strengths and weaknesses of contemporary discussion. Even the most formal, and perhaps least controversial, interpretation may be seen to contain the seeds of a richer account, whose expanded meaning must be sought, concretely, in the basic principles of a particular legal system.

The idea of the rule of law, in contradistinction to rule by men, is an ancient one.[9] At its core is the conviction that law provides the means of protecting each citizen from the arbitrary will of others—including the most powerful. By being constrained to govern by means of general laws, the political rulers of society cannot single out particular persons for special treatment. The law is to constitute a bulwark between governors and governed, shielding the individual from hostile discrimination on the part of those with political power. The idea is that 'when we obey laws, in the sense of general abstract rules laid down irrespective of their application to us, we are not subject to another man's will and are therefore free'.[10] In this most general form the doctrine expresses a political ideal, and the extent to which any political society

[8] See generally Ch. 3, below.

[9] See e.g. Aristotle, *Politics*, III (trans. Jowett, ed. Davis), 16: 'The rule of law is preferable to that of any individual.' The idea finds its clearest expression in medieval political theory. See A. P. d'Entreves, *The Notion of the State* (Oxford, 1967), Part 2.

[10] F. A. Hayek, *The Constitution of Liberty* (London, 1960), 153. Cf. J. R. Lucas, *The Principles of Politics* (Oxford, 1966), 113.

can claim conformity to it must inevitably be a matter of degree. In particular, the greater the extent of government involvement in social affairs and economic management, the greater correspondingly is the need for discrimination between individuals and groups by means of more particular rules.[11]

Joseph Raz explains that the ideal of government by law and not by men makes sense only if 'law' means general, open, and relatively stable law.[12] We cannot escape the necessity for more particular laws and regulations, but the making of such laws should be guided by relatively stable, published, general rules. On Raz's account, however, the doctrine is only a formal one: its various precepts derive from the basic idea that the law must be capable of guiding the behaviour of its subjects. The rule of law, on this view, plays an essentially procedural role, governing the *manner* in which government may pursue its ends. It does not place substantive limits on the content of the law. None the less, there is at least an indirect connection with ideas of generality and neutrality. Even the formal doctrine imposes important constraints on arbitrary power. The government is prevented from changing the law retrospectively or abruptly or secretly whenever that would suit its purposes; and possibilities for abuse of power are greatly reduced if executive powers must be exercised within the limits of general rules.

But since the rule of law, in Raz's view, is only one virtue which a legal system might possess, its importance should not be exaggerated. Like a sharp knife, the rule of law is morally neutral—an efficient instrument for good purposes, or wicked:

> It is not to be confused with democracy, justice, equality (before the law or otherwise), human rights of any kind or respect for persons or for the dignity of man. A non-democratic legal system, based on the denial of human rights, on extensive poverty, on racial segregation, sexual inequalities and religious persecution may, in principle, conform to the requirements of the Rule of Law better than any of the legal systems of the more enlightened western democracies.[13]

Lon Fuller had attempted a rather more ambitious interpretation, seeking to show a necessary connection between legality and justice. He expounded eight canons of legality, which were essential features of what he termed the 'inner morality of law': a total failure to respect any one of these canons would result in failure to achieve anything that could properly be called a legal system.[14] The enterprise of govern-

[11] For a powerful defence of the political ideal, and comment on the perceived dangers of government social and economic management, see esp. F. A. Hayek, *The Road to Serfdom* (London, 1944).

[12] 'The Rule of Law and its Virtue' (1977) 93 LQR 195 at 197.

[13] Ibid. 196.

[14] Lon F. Fuller, *The Morality of Law*, revised edn. (New Haven, Conn., 1969), ch. 2.

ment according to law was intimately associated with a moral view of the relation between citizen and state. With a drastic failure of legality, government by law inevitably degenerated into the exercise of a 'lawless unlimited power'—expressing a brutal disregard for human rights.

The first requirement was generality: there must be general rules, as opposed to deciding every issue on an *ad hoc* basis. The rules must be published; they must be clear and comprehensible; the rules should not be contradictory; nor should they require the impossible—laws creating a strict criminal liability were the gravest infringement, serving the convenience of the prosecutor at the expense of justice. Laws should be prospective: retrospective laws must be exceptional, employed to correct lapses in other requirements of the law's internal morality. The precept *nulla poena sine lege* was generally respected by civilized nations: 'It is the retroactive criminal statute that calls most directly to mind the brutal absurdity of commanding a man today to do something yesterday.'[15] There must be constancy of law through time, in the sense that too frequent changes in the rules render obedience impossible. Finally, there must be congruence between official action and the law: there should be no discrepancy between the law as declared and as actually administered. The law concerning, *inter alia*, procedural due process, habeas corpus, rights of appeal and standing dealt with the requirements of this principle of legality.[16]

Like Raz, many philosophers have questioned the connection between legality and justice, insisting that the rule of law merely enhances the ability of law to achieve its purposes, whatever these are. There is, however, an implicit assumption here that the law consists only in rules directed at the attainment of particular purposes—essentially governmental purposes. Raz's denial of the overriding importance of the rule of law,[17] and his attempt to sever its content from the values of justice and equality, alike reflect the serious limitations of legal positivism, which views every law as a species of 'command'. If the law were largely a mechanism for the execution of government objectives, it would be right to accept his contention that the rule of law was only a 'negative' virtue,[18] restraining government from certain kinds of arbitrary rule.

But this perspective overlooks the fundamental role of law as constituting a stable *framework* of rules, which enables everyone to pursue his own aims in reasonable confidence about the likely conduct of others. In ensuring the regular and consistent application of the ordinary private law, including the criminal law, the rule of law makes possible a free society in which each person, while respecting the constraints

[15] Ibid. 59. [16] Ibid. 81.
[17] 'The Rule of Law', 195. [18] Ibid. 206.

which the rules impose on all, has equal opportunity—in so far as the law can provide it—to further his own ends. The rule of law therefore serves to promote and protect legitimate expectations, which in turn provide a basis for individual planning and action.

Hayek explained that *the law*, as it features in the idea of the rule of law or government under law, as well as in the real meaning of the separation of powers, should be understood as those abstract rules which derive from the articulation of previously existing practices and understandings.[19] In particular, the English common law was not *commanded* by anyone: it evolved from custom and was adapted in response to changing circumstances, requiring the judges to announce 'new' rules which sought merely to resolve ambiguities and inconsistencies within the existing law. These abstract rules are not, then, primarily the product of deliberate legislation and do not serve the purposes of government, but rather form a basis for the successful pursuit of countless purposes of different individuals: 'The law will consist of purpose-independent rules which govern the conduct of individuals towards each other, are intended to apply to an unknown number of further instances, and by defining a protected domain of each, enable an order of actions to form itself wherein the individuals can make feasible plans.'[20]

The rule of law ensures equality in the fundamental sense that it is only the consistent application of the ordinary law to every person—including public officials, in the absence of special powers, specifically conferred—which preserves the functioning legal order necessary for everyone to act freely in his own interests, while respecting the same freedom in others. Hayek's work establishes an important connection between legality and justice. Justice may be understood primarily as entitlement to the benefits conferred by the application of those general rules which constitute a functioning legal order. Of course, those rules should broadly reflect people's expectations about the sort of conduct which is generally appropriate in different circumstances. And they must be abstract and general, applying equally to everyone in the same situation. Understood in this way, justice is secured by adherence to the rule of law.[21]

A similar connection is made by John Rawls, who identifies the failure of judges and other officials to apply the appropriate rules, or to interpret them correctly, as a form of injustice.[22] The regular and impartial administration of public rules provides a basis for both individual liberty and social co-operation:

[19] F. A. Hayek, *Law, Legislation and Liberty* (London, 1982), i, chs. 4, 5.
[20] Ibid. 85–6; see also esp. 112–22.
[21] Ibid., ch. 8.
[22] *A Theory of Justice* (Oxford, 1972).

A legal system is a coercive order of public rules addressed to rational persons for the purpose of regulating their conduct and providing the framework for social co-operation. When these rules are just they establish a basis for legitimate expectations. They constitute grounds upon which persons can rely on one another and rightly object when their expectations are not fulfilled.[23]

Rawls proceeds to derive the precepts of 'formal' justice—or canons of legality—from this conception of a legal system. As these precepts are weakened, so the system degenerates into a 'collection of particular orders designed to advance the interests of a dictator or the ideal of a benevolent despot'.[24] The rule of law implies the precept that similar cases be treated similarly. Even if the criteria of similarity are provided by the legal rules themselves, the precept is not vacuous. It significantly limits the discretion of judges and officials, forcing them to justify the distinctions made between persons by reference to the relevant rules and principles.[25]

Inevitably, constitutional lawyers are more concerned with the exercise of governmental authority, in the sense of political power, than with the administration of the ordinary private law. And it may be thought that Raz's conception of the rule of law is an adequate model for the purposes of public law. However, the continuing controversy over Fuller's claims seems to reflect different assumptions about the purposes of political philosophy, and about the nature of the connection between legal theory and legal practice. Fuller's discussion contained a powerful critique of positivism, which he thought was preoccupied with matters of labelling and accurate definition, at the expense of the practical elaboration of morality and justice. He complained that positivism sought a 'conceptual model' of law-making in artificial abstraction from social reality. Analytical legal positivism lacked a social dimension. Perceptively, Fuller insisted on placing enquiries about the definition of law within a purposive context, reflecting the underlying point of the rule of law.[26]

Raz's formal conception achieves precision and coherence at the price of a somewhat impractical detachment. It describes an ideal to which any particular legal system should aspire, and by which it may be broadly evaluated. The constitutional theorist, however, needs a more practical conception which can serve as a truly *juridical* doctrine, providing a basis for adjudication as well as a model for legislation. A judge could not easily adopt Raz's view that conformity to the rule of law was merely a 'matter of degree', and that a lesser conformity is

[23] Ibid. 235. [24] Ibid. 236. [25] Ibid. 237.

[26] Hayek also condemned as unrealistic the notion of a 'science of norms': the compatibility of different norms could not be ascertained in isolation from facts because abstract rules of conduct determine particular actions only in the light of factual circumstances: *Law, Legislation and Liberty*, i. 105–6.

often preferable to the failure of conflicting social goals.[27] The public lawyer needs a broader and richer theory which explains the widely accepted view that, for the judge, there can be no compromise with the rule of law.

Even if the formal conception has advantages of definitional certainty and clarity for the political philosopher, it is too jejune to inform the practice of adjudication. A judge is bound to have constant regard to its underlying rationale, and the values which that rationale implies. These values, in turn, will have important implications for the substantive content of law. Although Raz denies that it has any bearing on political freedom, in the sense of freedom from governmental interference, he observes that the rule of law provides the foundation for the legal respect for human dignity. Respecting human dignity entails treating people as persons capable of planning and plotting their future. A legal system which observes the rule of law meets this requirement in the sense of attempting to guide people's behaviour by affecting their deliberations about what to do, thereby respecting their rationality and autonomy.

Here Raz seems to follow Fuller, who argued that every departure from the rule of law was an affront to man's dignity as a responsible agent: 'To judge his actions by unpublished or retrospective laws, or to order him to do an act that is impossible, is to convey to him your indifference to his powers of self-determination.'[28] And in defence of Fuller, John Finnis, while warning that the rule of law does not guarantee every aspect of the 'common good', has denied that it should be viewed as morally neutral. Fuller's discussion should be understood as asserting a connection between the inner morality of law and substantive justice, in the sense that a tyrant holds in contempt the very values of reciprocity, fairness, and respect for persons which constitute the rational point of the rule of law:

> The idea of the rule of law is based on the notion that a certain quality of interaction between ruler and ruled, involving reciprocity and procedural fairness, is very *valuable for its own sake*; it is not merely a means to other social ends, and they may not lightly be sacrificed for such other ends.[29]

Now, a judge who seeks to uphold the rule of law—like the constitutional theorist who wishes to explore its implications—cannot rest content with a purely descriptive analysis. Necessarily he must interpret its demands in particular cases, determining the practical content of each of the precepts of formal justice, and seeking to resolve conflicts between them in the manner which best respects the underlying point

[27] 'The Rule of Law', 210–11.
[28] *The Morality of Law*, 162.
[29] *Natural Law and Natural Rights* (Oxford, 1980), 273–4 (emphasis added).

of the rule of law. Fuller denied the possibility of a utopia of legality, in which all his desiderata were fully satisfied. In practice, they would sometimes conflict, requiring a resolution sensitive to the fundamental idea of reciprocity—akin to a contract between citizen and State. Even in seeking to reconcile conflicting requirements of the formal doctrine, then, we must have resort to underlying substantive values, and these will be rightly considered themselves part of the rule of law by constitutional lawyers. They will indicate what a court *should* decide in a case where the formal doctrine provides no answer.

The judge is therefore driven by the nature of his office, as the constitutional theorist is directed by the nature of *his* enterprise, to seek the full meaning of the rule of law in those fundamental legal values of personal dignity and autonomy, which explain our adherence to the precepts of formal justice. We are, then, bound to move beyond the purely formal conception of legality, to seek a broader political theory, which explains the legitimacy of judicial activity in defence of the rule of law, understood as embracing both form and substance.

The limitations of the formal interpretation of the rule of law reflect a more pervasive problem with legal positivism itself. As a theoretical, descriptive philosophy, legal positivism can give no account of the practical activity of adjudication. It draws arbitrary lines between legal rules and underlying principles—as though in deciding between competing interpretations of the law, in the event of dispute, the judge is not in any significant sense constrained by law at all. Such distortions of legal analysis are reflected, as we shall see, in those untenable doctrines (propounded by Dicey) which place an artificial barrier between law and convention, and insist on the absolute sovereignty of Parliament. The formal interpretation of the rule of law, resisting a substantive dimension, is ultimately consonant only with that irredeemably theoretical perspective.[30]

Legality and equity

The principles of natural justice find a place even within a formal doctrine of the rule of law: the requirements of a fair and open hearing and the absence of bias are recognized as essential for the correct application of the law. 'These are guidelines intended to preserve the integrity of the judicial process . . . The precepts of natural justice are to insure that the legal order will be impartially and regularly maintained.'[31] The modern law of procedural fairness, however, demonstrates the

[30] See Chs. 10 and 11, below. For the theoretical nature of legal positivism, see M. J. Detmold, *The Australian Commonwealth* (Sydney, 1985), ch. 14.

[31] Rawls, *A Theory of Justice*, 238–9. Cf. Raz, 'The Rule of Law', 201.

practical necessity of developing the rule of law more broadly. Where discretionary powers are granted to public authorities, the correct application of the law involves more than the efficient operation of legal rules. It requires an exercise of discretion which is sensitive to the particular circumstances of those directly affected.

The rules of natural justice have accordingly been extended to apply to 'quasi-judicial' and administrative decisions; and the content of procedural fairness has become more flexible, dependent on all the circumstances of the particular case. Inevitably, the court's perception of the significance of the substantive interests at stake will colour its assessment of the requirements of fairness. Administrative decisions which impinge on important individual rights or established expectations may be expected to meet more demanding procedural standards than those which are more routine in character. Indeed, the doctrine of legitimate expectations has now been developed, in response to such considerations, to the point where a line between procedural and substantive fairness can no longer be clearly drawn.[32]

A formal or 'instrumentalist' theory of natural justice overlooks its grounding in recognition of the moral status of the person affected by a decision. It is a legitimate expansion of the rule of law, which extends the scope of natural justice from judicial proceedings to a broader range of administrative decisions, because the purposes of granting a fair hearing are not limited to those of the efficient administration of law or policy. Granting a fair hearing helps to address to that person the reasons for applying general rules to him in his particular circumstances. It enables him to play a role in the process of decision, thereby acknowledging his autonomy and individuality. Quite apart from the desire to reach a correct decision, 'we think we owe it to a man as a human being to engage in argument with him, and allow him to engage in argument with us, rather than take decisions about him behind his back, completely disregarding, as it were, his status as a rational agent, able to appreciate the rationale of our decisions about him, possibly willing to co-operate in carrying them out'.[33]

From this perspective, we can also appreciate the reason for insisting that justice must not only be done, but be manifestly seen to be done.[34] The *appearance* of bias offends the rule of law as much as its actuality; and where the decision-maker has a pecuniary interest in the decision, the court will quash or overturn it without investigating the real likelihood of bias.[35] The correct application of legal rules to the actual facts of a case by a judge with an interest in the outcome, however unbiased

[32] Ch. 8, below.
[33] Lucas, *The Principles of Politics*, 132.
[34] Cf. *R.* v. *Sussex JJ., ex p. McCarthy* [1924] 1 KB 256, 259 (Lord Hewart).
[35] *Dimes* v. *Grand Junction Canal* (1852) 3 HLC 759.

in practice, violates the requirement of respect for the parties affected.[36] The suspicion of bias insults their dignity, even if the outcome is in accordance with the law, correctly understood.

The development of the principle of fairness, as a requirement of administrative decisions, though a rational extension of traditional rules of natural justice, nevertheless complicates our understanding of the rule of law. It demonstrates that the principles of generality and neutrality, which are secured by general rules, consistently applied, must be supplemented by moral principles whose impact is closely tailored to the circumstances of particular cases. Executive powers must be confined in their purposes and scope by general rules, preventing arbitrary discrimination; but their exercise in individual cases—inevitably with very different consequences—should be sensitive to the particular circumstances. There is no contradiction here, only a recognition that the rule of law encompasses conflicting ideals of legality and equity, and cannot be reduced without distortion to either.

J. R. Lucas has distinguished helpfully between these ideals.[37] A decision in accord with legality is purely deductive, based on a finite number of features antecedently specified as relevant. It has the merits of certainty and predictability. Legality should not, however, be equated with the rule of law. It is not identical with rationality, and is less just than equity. Equity is more truly rational: it attempts to reach the right decision in all the circumstances, leaving the judge with wide discretion, subject only to treating like cases alike. Common law adjudication, Lucas suggests, is characteristic of equity—involving a limited number of persons, but an indefinite number of possibly relevant factors, justification for those selected being given *ex post facto*.

We shall see that the difference between these two ideals is indeed reflected in the important distinction between statutory rules and common law principles. Obtaining their moral force from the fact of enactment, statutory rules must be faithfully applied by the courts according to their terms. Common law rules, however, are only convenient distillations of underlying principle, and therefore vulnerable to continual reformulation in the light of better knowledge or changing perceptions of justice. Their moral force is more directly dependent on the dictates of reason.[38]

These different faces of the rule of law none the less transcend the division between common law and legislation. The common law encompasses both ideals: the requirements of legality are everywhere

[36] Cf. Gerry Maher, 'Natural Justice as Fairness', in Neil MacCormick and Peter Birks (eds.), *The Legal Mind: Essays for Tony Honoré* (Oxford, 1986), 103.

[37] *The Principles of Politics*, 133–5; see also J. R. Lucas, *On Justice* (Oxford, 1980), 76–9.

[38] Chs. 4–6, below. Cf. Lon L. Fuller, *Anatomy of the Law* (New York, 1968), 84–112.

tempered by those of equity. In the criminal law, the principle of legality is of special importance. No one should be convicted of an offence whose constituents were not clearly determined before he acted: *nulla crimen sine lege*. That principle places important limitations on the possibilities for judicial creativity in interpreting both common law and statute.[39] On the other hand, equity plays a central role in the administration of the criminal law. In particular, the rules of procedure and evidence are adjusted to meet the overriding requirement that the defendant should be fairly tried. Even probative and admissible evidence may be excluded in the judge's discretion, where its reception would undermine the fairness of the trial. The exclusionary discretion is not confined to incriminating evidence to which the jury might attach an exaggerated weight, but extends to evidence unfairly obtained in breach of the rules governing the manner in which evidence is obtained from the accused, by search or interrogation.[40]

An important consequence of the interplay between legality and equity, in the context of the criminal trial, is that the common law repudiates a notion of 'fair trial' based solely on formal procedures. The judge's duty to ensure a fair trial commits him to determining the justice of the defendant's treatment prior to arraignment, where the conduct of police or prosecution is impugned. The defendant's privilege against self-incrimination affords him protection: he enjoys a qualified right of silence both before and during the trial. Although controversial, the privilege serves to ensure that the adversarial nature of the criminal trial does not leave the accused at too great a disadvantage; and the exclusionary discretion exists to preserve the integrity of the trial by providing an effective remedy against abuse.[41] The principle *nemo debet prodere se ipsum* applies, not merely to confessions, but to other evidence obtained from the defendant in circumstances where a confession, similarly obtained, might be excluded.[42] A formal account of the rule of law would emphasize the importance of conformity to settled rules. But it would be a distorted account of the doctrine, as it applies to the English (and Scottish) criminal trial, if it omitted the influence of equity.[43]

39 Cf. A. T. H. Smith, 'Judicial Law Making in the Criminal Law' (1984) 100 LQR 46.

40 See *Sang* [1979] 2 All ER 1222; cf. Police & Crim. Evid. Act 1984 s. 78.

41 See generally T. R. S. Allan, 'Fairness, Truth and Silence: The Criminal Trial and the Judge's Exclusionary Discretion', in Hyman Gross and Ross Harrison (eds.), *Jurisprudence: Cambridge Essays* (Oxford, 1992). For a very strong application of the privilege, see *Brophy* [1982] AC 476. The right of silence is qualified chiefly because judicial comment may sometimes be made on the defendant's failure to testify; and adverse inferences may sometimes be drawn from failure to provide evidence (e.g. *Smith* (1985) 81 Cr. App. R. 286).

42 *Sang*, n. 40 above.

43 Cf. *Lawrie* v. *Muir* 1950 SLT 37.

Notwithstanding the contrary strictures in *Sang*,[44] for example, the exclusionary discretion seems likely to outflank the rule that entrapment constitutes no defence to a criminal trial. Equity—or fairness—is inherently antagonistic to general rules, whose application is (necessarily) unable to accommodate all the details of particular instances.[45] In some cases, the circumstances of entrapment may render a subsequent trial so unfair as to demand an exercise of the exclusionary discretion.[46] Moreover, the ordinary separation of powers between judge and prosecutor also seems vulnerable to the impact of equity in exceptional cases. The courts' careful denials of any jurisdiction to review the propriety of decisions to prosecute are invariably accompanied by reservations of the right to prevent an abuse of process. Although the court does not, as a general rule, direct the institution or discontinuance of criminal proceedings, ultimately it cannot escape responsibility for the fairness of the trial, considered as the consummation of a lengthy process including police investigation and the preparation of charges.[47]

In *Sang*,[48] Lord Scarman was anxious to set clear boundaries to the judge's exclusionary discretion. Admissible evidence could be excluded only in defence of settled principles: the character of the trial was determined by law, rather than 'subjective' judicial choice. He was right to recognize that there must be a balance of interests between prosecution and defence: the prosecution had rights, which the judge could not override. Legality imposes genuine constraints on exercise of the judge's discretion—constraints which justify Lord Scarman's determination to 'emerge from that last refuge of legal thought—that each case depends on its facts', and to attempt an analysis of principle.[49]

A full understanding of the rule of law, however, must acknowledge the value of that last refuge. The principle of fairness is ultimately irreducible: each case is, in some respects, unique and the requirements of justice can never be fully ascertained in advance. There is a continuing interaction between legality and equity—conflicting, but complementary, ideals whose relationship must—to a degree—be renegotiated in every instance. Like the principle of fairness which applies to administrative decisions affecting rights and expectations, the principle of fairness in the criminal trial acknowledges the defendant's dignity and autonomy as a moral agent. In the sense that the right to a fair trial secures a quality of treatment which suitably reflects the defendant's

[44] The House of Lords denied that evidence could be excluded because the crime was instigated by an *agent provocateur* because it would amount to recognizing entrapment as a defence, but available only at the court's discretion: see [1979] 2 All ER 1227 (Lord Diplock).

[45] For the distinction between rules and principles, see Chs. 4 and 6 below.

[46] Cf. *Harwood* [1989] Crim. LR 285; *Gill & Ranuana*, ibid. 358.

[47] See Ch. 9, below.

[48] [1979] 2 All ER 1222, 1242–8.

[49] Ibid. 1244.

dignity and autonomy, it is an absolute right which constitutes one of the primary ingredients of the rule of law.[50]

Nulla poena sine lege

An interesting conflict of formal values was occasioned by the House of Lords' notorious decision in *Shaw* v. *DPP*,[51] which resurrected the common law offence of conspiracy to corrupt public morals, and invoked Lord Mansfield's authority for the residual power of the King's Bench, as *custos morum* of the people, to superintend offences prejudicial to the public welfare. H. L. A. Hart compared the decision to German statutes of the Nazi period, which condemned whatever was deserving of punishment according to 'the fundamental conceptions of a penal law and sound popular feeling'.[52] It flouted the principle of legality by opening a wide field of uncertainty: the citizen could no longer regulate his conduct so as to avoid specifically prohibited offences, free from the risk of punishment for what his fellow citizens might consider immoral. It seemed that almost any conduct which conflicted with widely held prejudices about what was immoral or indecent, where at least two people were involved, might *ex post facto* be pronounced a crime.[53]

Although the House of Lords subsequently disclaimed any residual power in the courts to create new crimes or to widen existing offences, a majority declined to overrule *Shaw*.[54] A conflict had evidently arisen between the various canons of legality. While Lord Diplock argued that *Shaw* had made the law uncertain, in the sense that its prescriptions could only be ascertained in retrospect, the majority resisted a departure from *Shaw* on the ground that that would undermine the requirement of stability or constancy. *Shaw* had established with certainty that the offence of conspiracy to corrupt public morals formed part of English criminal law. Lord Reid refused to reconsider the earlier decision even though he thought it wrong and anomalous.[55]

No doubt the demands of legal certainty, in the sense of constancy, must be partly judged over a range of judicial decisions. Each decision to overturn existing law, as previously declared, however justified in the particular case, serves to undermine the stability of law as a whole. It becomes harder to keep abreast of newly stated rules and so plan one's affairs with any confidence in the content of the law. There must inevitably be a balance, however, between longer-term systemic considerations and the requirements of justice in the particular case. Does

[50] Cf. Allan, 'Fairness, Truth and Silence'; see also Ch. 6, below.
[51] [1962] AC 220.
[52] Statute of 28 June 1935; H. L. A. Hart, *Law Liberty and Morality* (Oxford, 1962), 12.
[53] Cf. *Knuller* [1973] AC 435, 480 (Lord Diplock).
[54] *Knuller*, n. 53 above. Cf. *Withers* [1975] AC 842.
[55] Ibid. 455.

the court not deny justice to the particular defendant if it sustains his conviction under a rule which it concedes is wrong or anomalous? A court which is truly committed to the administration of *justice* according to law must surely confront the substantive values which support the ideal of legality—if only to balance the detriment to these against the systemic gains from leaving bad rules unchanged.

Lord Diplock's proposal to overrule *Shaw* did not itself threaten the precept *nulla poena*. No one would be cheated by acting in reliance on the previous criminal law, in the sense of being trapped by new restrictions. Stability in law is valuable because it serves the interests of personal autonomy and dignity; and the idea of autonomy is closely linked with that of liberty: if the rule of law protects a person's ability to make intelligent decisions about how to act, it also entails the freedom of choice which makes that ability worthwhile. It recommends the maximum personal freedom compatible with public order and decency and similar freedom for others. John Rawls observes that 'if the precept of no crime without a law is violated, say by statutes being vague and imprecise, what we are at liberty to do is likewise vague and imprecise. The boundaries of our liberty are uncertain.' The citizens of a well-ordered society would want the rule of law maintained to safeguard basic civil and political liberties: it enjoyed a 'firm foundation . . . in the agreement of rational persons to establish for themselves the greatest equal liberty'.[56]

From this perspective, the reasons for repudiating *Shaw* seem almost overwhelming. It becomes hard to dissent from Lord Diplock's view that 'the courts should be the vigilant guardians of the liberty of the citizen'. He thought that if that liberty had been mistakenly curtailed by judicial decision, it was 'self-evident' that the court should correct its mistakes unless there were 'compelling reasons to the contrary'.[57] Admittedly, there is a sense in which a decision in favour of stability or constancy favoured equality. The majority noted that there had probably been many convictions of conspiracy to corrupt public morals since *Shaw* was decided; and it may be inferred that they were conscious of the injustice done to those convicted if the law were changed. Justice requires that like cases should be decided alike: equality between past and present litigants, it may be argued, forms a principal justification for the doctrine of precedent. However, in criminal cases the doctrine of precedent is usually relaxed because it is widely considered that the interests of liberty should prevail, and that no one should be punished for conduct which has been wrongly held illegal.[58]

[56] *A Theory of Justice*, 239–40.

[57] [1973] AC 435, 479.

[58] The Criminal Div. of the Court of Appeal may depart from an earlier decision in the interests of the liberty of the accused: *Taylor* (1950) 2 KB 368, 371 (Lord Goddard CJ).

Moreover, in the present context, equality was more truly protected by Lord Diplock's approach, notwithstanding the differences in treatment between defendants. *Shaw* permitted, in effect, the delegation of power to a jury to administer what amounts to an *ex post facto* criminal sanction for immoral conduct. Permitting the state to impose penalties for harmful or immoral conduct which is not clearly within the ambit of existing laws, defined with reasonable precision, violates equality fundamentally. It constitutes an essentially *extralegal* determination of the issues of criminality and punishment, placing the accused at the mercy of an *ex post facto* 'law' tailored to his personal circumstances, and leaving him vulnerable to the whims of passion and prejudice:

> It is more safe that punishment should be ordained by general laws, formed upon deliberation, under the influence of no resentments, and without knowing on whom they are to operate, than that it should be inflicted under the influence of those passions which a trial seldom fails to excite, and which a flexible definition of the crime, or a construction that would render it flexible, might bring into operation.[59]

Similar considerations support the common law principle that penal statutes should be strictly construed. No one should be entrapped by ambiguous laws, even if that principle demands some restraint on judicial co-operation with apparent statutory purposes: 'A man is not to be put in peril upon an ambiguity, however much or little the purpose of the Act appeals to the predilection of the court.'[60] Of course, a statute cannot plausibly be interpreted independently of its perceived objective: its manifest purpose will rightly and necessarily colour its meaning. There is a tension apparent here between competing requirements of consistency and coherence of *law*, on the one hand, and clarity and prospectivity of *laws*, on the other: 'Counterbalancing the public interest in clear laws and political liberty is the public interest that the law shall be applied intelligently in accordance with its purpose, and not in such a way as to reduce it to a mere series of arbitrary and irrational prescriptions.'[61] If, however, it is also a requirement of the rule of law that a statute should be construed in conformity with the expectations of those whose conduct it regulates, its underlying purpose must be confined by the ordinary or well-established meaning of the enacted words.

The content of the principle of legality must, then, be stated with some care: 'its intention is not the neglect of the policy of a statute but the limitation of the range of that policy by the actual meaning of the

[59] *Ex p. Bollman* (1807) 4 Cranch 127 (Marshall CJ, American Sup. Ct.).

[60] *LNER* v. *Berriman* [1946] AC 278, 313 (Lord Simonds). See also *Bloxham* [1983] 1 AC 109, 114 (Lord Bridge).

[61] Glanville Williams, *Criminal Law: The General Part*, 2nd edn. (London, 1961), 589.

words . . .'.[62] In so far as the meaning of the words depends on the preconceptions and assumptions of author or audience—and these may differ—we should, so far as possible, take the latter as decisive.[63] It is an important aspect of the rule of law that all legislation should be construed in the light of constitutional standards and principles; and it is a theme of this book that judicial allegiance to more immediate governmental (or legislative) objectives must be qualified to reflect the consequences for individual rights. The principle of legality should, then, be understood to require strict construction of penal provisions, where there is genuine doubt about their scope and effect, and to preclude the analogical extension of such provisions. As Marshall CJ expressed the point:

> To determine that a case is within the intention of a statute, its language must authorise us to say so. It would be dangerous, indeed, to carry the principle, that a case which is within the reason or mischief of a statute, is within its provisions, so far as to punish a crime not enumerated in the statute, because it is of equal atrocity, or of kindred character, with those which are enumerated.[64]

The precepts *nulla poena, nulla crimen sine lege* also find common law expression in the presumption against according retrospective force to statutory provisions. It is buttressed by the further presumption that Parliament does not intend to contradict the international obligations of the United Kingdom, which include observance of the principle against retroactive penal laws proclaimed by Article 11(2) of the Universal Declaration of Human Rights, and reasserted by Article 7 of the European Convention on Human Rights.[65] A full account of the rationale of this principle would advance beyond the idea that people should be forewarned of the risk of punishment. Nor is it primarily a matter of how the criminal law should be fashioned to secure obedience.

The presumption against retrospective effect derives fundamentally from the idea of constitutionalism as a safeguard of individual freedom in the face of organized state power: 'The rationale of non-retroactivity . . . is opposition to the lawless infliction of suffering, aggravated by the fact that this is done by public officials claiming authority to inflict that

[62] Jerome Hall, *General Principles of Criminal Law*, 2nd edn. (New York, 1969), 37.

[63] Cf. *Black-Clawson Internat.* v. *Papierwerke Waldhof-Aschaffenburg* [1975] AC 591, 638 (Lord Diplock); 645 (Lord Simon); *Maunsell* v. *Olins* [1975] AC 373, 391 (Lord Simon). See also *Pepper* v. *Hart* [1993] 1 All ER 42, 52 (Lord Oliver).

[64] *US* v. *Wiltberger* 5 Wheat 76, 96 (1820) (Am. Sup. Ct.). For criticism of the English courts' record in regard to the construction of statutes, see A. T. H. Smith, 'Judicial Law Making'; Glanville Williams, 'Statutory Interpretation, Prostitution and the Rule of Law', in C. H. F. Tapper (ed.), *Crime, Proof and Punishment: Essays in Memory of Sir Rupert Cross* (London, 1981), 71. For recent judicial expansion of criminal liability see *R.* v. *R.* [1991] 4 All ER 481; comment by J. C. Smith [1991] Crim. LR 477; [1992] Crim. LR 208. For discussion of the limits of linguistic analysis, see Andrew Ashworth, 'Interpreting Criminal Statutes: A Crisis of Legality?' (1991) 107 LQR 419.

[65] Cf. *Waddington* v. *Miah* [1974] 1 WLR 683, 694 (Lord Reid).

"punishment".'[66] The liberties of the citizen are especially vulnerable to the encroachment of the criminal law, even where its legitimate purpose is to secure the order and stability necessary for the exercise of the liberties of others. It is because the criminal law embodies the powers of the state at their most coercive, imposing sanctions which inhibit the exercise of basic civil rights, that the courts should not themselves enlarge its compass to meet apparent threats to public order or decency: 'That they might curtail rights ought to be a reason for the courts to interpret the law in favour of the defendant whenever there is any genuine doubt about the scope of the coercive powers that the law represents.'[67]

It is often observed that the common law is inherently retrospective, in the sense that the scope of a common law offence is inevitably clarified after the defendant has acted. In one sense this is true, but equally true of judicial interpretation of statutes or codes: 'Legitimate interpretation passes by imperceptible shades into so-called illegitimate extension.'[68] *Nulla poena* focuses on the quality of adjudication: is a decision retroactive only in the limited sense which is inescapable, or 'is it also unexpected and indefensible by reference to the law which had been expressed prior to the conduct at issue'?[69] In another sense, the common law is not truly retrospective in operation. It attempts to apply previously articulated principles to new instances; and in its earlier development it gave concrete expression to understandings which, though implicit in previous practice or settled understandings, had not before been stated authoritatively.

Since, however, the principle of legality depends on distinguishing clearly between criminal and immoral conduct, any further extensions of criminal liability should today be made by Parliament alone, prospectively and democratically.[70] Nevertheless, the discipline of strict construction applicable to statutes cannot be applied to the common law: in so far as the common law embodies general principles of liability, they cannot be confined by reference to any authoritative definition akin to enacted terms.[71] The language of previous judgments will be influential, but cannot be decisive; and we are obliged to repair to the underlying values of the legal order, as these can be most

[66] Hall, *General Principles*, 63. Hall describes the 'central meaning' of the principle of legality as a 'definite limitation on the power of the state': ibid. 27.

[67] A. T. H. Smith, 'Judicial Law Making', 72.

[68] Williams, *Criminal Law*, 604.

[69] Hall, *General Principles*, 61.

[70] Cf. *Knuller* [1973] AC 435, 474 (Lord Diplock): 'Society is now able to express its collective view as to what conduct merits punishment by the state through a legislature now representative of all adult citizens.' See A. T. H. Smith, 'Judicial Law Making', 67–9.

[71] For elaboration of this point see Chs. 4–6, below.

plausibly ascertained. The extension of criminal liability in *Shaw* was abhorrent because it flouted the more fundamental values which the principle of legality serves.

It does not necessarily follow that justice will always indicate the narrowest possible interpretation of common law principle, where the appropriate level of generalization is controversial. It is perhaps surprising, in a criminal context, to find the Divisional Court stressing that, far from being a 'worn out jurisprudence rendered incapable of further development by the ever-increasing incursion of parliamentary legislation', the common law was a 'lively body of law capable of adaptation and expansion to meet fresh needs calling for the exertion of the discipline of law'.[72] In that case, the court denied that common law contempt was confined to the effect of publications on judicial proceedings which were either pending or imminent. It held, in deference to the right of an accused person to a fair trial, that it was unlawful actively to assist in the institution of a private prosecution while interfering with the course of justice by publishing material intended to prejudice the trial.[73]

Since common law principles are not susceptible of scientific, or wholly objective, means of interpretation in doubtful cases, the rule of law requires wise judgment, sensitive to all the constitutional implications of a decision. The court relied on earlier statements of the distinction between applying in novel circumstances a broad principle against interference with the administration of justice, on the one hand, and *widening* its application, on the other.[74] It is, inevitably, in practice a distinction of degree. But while it is generally right to adopt a narrower, rather than broader, interpretation of common law offences—leaving Parliament to expand the field of criminal liability if it be thought desirable—the demands of such basic rights as the right to a fair trial, free from adverse publicity which might affect its outcome, can hardly be ignored in fixing the boundaries of existing offences.[75]

It is part, at least, of the objection to the retrospective or ambiguous criminal law that a person cannot conform his actions to it and so be sure of escaping punishment. He cannot form and execute his plans in the confidence that, provided he observe a reasonably certain and

[72] *A.-G.* v. *News Group Newspapers* [1988] 2 All ER 906, 920 (Watkins LJ).

[73] There would be no liability in the absence of intent to prejudice the course of justice, but that intent could be inferred from the circumstances of publication: ibid. 914–17. (The court also considered that the proceedings could properly be described as imminent.)

[74] *A.-G.* v. *Newspaper Publishing* [1987] 3 All ER 276, 299 (Sir John Donaldson MR). The *News Group Newsps.* case was doubted in *A.-G.* v. *Sport Newsps.* [1992] 1 All ER 503 (esp. 515 and 536).

[75] For further discussion of conflicts between important rights see Ch. 6, below. The scope of the law of contempt and the requirement of certainty were considered in *Sunday Times* v. *UK*, Eur. Ct. HR, judgment of 26 Apr. 1979, series A, no. 30.

stable framework of rules, his liberty will remain inviolate. The same objection applies, however, to prospective laws which render him liable to punishment for events whose occurrence he cannot control. The rule of law entails, therefore, the general principle of individual responsibility which insists that punishment cannot justly be inflicted in the absence of fault.

The 'cardinal principle of our law that *mens rea*, an evil intention or a knowledge of the wrongfulness of the act, is in all ordinary cases an essential ingredient of guilt of a criminal offence'[76] is reflected, in the legislative context, in the well-established presumption that, 'in order to give effect to the will of Parliament', the court 'must read in words appropriate to require *mens rea*'.[77] Since the statutory language will often provide no guide, the court is entitled to consider the purpose of the Act and any other relevant circumstances in deciding whether an exception to the general principle should be made.[78] The presumption may be displaced by express words or necessary implication, but the greater the injustice its displacement would cause, the more convincing the arguments for imposing strict liability must be.[79] Its strength 'stems from the principle that it is contrary to a rational and civilised criminal code . . . to penalise one who has performed his duty as a citizen to ascertain what acts are prohibited by law (*ignorantia juris non excusat*) and has taken all proper care to inform himself of any facts which would make his conduct lawful'.[80]

Liberty and equality

It seems plain that constitutional theory cannot rest content with a narrow, formal conception of the rule of law, neutral between different accounts of justice and fairness. The formal conception directs our attention to matters of individual right and human dignity. We are obliged to confront wider questions of liberty, equality, and autonomy in order to make concrete our commitment to the rule of law in the circumstances of particular cases. Both judge and legal theorist must address substantive questions of political philosophy in seeking justification of legal decisions. The judge must give appropriate weight in his decisions to personal liberty and develop a conception of equality, for these values will inevitably inform the judgments he makes in service of any plausible conception of the rule of law.

In interpreting a criminal statute, the court will not apply the presumption in favour of requiring *mens rea* with the sole objective of

[76] *Sweet* v. *Parsley* [1970] AC 132, 152 (Lord Morris).
[77] Ibid. 148 (Lord Reid).
[78] *R.* v. *Tolson* (1889) 23 QBD 168, 173–5.
[79] Ibid. 182.
[80] *Sweet* v. *Parsley* [1970] AC 132, 163 (Lord Diplock).

ensuring the efficiency of the criminal law, in the sense of maximizing its capacity for guiding people's behaviour. It will be primarily conscious of the *injustice* of punishing the defendant in the absence of fault, and sensitive to the close association of the presumption with basic freedoms:

> *It is of the utmost importance for the protection of the liberty of the subject* that a court should always bear in mind that, unless a statute, either clearly or by necessary implication, rules out *mens rea* as a constituent part of a crime, the court should not find a man guilty of an offence against the criminal law unless he has a guilty mind.[81]

Understood as a complex tapestry of constitutional principle, the rule of law embodies the traditional bias of the common law in favour of individual liberty. The common law has been generally regarded as providing a bulwark against erosion of the most important civil liberties, even if its capacity to resist encroachments by government and Parliament today seems insufficient.[82] And a special concern for personal liberty has long been a marked characteristic of common law adjudication, even if the courts' modern treatment of coercive powers of arrest and detention has sometimes failed adequately to live up to that underlying tradition.[83]

The principle in *Entick* v. *Carrington*,[84] that the burden of establishing requisite authority is borne by the official who asserts it, was applied with startling results in *McLorie* v. *Oxford*.[85] In the former case, the King's messengers were liable for trespass in the absence of authority indicating the legality of general warrants of search and seizure: the 'silence of the books' was held to be authority against them. In the latter instance, police officers were held to have no right to enter premises—with or without a warrant—in order to seize an instrument used to commit a serious crime known to be there. In view of 'the importance attached by the common law to the relative inviolability of a dwelling house', the court could not believe that there was 'a common law right without warrant to enter one either in order to search for instruments of crime, even of serious crime, or in order to seize such an instrument which is known to be there'.[86] If there were such a right, the court 'would expect it to be reflected in the books', which it was not.

The rule of law also entails the conservative construction of statutory provisions which grant powers of arrest and search. Pollock CB expressed

[81] *Brend* v. *Wood* (1946) 175 LT 306, 307 (Lord Goddard CJ).

[82] See e.g. Sir Leslie Scarman, *English Law—The New Dimension*, Hamlyn Lectures, 26th series (London, 1974); Eric Barendt, 'Dicey and Civil Liberties' [1985] PL 596.

[83] See discussion of *Wills* v. *Bowley* [1982] 2 All ER 654, below. Compare decisions of House of Lords and Court of Appeal in *IRC* v. *Rossminster* [1980] AC 952 (exercise of powers of search and seizure under Taxes Management Act 1970).

[84] (1765) 19 State Trials 1030.

[85] [1982] 3 All ER 480.

[86] Ibid. 485.

this principle in *Bowditch* v. *Balchin*: 'In a case in which the liberty of the subject is concerned, we cannot go beyond the natural construction of the statute.'[87] In *Morris* v. *Beardmore*,[88] in more recent times, Lord Scarman invoked *Entick* v. *Carrington* in support of his conception of 'the importance attached by the common law to the privacy of the home'. The House of Lords held that a constable could not lawfully require a person to provide a breath specimen, under the Road Traffic Act 1972, section 8, if he were present on that person's property without permission. Police officers had not been acting in the execution of their duty, as was necessary for a valid exercise of the power, because they were trespassers.

The statutory provisions made serious inroads on common law rights and were to be construed accordingly. If Parliament intended to authorize acts which would otherwise amount to torts actionable at common law, there must be express statutory provision: the presumption was that 'in the absence of express provision to the contrary Parliament did not intend to authorise tortious conduct'.[89] Lord Edmund-Davies rejected the view expressed in the Divisional Court that it was sufficient to satisfy the express terms of the statute granting the power to require a breath test: 'A statute does not exist in limbo. It has a background; it rests on an assumption that it will operate only in a certain climate and that circumstances of a certain sort will prevail.'[90] The statute conferred no power on a constable acting 'in circumstances of known illegality' which placed him in a situation where he had 'no business to be at all'.

The speeches in *Wills* v. *Bowley*[91] reflected sharply contrasting opinions about the application of the 'strong presumption in favour of the liberty of the innocent subject'[92] in the circumstances of that case. The House of Lords held that the power of a constable under the Town Police Clauses Act 1847, section 28, to arrest a person who 'within his view commits' one of a prescribed series of offences, extended to cases where the constable honestly believed on reasonable grounds that an offence had been committed, even though the suspect was subsequently acquitted. The appellant was acquitted of the offence of using obscene language in the street to the annoyance of 'passengers', but was convicted of assaulting three police constables in the course of her attempt to resist arrest. The validity of that conviction depended on whether the constables had been acting in the execution of their duty, which in turn depended on whether the appellant's arrest was lawful. After a lengthy examination of conflicting authority, Lord Bridge held that, since the offender's guilt could only be established subsequently, it must have been intended that an honest belief on reasonable grounds

[87] (1850) 5 Exch 378, 381. [88] [1980] 2 All ER 753. [89] Ibid. 757 (Lord Diplock).
[90] Ibid. 760. [91] [1982] 2 All ER 654. [92] Ibid. 680 (Lord Bridge).

would suffice to make exercise of a power of arrest in *flagrante delicto* lawful. The statute imposed a duty to arrest; and a constable should not be forced to choose between the risk of making an unlawful arrest and that of committing a criminal neglect of duty.

Lord Lowry's powerful dissenting speech, refusing to embroider the plain language of the statute, made a significant contribution to the common law tradition in favour of personal liberty—even if it perhaps gave exaggerated emphasis to the 'literal meaning'.[93] It is difficult to distinguish a 'literal' meaning of words from their ordinary grammatical meaning, taken in context. The distinction sometimes made between primary and secondary meanings is hard to sustain if (within appropriate limits) a 'purposive' construction is adopted, reading a clause in the light of the apparent legislative purpose.[94]

In *Barnard* v. *Gorman*,[95] the House of Lords had construed the term 'offender' as including a person suspected on reasonable grounds of having committed an offence. Such a reading was necessary to make sense of a provision that the 'offender' might be proceeded against by summons: a narrower, technical meaning would have reduced the clause to nonsense. Viscount Simon LC had denied that the statutory words could be given a wider meaning merely in order to close a loophole. The court's duty was to give the words 'their true construction, having regard to the language of the whole section, and, as far as relevant, of the whole Act, always preferring the natural meaning of the words involved, but none the less always giving the word its appropriate construction according to the context'.[96] It could certainly be argued, by analogy with that case, that the Town Police Clauses Act should be accorded a similarly contextual meaning.

The force of Lord Lowry's dissent, however, lay in its opposition to the general rule of construction, affording similar scope for reasonable error on the part of the person making the arrest, which Lord Bridge thought must apply to 'all cases where a power of arrest in *flagrante delicto* is coupled with a duty to convey the person arrested "forthwith" . . . before a justice'.[97] In *Barnard*, Lord Simon had stressed the need to examine the particular statute, repudiating 'any supposed general rule of construction'. Lord Lowry firmly asserted the priority of liberty over public order, citing Lord Simonds's remark, in *Christie* v.

[93] Ibid. 659–60, 667.

[94] Cf. E. A. Driedger, 'Statutes: The Mischievous Literal Golden Rule' (1981) 59 Can. Bar Rev. 780; Sir Rupert Cross, *Statutory Interpretation*, 2nd edn. by John Bell and Sir George Engle (London, 1987), 83–96. The appropriate limits must be determined in the light of constitutional considerations.

[95] [1941] AC 378.

[96] Ibid. 384.

[97] [1982] 2 All ER 654, 681. (The rule of construction applied to arrests by private citizens as well as constables.)

Leachinsky,[98] that the liberty of the subject and the convenience of executive authority were not to be weighed in the same scales. The principle that '"ambiguous" statutory provisions, not least those dealing with the power of arrest, should be construed in favour of the liberty of the subject' was not a 'mere incantation' to be recited only where its observance could do no possible harm to the cause of public order. It was a 'real and compelling guide . . . hallowed by authority and usage', whose application might properly have inconvenient consequences.[99]

The rule of law protects both liberty and equality. Raz denies a connection between the rule of law and equality on the ground that discrimination of all kinds is compatible with general rules.[100] However, the formal version of the rule of law treats all law as if it were *statute* law, because legislation is composed of discrete legal rules, whose meaning is confined, and scope determined, by their enacted terms. I have suggested that the common law cannot be reduced to rules in this manner, but exists primarily as a corpus of principles, whose articulation in new cases enables the rules to be adapted and modified in response to the perceived requirements of justice. Hayek described how the judge must constantly resort to principles, distilled from the *ratio decidendi* of earlier decisions, in order to prevent conflict between existing rules, or to resolve ambiguities, as new situations arise to challenge the existing legal order.[101]

In the sphere of common law, therefore, the rule of law entails a search for equality in the sense of the consistent application of underlying principles. The distinction often drawn between the regular application of the law, on the one hand, and the inequalities which it may impose in substance, on the other, therefore starts to break down. When we see that the common law is primarily a body of principle, awaiting continual elaboration and development, the connection between the rule of law and equality becomes clear. The consistent application of legal principle, required by the ideal of legality, involves a process of moral reasoning in which inequalities in treatment at the hands of the state have to be justified. Rawls observes that the 'requirement of consistency holds . . . for the interpretation of all rules and for justifications at all levels. Eventually reasoned arguments for discriminatory judgments become harder to formulate and the attempt to do so less persuasive.'[102]

98 [1947] AC 573, 595.

99 [1982] 2 All ER 670. Lord Elwyn-Jones, also dissenting, rejected any general rule of construction on the ground that where 'the liberty of the subject is concerned, the court should not go beyond the natural construction of the statute and the strict terms of the grant of the power . . .': ibid. 658.

100 'The Rule of Law', 200.

101 *Law, Legislation and Liberty*, i. 118–20. Cf. Dworkin, *Taking Rights Seriously*, chs. 2–4.

102 *A Theory of Justice*, 237.

Equality and integrity

The interpretation of the rule of law offered here may be thought to find some support in Ronald Dworkin's *Law's Empire.*[103] He commends the political ideal of 'integrity' for a world of ordinary politics, where the requirements of justice and fairness conflict. Fairness requires a political structure which distributes power correctly. Justice requires a morally acceptable distribution of material resources and the protection of civil liberties. If in practice we disagree about how these ideals should be reconciled, we may none the less require government to display consistency of principle, so that all are treated equally. Integrity assumes an (essentially metaphorical) personification of the state, which is to be treated as a moral agent: 'we insist that the state act on a single, coherent set of principles even when its citizens are divided about what the right principles of justice and fairness really are.'[104]

Dworkin's model of adjudication mirrors his general political theory. It requires a court to interpret all legal material as parts of a seamless, self-consistent unity. Judges should assume that the law is structured by a coherent set of principles about justice and fairness, which must be applied in every case so that each person's situation is fair and just according to the same standards.[105] Integrity is more than merely deciding like cases alike, however: it demands a more thoroughgoing consistency of principle in settling the rights of citizens. A judge's own convictions about justice and fairness may properly play their part in this process, but his decisions are constrained by the actual political history of his community. His conclusions of law, in other words, must respect the 'requirement of fit' with previous judicial decisions and statutory enactments: 'Judges who accept the interpretive ideal of integrity decide hard cases by trying to find, in some coherent set of principles about people's rights and duties, the best constructive interpretation of the political structure and legal doctrine of their community.'[106]

I have suggested that the common law requirement that like cases should be decided alike may be understood to embody a fundamental component of its underlying philosophy—the idea of equality. The importance of equality emerges in Dworkin's discussion of the common law, where he rejects an 'economic' interpretation—based on the principle that people should always act in whatever way will be financially least expensive for the community as a whole—in favour of an egalitarian one. Dworkin argues that if the common law is understood as protecting equality of resources, we can best explain a familiar division of public and private responsibility. We believe that each citizen should be free to use or exchange property lawfully assigned to him as he chooses,

[103] London, 1986. [104] Ibid. 166. [105] Ibid. 243. [106] Ibid. 225.

but that government should adjust the rules of property so as to treat people as equals: government has a duty to treat all members of the community with equal care and concern.[107] That fundamental idea of political morality is violated by laws which treat people differently when their different treatment cannot be justified in principle. Our interpretation of *fairness* depends on the same basic idea. We believe that our legislative institutions should be framed so as to ensure the equal distribution of political power.

It is also the notion of equality which explains our hostility to 'chequerboard laws', embodying compromises which reflect different shades of opinion about questions of justice. Dworkin defends the idea of integrity primarily by appeal to that widely shared attitude; and it seems clear that integrity reflects the demands of equality. Fairness might indicate that Parliament should recognize conflicting views about the morality of abortion by making it 'criminal for pregnant women who were born in even years but not for those born in odd ones'.[108] Dworkin identifies a failure of integrity as the source of our opposition to such chequerboard solutions because they cannot rationally be rejected on grounds of justice. 'For in the circumstances of ordinary politics the chequerboard strategy will prevent instances of injustice that would otherwise occur, and we cannot say that justice requires not eliminating any injustice unless we can eliminate all.'[109]

In some cases the ideal of equality may be overridden by other, more pressing demands of political morality. We will sometimes prefer to sacrifice equality, at least in the short term, in order to avoid a great injustice. Dworkin notes, for example, that people who believe very strongly that abortion is always murder may prefer the chequerboard solution to a wholly permissive law: 'They think that fewer murders are better than more no matter how incoherent the compromise that produces fewer.'[110]

The appeal of integrity, then, lies chiefly in the idea of equality. Hercules—Dworkin's model judge—will generally reject an interpretation of justice which is inconsistent with previous judicial decisions because it would undermine equality; although he will readily accept a novel explanation of those decisions if it better accords with what he conceives to be the litigants' moral rights.[111] In some cases, his convictions about justice will be sufficiently clear and strong to justify repudiating previous decisions altogether, even at the price of damage to equality between past and present litigants. Lord Diplock's unwillingness to be bound by *Shaw's* case reflected the strength of his

[107] Ibid., ch. 8. [108] Ibid. 178. [109] Ibid. 181. [110] Ibid. 183.

[111] The identification of legal with moral rights (subject only to inconsistent statute or precedent) is made most clearly in Dworkin, *A Matter of Principle*, ch. 1. Cf. *Taking Rights Seriously*, ch. 4.

objections to that decision on grounds of justice.[112] A judge will sometimes adopt a restrictive approach to previous decisions, when he is formally bound by their *rationes decidendi*, distinguishing them so far as possible. In attempting to reconcile the different results in principle, he will be seeking to reconcile equality and justice.[113]

Significantly, Dworkin makes the connection between integrity and equality explicit in his discussion of the United States Constitution, where he notes that the equal protection clause of the Fourteenth Amendment is understood to forbid internal compromises over matters of principle. It would not permit a state to enact the chequerboard abortion statute: 'This connection between integrity and the rhetoric of equal protection is revealing. We insist on integrity because we believe that internal compromises would deny what is often called "equality before the law" and sometimes "formal equality".'[114]

Dworkin's theory of law confirms the wisdom of A. V. Dicey's attempt to formulate a substantive doctrine of the rule of law. The notion of 'legal equality'—that 'every man . . . is subject to the ordinary law of the realm and amenable to the jurisdiction of the ordinary tribunals'[115]—should not be understood in a purely formal or procedural sense. The rule of law is not satisfied by the meticulous application of different rules to different persons, according to their terms, when the rules are intrinsically unjust, discriminating between classes of people without good reason. The ideal of equality may instead be a powerful force in the interpretation of the substantive content of the common law.

It would therefore be mistaken too readily to dismiss Dicey's doctrine on the grounds that it cannot provide a safeguard against the systematic abuse of power. It contains the seeds, perhaps, of a political philosophy capable of generating important conclusions about the standards of justice and fairness which government may be expected to meet. An analogy is provided by Dworkin's repudiation of the 'fashionable' tendency to denigrate the idea of equality before the law: 'The equal protection cases show how important formal equality becomes when it is understood to require integrity as well as bare logical consistency, when it demands fidelity not just to rules but to the theories of fairness and justice that these rules presuppose by way of justification.'[116]

For all its lack of philosophical sophistication, Dicey's analysis was an attempt to give content to the rule of law as a body of constitutional

[112] See discussion of *Shaw* [1962] AC 220, above.

[113] The *ratio* of a decision is not to be equated with the court's explanation, which may—with hindsight—be regarded as incorrect: see A. L. Goodhart, 'Determining the *Ratio Decidendi* of a Case', in *Essays in Jurisprudence and the Common Law* (Cambridge, 1931); M. J. Detmold, *The Unity of Law and Morality* (London, 1984), 188–92.

[114] *Law's Empire*, 185. [115] *Law of the Constitution*, 193. [116] *Law's Empire*, 185.

doctrine. Although it failed to distinguish clearly between constitutional doctrine and contingent features of English legal institutions, his emphasis on general principles has aptly been called the 'abiding merit' of his exposition.[117] Proposing that the rule of law consisted in the application by the courts of the 'general principles of the constitution', instancing the rights to personal liberty and of public meeting,[118] he insisted on the need to study the content of English law, as it applied to civil and political liberties and governmental powers. No doubt Dicey exaggerated the merits of the British version of the doctrine, at the expense of other Western democracies, but he made no fundamental mistake in seeking to ground his analysis in substantive law.

117 Marsh, 'The Rule of Law as a Supra-National Concept', 241.
118 *Law of the Constitution*, 195; chs. 5–7.

3
Law, Liberty, and the Separation of Powers

> Therefore in well-ordered commonwealths, where the good of the whole is so considered as it ought, the legislative power is put into the hands of divers persons who, duly assembled, have by themselves, or jointly with others, a power to make laws, which when they have done, being separated again, they are themselves subject to the laws they have made; which is a new and near tie upon them to take care that they make them for the public good.
>
> John Locke, *Second Treatise of Government*, xii, para. 143.

Although he failed to distinguish the judicial function from the executive, Locke captured the essential feature of the separation of powers. Government can be made subject to law only when the legislative function is clearly distinguished from policy-making and administration. The possibilities for arbitrary action, perhaps directed at unpopular groups or political opponents, are much reduced where the executive acts under general rules—applying to a substantial number of future cases—promulgated in advance.[1]

Accordingly, Locke insisted that the legislature should limit itself to the passing of general rules, and should not be constantly in session: 'They are to govern by promulgated establish'd Laws, not to be varied in particular cases'.[2] Legislature and executive were to be autonomous and independent within their own proper spheres, the former refraining from assuming power to rule by 'extemporary Arbitrary Decrees'. The separation of powers therefore serves in principle to secure the *generality* of law-making; and a body of considered, consistent, and public rules acts as a constitutional barrier shielding the citizen from passionate, hasty, or discriminatory executive action.

It is far from obvious that the character of the modern relationship between government and Parliament is compatible with Locke's conception. The ideal of government under law has come into conflict with our aspiration for democratic control.[3] Hayek complained that the

[1] Cf. F. A. Hayek, *The Constitution of Liberty* (London, 1960), 278–9. See further id., *Law, Legislation and Liberty* (London, 1982), iii, esp. ch. 13.

[2] *Second Treatise of Government*, xi, para. 142.

[3] Cf. M. J. C. Vile, *Constitutionalism and the Separation of Powers* (Oxford, 1967), 229. Vile notes the tension between the 'theory of government', under which Parliament exercised

character of modern assemblies had been determined by the needs of their *governmental* tasks, which necessitate continuous support of the executive authority by an organized majority committed to particular schemes for the control and use of resources. In issuing commands which can be 'executed' in the modern sense—the implementation of policies as opposed to the application of general rules—a parliamentary assembly acts as an instrument of responsible government, but not as a legislature as traditionally understood.[4] Members of Parliament have become advocates of their constituents' interests, and dependent on voters' satisfaction with governmental measures, rather than representatives whose task is to constrain the executive by framing general rules or principles of justice.[5] The rule of law implied the authorization of every coercive act of government by a 'universal rule of just conduct' adopted by an independent body:

> If we now call 'law' also the authorisation of particular acts of government by a resolution of the representative assembly, such 'legislation' is not legislation in the sense in which the concept is used in the theory of the separation of powers; it means that the democratic assembly exercises executive powers without being bound by laws in the sense of general rules of conduct it cannot alter.[6]

The force of Hayek's analysis is hard to deny; but it must be set in the context of British constitutional convention and the tripartite classification of powers which Blackstone adopted from Montesquieu. Blackstone sought to reconcile the doctrine with the older theory of mixed government, whereby a constitutional balance was preserved by a blending of elements of monarchy, aristocracy, and democracy. The result was a partial separation of persons and functions, in which the executive was a *branch* of the legislature: either total union or total disjunction would in the long run lead to tyranny.[7] The House of Commons Disqualification Act 1975 maintains this institutional arrangement today by limiting the number of ministerial office-holders entitled to sit and vote in the lower House; civil servants and members of the police and armed forces are excluded entirely.

Most importantly, Blackstone emphasized the separateness and independence of the judiciary—an independence central to the notion of the common law as the foundation of civil liberty and protection from arbitrary power:

control over government, and the 'theory of law', which required that the executive obey the legislature.

[4] *Law, Legislation and Liberty*, i, ch. 6; iii, ch. 13.
[5] For further discussion, see Ch. 5 below.
[6] *Law, Legislation and Liberty*, iii. 24–5.
[7] *Commentaries*, i. 154.

In this distinct and separate existence of the judicial power in a peculiar body of men, nominated indeed, but not removable at pleasure, by the crown, consists one main preservative of the public liberty; which cannot subsist long in any state, unless the administration of common justice be in some degree separated both from the legislative and from the executive power. Were it joined with the legislative, the life, liberty, and property, of the subject would be in the hands of arbitrary judges, whose decisions would be then regulated only by their own opinions, and not by any fundamental principles of law; which, though legislators may depart from, yet judges are bound to observe.[8]

In view of the crucial importance of the separation of powers to the maintenance of the rule of law, its generally unsympathetic treatment by constitutional lawyers is surprising. No doubt Bagehot's distorted account of constitutional arrangements bears much of the blame. His emphasis on the 'close union, the nearly complete fusion'[9] of the legislative and executive powers was superficially attractive, but exaggerated the significance of the overlap of personnel between the different branches. The nineteenth-century theory of the balanced constitution, based on a subtle division and interdependence of government and Parliament, has been well described by M. J. C. Vile, who noted that 'virtually the whole history of English constitutionalism has been characterised by the recognition of the need for a *partial* separation of the personnel of government, and a *partial* separation of the functions of government'.[10]

The development of mass political parties and party discipline, of course, undermined the earlier balance of institutions. However, a division of functions has remained a central component of legal theory, and therefore of constitutional law—which the independence of the judiciary serves to uphold. The courts rightly insist that the law-making and administrative functions must be sharply differentiated. Even if the Cabinet is for practical purposes the master of both legislative and executive powers of the state, these powers are none the less cast into 'differentiated and clear-cut organizational moulds and procedural channels'.[11] The courts perform their mediating function between government and governed largely by ensuring that the executive observes the limits of its statutory powers, as those limits are finally determined, in cases of doubt, by the judges. The law which regulates the activities of government can be changed only by formal *enactment*, whose meaning, as Dicey emphasized, is subject to judicial interpretation.

It follows that even subordinate legislation—the most obvious vio-

[8] Ibid. 269.
[9] *The English Constitution*, 7th edn. (London, 1894), 10.
[10] *Constitutionalism*, 226.
[11] Frederic S. Burin, 'The Theory of the Rule of Law and the Structure of the Constitutional State' (1966) 15 Am. UL Rev. 313, at 325.

lation of any 'pure' theory of separation of powers—is subject to common law constraints similar to those imposed on other ministerial orders and decisions.[12] And these constraints cannot be defeated by the simple expedient of delegating the widest amplitude of legislative power: the power will be treated as limited by the ordinary principles of judicial construction. There is a legal presumption that where Parliament confers powers, 'they will seldom if ever be conferred in gross, devoid of purposes or criteria, express or implied, by reference to which they are intended to be exercised'.[13] Nor can Parliament sanction *ad hoc* deviations from the legislative scheme previously enacted: there must be further formal legislation in accordance with the ordinary procedure. Lord Denning's suggestion, in *Hoffman-La Roche* v. *Secretary of State for Trade and Industry*,[14] that the court could not declare invalid a statutory order, made by a minister, which had been approved by resolutions in each House, was repudiated by the House of Lords:

> . . . in constitutional law a clear distinction can be drawn between an Act of Parliament and subordinate legislation, even though the latter is contained in an order made by statutory instrument approved by resolutions of both Houses of Parliament. Despite this indication that the majority of members of both Houses of the contemporary Parliament regard the order as being for the common weal . . . the courts have jurisdiction to declare it to be invalid if they are satisfied that in making it the Minister who did so acted outwith the legislative powers conferred upon him by the previous Act of Parliament under which the order purported to be made . . .[15]

Vile observed that an implicit commitment to some form of separation of powers formed the basis of Dicey's rejection of *droit administratif*, and of the claim of the ordinary courts to a monopoly of judicial power. The entire Diceyan scheme assumed such a division of powers: 'the whole burden of the *Law of the Constitution* was that the making of law, and the carrying out of the law, were distinct and separate functions, and that those who carry out the law must be subordinated to those who make it'. Dicey did not consider how far the different functions should be distributed between different *persons*, 'but if the subordination of the executive to the law was the keynote of his work, it would reduce this principle to nonsense to assume that legislators and executives were identical, that the powers of government were "fused"'.[16]

[12] See Sir William Wade, *Administrative Law*, 6th edn. (Oxford, 1988), 863–78.

[13] *R.* v. *Toohey, ex p. Northern Land Council* (1981) 151 CLR 170, 204 (Stephen J., High Court of Australia). See esp. *Commrs. of Customs & Excise* v. *Cure and Deeley* [1962] 1 QB 340.

[14] [1975] AC 295, 321.

[15] Ibid. 365 (Lord Diplock).

[16] *Constitutionalism and the Separation of Powers*, 230. For useful discussion of the importance of the separation of powers to the rule of law, see also Peter E. Quint, 'The

The force of the separation of powers principle must be found, then, in the conventions and 'spirit' of the constitution, interpreted in the light of the requirements of the rule of law.[17] The separation and independence of legislature and judicature has been judicially described as a 'constitutional convention of the highest importance'.[18] If as judge, legislator, member of Cabinet, and head of an administrative department, the Lord Chancellor is 'the spectacular exhibit in the museum of constitutional curiosities',[19] he is rightly subject to firm conventions governing his various roles. He is expected to divorce his judicial from his political roles.[20] The Attorney-General is expected to maintain a similar detachment in deciding whether or not to institute criminal proceedings: his acting at the dictation of government colleagues, or failing to exercise independent and impartial judgement, would clearly be unconstitutional.

O. Hood Phillips rejected the analogy drawn by Lord Diplock, in *Hinds* v. *The Queen*,[21] between the Jamaican Constitution, based on the 'Westminster model', and 'the basic concept of separation of legislative, executive and judicial power as it had been developed in the unwritten constitution of the United Kingdom'. But his observation that Lord Diplock and his colleagues adjudicated as members of an executive body—the Privy Council—and were also members of the legislature surely misfired. The convention which constitutes the Judicial Committee an impartial and independent court of law suffices to preserve the separation of powers: 'According to constitutional convention it is unknown and unthinkable that His Majesty in Council should not give effect to the report of the Judicial Committee, who are thus in truth an appellate court of law . . .'[22]

The modern history of Western constitutionalism consists in the attempt to fix the legitimate boundaries of political power, while according that respect to the different organs of state required by the separation of powers. Experience of more thoroughgoing versions of the doctrine, in the revolutionary state constitutions in America, led to the adoption of a modified form for the Federal Constitution in 1789. A pure separation of powers, unaccompanied by checks and balances,

Separation of Powers under Nixon: Reflections on Constitutional Liberties and the Rule of Law' (1981) Duke LJ 1.

[17] Cf. C. K. Allen, *Law and Orders*, 3rd edn. (London, 1965), 18–20; Colin Munro, 'The Separation of Powers: Not such a Myth' [1981] PL 19.

[18] *R.* v. *HM Treasury, ex p. Smedley* [1985] 1 All ER 589, 593 (Sir John Donaldson MR).

[19] Allen, *Law and Orders*, 16.

[20] Ibid. 20. See also Sir Nicholas Browne-Wilkinson, 'The Independence of the Judiciary in the 1980s' [1988] PL 44; A. W. Bradley, 'Constitutional Change and the Lord Chancellor' [1988] PL 165.

[21] [1977] AC 195, 212–13.

[22] *British Coal Corporation* v. *R.* [1935] AC 500, 510–12 (Lord Sankey LC). Cf. *Ibralebbe* v. *R.* [1964] AC 900, affirming the judicial character of the Order in Council implementing the decision of a Privy Council appeal.

seemed inherently unstable; the danger was that, as with the Long Parliament in seventeenth-century England, all power would gravitate to the legislature. It was always possible, by adopting the necessary legislative 'manner and form', for the legislature to use its power to attain improper ends, thereby subverting the constitutional scheme. Defending the adoption of a partial separation of powers and functions for the United States, Madison argued that Montesquieu should not be understood as denying the need for one department of government to control another. There must be a connection and blending of departments precisely in order to ensure that the separation of powers, which remained fundamental, was preserved.[23] The effect was described judicially as follows:

> While the Constitution diffuses power the better to secure liberty, it also contemplates that practice will integrate the dispersed powers into a workable government. It enjoins upon its branches separateness but inter-dependence, autonomy but reciprocity.[24]

Principle and policy

The division of powers and functions between government and judiciary assumes a fundamental distinction between administrative policy and legal right. If government is to be free to govern it must be permitted an appropriate sphere for the formulation and implementation of policy. But it is equally necessary for the courts—which have neither the democratic 'mandate' nor the requisite expertise to intervene on grounds of public policy—to exercise supervision to preserve legality. Judicial review of administrative action, in particular, is founded on this dichotomy. Government must be accountable to Parliament for its actions in defence of the public interest or the general welfare: the doctrine of ministerial responsibility provides the principal means of *democratic* control. But political responsibility cannot be substituted for judicial control in respect of legality. Hence the importance of judicial review of the actions of the central government departments: 'They are accountable to Parliament for what they do so far as regards efficiency and policy, and of that Parliament is the only judge; they are responsible to a court of justice for the lawfulness of what they do, and of that the court is the only judge.'[25]

[23] *The Federalist*, No. 47.

[24] *Youngstown Sheet & Tube Co.* v. *Sawyer* 343 US 579, 635 (1952) (Jackson J.). Marshall CJ established the power of federal judicial review of Congressional legislation accompanied by deference to the legislature's interpretation of its powers: *Marbury* v. *Madison* 5 US (1 Cranch) 137 (1803); *McCulloch* v. *Maryland* 17 US 316 (1819).

[25] *IRC* v. *Nat. Fed. of Self-Employed & Small Businesses* [1982] AC 617, 644. See also *City of Edinburgh DC* v. *Secretary of State for Scotland* 1985 SLT 551, 561 (Lord Robertson). Cf. Sir Gerard Brennan, 'The Purpose and Scope of Judicial Review', in Michael Taggart (ed.), *Judicial Review of Administrative Action in the 1980s* (Oxford, 1986), 33.

In practice, the distinction between law and policy entails careful analysis in the context of particular cases, and it will sometimes be controversial. W. A. Robson rejected the distinction altogether, consistently with his repudiation of the separation of powers.[26] In extolling the freedom of specialized tribunals from the constraints of legal doctrine, based on individual rights, Robson ably defended their distinctive constitutional role. He argued that the chief merit of administrative law was 'the power of the tribunal to decide the cases coming before it with the avowed object of furthering a policy of social improvement in some particular field; and of adapting their attitude towards the controversy so as to fit the needs of that policy'.[27] But this explanation only served to reinforce the distinction, drawn by the Donoughmore Committee,[28] between the judicial and the quasi-judicial—a distinction Robson scorned because it relied on the difference between law and policy.

According to Donoughmore, both judicial and quasi-judicial functions presupposed a dispute between opposing parties (unlike purely 'administrative' decisions). But only the former required the application of existing law to the facts, without regard to general considerations of the public interest. A minister's decision was quasi-judicial where it was governed 'not by a statutory direction . . . to apply the law of the land to the facts and act accordingly, but by a statutory permission to use his discretion after he has ascertained the facts and to be guided by considerations of public policy'—a course which 'would not be open to him if he were exercising a purely judicial function'.[29]

Ronald Dworkin's account of the distinction between principle and policy explains the difference of functions which forms the basis of the separation of powers. Arguments of principle appeal to the legal and political rights of individuals; arguments of policy claim that a particular decision will work to promote some conception of the general welfare or public interest. Dworkin argues persuasively that judicial decisions should be grounded on considerations of principle rather than policy: the court's function is to determine the legal rights of the parties. Wider considerations of the public interest are properly the concern of government and legislature.[30] Individual rights are worthless if they

[26] *Justice and Administrative Law*, 3rd edn. (London, 1951), 16: 'that antique and rickety chariot . . . so long the favourite vehicle of writers on political science and constitutional law for the conveyance of fallacious ideas'.

[27] Ibid. 573.

[28] Committee on Ministers' Powers, Cmd. 4060, 1932.

[29] Ibid. 74.

[30] *Taking Rights Seriously* (London, 1977), ch. 4. Dworkin distinguishes between background moral rights and institutional rights. Legal rights are those moral or political rights assumed by the most persuasive and morally compelling interpretation of the constitution and other sources of law, considered as a coherent and consistent body of principle. See also *Law's Empire* (London, 1986), 221 ff.

are wholly subject to either utilitarian considerations or majoritarian preferences: their protection cannot therefore be left to the ordinary political process.[31] The legitimacy of the judicial function within a democratic polity, where Parliament is the ultimate judge of government policy, stems primarily from recognition that 'the doctrine of ministerial responsibility is not in itself an adequate safeguard for the citizen whose rights are affected'.[32]

A judge is properly concerned with policy only when interpreting legislation: he takes account of policy in the sense that his application of a statute to the case in hand naturally depends on his understanding of the statute's purpose or intent. He is not, however, a creative agent of public policy in the manner in which his elaboration of legal principle must be creative.[33] In determining legal rights and duties, in other words, he does not *make* policy—in any ordinary sense of that expression. He employs his view of the statutory policy—what conception of the public interest has been adopted by those charged with legislative responsibility—in deciding questions about the rights of those involved in the case before him.

Accordingly, in the well-known *Padfield* case,[34] the House of Lords rejected a contention that South-Eastern Region milk producers had any right that the minister appoint a committee of investigation under the Agricultural Marketing Act 1958: he had a discretion whether or not to refer a complaint to such a committee. The language and context of the Act did not 'support the view that an absolute right to an enquiry is given to an aggrieved person'.[35] Since, however, the minister must act to promote the policies and objects of the statute, he could only refuse to refer a complaint on limited grounds. The producers aggrieved by the operation of the marketing scheme therefore had corresponding rights to the proper exercise of the statutory discretion. The Act imposed a duty to have any relevant and substantial complaint investigated: by failing to act, the minister was 'rendering nugatory a safeguard provided by the Act' and depriving the complainants of a 'remedy which . . . Parliament intended them to have'.[36] The fact that

[31] *Taking Rights Seriously*, ch. 7; *A Matter of Principle* (Oxford, 1985), ch. 17.

[32] *R.* v. *Toohey; ex p. Northern Land Council* (1981) 151 CLR 170, 222 (Mason J.).

[33] See esp. *Taking Rights Seriously*, ch. 4; *Law's Empire*, ch. 7. Cf. Hayek, *Constitution of Liberty*, 212: 'The task of the judge is to discover the implications contained in the spirit of the whole system of valid rules of law or to express as a general rule, when necessary, what was not explicitly stated previously in a court of law or by the legislator. That this task of interpretation is not one in which the judge has discretion in the sense of authority to follow his own will to pursue particular concrete aims appears from the fact that his interpretation of the law can be . . . made subject to review by a higher court.' (See also Luke K. Cooperrider, 'The Rule of Law and the Judicial Process' (1961) 59 Mich. LR 501, esp. 506.)

[34] *Padfield* v. *Minister of Agriculture* [1968] AC 997.

[35] Ibid. 1045–6 (Lord Hodson). [36] Ibid. 1032 (Lord Reid).

the complaint raised wide issues concerning the public interest did not detract from the complainants' rights to have it properly considered. They could not, of course, assert any rights in respect of the committee's conclusions regarding the public interest, or of the minister's decision whether to implement the report: at that stage the minister was answerable only to Parliament for the policy he adopted.[37]

The court, then, determines the *existing legal rights* of the parties, whereas a tribunal or agency—where it is granted power to decide matters of public interest—adjusts the *future relations* between the parties. The former is retrospective, seeking consistency with previous cases as a matter of legal justice. The latter is prospective: consistency with other decided cases may be desirable on general policy grounds (fostering certainty and predictability) but is not an integral requirement of justice between the parties. This was the fundamental division between judicial and arbitral functions affirmed by the Privy Council in relation to the Australian Constitution.[38] The Dominion Parliament was unable to confer arbitral and judicial functions on the same institution; with the result that an attempt to vest judicial power in the Court of Conciliation and Arbitration had failed. In distinguishing between the judicial power, and the arbitral function conferred on the Court for the purpose of settling industrial disputes, the court adopted the previous analysis of Isaacs and Rich JJ.[39] Both functions presupposed a dispute, a hearing or investigation, and a decision:

> But the essential difference is that the judicial power is concerned with the ascertainment, declaration and enforcement of the rights and liabilities of the parties as they exist, or are deemed to exist, at the moment the proceedings are instituted; whereas the function of the arbitral power in relation to industrial disputes is to ascertain and declare, but not enforce, what in the opinion of the arbitrator ought to be the respective rights and liabilities of the parties in relation to each other.

The arbitral function was ancillary to the legislative function, providing the '*factum* upon which the law operates to create the right or duty'. Whereas the judicial function was to ascertain pre-existing legal rights, whose content preceded the dispute and governed its resolution, an industrial dispute involved a claim that existing relations should be altered: 'It is therefore a claim for new rights.' Subsequent decisions of the High Court of Australia have attempted to relax the doctrine of

[37] Ibid. 1054 (Lord Pearce).

[38] *A.-G. for Australia* v. *The Queen and the Boilermakers' Society of Australia* [1957] AC 288.

[39] *Waterside Workers' Fed. of Australia* v. *Alexander* (1918) 25 CLR 434, 463–4. See also *R.* v. *Commonwealth Industrial Court; ex p. Amalgmd. Engineering Union* (1960) 103 CLR 368, 376 (Fullagar J.); and M. J. Detmold, *The Australian Commonwealth* (Sydney, 1985), 230–6. Detmold observes that 'the conception of an "existing legal right" cannot be limited to something already actually formulated in a statute or decision, but must include that which is in accordance with the balance of existing reasons . . .' (234).

separation of powers in its application to the statutory conferment of powers; but as the New Zealand Court of Appeal recently noted, the 'basic distinction between industrial arbitration and the determination of legal rights' remains unimpaired.[40] That court upheld a regulation, made under statutory authority and prohibiting the Arbitration Court from proceeding with disputes, on the ground that it applied only to disputes of interest 'remote from typical judicial functions'.[41] The court's jurisdiction over disputes in respect of existing rights was unaffected.

In judicial proceedings, then, attention is focused on pre-existing legal rights and duties, the court having no creative role in respect of the development of policy. Conceptually, law and policy—where the latter permits a genuine *choice* of outcomes—are fundamentally opposed: 'justice is "owed"; it is not granted by favour or accorded at discretion'.[42] By contrast, policy plays an active and commanding role in the quasi-judicial function entrusted to many tribunals, where Parliament has conferred jurisdiction, not to determine rights and duties already given, but to determine some facet of the public interest or administer a scheme, where executive 'discretion' (or choice) is an integral component of each decision.[43]

The quasi-judicial function can be clearly distinguished in matters of procedure, where the courts have recognized that the imposition of curial arrangements may be inappropriate. In *Local Government Board* v. *Arlidge*,[44] the House of Lords held that the minister could dismiss an appeal against a local authority's closing order without disclosing his inspector's report or granting an oral hearing. Viscount Haldane LC denied that the case involved a *lis inter partes*: the authority's decision was not a determination of existing rights. In hearing the appeal, the Board was required to act judicially—but only in the sense that it must act in good faith, affording each party an opportunity to present its case. The procedural rights of the parties were therefore determined in the light of statutory policy and the nature of the governmental power. It was Parliament's prerogative to entrust the matter to a department of state, but the court's function to settle, as a matter of law, what procedural rights accompanied the exercise of executive power.

In *Ridge* v. *Baldwin*,[45] Lord Reid classified as quasi-judicial cases involving such diverse bodies as boards of works, colonial governors,

[40] *New Zealand Drivers' Assocn.* v. *NZ Road Carriers* [1982] 1 NZLR 374, 391 (Cooke, McMullin, and Ongley JJ.).

[41] Ibid.

[42] *Ibralebbe* v. *R* [1964] AC 900, 919.

[43] Cf. D. J. Galligan, *Discretionary Powers* (Oxford, 1986), esp. ch. 1; Hayek, *Constitution of Liberty*, 212–15.

[44] [1915] AC 120. See also *Board of Education* v. *Rice* [1911] AC 179.

[45] [1964] AC 40.

and club committees. These bodies dealt with single cases, but did not determine legal rights. None the less, there was an analogy with the judge's function in sentencing offenders. Policy would play a role in any decision, but the proceedings were of sufficiently 'judicial' a character to attract the principles of natural justice. The judicial quality was an attribute of the power conferred, involving the treatment of individuals to the prejudice of their rights or interests. In an important judgment, Atkin LJ had affirmed the extension of the prerogative writs to quasi-judicial bodies, which did not 'possess legal authority to try cases, and pass judgments in the strictest sense'.[46]

The distinction between legal principle and public policy, then, is fundamental to the separation of powers. It underlies the conviction, basic to the rule of law, that 'the judicial power of the state exercised through judges appointed by the state remains an independent, and recognisably separate, function of government'.[47] The dichotomy of law and policy corresponds to that distinction, and explains the nature of the quasi-judicial function—inserted, sometimes uneasily, between the judicial and executive paradigms.[48] The requirements of procedural fairness must be adjusted to the circumstances of each public authority, according to the impact of its decisions on individual rights. But that conclusion does not contradict the distinction between principle and policy. The Privy Council rightly denied that the distinction between judicial and arbitral functions was refuted by the relevance of natural justice to both.[49] In a passage reminiscent of Robson's argument for rejecting the distinction in favour of an undifferentiated function of fair decision-making—but to precisely the opposite effect—Viscount Simonds stated:

> Such facts as that the same qualities of fairness, patience and courtesy should be exhibited by conciliator, arbitrator or judge alike, and that none of them should act without hearing both sides of the case do not weigh against the fact that the exercise of the judicial function is concerned, as the arbitral function is not, with the determination of a justiciable issue.[50]

Clarity of thought is not assisted by denial of the distinction between law and policy, even if their reconciliation is sometimes problematic. Dicey had pointed out that the functions entrusted to government in the modern state demanded extended powers, which could not be confined by rules appropriate to the administration of justice.[51] He was

[46] *R.* v. *Electricity Cmmrs., ex p. London Elec. Jt. Cttee.* [1924] 1 KB 171, 206.

[47] *A.-G.* v. *BBC* [1980] 3 All ER 161, 182 (Lord Scarman).

[48] Cf. Geoffrey Marshall, 'Justiciability', *Oxford Essays in Jurisprudence*, 1st series, ed. A. G. Guest (Oxford, 1961), 285: 'an administrative tribunal is in a position of unstable equilibrium between the judicial and political processes'.

[49] *A.-G. for Australia* v. *The Queen and the Boilermakers' Society of Australia* [1957] AC 288.

[50] Ibid. 319. For discussion of the concept of justiciability, see Ch. 9 below.

[51] 'The Development of Administrative Law in England' 31 LQR 148 (1915).

also, of course, well aware that extended political and social control inevitably threatened the traditional values of individual autonomy embraced within the rule of law. In Hayek's terms, modern public administration cannot be wholly conducted within a framework of purpose-independent general rules. As Robson states the point, from a different ideological perspective: 'Social interests cannot be secured, or a social policy effected, by the application of abstract principles of justice as between man and man.'[52]

Public interest immunity and legal principle

It is often thought that the courts' determination of claims of public interest immunity—an immunity from the ordinary process of disclosure of documents in the course of litigation, asserted on the grounds of a public interest in confidentiality—demonstrates their involvement in policy-making. Since the courts no longer accept ministerial certificates automatically, but undertake to balance the public interest in secrecy against the needs of the administration of justice in each case, are they not bound to decide broad questions of public interest?[53] How in such circumstances can principle be distinguished from policy?

We should be cautious about taking judicial language at face value. References to public interests might more accurately be interpreted as allusions to legal rights. It is clear that there is generally little public interest in the disclosure of information sought by a litigant for his own purposes, *except in the sense* that it is strongly in the public interest (other things being equal) that he should be able to enforce his legal rights. The public interest in the administration of justice consists in the effective protection of legal rights, even if the procedural conditions for their enforcement must make appropriate allowance for important, opposing public interests. What is appropriate, as the law reports reveal, will depend on the strength of the litigant's right and the cogency of the public immunity claim in the circumstances of each case.[54]

Ronald Dworkin has denied that the balancing of public interests should be understood as a purely utilitarian calculation.[55] In weighing the requirements of justice, in the context of a claim to withhold documents on public interest grounds, the court gives effect to the

[52] *Justice and Administrative Law*, 549.

[53] See *Conway* v. *Rimmer* [1968] AC 910; *Sankey* v. *Whitlam* (1978) 142 CLR 1: e.g. Gibbs ACJ: 'In some cases . . . the court must weigh the one competing aspect of the public interest against the other, and decide where the balance lies.' (142 CLR 39)

[54] See e.g. *Burmah Oil* v. *Bank of England* [1979] 3 All ER 700, 720–1 (Lord Edmund-Davies); 725 (Lord Keith). Lord Keith thought that 'the nature of the litigation and the apparent importance to it of the documents in question may in extreme cases demand production even of the most sensitive communications at the highest level'.

[55] *A Matter of Principle*, ch. 3.

procedural rights of the parties (much as it does in the case of quasi-judicial powers, considered above). Procedural rights are a necessary concomitant of substantive rights. (Substantive rights would otherwise lack means of enforcement and their recognition would be insincere.) When a court fails to protect a person's legal rights (or where in a criminal case a defendant is wrongly convicted) because of defects in the court's procedure, that person suffers an injustice, or 'moral harm'. This 'injustice factor' or 'moral harm' reveals the inadequacy of simple utilitarian calculation. For example, we believe that it would be wrong deliberately to convict the innocent, even if there were a long-term utilitarian benefit to be gained. But a similar injustice exists where an innocent person is mistakenly convicted, as a result of imperfect procedures, and this is quite independent of the actual suffering any punishment may cause.

Although no litigant can insist on faultless procedures—guaranteeing perfect accuracy in the determination of relevant facts regardless of their social cost—he can expect the risk of injustice inherent in less perfect procedures to be properly assessed and taken into account. The litigant is entitled, Dworkin argues, to procedures consistent with that evaluation of moral harm which is reflected in the (civil) law as a whole.[56] Only then is he fairly treated, on principles applied to everyone else. Cases about public interest immunity—such as those concerning the claims of certain bodies to protect their sources of information—do not therefore turn on ordinary utilitarian arguments, based solely on the general welfare:

> For the central question raised in such cases is the question whether the party claiming some procedural advantage or benefit is entitled to it as a matter of right, in virtue of his general right to a level of accuracy consistent with the theory of moral harm reflected in the civil law as a whole . . . References to the public's interest in disclosure or in justice make sense only as disguised and misleading references to individual rights, that is, as references to the level of accuracy that litigants are entitled to have *as against* the public interest in, for example, the flow of information to useful public agencies or newspapers . . . What is in question, in these cases, is whether the litigant is entitled to a level of accuracy, measured in terms of the risk of moral harm, that must trump these otherwise important and legitimate social concerns.[57]

Dworkin rightly insists that the matter is not purely one of public policy. The relevant instrumental and consequential calculations are

[56] The special injustice caused by erroneous conviction of a criminal offence is acknowledged by the more restricted operation of public interest immunity: see Colin Tapper, *Cross on Evidence*, 7th edn. (London, 1990), 472–5. Claims to legal professional privilege (an analogous exception to disclosure of evidence) are overridden when necessary to enable the defendant to establish his innocence: *Barton* [1972] 2 All ER 1192.

[57] *A Matter of Principle*, 95. Dworkin refers specifically to *D.* v. *NSPCC* [1978] AC 171 and *British Steel Corp.* v. *Granada TV* [1981] AC 1096.

fully embedded in arguments of principle: 'Consequences figure not in deciding whether to admit evidence to which no party is entitled, but in deciding whether one party is entitled to have that evidence.'[58] It is not a question of asking whether a minimum level of procedural accuracy has been achieved, followed by an independent policy judgment on grounds of public interest. It is a question of whether the risk of injustice or moral harm is properly weighed—a matter which necessarily connects the two judgments about accuracy and the public interest.

It might none the less be argued that the inherent capacity of the common law for gradual development and change blurs the neat conceptual division of powers. New heads of public interest may come to be accepted in recognition of altered political or social conditions, and the weight to be accorded established immunities is intrinsically vulnerable to changing perceptions of the public interest. It would be mistaken, however, to think that this point necessarily undermines the separation of powers. The scope of legal rights develops by appeal to analogy with existing principle, and there is therefore a genuine sense in which the court is constrained by established standards and accepted modes of reasoning.

In *D.* v. *National Society for the Prevention of Cruelty to Children*,[59] the House of Lords rebuffed a submission that whenever an identifiable public interest in non-disclosure of a source of information could be established, the court should balance the relevant considerations in exercise of a wide discretion whether or not to order disclosure. The court preferred a more cautious approach, Lord Hailsham rejecting the submission as contrary to 'the general tradition of the development of doctrine preferred by the English courts'. This tradition proceeded 'through evolution by extension or analogy of recognised principles and reported precedents'.[60] Those who gave information to the Society about neglect or ill-treatment of children would have their identity protected by analogy with the protection traditionally afforded police informers. There was a similar risk that sources of information would dry up if anonymity could not be preserved; and the Society, even if it were not a public agency, had statutory powers to bring care proceedings and therefore a public responsibility. The court had already extended the immunity to persons from whom the Gaming Board received information for the purposes of its statutory functions under the Gaming Act 1968.[61]

The decision to refuse an order for disclosure of the Society's informant, in the circumstances of that case, was therefore based on a

[58] *A Matter of Principle*, 97. [59] [1978] AC 171.
[60] Ibid. 225. [61] *Rogers* v. *Home Secretary* [1973] AC 388.

narrow extension of existing authority: it did not entail the assumption of a policy-making role by the court. Lord Simon stressed the importance of resting the decision on an existing head of public policy already recognized by law, citing Lord Thankerton's view of the role of the courts in *Fender* v. *Mildmay*:[62] 'Their duty is to expound, and not to expand, such policy. That does not mean that they are precluded from applying an existing principle of public policy to a new set of circumstances, where such circumstances are clearly within the scope of the policy.'

Legislative supremacy and judicial deference

In order to maintain the separation of powers between the courts and Parliament there must be appropriate judicial deference to the legislative command. In the absence of a tradition of judicial review of primary legislation, ultimate responsibility for reconciling individual rights with the needs of the public interest rests, in ordinary circumstances, with the legislature. Although the courts can impose important restraints on (potentially) unjust legislation, in accordance with their role in defence of the rule of law, the separation of powers would be undermined—and the independence of the judiciary made more vulnerable—if the interpretative function were to permit wholesale judicial revision of statutes which infringed individual rights. Even if clear words are needed before basic rights may be curtailed, it must be recognized that the words are sometimes all too clear.

Lord Diplock made this point forcefully in a case which was treated as raising 'some profound questions' about the separation of powers.[63] Legislation often gave effect to policies which were the subject of acute political controversy. In such circumstances it could not be too strongly emphasized that the British constitution, though largely unwritten, was 'firmly based on the separation of powers: Parliament makes the laws, the judiciary interpret them'. Where the meaning of a statute was plain and unambiguous, it was not for the courts 'to invent fancied ambiguities as an excuse for failing to give effect to its plain meaning because they themselves consider that the consequences of doing so would be inexpedient, or even unjust or immoral'.[64] In such matters as industrial relations, it was Parliament's view about what was expedient, just, or moral which was paramount.

The House of Lords interpreted the Trade Union and Labour Relations Act 1974, section 13, which granted immunity from liability in tort for damage caused by industrial action taken 'in furtherance of a trade

[62] [1938] AC 1, 23.
[63] *Duport Steels* v. *Sirs* [1980] 1 All ER 529, 550–1 (Lord Scarman).
[64] Ibid. 541 (Lord Diplock).

dispute', as sanctioning a wholly subjective test of intent. A trade union therefore enjoyed a power, limited by self-restraint alone, to inflict 'untold harm' even on parties unconnected with a particular dispute—harm 'to the employees of such enterprises, to members of the public and to the nation itself'—provided only that its leaders honestly considered that to do so might advance its objectives, even slightly. In the Court of Appeal, Lord Denning had proposed a test of remoteness to limit the otherwise open-ended nature of the statutory terms: some actions, causing loss to innocent third parties, would be too remote from a trade dispute to be in furtherance of it. Each of the court's various suggestions for confining the scope of the immunity, however, was rejected by the House of Lords. It endangered 'continued public confidence in the political impartiality of the judiciary' if, 'under the guise of interpretation', judges provided 'their own preferred amendments' to statutes whose operation had had what they considered injurious results.[65]

That description of restrictive interpretation, however, seems tendentious. The exception of particular groups or organizations from ordinary legal constraints—where such groups serve only private interests and have no special status in public law—is wholly antagonistic to the rule of law.[66] It is a fundamental principle that the law should afford equal protection to, and impose equal restraints on, all persons—except where departures from equality before the law can be specially justified (as in the case of public bodies or agencies acting deliberately in the public interest). A sovereign Parliament can authorize departures from this general principle. But the courts might be expected to adopt a sceptical stance, when the consequent injustice appears to be grave, requiring clear language before embracing the widest construction of an immunity from the ordinary civil law.[67]

Lord Diplock explained that the court must focus on the terms in which Parliament has defined the category of actions entitled to immunity: 'Do the acts done in this particular case fall within that description?' It was not legitimate to ask whether Parliament intended that the actions taken in the particular case should enjoy the benefit of the immunity. That amounted to assuming a discretion to decide 'whether or not to apply the general law to a particular case'. But where the category of relevant actions is uncertain—where cogent arguments for opposing interpretations can be made by competent

[65] Ibid. 542 (Lord Diplock). The Court of Appeal had also sought to distinguish a 'trade dispute' from a dispute between a union and the government: 536 (Lord Denning MR); 539–40 (Lawton LJ); 540 (Ackner LJ).

[66] Cf. Hayek, *Law, Legislation and Liberty*, i. 141–4; ii, ch. 11.

[67] Lord Diplock thought the immunity 'intrinsically repugnant to anyone who has spent his life in the practice of the law or the administration of justice': [1980] 1 All ER 529, 541.

lawyers—Lord Diplock's distinction proves elusive. Inevitably, a doubtful case poses questions about the boundaries of the category, and the questions Lord Diplock distinguished begin to converge. Moreover, it is surely permissible to take account of the consequences of an interpretation—even in the particular case—when deciding what the statute means. It is precisely our conviction that the statute might have unjust or unreasonable results which causes us (justifiably) to think its meaning uncertain.[68]

In his dissenting speech in a previous case on the same provision,[69] Lord Wilberforce defended a reading which would limit the immunity to action which was reasonably capable of furthering a trade dispute. There was an objective element which the court must appraise, although it should be slow to question the judgment of experienced trade union officials. It was the duty of the courts, faced with 'open-ended expressions such as those involving cause, or effect, or remoteness . . . to draw a line' beyond which such an expression ceased to apply. He accepted the view that the statute should be given its 'natural meaning', but his interpretative method was quite as plausible as Lord Diplock's approach. It was 'simply the common law in action'. It did not amount to 'cutting down' what Parliament had given: it involved an interpretation 'in order to ascertain how far Parliament intended to go'.[70]

The restrictive reading seems more in accordance with the court's approach in public law cases, where broadly framed powers are generally given a strict construction. Lord Diplock's denial that the damage caused to the victim of strike action need be proportionate to the assistance afforded the union would carry little conviction if applied, by analogy, to the exercise of coercive powers by ministers or official agencies.[71] The weakness of the result is confirmed, perhaps, by Lord Scarman's assertion that the court had power in an 'altogether exceptional case' to grant an interlocutory injunction, restraining industrial action, even where the statutory defence was likely to succeed at trial.[72] Would not such an injunction contradict the court's interpretation? In a similar context Frankfurter J. observed, in the United States Supreme Court, that 'balancing the equities' in deciding whether an injunction should issue was 'lawyers' jargon' for choosing between conflicting interests. When Congress had itself struck the balance, a court of equity was 'not justified in ignoring that pronouncement under the guise of exercising equitable discretion'.[73]

[68] Cf. Dworkin, *Law's Empire*, 352–3; and see Ch. 4 below.

[69] *Express Newspapers* v. *MacShane* [1980] 1 All ER 65.

[70] Ibid. 70.

[71] For the (contested) requirement of proportionality in administrative law, see Ch. 8 below.

[72] [1980] 1 All ER 529, 553.

[73] *Youngstown Sheet & Tube Co.* v. *Sawyer* 343 US 579, 609–10 (1952).

Judicial resistance to privative clauses

It seems reasonable to argue that the degree of deference to legislative supremacy (or style of interpretation) should depend on the nature of the statutory command and its implications for the rule of law—in the sense that judicial co-operation with the statutory purpose should be tailored to the implicit requirements of liberal constitutionalism. Those presumptions of legislative intent which operate to protect established rights reflect a legitimate bias in favour of traditional liberties—preventing serious encroachments by general rules of uncertain scope, which betray no sign that such effects were truly intended or even considered, but not frustrating explicit statutory provision. In particular, the rule of construction which protects ordinary rights to invoke the courts' jurisdiction for the determination of other legal rights and duties is an important adjunct of the separation of powers. The role of the law as a bulwark between government and governed, excluding the exercise of arbitrary power, is destroyed if the citizen is deprived of his recourse to independent courts.[74]

If the style of statutory interpretation should reflect the nature of any threat to individual rights—in defence of the court's understanding of the demands of the separation of powers and the rule of law—the *Anisminic* case[75] showed that, in appropriate circumstances, interpretation can come acceptably close to disobedience. Perhaps talk of disobedience is too histrionic: since a provision must always be read in its general legal context, restrictive interpretation may often be fairly justified as obedience to the parliamentary will, properly—constitutionally—understood. However, we should recognize that for practical purposes the distinction between application and interpretation of statutes is (in a sense) a matter of degree: there is necessarily an uncertain border between restrictive interpretation and non-application (in the particular case). To pretend otherwise is to overlook the ineradicable tension between legislative supremacy and individual autonomy—between democracy and the rule of law.[76]

In *Anisminic*, the House of Lords ruled that a clause providing that 'the determination by the Commission of any application made to them under this Act shall not be called in question in any court of law' did not preclude the court from setting aside what purported to be a determination, but was in fact a nullity. In basing its rejection of the

[74] See e.g. *Pyx Granite Co.* v. *Ministry of Housing and Local Govt.* [1960] AC 260, 286 (Viscount Simonds); and Ch. 6 below.

[75] *Anisminic* v. *Foreign Compensation Commission* [1969] 2 AC 147.

[76] See Ch. 11 below. Cf. Sir William Wade, *Constitutional Fundamentals*, Hamlyn Lectures, 32nd series, revised edn. (London, 1989), ch. 5 (Wade talks of 'disobedience' and 'rebellion').

appellant's claim to compensation on matters which were irrelevant to a proper determination, the commission had exceeded its jurisdiction. An ouster clause would not serve to protect from judicial control action by a public body which was *ultra vires*. The court's reasoning can clearly be defended as a matter of constitutional theory. If the rule of law means rule by a body of consistent legal principle, it is hard to defend the complete exclusion from review of a specialist tribunal by the ordinary courts of law. Justifiably, Lord Wilberforce denied any true conflict with parliamentary intent: 'What would be the point of defining by statute the limit of a tribunal's powers if, by means of a clause inserted in the instrument of definition, those limits could safely be passed?'[77]

We should, however, be cautious in embracing Lord Diplock's view that the decision destroyed the previously accepted distinction between *ultra vires* and *intra vires* errors of law, at least in the case of administrative tribunals: 'Any error of law that could be shown to have been made by them in the course of reaching their decision on matters of fact or of administrative policy would result in their having asked themselves the wrong question with the result that the decision they reached would be a nullity.'[78] It all depends on what is meant by 'error of law'.

Although a tribunal may be accorded a comparative freedom in deciding the relevant facts of a case, its application to those facts of any legal provision—and therefore also the matter of which facts are relevant—is necessarily (to some degree) a question of law.[79] The result is that decisions entrusted to administrative bodies may become instead ultimately decisions for the court. The court would then be usurping statutory powers granted by Parliament to other agencies. A tribunal would be free to determine policy where the statute envisaged the necessary discretion. But where the scope for policy-making is severely curtailed or non-existent—where the statutory function is to determine existing rights—a tribunal may be left with no independent jurisdiction at all. It could lawfully decide only what a court of review itself would decide. In those circumstances, or course, there would be nothing to which a privative clause (like that in *Anisminic*) could attach.

It is no answer to this objection that the determination of questions of law (for the courts) might be distinguished from the *application* of law to the facts of particular cases (for the tribunal). For the meaning of a rule of law cannot logically be distinguished from its application. Each new case which raises a question about a statute's application—

[77] [1969] 2 AC 147, 208. And see H. W. R. Wade, 'Constitutional and Administrative Aspects of the *Anisminic* Case' (1969) 85 LQR 198.
[78] *Re Racal Communications* [1980] 2 All ER 634, 639.
[79] Cf. M. J. Detmold, *Courts and Administrators* (London, 1989), ch. 5.

do the circumstances fall within its scope?—*ipso facto* tests its meaning. The mistake we reviewed above, where Lord Diplock attempted to divorce the meaning of a stipulated category of acts from its application to particular actions, was an example of this misunderstanding.[80]

The same point was actually taken by Lord Diplock himself against Lord Denning, who had asserted that 'no court or tribunal has any jurisdiction to make an error of law on which the decision of the case depends'.[81] The Court of Appeal had improperly overturned the decision of a county court judge that an installation of central heating did not amount to 'structural alteration, extension or addition' under the Housing Act 1974. As Lord Diplock fairly objected: 'If the meaning of ordinary words when used in a statute becomes a question of law, here was a typical question of mixed law, fact and degree which only a scholiast would think it appropriate to dissect into two separate questions, one for decision by the superior court, viz. the meaning of those words . . . and the other for decision by the county court, viz. the application of the words to the particular installation . . .'[82] The scholiast would clearly be confused. The statute had given the judge jurisdiction to decide 'finally and conclusively' a matter involving 'interrelated questions of law, fact and degree'.[83]

We must accept, then, that Parliament sometimes leaves the meaning of its enactments in the hands of courts or tribunals, without further recourse to the superior courts. The superior court should sometimes defer to parliamentary sovereignty by acknowledging that statutory provisions should be applied in the light of the tribunal's specialist experience and expertise. There is nothing here necessarily contrary to the rule of law: the court's constitutional role includes the task of deciding, as a matter of overall interpretation, whether the meaning of particular terms is remitted to the tribunal's decision. The court acknowledges what might be considered a quasi-legislative power: the tribunal enjoys authority to *determine* the meaning of a provision, acting within the scope of its jurisdiction.[84]

That final qualification, however, is of some importance. The scope of jurisdiction must always be ultimately a matter for the courts: any other view would destroy the principle of government according to law. A tribunal which could determine the sense of its own empowering statute, however far its interpretation diverged from that of the superior

[80] *Duport Steels* v. *Sirs*, considered above.

[81] *Pearlman* v. *Keepers & Governors of Harrow School* [1979] QB 56, 70.

[82] Re Racal Communications [1980] 2 All ER 634, 639.

[83] Ibid. approving Geoffrey Lane LJ's dissenting judgment in *Pearlman*. See generally J. Beatson, 'The Scope of Judicial Review for Error of Law' (1984) 4 OJLS 22.

[84] Cf. *Edwards* v. *Bairstow* [1956] AC 14, 33: commissioners' determination of existence of a 'trade', for the purposes of Income Tax Act, conclusive if 'the facts of any particular case' were 'fairly capable of being so described' (Lord Radcliffe).

courts, would not be a body operating under the law.[85] It follows that deference to the legislative will—if that means taking literally extravagant attempts to curtail judicial review—cannot proceed too far without altogether repudiating constitutionalism. But we need not assume any ultimate irreconcilability as a matter of legal principle. For legislative sovereignty inheres in the words enacted—interpreted correctly in accordance with the constitutional premisses of the rule of law—and not in the aspirations of government or even parliamentary majority.[86] Accordingly, the court's authority to decide the limits of an agency's powers is ultimately—fundamentally—invulnerable to legislative abrogation.

Privative clauses may help, 'according to the width and emphasis of their formulation', to ascertain the extent of a tribunal's jurisdiction; but they cannot—'unless one is to deny the statutory origin of the tribunal and of its powers'—preclude all examination of the question. Such clauses 'in their nature can only relate to decisions given within the field of operation entrusted to the tribunal'.[87] Sir Robin Cooke has spoken of a 'fundamental rule of our mainly unwritten constitution' in this connection: determination of questions of law is always the ultimate responsibility of courts of general jurisdiction. Privative clauses must be as subject to judicial (principled) construction as any other provisions:

> Inherent in our system of checks and balances is the practical truth that every Act of Parliament, even one touching the jurisdiction of the courts themselves, is ultimately subject to interpretation by the superior courts of general jurisdiction . . . If these courts were to accept that some Act deprived them of a significant part of that function, they would be acquiescing *pro tanto* in a revolution.[88]

Constitutionalism and the limits of sovereignty

If there were ultimately no limits to legislative supremacy, as a matter of constitutional theory, it would be difficult to speak of the British

[85] It is not the case (as I stress in Ch. 5) that the superior courts enjoy a monopoly of the powers of legal reasoning; but the separation of powers requires that legal *authority* (in respect of particular cases) should rest finally with the superior courts. Only then are the other organs of *government* truly subject to law.

[86] Cf. *Black-Clawson Internat.* v. *Papierwerke Waldhof-Aschaffenburg* [1975] AC 591, 638 (Lord Diplock).

[87] *Anisminic* case [1969] 2 AC 147, 207 (Lord Wilberforce). Cf. *Minister of Health* v. *R., ex p. Yaffe* [1931] AC 494: court's jurisdiction could not be entirely excluded by provision that a minister's order should 'have effect as if enacted in this Act'. The minister had no power to make an order inconsistent with the Act.

[88] 'The Struggle for Simplicity in Administrative Law', *Judicial Review of Administrative Action in the 1980s*, ed. Michael Taggart (Oxford, 1986), 10. Sir William Wade has also suggested that the courts were 'discovering a deeper constitutional logic than the crude absolute of statutory omnipotence': *Constitutional Fundamentals*, 87.

polity as a constitutional state grounded in law. Although the form of the separation of powers may vary between constitutions, the independence of the superior courts from government and legislature seems fundamental to the rule of law. It follows that if we deny all restrictions on legislative competence—even in respect of the adjudication of particular cases—we thereby reject constitutionalism. The scope of such restrictions is admittedly hard to identify, and largely untested: our jurisprudence has been impoverished by lawyers' uncritical adherence to Dicey's dogma of parliamentary omnipotence—a dogma rendered plausible only by its counterpart doctrine rejecting the integral connection between law and convention.[89]

Parliamentary competence undoubtedly extends to the alteration of legal rights, even where such rights are simultaneously the subject of judicial decision. The legislative process could not be impeded by the fortuitous circumstances of current litigation. A distinction must therefore be drawn between legislation which affects rights in issue before the courts, and enactments which invade the judicial process by interfering directly with the exercise of judicial powers. Legislation of the latter kind strikes unacceptably at the kernel of the rule of law, which depends on the distinction between the formulation of general rules and their application, by an independent judiciary, to particular cases. As Street CJ emphasized, in the New South Wales Court of Appeal, the protections of natural justice, appellate control, and other concomitants of ordinary judicial process are fundamental safeguards of individual rights: 'For Parliament, uncontrolled as it is by any of the safeguards that are enshrined in the concept of due process of law, to trespass into this field of judging between parties by interfering with the judicial process is an affront to a society that prides itself on the quality of its justice.'[90]

Unfortunately, that distinction between permissible and impermissible invasions of the judicial sphere proves insecure. Legislation which on its face respects the integrity of the judicial process may be enacted for the purpose of frustrating particular legal proceedings. Accordingly, the separation of powers, even in its most conservative formulation, must entail a principle against *ad hominem* legislation. In one sense, of course, if the judicial function involves the application of law in the ascertainment of pre-existing rights, the 'legislative judgment', providing *ex post facto* for the outcome of a particular case, is not itself an exercise of judicial power.[91] In substance, however, it

[89] See Chs. 10 and 11 below.

[90] *Building Construction Employees & Builders' Labourers Fed. of NSW* v. *Minister for Industrial Rels.* (1986) 7 NSWLR 372. 376. For the distinction between permissible and impermissible legislation, see *Australian BCE & Builders' Labourers Fed.* v. *The Commonwealth* (1986) 60 ALJR 584.

[91] Cf. Geoffrey Marshall, *Constitutional Theory* (Oxford, 1971), 122–3.

invades the judicial function in precisely the manner that the separation of powers forbids. It permits a 'political' arm of government to act directly against an individual or private organization without any of the intermediate safeguards of legal process, based on general rules. It is an exercise of legislative power which circumvents, and thereby frustrates, the judicial function.

That was the principal thrust of Powell J.'s objection to the reasoning (though not the decision) of the United States Supreme Court in *Chadha's* case.[92] An attempt by the House of Representatives to retain and exercise a 'legislative veto' over certain executive decisions was held unconstitutional. After a hearing, the Immigration Service granted Chadha's appeal against deportation on the expiry of his student visa: it decided that he met the statutory criteria for permanent residence. The House subsequently adopted a resolution, submitted by its Judiciary Committee, rejecting the Service's decision in the case of six persons, including Chadha. The court denied the validity of the resolution, notwithstanding its purported statutory authority,[93] holding that Congress was bound by its delegation of authority in respect of aliens to the executive until such delegation was 'legislatively altered or revoked'.

The House had none the less taken action which was 'essentially legislative in purpose and effect'. Its action had deliberately altered the legal rights, duties, and relations of persons (including Chadha). The exercise of the veto was analogous to new legislation requiring Chadha's deportation.[94] Powell J. disagreed. In his view, the Congressional action was adjudicatory rather than legislative, and unconstitutional on that ground. He thought it necessary to ask whether it raised the danger which the Framers had sought to avoid. The separation of powers doctrine, like the Bill of Attainder clause, reflected the Framers' concern that trial by a legislature lacked the safeguards necessary to prevent abuse of power. In a fundamental sense, Congress had invaded the judicial sphere: 'The House did not enact a general rule; rather it made its own determination that six specific persons did not comply with certain statutory criteria.'[95] Powell J. observed that the deportee enjoyed none of the protection of substantive rules or procedural safeguards which existed when a court or agency determined individual rights: 'The only effective constraint on Congress' power is political, but Congress is most accountable politically when it prescribes rules of

[92] *Immigration & Naturalization Service* v. *Chadha* 462 US 919 (1983).
[93] Immigration & Nationality Act s. 244(c)(2).
[94] Cf. White J. (dissenting), who suggested that the Attorney-General's suspension of deportation, subject to the Congressional veto, was equivalent to a proposal for legislation: 462 US 1001.
[95] 462 US 919, 964–5.

general application. When it decides rights of specific persons, those rights are subject to "the tyranny of a shifting majority".'[96]

Since the resolution in *Chadha* was apparently based on the Committee's view that the aliens concerned did not meet the statutory requirements for permanent residence, it would indeed appear to be adjudicatory rather than legislative in character. As Powell J. emphasized, however, the classification is ultimately inconclusive: in substance, the procedure (even if truly 'legislative') permitted precisely the kind of exercise of power *ad hominem* against which the Framers had sought to guard.

The difficulty of ascertaining the ambit of limits to parliamentary sovereignty on analogous grounds is compounded by constitutional history. Parliament's gradual evolution from court to legislature makes it hard to assess the relevance of tradition in determining the nature of the modern separation of powers. In addition to such striking instances of 'legislative adjudication' as impeachment and attainder, Parliament exercised judicial power by private Act in response to petitions, for example in respect of divorce. In the *Builders' Labourers Federation* case, the New South Wales Court of Appeal condemned legislation which constituted an exercise of judicial power, but held that the Parliament was none the less competent to pass it.[97] That decision rested ultimately on Dicey's distinction between law and convention which I examine more closely in Chapter 10. The New South Wales legislature enjoyed judicial power; but it was 'contrary both to modern constitutional convention, and to the public interest in the due administration of justice, for Parliament to exercise that power by legislation interfering with the judicial process in a particular case pending before the court'.[98]

An earlier statute had provided for the cancellation, by way of ministerial declaration, of the Federation's registration as a trade union because it had engaged in activities contrary to the public interest. The Federation brought proceedings challenging the minister's action, taken under that statute, on grounds of natural justice. Before the Federation's appeal against dismissal of those proceedings at first instance, Parliament enacted the Builders' Labourers Federation (Special Provisions) Act 1986, providing for the minister's action to be treated as valid, notwithstanding any decision in proceedings previously instituted, and for the costs of such proceedings to be borne by the party incurring them.

[96] Ibid. 966, citing Levi, 'Some Aspects of Separation of Powers' (1976) 76 Colum. L. Rev. 369, 374–5.

[97] *Builders' Labourers Federation* case (n. 90 above).

[98] (1986) 7 NSWLR 372, 381 (Street CJ).

The Act was characterized by the Court of Appeal as *ad hominem* legislation: it was addressed to a particular legal person, the Federation, and dealt specifically with incidents of litigation currently involving the Federation. The Parliament had 'intruded its power into the judicial process by directing the outcome of a specific case between particular litigants awaiting hearing at the time the legislation in question was passed'.[99] The Chief Justice roundly condemned such interference, the harm which the Federation was widely considered to have done the nation notwithstanding: 'The greater the hostility directed against a person or organisation, the greater the temptation to distort the fundamental precepts of our democracy by setting at nought the great principles of British justice.'[100]

In the absence, however, of a well-established separation of powers doctrine such as applied under the Federal Constitution, or special entrenchment of the judicial power in the existing courts, the validity of the statute was upheld. The 'constitution, organisation and business' of the Supreme Court were wholly subject to the power of the Parliament. 'Any limitations . . . must be derived from politics and convention, grounded in history. They are not based upon legal restrictions.'[101] Here we anticipate the observations concerning both legislative sovereignty and the law/convention dichotomy of later chapters.[102] If, however, the court's refusal to reject the statute rested, in the final analysis, on the distinction between law and convention, its basis was insecure.

Although a statutory rule may be readily distinguished from convention—the former valid by virtue of formal enactment, the latter deriving from constitutional custom—the distinction proves harder to draw in respect of the common law. As a body of principle, whose content is largely dependent on reasoning from fundamental (including constitutional) axioms, the common law must take account of (legitimate) expectations. Expectations, based on accepted practice, form part of the material from which political principle is derived—necessarily so, if we are talking of a particular legal system rather than abstract, ideal theory. And no distinction can be made between legal and political principle: these are ultimately different labels for the same phenomenon—legitimate constitutional behaviour. Dicey's dichotomy cannot finally be sustained; and invasion of the judicial sphere—if unconstitutional—must, it follows, be equally illegal.

A historical precedent for the prevention of interference with the judicial function, based on convention, is provided by Coke CJ's denial of executive pretensions to judicial power. In holding that James I

[99] Ibid. 378 (Street CJ); cf. Kirby P. at 395. [100] Ibid. 379.
[101] Ibid. 401 (Kirby P.). [102] Chs. 10 and 11 below.

could not sit in person to decide cases, Coke relied on constitutional practice rather than previous judicial authority.[103] As a primary modern convention, the separation of powers must, as a matter of (legal) principle, impose limits on the legislative sovereignty of Parliament. Acts of attainder would today be universally condemned as contrary to fundamental principle. As the 'archetypal violation of the generality of law' the Act of attainder is a law only in form: 'In substance it is a *measure* bearing all the earmarks of an arbitrary executive act.'[104] Is it not grotesque today to insist that constitutional theory permits any and every legislative invasion of the judicial function because Parliament once decided that the Bishop of Rochester's cook should be boiled to death?[105]

As a legislative adjudication of guilt of a criminal offence, the Act of attainder is the most serious, and brutal, violation of the separation of powers. It was an analogous exercise of legislative power which the Privy Council held invalid in the celebrated case, *Liyanage* v. *R.*[106] Following an abortive *coup d'état* in Ceylon, the first Criminal Law (Special Provisions) Act 1962 was passed to deal specifically with the participants. In addition to authorizing breaches of criminal procedure which had previously occurred, the Act created a new criminal offence *ex post facto* and provided for a minimum sentence of ten years' imprisonment and mandatory forfeiture of property on conviction. It empowered the Minister of Justice to direct that the accused should be tried by three judges without a jury, and to nominate the judges; and it sanctioned the admission in evidence of confessions which would otherwise have been excluded. A subsequent Act vested the power of nomination in the Chief Justice when executive nomination was ruled unconstitutional. Although the Judicial Committee accepted that the Ceylon Parliament enjoyed the full legislative powers of a sovereign independent state, it struck down the legislation as an invalid attempt to usurp the judicial power.[107] Although the judicial power was not explicitly vested in the courts, a basic separation of powers was inferred from the general constitutional scheme.

It has been objected that the constitutional provisions regarding the appointment and dismissal of judges—which evinced 'an intention to secure in the judiciary a freedom from political, legislative and executive

[103] *Prohibitions del Roy* (1607) 12 Co. Rep. 63; see W. S. Holdsworth, *A History of English Law*, 3rd edn. (London, 1922), i. 194, 207 (cited by Street CJ at 7 NSWLR 380). (Coke CJ is cited below, Ch. 10.)

[104] Frederic S. Burin, 'The Theory of the Rule of Law and the Structure of the Constitutional State' (1966) 15 Am. UL Rev. 313, at 315.

[105] 22 Hen. 8, c. 9; cited by Committee on Ministers' Powers (1932) Cmd. 4060, 20–1.

[106] [1967] AC 259.

[107] The Ceylon (Constitution) Order in Council, 1946 and Ceylon Independence Act, 1947 provided for full legislative competence.

control'[108]—did not necessarily imply the reservation of exclusive judicial power to the judicature.[109] However, it would be hard to envisage a more flagrant denial of the underlying purpose of the separation of powers as a protection against arbitrary power: 'The pith and substance of both Acts was a legislative plan *ex post facto* to secure the conviction and enhance the punishment of those particular individuals.'[110] In such circumstances, an interpretation which had not imported the doctrine, when the constitution clearly permitted that implication, would surely have been pusillanimous, if not indefensible. The court conceded that a lack of generality in criminal legislation would not, *ipso facto*, invade the judicial function; nor would every *ad hominem* enactment inevitably usurp the judicial power. The present case, however, involving in particular removal of the judges' ordinary sentencing discretion, was an unconstitutional abuse of power.

Despite similarities between the constitutions of Ceylon and New South Wales—in each case the judicial system had been established by a Charter of Justice—the analogy of *Liyanage* was rejected in the *Builders' Labourers Federation* case on the ground that the Constitution of Ceylon entrenched the judicial power by preventing constitutional amendment by ordinary legislative majority. But it is not clear that the limits of legislative power can ultimately be dependent on the existence of entrenched provisions alone. Would the court have found the distinction as persuasive if the facts of the two cases had been truly analogous—involving a similar usurpation of the judicial function in respect of the criminal law? Significantly, perhaps, Kirby P. noted that the 1986 Act would not have offended the express prohibition on legislative judgments in the United States Constitution. Since no final judgment had been given in the litigation concerning the Federation, the Act would not be considered an impermissible invasion of the judicial domain. Since it was not criminal legislation, it would not attract the express constitutional prohibition against Acts of attainder and retroactive laws.

It is reasonable to suppose that there are some constraints on the exercise of legislative sovereignty, implicit in the constitutional scheme of the separation of powers as settled by modern convention, even in the absence of entrenched provisions. In giving the court's advice in *Liyanage*, Lord Pearce stated that any analogy with the British Constitution must be indirect: an unwritten constitution could provide no helpful guidance in interpreting a written document. That view was contradicted, however, by Lord Diplock's more recent judgment,

[108] [1967] AC 259, 287.
[109] S. A. de Smith, 'The Separation of Powers in New Dress' (1967) 12 McGill LJ 491.
[110] [1967] AC 259, 290.

mentioned above.[111] He described written constitutions, established by United Kingdom statute or order in council, as 'drafted by persons nurtured in the tradition of that branch of the common law of England that is concerned with public law and familiar in particular with the basic concept of separation of legislative, executive and judicial power as it had been developed in the unwritten constitution of the United Kingdom'.[112] The legislature might provide for the establishment of new courts, in exercise of its power to make laws for the 'peace, order and good government' of the state. It was none the less 'implicit in the very structure of a constitution on the Westminster model' that judicial power, however it be distributed from time to time between various courts, should continue to be vested in persons appointed to hold judicial office in the traditional manner.[113]

It seems to follow that the independence of the judiciary and of the judicial process may be regarded as ineradicable features of the 'Westminster model' of constitutions—including, therefore, the constitution of the United Kingdom. In the absence of a single, venerated document, legal reasoning must depend on 'what, though not expressed, is none the less a necessary implication from the subject-matter and structure of the constitution . . .'.[114] The doctrine of legislative sovereignty, conventionally taken to preclude any notions of 'entrenched' or fundamental principles, is plainly unable to provide a convincing ground of distinction. The advice in *Liyanage* affirmed that the Ceylonese legislature enjoyed full sovereign power.[115]

Admittedly, the court in *Liyanage* also denied that legislative supremacy was inhibited by 'fundamental principles' of justice; and the Court of New South Wales similarly denied the existence of fundamental rights invulnerable to parliamentary interference. But though constrained by authority in that quarter, the Australian court acceded to the demands of reason in another. Priestly JA acknowledged that the Parliament's powers to make laws for 'the peace, welfare and good government of New South Wales' might be qualified by those purposes. A statute providing, in Stephen's familiar example, for the murder of

[111] *Hinds* v. *R.* [1977] AC 195.

[112] Ibid. 212–13. Cf. *Chokolingo* v. *A.-G. of Trinidad* [1981] 1 All ER 244, 247–8 (Lord Diplock).

[113] Parliament could not, consistently with the separation of powers, transfer from judiciary to the executive the discretion to decide the severity of punishment to be inflicted on particular offenders. Cf. *Ali* v. *R.*; *Rassool* v. *R.* [1992] 2 All ER 1: DPP could not lawfully (under the Constitution of Mauritius) be granted a discretion to select the form of criminal proceedings where the effect would be to enable him to choose the penalty to be imposed in a particular case.

[114] [1977] AC 195, 211.

[115] See also *Bribery Commr.* v. *Ranasinghe* [1965] AC 172; cf. *Ibralebbe* v. *R.* [1964] AC 900, 922.

all blue-eyed babies could be held *ultra vires* as not for the peace, welfare, and good government of the State.[116]

Street CJ made similar observations, explaining that 'New South Wales' had a conceptual meaning. It referred to the body politic, which was essentially a parliamentary democracy—'an entity ruled by a democratically elected Parliament whose citizens enjoy the great inherited privileges of freedom and justice under the protection of an independent judiciary'.[117] Laws enacted by Parliament must meet the test of being for 'the peace, welfare and good government' of that parliamentary democracy 'as it is perceived at the time when the question arises'. The independence of the judiciary, moreover, like universal suffrage, inhered in the very substance of that democracy. Laws which were inimical to, or which did not serve, the peace, welfare and good government of the State, in the sense explained, would be struck down as unconstitutional.[118]

Finally, we should question the New South Wales court's assumption that the Constitution Act placed limits on legislative competence which were not applicable to Parliament at Westminster.[119] Kirby P., who doubted whether the court could declare a law repugnant to the constitution even in New South Wales, thought the problem of defining ultimate constraints insuperable: 'Substituting judicial opinion about entrenched rights for the lawful powers of Parliament, unless anchored in a Bill of Rights duly enacted, inevitably runs into the difficulties of defining what those "common law rights" are and of explaining how they are so basic that they cannot be disturbed.'[120] But such difficulties are the ordinary concerns of common law adjudication; and they do not disappear with the adoption of a bill of rights, which provides no new 'objective' basis for the assertion of rights in concrete cases. Similar problems of definition and delimitation arise. Indeed, the rights enacted are in basic conception only the rights existing at common law.[121]

Can it be supposed that Parliament has authority to legislate for purposes inimical to the peace, welfare, and good government of the United Kingdom? Or that any presumption that its enactments satisfy such implicit conditions is irrebuttable—whatever the circumstances?

[116] L. Stephen, *Science of Ethics* (London, 1882), 143; A. V. Dicey, *The Law of the Constitution*, 10th edn. (London, 1959), 81; 7 NSWLR 372, 420–1: see Constitution Act 1902, s. 5.

[117] 7 NSWLR 382.

[118] Ibid. 384. Mahoney JA refused to recognize such limits on legislative sovereignty, stressing instead the possibility of restrictive interpretation. But if it is legitimate to adopt a restrictive approach to morally offensive legislation, duly enacted, it must also be legitimate—for similar reasons—to repudiate legislation where, in the most extreme case, it is sufficiently abhorrent. (See further Ch. 11 below.)

[119] Ibid. 383 (Street CJ); 421–2 (Priestly JA).

[120] Ibid. 406.

[121] See Ch. 6 below.

The (common law) doctrine of sovereignty is but one component of the conceptual body politic to which Street CJ referred. The objection that the powers of the New South Wales Parliament derive from the Constitution Act 1902, and so cannot properly be analogous to their British counterparts, misses the point. The 'conceptual' interpretation which the Chief Justice favoured had its source, not in the statute, but in the common law. It is therefore equally valid in respect of the unwritten British constitution. Recognition of sovereign legislative power could make no sense in any other circumstances. Legislative supremacy is accepted, in a democratic polity, as part of a constitutional scheme intended to secure good government and the general welfare.

Locke was emphatic that the legislature, 'though it be the supreme power in every commonwealth', did not enjoy unlimited authority: 'Their power in the utmost bounds of it is limited to the public good of the society.'[122] In particular, it could not usurp the executive or judicial functions: 'the legislative or supreme authority cannot assume to itself a power to rule by extemporary arbitrary decrees, but is bound to dispense justice and decide the rights of the subject by promulgated standing laws, and known authorised judges'.[123] It is hard to believe that, as a body of principle (reason), the common law could take a different view. It follows that a statute which violates the constitutional scheme fundamentally could derive no legal authority from the doctrine of sovereignty, properly understood.[124]

One writer has argued that 'the combination of legislative supremacy offset by an independent judiciary suggests that the individual enjoys one right, at least, against the British government—the right not to be deprived of the fruits of a successful law-suit'.[125] On this view, the War Damage Act 1965, overturning the House of Lords' decision in *Burmah Oil Co.* v. *Lord Advocate*,[126] was unconstitutional. It is a vexed question since it might plausibly be argued that the Act constituted only an interference with substantive rights, rather than any invasion of the judicial process. In one sense, it merely rendered redundant the legal proceedings taken by Burmah Oil against the government, much as Commonwealth legislation did in respect of the Builders' Labourers Federation's litigation in the High Court of Australia.[127] A. L. Goodhart argued that the constitutional objection to retrospective legislation was

[122] *Second Treatise of Government*, xi, para. 135.

[123] Ibid. para. 136. (The judicial and executive functions are not distinguished.)

[124] See further Ch. 11 below. Cf. Lord Hailsham, *Dilemma of Democracy*, 104: 'the independence of the judiciary from the government is every bit as fundamental to the maintenance of a free society enjoying liberty under law as is representative government or a multiplicity of political parties . . .'.

[125] Joseph Jaconelli, *Comment* [1985] PL 629, at 631.

[126] [1965] AC 75.

[127] *Australian BCE & Builders' Labourers Fed.* v. *The Commonwealth* (1986) 60 ALJR 584.

limited to penal statutes; and he pointed out that Burmah's claim had been founded on an anomaly, since the more restrictive provisions of the Compensation (Defence) Act 1939 had by oversight not been extended to the colonies.[128] Nevertheless, the 1965 statute is hard to defend: where rights against the government have been crystallized in the final judgment of a court, their deliberate negation by legislation seems to mock the independence of the judiciary: 'It secures, by less unpalatable means, the same result as would the brow-beating of the judges who heard the case.'[129]

In *Chokolingo* v. *Attorney-General of Trinidad*,[130] Lord Diplock declared it 'fundamental to the administration of justice under a constitution which claims to enshrine the rule of law . . . that if between the parties to the litigation the decision of that court is final . . . the relevant law as interpreted by the judge in reaching the court's decision *is* the law so far as the entitlement of the parties to "due process of law" . . . and the "protection of the law" . . . are concerned'. It follows that retrospective legislative amendment of final determinations of rights in particular cases is inconsistent with, and a denial of, the rule of law. It is also, therefore, incompatible with fundamental (legal) principle.

[128] 'The *Burmah Oil* Case and the War Damage Act 1965' (1966) 82 LQR 97.
[129] Jaconelli, *Comment*, 631.
[130] [1981] 1 All ER 244, 248.

4
Legislation and the Common Law

> This power which has been devolved upon the judges from the earliest times is an essential part of the constitutional process by which subjects are brought under the rule of law—as distinct from the rule of the King or the rule of Parliament . . . The saying that it is the function of the courts to ascertain the will or intention of Parliament is often enough repeated . . . If too often or unreflectingly stated, it leads to neglect of the important element of judicial construction; an element not confined to a mechanical analysis of today's words, but . . . related to such matters as intelligibility to the citizen, constitutional propriety, considerations of history, comity of nations, reasonable and non-retroactive effect and, no doubt, in some contexts, to social needs.
>
> *Black-Clawson* v. *Papierwerke Waldhof-Aschaffenburg* [1975] AC 591, 629–30 (Lord Wilberforce).

Although the rules of common law are subject to legislative alteration and abrogation, there is an important sense in which the common law is superior to statute. As a body of evolving principle, the common law provides stability and continuity. Its settled doctrines and assumptions, though always open to reconsideration and challenge, constitute a framework into which legislation must be fitted. No statute, however radical or important its objectives, can be interpreted in isolation from the legal system of which it forms a part. Its meaning will inevitably be dependent, to some degree, on the expectations and preconceptions of those subject to its requirements; and those expectations will rightly be reflected in the process of judicial interpretation. The familiar presumptions of legislative intent—such as that neither extensions of the criminal law nor enactments curbing individual rights are retrospective, and that property is not to be taken without compensation—embody traditional attitudes of the common law to the requirements of freedom and justice.[1] Sir Owen Dixon, as we have seen, expressed his understanding of the relation between common law and statute in his treatment of the common law as 'an ultimate constitutional foundation'.[2]

Some readers may dislike the primacy given here to the common law. They may think that common law presumptions unduly inhibit

[1] See generally Ch. 2, above; and Sir Rupert Cross, *Statutory Interpretation*, 2nd edn. by John Bell and Sir George Engle (London, 1987), ch. 7.

[2] Sir Owen Dixon, 'The Common Law as an Ultimate Constitutional Foundation' (1957) 31 ALJ 240 (see Ch. 1, above).

the effectiveness of legislation, permitting too conservative an approach to contemporary measures for implementing social and political change.[3] Perhaps it will be granted that the common law may be conceived as an evolving corpus of principle, subject to reinterpretation in the light of changing perceptions of justice. But could not legislation, representing the product of the popular will, be accorded at least equal place in the proposed debate about legal principle? It is sometimes suggested that statutes should be treated like precedent—Dicey himself regarded statutes as 'judgments pronounced by the High Court of Parliament'[4]—and invoked as sources for the elaboration of common law rules by means of analogy. Roscoe Pound made that proposal; and Sir Rupert Cross considered that statutes were in practice fully received by English judges into the body of the law, to be reasoned from by analogy in the same manner as decided cases.[5] Ronald Dworkin also condemns a view of legislation as a series of 'negotiated compromises that carry no more or deeper meaning than the text of the statute declares'. He defends an account of the legal order as a 'community of principle', which 'treats legislation as flowing from the community's present commitment to a background scheme of political morality'.[6]

I have suggested, following Dworkin, that the courts must attempt, in particular cases, to accommodate the requirements of both fairness and justice.[7] Legislative supremacy dictates obedience to statutes in accordance with the demands of fairness: a statute is the product of the procedure devised to ensure the equal participation in government of every citizen. Justice, however, makes its own independent claims. It requires the court to decide a case in accordance with the moral rights of the parties—what justice, properly understood, truly requires—subject always to the requirements of the law as a whole, interpreted as a body of consistent principle. Lord Goff has frankly acknowledged this interdependence of law and justice in emphasizing the importance of the facts of a case as a basis for legal decision. The inherent particularity of adjudication must govern—even qualify—the application of settled rules of law: 'The function of judges is, literally, to decide cases . . . The judicial act can not unreasonably be epitomised as an

[3] See e.g. H. W. Arthurs, 'Rethinking Administrative Law: A Slightly Dicey Business' (1979) 17 Osgoode Hall LJ 1. Arthurs denies that statutes have a 'parasitic and contingent existence within the body of the common law' (ibid. 22), a view which is ultimately inconsistent with the conception of the rule of law defended in this book.

[4] *The Law of the Constitution*, 10th edn. (London, 1959), 197.

[5] Roscoe Pound, 'Common Law and Legislation' (1908) 21 Harv. LR 383 at 385; Sir Rupert Cross and J. W. Harris, *Precedent in English Law*, 4th edn. (Oxford, 1991), 173–7.

[6] *Law's Empire* (London, 1986), 345–6.

[7] Ch. 2, above.

educated reflex to facts, though always within the framework of established legal principle.'[8]

It seems clear, none the less, that a court is justified in denying a litigant the decision which his moral rights would otherwise require, when an adverse decision is (clearly) commanded by statute. Although there may be important exceptions to this approach—it would be wrong to assume that parliamentary sovereignty authorizes any and every invasion of individual rights—a statute will in ordinary circumstances override inconsistent judicial conceptions of justice, even where those conceptions are embodied in the common law.[9] The power of statute to overturn the common law, however, may easily be exaggerated: in constitutional theory there would seem to be significant, and inherent, limitations. The requirements of justice defer to those of fairness only up to a point; and the identification of that point of intersection is of fundamental constitutional importance.

The proposal that a statute might be applied by way of analogy misunderstands the nature of the distinction between common law and statute. It overlooks the philosophical distinction between enacted rule—whose compass is necessarily determined by its enacted terms—and general principle, whose scope knows no such predetermined (stipulated) boundaries. It also ignores the constitutional importance of the common law as a settled framework for the protection of individual rights. An extension of statutory requirements, beyond the scope of the rules actually enacted, therefore violates the requirements of justice by circumscribing the common law. And it is illegitimate because it cannot be justified—as the moral force of statute must be justified—by the requirements of fairness.

I have argued that fairness requires the loyal application of the decisions of a democratic (and thus egalitarian) legislative procedure. Those decisions are enshrined in statutes, duly enacted. Now statutes must be interpreted, and fairness undoubtedly demands an interpretation which respects the general point or purpose of a statute, so far as that can be ascertained. An overly 'literal' or wooden construction may be justly condemned for failure to honour the demands of fairness. Language can be understood only by attending to its context; and a court must therefore examine a statute's apparent objectives when it seeks to make sense of its provisions. In stressing that words derive their colour and content from their context, Viscount Simonds explained that the 'context' should be broadly understood, as 'including not only

[8] 'Judge, Jurist and Legislator' (Child & Co. Oxford Lecture 1986) [1987] Denning LJ 79 at 82; see also *Elliott* v. *C.* [1983] 1 WLR 939, 947–8 (Robert Goff LJ).

[9] See generally Ch. 3, above; and more detailed discussion of Dworkin's theory of adjudication below.

other enacting provisions of the same statute, but its preamble, the existing state of the law, other statutes *in pari materia*, and the mischief which . . . the statute was intended to remedy'.[10]

However, using statutes by way of analogy is not a process of construction at all. It entails their use to draw conclusions, or formulate rules, which the legislation in question does *not* enact.[11] And it is fundamental to our constitutional arrangements that legal authority attaches, not to the general desires or intentions of Members of Parliament—let alone to those of government ministers—but to the statutory text: 'Parliament, under our constitution, is sovereign only in respect of what it expresses by the words used in the legislation it has passed.'[12] Restrictive interpretation of statute in defence of individual rights—a well-established feature of the rule of law—reflects this basic principle. It is embodied too in the traditional idea that a statute makes no change in the existing law beyond what is expressly stated by, or follows by necessary implication from, its language: 'To alter any clearly established principle of law, a distinct and positive legislative enactment is necessary and statutes are not presumed to alter the common law further or otherwise than the Act expressly declares.'[13]

The whole of our public law, in particular, is premissed on the view that the statutory powers of officials and public authorities are confined by the words of the relevant statute, properly construed. No one may be obliged to act contrary to his own wishes—whether for the public good or his own—because government ministers or officials think it desirable. In accordance with that basic principle, for example, it is clear that coercive powers in respect of those suffering mental illness cannot be widened to enable doctors to conform more easily with accepted psychiatric practice.[14] There is no presumption 'that Parliament intended that people should, against their will, be subjected to treatment which others, however professionally competent, perceive, however sincerely and however correctly, to be in their best interests'.[15] There is instead 'a canon

[10] *A.-G.* v. *Prince Ernest Augustus of Hanover* [1957] AC 436, 461. For an account of the co-operation necessary between legislator and interpreter, see Lon L. Fuller, *Anatomy of the Law* (New York, 1968), 59 ff. The meaning of the statutory words cannot, however, be *identified* with the legislative purpose: see Gerald C. MacCallum Jr., 'Legislative Intent' (1966) 75 Yale LJ 754, reprinted in Robert S. Summers (ed.), *Essays in Legal Philosophy* (Oxford, 1968).

[11] P. S. Atiyah, 'Common Law and Statute Law' (1985) 48 MLR 1 at 6.

[12] *Black-Clawson Internat.* v. *Papierwerke Waldhof-Aschaffenburg* [1975] AC 591, 638 (Lord Diplock).

[13] *Wills* v. *Bowley* [1982] 2 All ER 654, 662 (Lord Lowry). Cf. *Nat. Assistce. Bd.* v. *Wilkinson* [1952] 2 QB 648, 661: 'It is a well-established principle of construction that a statute is not to be taken as effecting a fundamental alteration in the general law unless it uses words that point unmistakably to that conclusion' (Devlin J.). See further P. St. J. Langan, *Maxwell on the Interpretation of Statutes*, 12th edn. (London, 1969), 116.

[14] *R.* v. *Hallstrom, ex p. W. (No. 2)* [1986] 2 All ER 306.

[15] Ibid. 314 (McCullough J.).

of construction that Parliament is presumed not to enact legislation which interferes with the liberty of the subject without making it clear that this was its intention'.[16] If statutes confer powers on public authorities, or impose duties on the ordinary citizen, they do so to the extent that the enacted words, properly interpreted, have those consequences. They do not thereby authorize any further encroachments on traditional liberties, even by way of consistency.

Lord Bridge's proposal in *Wills* v. *Bowley*,[17] for a *general rule* of construction to govern statutes conferring powers to arrest persons 'found committing' offences, sought overall coherence at the expense of the traditional bias in favour of liberty. He invoked the analogy provided by the Criminal Law Act 1967, section 2(2), in support of his construction of the Town Police Clauses Act 1847, section 28, even though the modern statute granted powers of arrest only in respect of serious ('arrestable') offences.[18] He thought that extension of the power of arrest, in the modern statute, to a person who acted on reasonable suspicion that an offence was being committed, even where it was not, reflected the rationale which underlay his construction of statutes conferring powers of arrest *in flagrante delicto*, enacted 'in an age when Parliament was less articulate than it is now'.[19]

Lord Lowry rejected the proposed rule of construction precisely because it had the effect of extending the scope of powers of arrest without explicit statutory sanction. He found it impossible to accept that statutes which had conferred on ordinary citizens (as well as police officers) in 'plain, unadorned language' a power of arresting without warrant persons who committed offences 'within their view', or were 'found committing' offences, had 'at the same time *as a general principle* so altered the common law' that an ordinary citizen could arrest such a person where no offence had actually been committed, however reasonably the ordinary citizen might believe that it had.[20] Lord Bridge's approach gave the ordinary citizen a power of arrest which had never been recognized at common law, and was only granted expressly in 1967 in the case of arrestable offences.

The possibility that statutes might be extended by analogy to enlarge the sphere of criminal liability at common law is a particularly alarming one. Its consequences are illustrated by the failure of the House of Lords, in *Lemon*,[21] to adhere to the basic principle that a defendant should not be convicted of a criminal offence in the absence of *mens rea*.

16 Ibid.
17 [1982] 2 All ER 654, considered above, Ch. 2.
18 An arrestable offence included any offence punishable on first conviction by imprisonment for at least five years. See now Police & Crim. Evid. Act 1984 s. 24.
19 [1982] 2 All ER 682.
20 Ibid. 664 (Lord Lowry's emphasis).
21 [1979] 1 All ER 898.

The majority upheld a conviction for publishing a blasphemous libel even though the defendant was not shown to have intended to provoke shock or resentment among believing Christians. Despite the inconclusive nature of previous authority, it was held to be sufficient for the prosecution to prove an intention to publish material which the jury considered blasphemous.[22]

Lord Scarman sought to justify this conclusion by invoking the analogy of recent statutes in support of his own conception of 'legal policy in the society of today'.[23] The Obscene Publications Act 1959 focused attention on the words or article published, rather than the intention of the author or publisher; and the Public Order Act 1936 had been amended to make it unnecessary to prove an intention to provoke a breach of the peace in order to secure a conviction for inciting racial hatred. Perhaps there was some merit in Lord Scarman's view that an author's right of free speech should not be interpreted to allow him to outrage the religious sensibilities of others. But if so, it was certainly not the court's function to make that decision in pursuit of desirable policy. Nor was it legitimate to plead in support statutes concerned with other matters, attempting to strike a balance of public interests in their own special contexts. The dissenting speeches, which emphasized the general principle that a person is not to be held guilty of a serious criminal offence unless he intended to commit it, would seem more faithful to the judicial role under the rule of law.[24]

Purposive construction and common law rights

If it were legitimate to apply a statute by means of analogy, it would presumably be permissible to fill a *casus omissus* in order to give a statutory policy full rein, notwithstanding the shortcomings of the terms enacted. But that has never been the constitutional position. It is well established that a legislative policy must be applied to the extent that the statute in terms directs, but beyond that point the previous law remains unchanged. A purposive interpretation may sometimes permit the insertion of words needed to prevent 'manifest absurdity or repugnance'.[25] But judicial attempts to repair legislative omissions are generally thought to cross the accepted boundary between interpretation and legislation, usurping a function which belongs properly to

[22] For analysis, see J. R. Spencer, 'Blasphemous Libel Resurrected—Gay News and Grim Tidings' [1979] CLJ 245.

[23] [1979] 1 All ER 927.

[24] Lords Diplock and Edmund-Davies would have upheld the defendants' appeals against conviction.

[25] *Becke* v. *Smith* (1836) 2 M & W 191, 195 (Parke B.) Cf. *Grey* v. *Pearson* (1957) 6 HL Cas. 61, 106 (Lord Wensleydale).

Parliament.[26] The traditional role of the courts as mediators between government and governed depends on that separation of functions: existing rights could otherwise be curtailed or removed without express parliamentary sanction. Lord Reid clearly affirmed the critical role of the statutory text: 'We often say that we are looking for the intention of Parliament, but that is not quite accurate. We are seeking the meaning of the words which Parliament used. We are seeking not what Parliament meant but the true meaning of what they said.'[27]

Admittedly, the courts have sometimes lapsed from this position. The decision of a majority of the House of Lords in *Francis and Francis* v. *Central Criminal Court*[28] is a recent example, worth close examination. A question arose concerning the scope of the Police and Criminal Evidence Act 1984, section 10(2), which excluded 'items held with the intention of furthering a criminal purpose' from the definition of legal privilege provided by section 10(1). The appellants, a firm of solicitors, sought judicial review of an order made under the Drug Trafficking Offences Act 1986, section 27, which required them to allow the police access to material in their possession relating to a purchase of property made by a client. The police suspected that the purchase-money represented part of the proceeds of drug trafficking by one of the client's relatives.

The 1986 Act protected from disclosure 'items subject to legal privilege' within the meaning of section 10 of the Police and Criminal Evidence Act; and the appellants argued accordingly that the relevant files could not be seized: there was no suggestion that they held them with any criminal purpose or intention. The majority of the court, however, affirmed the decision of the Divisional Court that section 10(2) removed the protection of privilege where a relevant criminal intention existed, *regardless of whether the intention was that of the person holding the documents or any other person*. Although, therefore, the documents might be held in perfect good faith by the solicitors, legal professional privilege would not attach where a criminal purpose was entertained by their client—or even by a third party 'using the client as his innocent tool'.

The construction adopted flew in the face of the natural grammatical meaning. Lord Oliver, who dissented, took it to be 'a primary canon of statutory construction that words are to be read in their ordinary, natural meaning unless there is some compulsive reason for reading them in some other and secondary sense'.[29] There was no doubt about the ordinary, natural meaning of the relevant words. They were clear, concise, and unequivocal. The expression 'items held with the intention

[26] Cf. *Jones* v. *Wrotham Park Estates* [1980] AC 74, 105–6; *Magor & St Mellons RDC* v. *Newport Corp.* [1952] AC 189, 191 (Lord Simonds).

[27] *Black-Clawson* v. *Papierwerke* [1975] AC 591, 613.

[28] [1988] 3 All ER 775.

[29] Ibid. 792.

of furthering a criminal purpose' could not, as a matter of ordinary language, refer to items in relation to which the holder had no such intention but which figured in the intentions of someone else.

Perhaps some members of the legislature—if they had considered the question—envisaged a broader exclusion of legal privilege than the statutory words strictly permitted. Since solicitors would only rarely be party to a criminal purpose, but were obliged to claim privilege on behalf of their clients, applications for access to material held by solicitors in criminal cases would almost invariably fail. Section 10(2) had probably been intended simply to incorporate the established common law rule that no privilege attached to legal advice obtained for the purpose of committing crime.[30] Lord Goff was unwilling to countenance the 'extraordinary' result of a literal construction, that the police could be prevented by legal privilege from calling for the production of documents which, if obtained, would be admissible at the defendant's trial.[31] Lord Brandon adopted a frankly purposive approach. The power of search and seizure was conferred on the police in the public interest, for the easier and more effective investigation of serious crimes. Since a broad construction would materially assist in achieving the legislative purpose, Parliament must have intended that wider meaning.

It is suggested that the dissenting speeches of Lords Bridge and Oliver were more persuasive. If the rule of law recommends strict scrutiny of grants of coercive powers of search and seizure, it seems wrong to adopt a broad construction, at variance with the ordinary grammatical meaning,[32] extending the scope of such powers in order to render the legislation more effective. Although the courts must interpret a statute in the light of its context and general purpose, a departure from the ordinary meaning cannot be justified here. The courts owe dutiful obedience to legislative provisions passed in support of the public interest in combating drug trafficking. But they have no authority to amend the statutory text in order to improve the machinery chosen for that purpose. Lord Oliver's speech contained a powerful indictment of the majority's approach, condemning as illegitimate the judicial correction of an 'anomalous omission' thought to impede the effective fulfilment of the legislative purpose:

> It is not clear to me by what principle of statutory construction such a process is regarded as permissible unless it be by the invention of a new doctrine of judicial rectification, in exercise of which the court, by virtue of its superior perception of what public policy requires, is entitled to arrogate to itself the function of legislating where Parliament has not seen fit to do so.[33]

[30] *Cox and Railton* (1884) 14 QBD 153. [31] [1988] 3 All ER 775, 797.

[32] Lord Bridge insisted on a strict *grammatical* meaning; Lord Oliver declined to rely on grammatical analysis.

[33] [1988] 3 All ER 793.

Moreover, Members of Parliament might have considered that a solicitor should not be obliged to decide his duty in respect of legal privilege on the basis of another's criminal intention, of which he knows nothing. And a differently worded provision might have attracted representations from interested professional bodies during the Bill's passage through Parliament. But in any case, parliamentary intention was inevitably a matter of speculation. If such speculation led the court to adopt a forced construction in order to fill a supposedly unintentional lacuna, the court had abandoned the judicial role, 'assuming, without the benefit of public discussion or debate, that mantle which is properly reserved to the legislature alone'.[34]

If statutory interpretation is to proceed in a principled manner, it should reflect those deep-seated, relatively enduring, values of the legal order, whose identification and protection are tasks falling chiefly to the judiciary. Since those values embrace the loyalty to statute which representative democracy plainly demands, judicial deference to the legislative purpose, and co-operation in securing its achievement, are themselves important requirements of the rule of law. However, the attainment of immediate legislative purposes, even though securely grounded in an intelligent and persuasive view of the public interest, cannot be too readily permitted to eclipse settled legal principles—at least not without the legislative deliberation implied (if not in practice guaranteed) by the use of clear statutory words.

It therefore seems wrong to extend the ambit of compulsory police powers of search and seizure by adoption of a non-literal, purposive construction. The majority decision not only adapted the statute to conform to the common law position, but extended the scope of the established exception to deny privilege where a criminal intention was held by a third party. If legal privilege attaching to private communications between lawyer and client, made for the purposes of obtaining confidential advice, is to be seriously eroded in that way, it should surely be in consequence of clear statutory authorization. For the ability to obtain such confidential advice in respect of one's legal position is a well-established feature of the legal order. In criminal cases, the privilege is taken to be a fundamental of civilized legal procedure, a necessary component of the right of the accused to legal advice and ancillary to his privilege against self-incrimination.[35]

[34] Ibid. 794–5.

[35] See esp. *Baker* v. *Campbell* (1983) 49 ALR 385: High Ct. of Australia held that documents to which legal professional privilege attached could not lawfully be made the subject of a search warrant issued under Crimes Act 1914 s. 10(b). For the dependence of the right to silence on legal privilege, see Brennan J., ibid. 427–8. See also Canadian decisions, *Descoteaux* v. *Mierzwinski* (1982) 70 CCC (2d) 385; *Solosky* (1979) 105 DLR (3d) 745. For privilege treated as an aspect of the right to assistance of counsel under 6th

I do not contend that the rule of law invariably justifies a strict or 'literal' interpretation of statutes. On the contrary, it recommends an interpretative approach which is sensitive to settled principles protecting individual rights and expectations. Lord Reid's well-known remarks in *Hinchy*[36]—although entirely consistent with his insistence on the critical role of the statutory text—should therefore be treated cautiously. Lord Reid was there concerned with a case where the statute, in its ordinary meaning, appeared to produce injustice. Since the court could only take the intention of Parliament from the words of the Act, the question was whether those words were 'capable of a more limited construction'. If they were not, he thought that the court 'must apply them as they stand, however unreasonable or unjust the consequences'.

Now, it cannot be true that construction should be unaffected by considerations of justice and reasonableness; and words are almost invariably capable of a 'more limited construction'. The objection to the decision in *Francis* is that there they were given a *wider* construction. In his (dissenting) speech, Lord Bridge explained the distinction between a 'positive' and 'negative' absurdity. It was legitimate to abstain from ascribing to the language of an Act the full effect of its ordinary grammatical meaning in order to avoid 'some positively harmful or manifestly unjust consequence'. It was not permissible, however, to read into a statute a meaning which the language used would not bear in order to remedy a supposed defect or shortcoming which, unless remedied, made the Act less effective. Lord Bridge knew of 'no legitimate principle of construction which permits such a negative absurdity to be remedied by implying words which the court thinks necessary to enhance the operation of the statutory machinery'.[37]

A permissible instance of *restrictive* construction, in defence of a right which is 'deep rooted in English law',[38] was perhaps the decision of the Divisional Court that the compulsory powers of interrogation enjoyed by the Director of the Serious Fraud Office were sharply curtailed once a suspect was charged.[39] Although the Criminal Justice Act 1987, section 2 enabled the Director to require information from a person 'under investigation' in connection with a suspected offence involving serious fraud, the court was naturally unwilling to accept that incriminating information might be demanded after he had been charged, or even during his trial for such an offence. It was 'almost unthinkable' that

Amendment to US Constitution, see esp. *Coplon* 191 F 2d 749 (1951); *Caldwell* 205 F 2d 879 (1953); *Black* 385 US 26 (1966). See also *AM & S Europe* v. *European Comm.* [1983] 1 QB 878.

[36] *IRC* v. *Hinchy* [1960] AC 748, 767 (cited by Lord Oliver in *Francis and Francis* at [1988] 3 All ER 793).

[37] [1988] 3 All ER 775, 783.

[38] *Lam Chi-ming* v. *R* [1991] 3 All ER 172, 179 (Lord Griffiths).

[39] *R.* v. *Director of Serious Fraud Office, ex p. Smith* [1992] 1 All ER 730.

Parliament should have authorized the exercise of inquisitorial powers in such circumstances, and 'only the very clearest statutory language could produce such a result'.[40]

Reversing that decision, however, the House of Lords declined to accord a similar deference to the privilege against self-incrimination, or right of silence, on the (somewhat circular) ground that the ordinary rule prohibiting interrogation after charge was related to the common law requirement that any confession should be voluntary—a requirement which the statute had overridden.[41] But the requirement of voluntariness is not derived solely from the desirability of excluding unreliable confessions: it is ultimately grounded itself in the more fundamental privilege against self-incrimination.[42] And the *scope* of the statute's encroachment on that privilege was what the court had to determine.

Lord Mustill's insistence that the 'right of silence' was constituted by a 'disparate group of immunities', which differed in 'nature, origin, incidence and importance', plainly reflected a disenchantment with the (wider) right itself—a disenchantment evidently shared by a number of senior judges.[43] A more sympathetic treatment of the idea of 'fair play'—to which Lord Mustill briefly alluded—would weaken his assertion that 'objections to the curtailment of one immunity may draw a spurious reinforcement from association with other, and different, immunities' within the group.[44] In the result, the defendant's right of silence at his trial—which included, but was not exhausted by, his right not to testify—was left dependent on the ability of the trial judge to prevent an 'abuse of power' by the Director, or the possibility of judicial review.[45] An available interpretation of the statute, fashioned to ensure a fair trial, was rejected in favour of reliance on the judge's discretion—a safeguard which the Divisional Court had considered inadequate. A 'positive absurdity' was allowed to stand because the more senior judges were once again unwilling to allow settled common

[40] Ibid. 738. The Police and Crim. Evidence Act 1984 and Codes of Practice (applicable to the Director as to other persons investigating offences) reflected the earlier provisions of the Judges' Rules (at common law) and 'effected no diminution in the general right of an accused person to remain silent' (ibid. 735).

[41] *Smith* v. *Director of Serious Fraud Office* [1992] 3 All ER 456, 474 (Lord Mustill). Statements made in response to a requirement to provide information were generally inadmissible in evidence: s. 2(8).

[42] Cf. *Sang* [1979] 2 All ER 1222. Lord Mustill overlooks this point in his analysis of the right of silence in *Smith* at [1992] 3 All ER 465. An involuntary confession does not become admissible because its truth is independently established: *Lam Chi-ming, supra*. Cf. *Chalmers* v. *HM Advocate* 1954 JC 66.

[43] See e.g. *A T & T Istel* v. *Tully* [1992] 3 All ER 523, 530–2 (Lord Templeman), 533–4 (Lord Griffiths).

[44] [1992] 3 All ER 464. See Ch. 2, above.

[45] [1992] 3 All ER 474. Compare the view of the Div. Ct. at [1992] 1 All ER 740 (Nolan LJ).

law principle to inhibit fulfilment of the statutory purpose of combating serious crime.

Where presumptions of legislative intent, such as the presumption against abrogation of the right to silence,[46] are too easily overridden in response to the perceived requirements of public policy, the separation of powers on which the rule of law depends is clearly endangered. This is no less true because the policy enjoys current parliamentary support. A purposive approach to construction is capable, unless suitably constrained, of undermining well-established rights without proper (legislative) deliberation. The judges' failure to limit the scope of draconian inquisitorial powers recalls the decision of the Court of Criminal Appeal, that a defendant's examination before the Court of Bankruptcy could be admitted in evidence at his trial on a criminal charge.[47] The maxim of the common law—*nemo tenetur se ipsum accusare*—had been overruled by the legislature. Coleridge J., in dissent, rightly protested against a judgment which impaired a 'maxim of our law as settled, as important and as wise as almost any other in it'. He proposed a more subtle approach, more consistent with the constitutional status of the right which the maxim enshrined:

> How, then, upon general principles, are we to proceed in a seeming conflict between the common law and these provisions of the statute? Not, I apprehend, by assuming at once that there is a real conflict, and sacrificing the common law; but by carefully examining whether the two may not be reconciled, and full effect be given to both . . . If . . . it should be clear that the examination was authorized solely for the better discovery of the bankrupt's estate, and the bringing it into distribution amongst his creditors—that . . . he might lawfully refuse to answer any question put merely for the purpose of extracting evidence against him on a criminal charge, then . . . you would be far advanced on your way to a conclusion which will prevent the statute from breaking in upon the common law.[48]

Parliamentary sovereignty undoubtedly permits radical change and even abrogation of well-established rights and expectations: ordinarily, fairness requires that explicit enactment be given full respect. Presumptions of legislative intent should not be applied to defeat the parliamentary will, where that is clearly expressed. In *Attorney-General for*

[46] Stuart-Smith LJ acknowledged the presumption in *Bishopsgate Investment Management* v. *Maxwell* [1992] 2 All ER 856, 883, but again the court resorted to purposive statutory construction in order to defeat it. For analysis, see Adam Tomkins and Brian Bix, 'The Sounds of Silence: A Duty to Incriminate Oneself?' [1992] PL 363.

[47] *R.* v. *Scott* (1856) Dears & B 47.

[48] Ibid. 62. To admit the accused's answers in evidence against him, if wrongfully obtained, would be a 'fraud upon' the common law and the 'principles of justice' (ibid. 63). There is, of course, no *direct* analogy with *Smith* because the Director's powers were designed to obtain information for the purposes of criminal proceedings. See generally J. D. Heydon, 'Statutory Restrictions on the Privilege Against Self-Incrimination' (1971) 87 LQR 214.

Canada v. *Hallett and Carey*,[49] the House of Lords rejected a principle of construction whereby general words in a statute were incapable of authorizing the 'gravest possible inroads upon private rights'. The court affirmed the 'well-known general principle that statutes which encroach upon the rights of the subject, whether as regards person or property, are subject to a "strict" construction'.[50] None the less, most statutes made such an encroachment—that was usually a concomitant of changing the common law—and the scope of the general principle should not be exaggerated. It meant 'no more than that, where the import of some enactment is inconclusive or ambiguous, the court may properly lean in favour of an interpretation that leaves private rights undisturbed'.[51]

Nor should the presumption against radical changes in the common law be overstated, even though it sharply limits the possibilities for reasoning by analogy from statutes. It reflects the ideal of government by stable, general laws.[52] The citizen, in principle, is entitled to act in reliance on the existing law—both common law and statute[53]—until it is changed with reasonable certainty and precision. All the more is he entitled to assume that fundamental principles of law will not be altered lightly and obscurely. The presumption cannot be applied to frustrate a legislative purpose which is expressed with sufficient clarity; but it confines the scope of the statute to what is necessary to remedy the 'mischief' against which it is directed: 'the principle is that if the enactment is ambiguous, that meaning which relates the scope of the Act to the mischief should be taken rather than a different or wider meaning which the contemporary situation did not call for'.[54]

It must be recognized, however, that 'ambiguity' is not a 'neutral' quality of language, independent of the interpreter's substantive convictions. We will think a statute ambiguous, or not clear, when its 'literal' application would have unjust results. In practice, legal argument rarely concerns the meaning of a single word or phrase in isolation. To a high degree, therefore, a finding of 'ambiguity' expresses an interpretative conclusion, rather than asserting a need for interpretation.[55] The preservation of vested rights and the maintenance of traditional liberties are therefore desiderata fully embedded in an approach to interpretation faithful to the requirements of the rule of law.

There is, then, no denial of fairness—or repudiation of the democratic

[49] [1952] AC 427.
[50] Ibid. 450–1 (Lord Radcliffe).
[51] Ibid.
[52] See Ch. 1, above.
[53] There is also a presumption against ambiguous changes to existing legislation: see e.g. *Bennett* v. *Chappell* [1966] Ch. 391.
[54] *Black-Clawson* v. *Papierwerke* [1975] AC 591, 614 (Lord Reid).
[55] Cf. Dworkin, *Law's Empire*, 350–4.

will—in an interpretation which assumes a background of settled principle at common law. A statute can only be understood in its context, which extends to the expectations of the interpreter. Chief among these is the expectation that Parliament will conform to well-established notions of justice—that punishment will not be authorized for acts which were lawful when committed, that vested rights will not be destroyed without compensation, that the powers of officials must be limited by proper respect for the familiar liberties of the citizen, etc. 'If the words are not conclusive in themselves, the reasonableness or otherwise of the construction contended for has always been recognised as a matter fairly to be taken into account.'[56] Legislative supremacy is itself ultimately acknowledged only on the basis that Parliament is an institution committed to the attainment of justice; and that consideration properly affects the process of interpretation, imposing in the last resort limits to the exercise of sovereign power.[57]

Rules and principles

Even if it be accepted that in 'constitutional' cases—concerning the extent of government powers or the duties of the ordinary citizen under the criminal law—statutes should be strictly construed, it might none the less be thought legitimate to apply a statute by analogy in other cases. Where a case involves a conflict of individual rights, and the correct resolution at common law is controversial, might the court not properly invoke a statutory analogy in support of its decision?

Quite apart from constitutional considerations, however, it is not clear how a statute might exert an influence beyond the compass of its enacted terms. In what sense may a statute be applied by analogy? Perhaps its underlying principle, where that can be sufficiently ascertained, could be applied to other cases outside its (literal) scope. But it is hard to see what the statute would contribute. The relevant principle would presumably be relevant, and must be equally as strong, without the statute. It is a mistake, though one commonly made, to think that a statute can introduce a novel principle, or strengthen a principle already held.

[56] *Tolson* (1889) 23 QBD 168, 175 (Wills J.). Cf. *Maxwell on the Interpretation of Statutes*, 208–12; Francis Bennion, *Statutory Interpretation*, 2nd edn. (London, 1992), 549–51.

[57] See further Chs. 3 and 11. Cf. Lord Browne-Wilkinson, 'The Infiltration of a Bill of Rights' [1992] PL 397. See also *Marcel* v. *Commr. of Police of Metropolis* [1991] 1 All ER 845, 851: 'Search and seizure under statutory powers constitute fundamental infringements of the individual's immunity from interference by the state with his property and privacy—fundamental human rights . . . [I]n the absence of clear words . . . Parliament cannot be assumed to have legislated so as to interfere with the basic rights of the individual to a greater extent than is necessary to secure the protection of [the] public interest' (cited with approval by the Court of Appeal at [1992] 1 All ER 80–1).

It seems helpful here briefly to rehearse the jurist's familiar distinction between rules and principles. I shall argue that while the common law should be understood primarily as a corpus of principle, statute consists only of rules. Rules apply in an all-or-nothing fashion, and operate largely by definition: a rule stipulates a particular result whenever the facts arise to which its terms apply. It applies absolutely, dictating a particular outcome, subject only to any specified exceptions. By contrast, a principle has the attribute of 'weight': it argues in favour of a judgment on particular facts, but need not demand a certain result. It may be overridden or counterbalanced by conflicting principles, or displaced by operation of a legal rule. Above all, its weight (or 'force') will vary according to all the circumstances of a particular case.[58]

Now, legislation consists entirely of rules in the sense that its terms are uniquely authoritative in the resolution of particular cases. Statutory interpretation proceeds by analysis of a canonical form of words. It is the words enacted which must be construed, and the statute itself is necessarily silent about matters beyond their scope. Although courts are sometimes tempted to draw conclusions from a statute's silence, they are speculating about a 'parliamentary intention' which is not only fictional—whose intention is to be taken when Members probably entertained conflicting views?—but almost certainly imaginary.[59] Where it applies to a state of facts, a statute gives a definitive answer: it is authoritative within the scope of its terms. It is the nature of rules that they have mandatory force within a limited compass. But a statute plainly cannot *govern* a case about which it says nothing, and to which therefore it does not, according to its terms, apply.[60]

It is not possible for *principles* to be enacted, rather than rules, because a principle has no real existence apart from its weight. (A principle which had no weight would not, in any intelligible sense, be a principle at all.) And weight or force cannot be enacted: it clearly cannot be determined in advance of any particular case arising for decision. A principle's weight will vary infinitely within an infinite range of facts and circumstances: it is precisely this elastic quality which eludes the straitjacket-nature of rules. A principle is applied to particular facts because—and only to the extent that—it is *understood* to be appropriate; and such understanding (or according of weight) cannot be enacted. It is precisely the character of a principle, as opposed to a rule, that its weight is a function of its intrinsic appeal to reason. (It

[58] See Ronald Dworkin, *Taking Rights Seriously* (London, 1977), 22–8; 71–80.

[59] Cf. Atiyah, 'Common Law and Statute Law', 25–7.

[60] As Atiyah observes, 'There is one, and only one, way in which Parliament is entitled to make its intentions known to the judges, and that is by passing an Act. The intentions of Parliament, when not enshrined in a statute, have no legal or constitutional validity . . . [T]he courts should completely eschew the attempt to ascertain the intentions of Parliament as to a piece of non-existent legislation': ibid. 26.

could derive no additional weight by being expressly *asserted* in a statute. How could such an addition of weight conceivably be measured?) It is ultimately a question of moral education: a statute—even one passed by a sovereign Parliament—can be no substitute for education.[61]

The decision of cases by application of principle is characteristic of common law adjudication. In the absence of any unique, canonical form of words, even a common law *rule* must be applied in the light of underlying principle. It cannot be applied, that is, purely by a process of definition. In the event of dispute about either the scope or meaning of a common law rule, there are no authoritative words to construe. The doctrine of precedent ties the decision of even the highest court to the material facts of the case. It may always be distinguished in subsequent cases for adequate reason—even if that involves some departure from, or qualification of, statements of principle (or formulations of rule) previously made. No common rule is therefore immutable—it is inherently subject to adaptation and change in the course of succeeding cases—and no verbal formulation carries unique authority. Whereas statutes operate by means of fiat, expressing the parliamentary will, the common law enjoins a process of reason.[62] Subject only to the doctrine of precedent, it brings the demands of principle—with all its varying degrees of weight—directly to bear on the facts of particular cases.

Confusion about the interrelation of statute and precedent is rife. A recent example was the Master of the Rolls' assertion that section 10 of the Contempt of Court Act 1981—which grants journalists a limited immunity from orders to reveal their sources—had 'profoundly changed the balance of competing public interests'.[63] The provision forbids a court from requiring a person to disclose the source of published information 'unless it be established to the satisfaction of the court that disclosure is necessary in the interests of justice or national security or for the prevention of disorder or crime'. It is clear that section 10 enacts a rule against ordering disclosure of sources: an order is prohibited unless one of the specified exceptions applies. However, the mandatory force of a statutory rule depends on its enacted terms. And the width of the specified exceptions ensures that section 10 will function in substance as a principle.

It had previously been accepted that the courts should, where possible, respect the journalist's wish to protect his informant in deference to the

[61] Cf. M. J. Detmold, *The Unity of Law and Morality* (London, 1984), ch. 4. Detmold's work contains a helpful analysis of the distinction between rules (norms) and principles (reasons).

[62] For full discussion of this distinction, see M. J. Detmold, 'Law as Practical Reason' [1989] CLJ 436.

[63] *X.* v. *Morgan-Grampian* [1990] 1 All ER 616, 627.

public interest in press freedom. In *Attorney-General* v. *Mulholland*, where the court rejected a claim of privilege, Lord Denning none the less thought that the court would respect such professional confidences, directing the witness to answer only if it were 'a proper and, indeed, necessary question in the course of justice to be put and answered'.[64] The general principle, then, was well established. As regards the statute, 'the only reasonable inference is that the purpose of the protection is the same as that which underlay the discretion vested in the judge at common law . . . *videlicet*—unless informers could be confident that their identity would not be revealed sources of information would dry up'.[65]

Moreover, the balance of competing public interests remains entirely unchanged. In almost every case—the 'interests of justice' alone would appear to cover all eventualities[66]—the court must resort to a balancing of principles in order to determine the 'necessity' for disclosure. Does the freedom of the press (in the form of the protection of sources) outweigh the requirements of justice (or national security etc.) in the particular case? Since the weight of each principle depends on all the circumstances of the case, the statute necessarily adds nothing. The position is the same as it was at common law, where the balance of interests (general principles) was settled as a matter of judicial 'discretion'. It has been aptly described as a process which 'involves the exercise of judgment on the established facts'.[67]

It seems clear that at common law, as much as under statute, a journalist is entitled to maintain the confidentiality of his source except when countervailing public interests of greater weight, antecedently specified, require him to break it. In *British Steel Corporation* v. *Granada*,[68] the House of Lords affirmed that the court should not compel such confidences to be breached unless it were necessary in the interests of justice: 'To succeed in proceedings aimed at compelling disclosure the plaintiff will always have to satisfy the court that he has a real grievance . . . which, in the interest of justice, he ought to be allowed to pursue, and that this ought, in the particular case, to outweigh whatever public interest there may be in preserving the confidence.'[69]

[64] [1963] 2 QB 477, 489.

[65] *Secretary of State for Defence* v. *Guardian Newspapers* [1985] AC 339, 349 (Lord Diplock).

[66] Although 'justice' is thought to be narrower than its sense as the antonym of 'injustice', it is not confined to the 'technical sense of the administration of justice in the course of legal proceedings': *Guardian* case [1985] AC 339, 350 (Lord Diplock). It is hard to dissent from the view that it is in the interests of justice (within the sense of s. 10) 'that persons should be enabled to exercise important legal rights and to protect themselves from serious legal wrongs . . .': *Morgan-Grampian* case [1990] 2 All ER 1, 9 (Lord Bridge).

[67] *Re an Inquiry under the Company Securities (Insider Dealing) Act 1985* [1988] AC 660, 704 (Lord Griffiths).

[68] [1981] AC 1096 (decided at common law before the Contempt of Court Act was passed).

[69] Ibid. 1173. See also ibid. 1184 (Viscount Dilhorne).

Both common law discretion and statutory value-judgment are alike dependent on analysis of the strength of the respective public interests, as the *Granada* case reveals. British Steel had sought an order that Granada disclose the identity of an informant, who had supplied Granada with copies of confidential documents for use in a television programme, broadcast during a national steel strike. The House of Lords did not deny the public interest in preserving the confidence between journalists and their sources, but held that disclosure was required in the interests of justice in the circumstances of the case. No 'iniquity' or misconduct had been revealed. British Steel had suffered a grievous wrong, in which Granada had actively participated. The interest in maintaining the free flow of information to the press, and against obstructing informers, was outweighed by British Steel's right to preserve confidentiality within its operations, free from suspicion that it harboured disloyal employees. There is no reason to doubt Hoffmann J.'s conclusion, expressed more recently, that the House of Lords would have reached exactly the same decision *after* the passing of the 1981 Act.[70]

In the *Morgan-Grampian* case,[71] Lord Oliver attempted to separate the statutory test from the common law discretion. He sought to distinguish between the court's *jurisdiction* to order disclosure of sources (governed by the statute) and its discretion (at common law). Moreover, Lord Diplock had previously explained that 'section 10 requires actual necessity to be established; and whether it has or not is a question of fact that the judge has to find in favour of necessity as a condition precedent to his having any jurisdiction to order disclosure of sources of information'.[72] The idea here is that the journalist's privilege is defined by the scope of the court's jurisdiction: once disclosure is found to be necessary within one of the statutory exceptions, he is at the mercy of the court's discretion.

However, the supposed distinction between jurisdiction and discretion is meaningless, for each requires precisely the same balancing of interests in the light of all the relevant facts. Lord Bridge acknowledged that whether disclosure were *necessary*—although 'certainly a question of fact rather than an issue calling for the exercise of the judge's discretion'—was a matter calling for 'the exercise of a discriminating and sometimes difficult value-judgment'.[73] How could the exercise of discretion, if it were to be principled rather than arbitrary, possibly be any different?

Lord Oliver's two-stage analysis left the discretion with nothing to

[70] *X.* v. *Morgan-Grampian*; sub nom. *Re Goodwin* [1990] 1 All ER 608, 614.
[71] [1990] 2 All ER 1, 14. The facts of the case are set out in Ch. 5, below.
[72] *Guardian* case [1985] AC 339, 350.
[73] [1990] 2 All ER 9.

do. It became an embarrassing abstraction, devoid of practical significance. There was a conflict of public interests to be resolved:

It is here . . . that the balancing exercise comes in . . . Once it has been performed (and it will have embraced the consideration of all the features which favour and which militate against disclosure), there will, no doubt, theoretically remain a residual true discretion which is inherent in the common law position to which a positive answer to the question of necessity will have brought the court. But the exercise of balancing will in fact have already been done at that stage and it is not easy to imagine a case in which it would be necessary for it to be gone through again, *for once it has been determined that the need for disclosure is predominant over the public interest in non-disclosure there is nothing more to be asked.*[74]

In so far as the Contempt of Court Act, section 10, invokes a principle in favour of protecting the anonymity of sources, then, it contributes nothing to the solution of particular cases. The provision makes sense only because that principle was previously recognized and understood. The importance of a free press was already acknowledged; and its weight depends on all the facts of a particular case, a matter about which the statute (necessarily) has nothing to say. In so far as the statute enacts a rule, it is largely vacuous. The scope of its stated exceptions compels the court to decide each case on grounds of principle. If section 10 has changed the previous law, it is only in the sense of shifting the burden of proof. In the event of doubt, the court may not order disclosure of sources. There is, to that (limited) extent, a presumption in favour of privilege.[75]

A principle exists solely in the sphere of reason. Its statutory endorsement gains no purchase—in the sense of changing its weight—because it remains an abstraction. No practical consequences result from acknowledging a public interest or value in general terms: it can only have weight in the actual circumstances of particular cases. It was for this reason that, in *Granada*, Lord Wilberforce declined to attribute any value to the public interest in encouraging 'leaks' of information:

'Leaks' may vary all the way from mere gossip or scandal to matters of national or international importance. A general proposition that leaks should be encouraged, or at least not discouraged, cannot be made without weighing the detriments in loss of mutual confidence and co-operation which they involve. The public interest involved in individual leaks can be taken account of and weighed by the court in deciding whether to grant the remedy in a particular case.[76]

[74] Ibid. 16 (emphasis added).

[75] Lord Diplock thought that, at common law, the right to disclosure of sources prevailed unless the balance of competing public interests tilted *against* disclosure: *Guardian* case [1985] AC 339, 347.

[76] [1981] AC 1096, 1174.

A statutory affirmation of public policy or general principle inevitably meets the same objection: its cogency is necessarily a function of the material facts of particular cases.

Lord Donaldson's judgment in *Morgan-Grampian* illustrates the point to perfection. He purports, in the final balancing of interests, to weigh the '*general* public interest in maintaining the confidentiality of journalistic sources' against the necessity for disclosure (in the interests of justice) in the particular case. Since the general interest is largely abstract, it has in practice no weight at all; the interests of justice inevitably carry the day: 'The general public interest in maintaining the confidentiality of journalistic sources exists, *but the facts of this particular case add absolutely nothing to it*. No "iniquity" has been shown . . . This is in reality a piece of wholly unjustified intrusion into privacy.'[77]

Lord Oliver's speech in *Morgan-Grampian* can be better understood from this perspective. He rejected Lord Donaldson's approach to the section, which separated the question whether disclosure were 'necessary in the interests of justice' from the principle of journalistic privilege. He considered that, by divorcing necessity from the context of privilege, the scales were likely to be weighted in favour of disclosure. Only special circumstances would then be capable of overriding the requirements of justice and preventing an order for disclosure. Lord Oliver's argument here is precisely the point that Lord Donaldson's approach leaves the public interest in non-disclosure as an abstract one, lacking any purchase on particular cases (except in the event of special circumstances). He rightly stressed the importance of striking a balance between the respective public interests in the context of each case. The true question was not whether the information was needed to serve the interests of justice—a question which leaves the interest in non-disclosure without connection to the case—but whether the interests of justice were sufficiently pressing to outweigh the grounds for non-disclosure:

> Thus the sense of the section is . . . this: the court is not permitted to require the disclosure of a journalistic source unless it is satisfied that one or more of the four enumerated considerations (i.e. the interests of justice etc.) are of such preponderating importance in the individual case that the ban on disclosure imposed by the opening words of the section really needs to be overridden.[78]

Justice and fairness

In an earlier chapter,[79] we considered Ronald Dworkin's theory of 'law as integrity', where 'integrity' envisages an appropriate accommodation between the ideals of justice and fairness, which in practice often

[77] [1990] 1 All ER 616, 630 (emphasis added).
[78] [1990] 2 All ER 1, 16. [79] Ch. 2, above.

conflict. Justice is a matter of the right distribution of goods, opportunities, and other resources—a question of the moral rights which individuals are understood to have against other persons and against the government. 'Fairness is a matter of the right structure . . . the structure that distributes influence over political decisions in the right way.'[80] The ideal of integrity expresses the coherence and consistency of underlying principle which the rule of law seems to require. It 'demands that the public standards of the community be both made and seen . . . to express a single, coherent scheme of justice and fairness in the right relation'.[81] It follows from the ideal of integrity that the judge should interpret legal rights and duties so as to express a coherent conception of political morality.[82] But it is not the case, as Dworkin's discussion appears to assume, that there must be an accommodation between justice and fairness at the level of every legal decision.

We should understand integrity as a goal for the legal system as a whole, providing a suitable reconciliation of common law and legislation. On closer inspection, the distinction between justice and fairness largely corresponds with that between common law and statute. No appeal to fairness seems justified in common law adjudication, where integrity should be understood to require respect for precedent on grounds of consistency and equality. The rights enforced are those moral rights which justice seems to require, provided that their recognition is compatible with previous judicial decisions. ('Fairness' is relevant here only in the different sense of equality between past and present litigants.[83]) Integrity (I argue below) requires an accommodation between justice and fairness only in the sense of reconciling legislative injunctions with those of common law. Law as integrity should be understood as committing the judge to decide cases according to justice, qualified only by proper respect for statutes (interpreted always in accordance with justice) and for consistency within the common law (the principle that like cases should be decided alike).

The distinction between justice and fairness is perhaps ambiguous. It is not at first clear whether Dworkin intends a distinction between the distribution of power (fairness) and the allocation of other resources (justice), or whether he envisages a distinction between procedure and substance. The most helpful interpretation, however, incorporates both

[80] *Law's Empire*, 404. [81] Ibid. 219.

[82] 'According to law as integrity, propositions of law are true if they figure in or follow from the principles of justice, fairness and procedural due process that provide the best constructive interpretation of the community's legal practice': ibid. 225. Due process is defined as 'a matter of the right procedures for enforcing rules and regulations the system has produced' (ibid. 405).

[83] Cf. *Taking Rights Seriously*, where Dworkin explained that the 'doctrine of fairness offers the only adequate account of the full practice of precedent'. This is a reference to the 'fairness of treating like cases alike' (p. 113).

these distinctions. Fairness is essentially a matter of the correct *procedures* for decision-making: they are correct in the sense that they constitute the appropriate vehicle for the distribution of political power. (John Rawls's theory of 'justice as fairness' seeks to derive principles of 'abstract' justice—for a perfectly just society—from agreement to a fair procedure: justice is the outcome of a decision-making *procedure* accepted as fair.)[84]

According to Dworkin's initial account of the conflict of these ideals, 'fairness in politics is a matter of finding political procedures—methods of electing officials and making their decisions responsive to the electorate—that distribute political power in the right way.'[85] Fairness clearly requires that the judge should respect the rules duly enacted by the legislature, at least where they are the product of a representative procedure, according every citizen (roughly) equal influence over political affairs. The ordinary process of statutory interpretation should be understood as an attempt to settle the appropriate accommodation between justice and fairness.

Dworkin's most important contribution to jurisprudence has perhaps been his insistence on the interconnection between law and morality, emphasizing the role of the judge's political morality in his judgments about the law. His earlier writing has, in particular, illuminated the close dependence of the content of law—at least of common law—on justice. The judge was enjoined to do justice—according to his lights—except where statute or precedent constrained his view of what justice would otherwise require. The moral or political rights actually enforced must obviously be consistent with existing legislation and precedent. 'The rights conception supposes that the rule book represents the community's efforts to capture moral rights and requires that any principle rejected in those efforts has no role in adjudication.'[86]

Although he should strive to determine and apply the *correct* moral and political rights in a 'hard' case—those rights which justice would recommend—the judge must reject any principle which is 'inconsistent with the vast bulk of the rules in the rule book'.[87] Where, however, competing moral principles are equally compatible with statute and precedent, the judge must apply his own judgments about what justice requires. If a case involving statutory construction requires a choice between competing moral principles, where neither is incompatible with the 'British rule book taken as a whole', the judge decides as he does 'because he believes his principle to be correct, or at least closer to correct than other principles that are also not excluded'.[88]

It seems right to conclude that fairness requires a judge loyally to

[84] *A Theory of Justice* (Oxford, 1972). [85] *Law's Empire*, 164.
[86] *A Matter of Principle* (Oxford, 1985), 17. [87] Ibid. [88] Ibid.

apply an Act of Parliament, in deference to the will of the parliamentary majority. He may not reject it—or deliberately misread it—because it conflicts with his own conception of justice. (He may none the less construe it strictly to prevent a real injustice which is not plainly authorized by its enacted terms.) Fairness is essentially a matter of the correct *procedures* for decision-making: it enjoins obedience to statutes as the outcome of the legitimate machinery for distributing political power. Fairness has no further or additional role to play: its demands are exhausted by loyal adherence to the statutory injunctions, properly (fairly) construed.

In his more recent work, however, Dworkin confuses the relation between justice and fairness by what seems to be an erroneous amendment. The judge's political morality should sometimes defer, Dworkin supposes, to *popular* morality—apparently because fairness may suggest that a principle widely endorsed by the public at large should override a conflicting principle which the judge himself prefers. The popular principle (which the judge rejects) may then determine his interpretation of the common law.[89] Dworkin imagines a court choosing between competing principles of liability in negligence in circumstances where each principle would provide adequate justification for previous decisions. The judge's choice would depend on his convictions about justice and fairness: 'It will depend, that is, not only on his beliefs about which of these principles is superior as a matter of abstract justice but also about which should be followed, as a matter of political fairness, in a community whose members have the moral convictions his fellow citizens have.'[90]

The injunction to take account of popular morality, however, seems unacceptable. The idea that popular morality could be an independent source of law endangers the separation of powers by making the courts vulnerable to the pressures of public opinion. The proposal that the judge's interpretation of the common law should make allowance for public opinion—even on issues of principle—seems inimical to the rule of law,[91] and quite inconsistent with Dworkin's previous analysis, in which fairness played a more limited role. The legal rights declared and enforced, in any particular case, were those moral or political rights which the court believed *ought*, as a matter of justice, to be acknowledged—those rights which 'abstract' justice would recommend, provided only that they were fully compatible with precedent and consistent with any relevant statute, properly construed.[92]

[89] *Law's Empire*, 240–50. [90] Ibid. 249.

[91] Cf. Dworkin, *A Matter of Principle*, contrasting the 'rights' model of law with the 'rule-book' one: 'The rule of law on this conception is the ideal of rule by an accurate public conception of individual rights' (pp. 11–12).

[92] Cf. *Law's Empire*, 97: 'Justice is a matter of the correct or best theory of moral and

The statutory language might properly limit the possible moral solutions to questions about rights because fairness required that deference to the popular will. Fairness, however, had no *further* role in judicial decision when a choice had to be made between competing principles, each of which sufficiently met the constraints of the statutory language. In the absence of any determinate legislative decision, there was no reason to depart from the judge's own scheme of moral rights *correctly* acknowledged—his vision of justice, unclouded by legislative intervention. Dworkin's earlier analysis was clear:

> If . . . some case arises as to which the rule book is silent, or if the words in the rule book are subject to competing interpretations, then it is right to ask which of the two possible decisions in the case best fits the background moral rights of the parties. For the ideal of adjudication . . . is that, so far as is practicable, the moral rights that citizens actually have should be available to them in court.[93]

A decision which took account of 'background' moral rights should be preferred to one that speculated about what the legislature might have done, if there were a statute in point.

It is hard to resist the conclusion that fairness is satisfied by scrupulous attention to any relevant statute—the authentic expression of the legislative will—and that no further recourse to popular morality, in the absence of statute or when the language is not clear, is either demanded or justified. If the judge defers to popular morality in such circumstances he denies the moral rights of the parties—what they are entitled to as a matter of abstract justice—when there is no legislative injunction to warrant that denial. The principle he adopts—the principle which enjoys public support, but which the judge thinks misguided or outweighed by countervailing principles—has not received the endorsement of the fair procedure (enactment) designed to secure the proper distribution of political power.

In one sense, of course, the common law does embody popular morality.[94] The principles of the common law naturally reflect popular understandings, as these have been ascertained and applied by the courts. But they have been applied only to the extent that the judges considered them appropriate in particular cases: they have not been substituted for principles which would otherwise have commended themselves to the courts. It seems reasonable to argue, for example, that moral rights may be founded on legitimate expectations which arise on the basis of familiar practices, or widely accepted principles of

political rights, and anyone's conception of justice is his theory, imposed by his own personal convictions, of what these rights actually are.'

[93] *A Matter of Principle*, 16.

[94] See e.g. F. A. Hayek, *Law, Legislation and Liberty* (London, 1982), i. 85–8; Geoffrey de Q. Walker, *The Rule of Law* (Melbourne, 1988), 162–70.

fair dealing between persons (for example, in contract or commercial cases). To the extent that such expectations are recognized at common law, these moral rights have been accorded legal protection. However, this does not mean that there has been a passive assimilation of popular morality, displacing the critical morality of individual judges.[95] The courts have rather determined that expectations based on widely held principles of fair dealing were legitimate—that political morality, properly understood, required their protection. Popular morality contributes to the content of the common law in so far as it is filtered through the critical morality of particular judges.

In fact Dworkin acknowledges that 'many judges will think the interpretive force of popular morality very much weaker in constitutional cases' because the (United States) Constitution is designed to protect individuals from majority opinion.[96] Similar considerations plainly apply to the British Constitution. The scope of common law rights such as those to freedom of speech[97] or personal liberty could hardly be thought to depend on public opinion. Dworkin's concession here is plainly much too weak: *any* judge who deferred to popular morality against his own convictions about the constitutional rights justice prescribed would misunderstand his function. He would destroy the point of rights which, as Dworkin has himself previously emphasized, insulate the private citizen from the exercise of public power based on majority (or utilitarian) preference and prejudice.[98] If a judge believes that some government order violates the right to freedom of speech, without statutory authorization, he should strike it down in defence of the principle of free speech which he believes the common law respects. He could hardly uphold it on the ground that popular morality supports it, even when the scope or content of that right is controversial.

Legal principles and popular morality

Our earlier analysis of legal principle—nothing of significance attaches to the label 'legal'[99]—further illuminates Dworkin's mistake. In a difficult case, a court must have regard to the balance of conflicting principles. (*Ex hypothesi*, no rule exists which settles the question at

[95] Cf. H. L. A. Hart, *Law, Liberty and Morality* (Oxford, 1963), 17–24. Hart distinguishes 'positive morality'—the morality 'actually accepted and shared by a given social group'—from 'critical morality'—the 'general moral principles used in the criticism of actual social institutions including positive morality'.

[96] *Law's Empire*, 250.

[97] For common law 'constitutional' rights, see Ch. 6, below.

[98] See esp. *Taking Rights Seriously*, chs. 5 and 7; 'Is there a Right to Pornography?' (1981) 1 OJLS 177.

[99] Principles, as matters of reason, know no subject-boundaries: cf. Detmold, *The Unity of Law and Morality*, ch. 4.

issue.) But it is not possible to defer to popular morality in determining this balance—even if it were legitimate—because there is no popular morality in respect of particular cases. Even if popular morality could be suitably ascertained—perhaps popular politicians are thought to articulate widely held views about matters of justice—it could only consist in general maxims or principles, broadly understood. But a judge cannot decide a case, where the law is not clear, by invoking a general maxim or abstract principle. He must *apply* the principle to the facts, making the *judgments* necessary to determine its appropriate weight in all the circumstances. (A principle's weight depends on the facts of a concrete case. If it were not so dependent, it would have to be applied as a rule.)[100]

Popular morality is inherently abstract: it cannot be tested in the manner necessary for legal decision. How far should a popular maxim be understood to apply in unusual cases? What exceptions or qualifications should be assumed? How should its weight be ascertained when other principles, which may also claim popular allegiance, seem to conflict? Particular cases can only be decided by a process of *deliberation*, in which relevant principles are tested and refined. Popular morality, therefore, can make no contribution at all to the decision of particular cases—except in so far as it is embodied in legislation, the legitimate vehicle for translating popular views about questions of justice into law.

A rule may be applied, at least in the case of statutes, by a process of definition. Where a set of circumstances fall within the ambit of the rule, as determined by its enacted terms, no further deliberation is normally required: the rule dictates a particular result. It is precisely the function of rules to foreclose such deliberation in advance of particular cases arising for decision. By contrast, a principle makes an appeal directly to reason. It follows that a judge can only apply a principle he understands and shares and therefore values. Since the weight of a principle inevitably depends on all the circumstances of the case, its application is always a matter of judgment—necessarily personal judgment.

It is hard to see how a judge could determine the weight of a principle whose results he thought unfortunate, perhaps pernicious. If he applied the principle to the extent he thought truly appropriate—ascertaining its weight—he would inevitably reject it altogether. He could not, then, discriminate between particular cases, distinguishing or following precedents in all their complexity, on the basis of a popular conception of principle he himself rejected. It follows that it makes no sense to attempt to compare principles one accepts with those one

[100] See earlier discussion above of the distinction between rules and principles.

rejects, even if the latter are popular. The comparison would be wholly theoretical: it could gain no purchase on the particular facts of concrete cases.[101]

The irremediable abstractness, and hence inutility, of popular morality may be better appreciated by close examination of ordinary common law reasoning from precedent. Although a court cannot escape the necessity of choosing between different principles, when a 'hard' case has to be resolved, it will usually confine that choice as narrowly as possible. The court will characteristically seek a principled explanation of that particular decision, rather than attempt a grand restatement of the relevant field of law. Since the court has no power to lay down general rules in the manner of legislation, its decisions are ultimately authoritative only in respect of their particular facts, and future cases closely analogous.

The *ratio decidendi* of a case, that is to say, is necessarily tied to its 'material facts'. It is not to be equated with the court's statement of reasons, which may be too widely or too narrowly expressed, or indeed erroneous.[102] Even the decisions of higher courts are binding on lower courts only to the extent that subsequent cases cannot be (rationally) distinguished on their facts. Assertions of general principle, or statements of legal rule, are always subject to qualification and adaptation in the face of new situations: they are inherently sensitive to other judges' perceptions of the requirements of justice in later cases.[103]

These limits on the judicial function, although constitutionally fundamental, are also a necessary consequence of the nature of common law adjudication. Since principles have no weight in the abstract, but only in respect of particular facts, it is only possible to choose between them—or attempt an appropriate reconciliation where they conflict—in the context of particular cases. Although, therefore, a systematic elaboration of principle beyond the requirements of the case in hand—as is sometimes attempted in the higher courts—may be instructive and helpful, it can clearly never be binding. Inevitably, the court's application of principles to determine a case creates only a decision on particular facts—with which future decisions must be reconciled, but where the weights of the relevant principles may be quite different.

[101] See the instructive discussion by Detmold, *The Unity of Law and Morality*, ch. 4. Detmold argues that Dworkin correctly denies a distinction between legal judgment and personal judgment, but wrongly proposes a contrast between legal and moral judgment.

[102] Cf. A. L. Goodhart, 'Determining the *Ratio Decidendi* of a Case', *Essays in Jurisprudence and the Common Law* (Cambridge, 1931); Detmold, *The Unity of Law and Morality*, 188–92; Sir Rupert Cross and J. W. Harris, *Precedent in English Law*, 4th edn. (Oxford, 1991), 63–73.

[103] Cf. Dworkin's own discussion of statute and case-law in *Taking Rights Seriously*, 107–15: judgments 'cite reasons, in the form of precedents and principles, to justify a decision, but it is the decision, not some new and stated rule of law, that these precedents and principles are taken to justify' (p. 111).

A study of the House of Lords' decision in *McLoughlin* v. *O'Brian*,[104] which Dworkin cites to illustrate his thesis, illuminates the interplay of fact and principle. Lord Scarman distinguished between policy considerations and the formulation of principle in a manner which closely reflects Dworkin's own account of that distinction.[105] It was the court's function to adjudicate according to principle, leaving matters of policy to legislative determination. Considerations of the general welfare (as the point might be expressed) could not be permitted to override or interfere with the moral rights of the parties, in so far as these were reflected in, and consistent with, existing precedent. However, Lord Scarman clearly understood the sense in which the elaboration of principle was itself only secondary to, or parasitic on, the main task of deciding the case before the court: 'The function of the court is to decide the case before it, even though the decision may require the extension or adaptation of a principle or in some cases the creation of new law to meet the justice of the case.'[106]

In *McLoughlin* the House of Lords decided that, whatever reasons there might be for limiting recovery for emotional distress, the plaintiff's case could not rationally—in justice—be distinguished from previous cases in which recovery had been permitted. The court refused to set arbitrary limits to the foreseeability principle. Lord Bridge stated: 'To attempt to draw a line at the furthest point which any of the decided cases happen to have reached . . . would be . . . an unwarranted abdication of the court's function of developing and adapting principles of the common law to changing conditions . . .'[107] The case is a good illustration of the incremental development of the common law, seeking out underlying principles to the limited extent necessary to avoid arbitrary, unjust distinctions. Lord Wilberforce considered that the plaintiff succeeded if one followed 'the process of logical progression': the courts had 'proceeded in the traditional manner of the common law from case to case, on a basis of logical necessity'.[108]

It should now be apparent why popular morality can make no contribution to common law adjudication. Since general principles which enjoy widespread support within the community are only abstract—*ex hypothesi* there is no formal institutional *record* of their application to particular cases—they cannot be compared or contrasted *as a matter of popular morality*. Where popular understandings or values appear to

[104] [1983] 1 AC 410; *Law's Empire*, 23–9.

[105] See Ch. 3, above.

[106] [1983] 1 AC 410, 430. The judicial task is creative only in the sense of seeking to determine the true content of moral rights. Lord Scarman adds that, 'whatever the court decides to do, it starts from a base-line of existing principle and seeks a solution consistent with or analogous to a principle or principles already recognised'. Cf. Lord Goff, 'Judge, Jurist and Legislator' [1987] Denning LJ 79 at 82, 86.

[107] [1983] 1 AC 441. [108] Ibid. 419.

conflict, they can only be reconciled by the allocation of weights in respect of the facts of individual cases. And that is necessarily a task which falls to the judge—or anyone else seeking to resolve a question of law—who must *supply* the judgments of weight required. He determines the correct principle, and its appropriate weight, in the light of the concrete facts before him.

To the extent that features of his political morality are attuned to moral ideas which are widely held, the judge's decisions will (loosely) reflect popular morality. But that will be largely coincidental. His legal judgments will be grounded in his own understanding and evaluation of relevant moral principle. Popular morality—even if it could be suitably ascertained—might sometimes discriminate generally between abstract principles (and this seems to be what Dworkin has in mind) but it cannot discriminate between different solutions to the particular case before the court. That is a responsibility, necessarily sensitive to the facts of the case—which determine the *weight* of relevant principles—which the judge cannot shift to the public at large.

Principle and policy

There is, perhaps, one qualification which follows from Dworkin's distinction between principle and policy. The separation of powers is preserved by confining the judicial role to the elaboration of principle—questions of individual rights and their corresponding duties; while matters of policy (or questions of the general welfare) are reserved for Parliament and government.[109]

Statutes, of course, are often enacted to give effect to policies thought to be in the general interest rather than to enforce moral rights. If several policies are equally consistent with the statutory language, and equally consistent with those moral rights of citizens recognized by existing law, fairness requires an interpretation which seems likely to enjoy public approval. A judge could have no reason in justice for preferring a less popular interpretation, even if he thought it more attractive on grounds of policy. In these circumstances, however, the judge is appealing to public opinion but not to popular morality: he does not defer to what he thinks is an erroneous, but popular, conception of individual rights. There is no competition between justice and fairness.

We may therefore accept Dworkin's account of judicial duty in the Snail Darter case.[110] Hercules—Dworkin's model judge—must decide whether the Endangered Species Act, passed by the United States Congress, required the construction of a dam to be halted, wasting

[109] See Ch. 3, above.

[110] *Tennessee Valley Authy.* v. *Hill* 437 US 153 (1978); *Law's Empire*, 20–3 and ch. 9.

large public funds, in order to save the habitat of the snail darter, a small fish which had been designated as an endangered species. Even if Hercules would himself prefer to halt the dam, he will think it right to bow to the popular view that it should be completed. There is no question of any conflict between justice and fairness. The fate of the snail darter involves no question of principle, in the sense of rights particular citizens may have against others or against the state:

> It is a question of what state of affairs is best for everyone: Hercules believes that everyone's life is diminished when a species becomes extinct, but he does not believe that allowing a species to disappear unjustly favours some people at the expense of others. So the conservation of species is a paradigm of the kind of decision that should be governed by the will of the people, the kind of decision that even legislators who accept the Burkean model of legislative responsibility should not impose on their constituents when the latter are united in the opposite opinion.[111]

Once issues of justice arise, however, it cannot be acceptable to pay regard to public opinion, or indeed parliamentary opinion—beyond that expressed in the statute, properly construed in accordance with justice. In any conflict between statutory policy and common law rights—those moral rights enshrined in precedent—Hercules would permit the curtailment of existing rights only to the extent necessary to give loyal effect to the statute. Fairness demands an interpretation of policy which seems likely to commend itself to the electorate, but it cannot justify deference to public opinion on issues of principle. The scope and content of moral rights, even when qualified by statute, remain questions of justice for personal, not popular, evaluation.[112]

Common law rights must give way to the legislative policy which best explains the statutory text. They should not, however, be at the mercy of an interpretation which, though widely approved or admired on grounds of policy, fits the text no better than other interpretations which leave individual rights intact, or erode them less seriously. It is not mere conservatism, for its own sake, which supports the doctrine that a statute makes no further change to the common law than its text expressly or by necessary implication requires. The doctrine enforces the requirements of justice, when fairness does not warrant their denial. Deference to popular morality, in the absence of clear statutory authority, would equally constitute an illegitimate denial of justice—even if, contrary to my analysis, the suggestion that such deference was required made any practical sense.

[111] *Law's Empire*, 341.

[112] The content of law is ultimately a matter of conscience for each individual. Anyone seeking an adequate interpretation of existing law must, like Hercules, invoke the standards of his own political morality in order to complete that task. See Ch. 5, below.

5
Disobedience, Dissent, and Freedom of Conscience

> A community of mutually respectful and self-respecting citizens would be one within which freedom of communication between and among persons would be maximised and most of all at a premium; this whether or not some citizens hold official positions and others not.
>
> Neil MacCormick, 'The Interest of the State and the Rule of Law', in Peter Wallington and Robert M. Merkin (eds.), *Essays in Memory of Professor F. H. Lawson* (London, 1986), 185.

The concept of individual autonomy, which we suggested was a basic value protected by the rule of law, entails important limitations on governmental authority in relation to thought and expression. The close association between freedoms of speech and conscience is apparent from Thomas Scanlon's defence of the 'Millian Principle' of freedom of expression.[1] It is not legitimate to prohibit speech merely on the grounds that it may inculcate false beliefs or encourage people to attach greater weight to the value of performing certain harmful actions. Scanlon explains this principle as a consequence of the Kantian view 'that a legitimate government is one whose authority citizens can recognise while still regarding themselves as equal, autonomous and rational agents'.[2]

A truly autonomous person is one who exercises independent judgment in deciding how to act. He must regard himself as 'sovereign in deciding what to believe and in weighing competing reasons for action'.[3] Although he may, of course, sometimes rely on the judgment of others, he must be able to advance independent reasons for trusting that judgment, and to assess their opinion in the light of contrary indications. If freedom of speech could be curtailed in order to prevent the spread of false beliefs—or even to forbid the advocacy of unlawful conduct—autonomy would be undermined. One cannot retain the ability to judge the wisdom of a course of action if the state is permitted to censor the information necessary for independent judgment. And it is

[1] Thomas Scanlon, 'A Theory of Freedom of Expression' (1972) *Philosophy & Public Affairs* 204. (Cf. J. S. Mill, *On Liberty*, ch. 2.)

[2] Ibid. 214.

[3] Ibid. 215.

fundamental to autonomy that a citizen cannot acknowledge any duty to obey the state's decrees without due deliberation.

The proper scope of freedom of conscience, and the nature and requirements of the rule of law, are questions raised acutely by the role of civil disobedience in a liberal democracy. John Rawls suggests that civil disobedience may be viewed as a political act guided and justified by the principles of justice which regulate the constitution.[4] It represents an appeal to the sense of justice of the majority and, unlike militant action or forcible resistance, it does not deny the legitimacy of the legal order but merely the justice of particular laws. On this interpretation, civil disobedience plays a role in ensuring the stability of a constitutional regime and, by resisting injustice through unlawful conduct which respects appropriate constraints, can serve to correct departures from fundamental principles of constitutional morality.[5]

It is no objection that each person must decide for himself when disobedience is justified. Rawls denies that the individual is free to decide as he pleases: 'To act autonomously and responsibly a citizen must look to the political principles that underlie and guide the interpretation of the constitution. He must try to assess how these principles should be applied in the existing circumstances.'[6] In all cases, in the context of democratic political theory, we are ultimately individually accountable for our actions and cannot divest ourselves of our responsibility or transfer the burden of blame to others.

Rawls distinguishes civil disobedience, narrowly interpreted, from 'conscientious refusal', which does not appeal to the community's sense of justice, but simply entails a refusal to comply with a legal injunction on grounds of conscience.[7] He observes that the law cannot always respect the dictates of conscience. It may be necessary, for example, to restrict religious expression where it violates the liberties of others. But it would also seem difficult to ground a moral right of civil disobedience (or conscientious refusal) on freedom of conscience alone. Where the law *does* meet those necessary standards of justice and fairness which the rule of law demands, the state would seem to be justified in enforcing compliance—even if, as a matter of personal morality, individual autonomy reserves the decision whether to obey to the private citizen.[8]

However, it will often in practice be a matter of controversy whether the law, properly understood, does meet acceptable standards of justice and fairness. A claim of right, on moral grounds, to disobey the law

[4] *A Theory of Justice* (Oxford, 1972), 363–8. (Rawls assumes the existence of a 'nearly just society', one that is 'well-ordered for the most part but in which some serious violations of justice nevertheless do occur'.)

[5] Ibid. 382–91. [6] Ibid. 389. [7] Ibid. 368–71.

[8] Cf. Frederick Schauer, *Free Speech: A Philosophical Enquiry* (Cambridge, 1982), 67–72.

may be hard to distinguish from a claim of right, on legal grounds, to resist an erroneous interpretation. Conduct which is portrayed as disobedience sometimes turns out, on better analysis, to be only the kind of conscientious dissent which (it may be argued) the rule of law truly invites and requires.

It is instructive to examine the character of disobedience, where it occurs within a polity which makes political morality directly relevant to the content of law. If, as I have urged, the common law should be understood as a body of principle which makes constant appeal to the requirements of justice, it must invite continuous debate and deliberation about questions of political morality. Properly understood, the common law serves the ideal of the rule of law by incorporating such deliberation within its ordinary process of evolutionary change and development. But the rule of law also places a premium on rational debate and communication between citizens, not merely between officials.[9] From this perspective, we must be cautious in identifying the content of legal duties with judicial pronouncements—even if, as a practical matter, the courts will have the last word on their enforcement. It is only judicial arrogance which insists on such an identification—an arrogance which reflects the élitism engendered by a positivist view of legal obligation.[10]

These questions may be illuminated by reflection on the *Morgan-Grampian* case, mentioned above.[11] The salient facts of that case may be quickly rehearsed. The young trainee journalist in question, Mr Goodwin, obtained information about two associated privately owned companies, after a copy of their draft business plan, prepared for the purpose of raising additional working capital, was stolen from the companies' premises. Goodwin's employers, who published *The Engineer*, were restrained by injunction from publishing an article about the companies, written by Goodwin and based on information obtained from the business plan. Both journalist and publishers were also ordered by Hoffmann J. to disclose the identity of their source, the judge accepting the plaintiffs' contention that the plan's publication would be likely to cause severe damage to their business.

The Court of Appeal subsequently dismissed appeals by Goodwin and his employers, refusing to hear argument on behalf of the journalist,

[9] Cf. Lon F. Fuller, *The Morality of Law*, revised edn. (New Haven, Conn., 1969), 185–6; MacCormick, 'The Interest of the State', 185.

[10] A 'positivist' view emphasizes authority rather than reason as the principal source of legal obligation, and accordingly insists on a clear separation between legal and moral reasoning. (See e.g. H. L. A. Hart, 'Positivism and the Separation of Law and Morals' (1958) 71 Harv LR 593; Lon L. Fuller, 'Positivism and Fidelity to Law—A Reply to Professor Hart', ibid. 630.) Cf. A. W. B. Simpson, 'The Common Law and Legal Theory', in A. W. B. Simpson (ed.), *Oxford Essays in Jurisprudence*, 2nd series (Oxford, 1973), esp. 88–91.

[11] [1990] 2 All ER 1; see Ch. 4.

who was in breach of an order to place the notes of his conversation with the source in a sealed envelope pending the outcome of the appeal. The House of Lords finally dismissed a further appeal, upholding the order for disclosure of the source, but disapproving the Court of Appeal's refusal to hear the journalist in support of his appeal. The court had a discretion to refuse to entertain an appeal, where a contemnor made clear his intention to defy the court's authority if its order should be affirmed; but if the appeal were entertained, his counsel should be heard in its support.

Goodwin had relied on section 10 of the Contempt of Court Act 1981 in support of his refusal to divulge his source of information; but his failure to comply with the court's order, when his plea of immunity was rejected, was treated as direct defiance of the rule of law. It was assumed that the scope of the journalist's duty of disclosure was conclusively determined by the court's decision. Whether loyalty to the ethics of his profession could ever justify disobedience, and in what circumstances, would on this view be a separate moral or political issue, quite independent of the question of legal obligation. But, of course, it would be surprising if disobedience could ever be morally justified under existing constitutional arrangements:

> Parliament makes the law and it is the duty of the courts to enforce that law, whether or not they agree with it. Every citizen, every corporate body and every authority, whether national or local, is entitled to campaign to change the law, but until the law is changed it is their duty to obey it. That is what parliamentary democracy and the rule of law is all about. Each one of us surrenders a part of his personal freedom of action and choice and in return is protected by the law from the consequences of others seeking to exercise an unfettered freedom of action and choice . . . In a parliamentary democracy personal and professional honour surely equates with the acceptance of, and obedience to, the rule of law.[12]

It is surely no answer to assert, as is sometimes done, that if a journalist accepts with good grace imprisonment or a fine, in consequence of his contempt, he does not truly place himself 'above the law'.[13] It is hard to see why credit should be claimed for accepting a punishment which is the inevitable outcome of disobedience, whether willingly embraced or not. Nor should we expect the state to be indifferent between obedience, on the one hand, and a willingness to pay the penalty, on the other. The rule of law surely demands a stronger commitment to the enforcement of the law than that. There is, then, some truth in Lord Donaldson's insistence, in the Court of Appeal, that 'any widespread refusal to obey the orders of the courts is a threat to the authority of the courts which is not any less such a threat,

[12] [1990] 1 All ER 616, 621–2 (Lord Donaldson MR in the Court of Appeal).
[13] Cf. Lord Bridge at [1990] 2 All ER 13.

because it is coupled with an acceptance that there will be a penalty to be paid'.[14]

None the less, it is possible for the courts to exaggerate the importance of unqualified submission to their interpretation of the law; and Goodwin's judicial rebuke begs important questions about the nature of legal obligation. A journalist might adopt the uncompromising stance that no legal duty of disclosure could ever override his personal moral obligation to respect the confidence in which he received his material. It would certainly seem difficult to square such a view with his obligations as a citizen under the rule of law. It is not simply that the law plainly rejects such an absolute immunity: it seems unlikely that any just and sophisticated legal system could countenance it. However much weight one attributes to the public interest in maintaining the anonymity of journalists' sources—as an adjunct to the freedom of the press—it is easy to visualize circumstances in which it would be overridden. If disclosure were necessary to forestall serious injury to person or property, almost certain to occur if the information were withheld, most people would think disclosure should be made. As Lord Bridge observed, it is difficult to accept that the journalist's immunity, however important, could be absolute.[15]

It may be mistaken, however, to treat a journalist's recalcitrance in a particular case as an instance of civil disobedience at all. If he accepts that the public interest in anonymity, and his own immunity derived from it, may sometimes be overridden by other more pressing public interests, his view would correspond to the present law, which grants an immunity from disclosure of sources, subject to exceptions designed to safeguard certain other major public interests. On this interpretation, the journalist's 'disobedience' may be plausibly viewed as itself an appeal to the rule of law: he denies any *legal* obligation to disclose his sources in the circumstances of the particular case. He repudiates the court's decision as mistaken. In addition to its character as an act of conscience, based on personal integrity—he is morally bound to respect the confidence in which he obtained his information—the journalist's recalcitrance may now be seen as a claim of right or justice, but one within, rather than in opposition to, the law.

None the less, the court has denied the journalist his immunity in the circumstances of a particular case. Does not the court's decision settle his legal obligation? Section 10 provides specifically that the necessity for disclosure must be 'established to the satisfaction of the court'. However, we have already considered the distinction which the House of Lords attempted to draw between the court's 'jurisdiction' under that section and its residual (common law) 'discretion'. We

[14] [1990] 1 All ER 623. [15] [1990] 2 All ER 13.

found that distinction empty, concluding that the court's decision (however described) depended on a balancing of interests in the light of the facts of the case. There was no scope for judicial 'choice' in any wider sense of the term 'discretion': it was solely a matter of whether, in the court's best judgment, an order for disclosure was necessary.[16]

It is certainly true that the journalist's view of the matter may be suspected to lack impartiality. Lord Donaldson observed that a journalist's view of the public interest seemed to march 'hand in hand with the commercial interests of the media';[17] and Lord Bridge denied that a journalist could 'be left to be judge in his own cause'.[18] That would amount to the grant of absolute privilege. It followed, he thought, that Goodwin's disobedience was morally indefensible:

> The maintenance of the rule of law is in every way as important in a free society as the democratic franchise. In our society the rule of law rests on twin foundations: the sovereignty of the Queen in Parliament in making the law and the sovereignty of the Queen's courts in interpreting and applying the law . . . Of course the courts, like other human institutions, are fallible and a journalist ordered to disclose his source may . . . feel that the court's decision was wrong. But to contend that the individual litigant, be he a journalist or anyone else, has a right of 'conscientious objection' which entitles him to set himself above the law if he does not agree with the court's decision, is a doctrine which directly undermines the rule of law and is wholly unacceptable in a democratic society . . . Freedom of speech is itself a right which is dependent on the rule of law for its protection and it is paradoxical that a serious challenge to the rule of law should be mounted by responsible journalists.[19]

But the paradox may be a product of the court's unduly narrow, desiccated conception of the rule of law. It seems better to perceive the journalist's resistance as a challenge to the court's interpretation of the law—an example, if truly conscientious, of the kind of dissension which the rule of law, properly understood, demands. Although the suspicion of bias counsels caution, it does not follow that the journalist's legal obligation is necessarily to be identified with the court's account of it. As Lord Bridge observed, judges are fallible. If it is sometimes right to disobey the law on moral grounds, it must equally be right on some occasions to stand by one's own understanding of the law, subject only to arguments of reason to the contrary.

The journalist's obligation is to make disclosure where that is necessary in the interests of justice (or national security etc.), and he may not be ordered to do so unless the court decides that that test is satisfied. If it is a matter of judgment, it is necessarily a matter of judgment for the journalist as much as the court. In ascertaining his legal duty, he asks the same question as the court: what is necessary in the interests of

[16] See Ch. 4, above.
[17] [1990] 1 All ER 622.
[18] [1990] 2 All ER 13.
[19] Ibid.

justice (or national security etc.)? It is a value judgment made in the light of the available evidence; and the court can claim no special endowments of reason or knowledge simply by virtue of being a court. The court consults its own judgment, just as the journalist should do, by asking whether it believes that the statutory test is satisfied on the facts of the case. It does not accord its own opinion any special weight merely because that *is* its opinion.

Lords Fraser and Scarman dissented in an earlier case under section 10 because they disagreed with the judgment of the majority about the legal obligation involved:[20] they did not believe that the evidence presented to the judge justified an order for disclosure in the interests of national security. If that legal obligation were equivalent to, or constituted by, the court's decision on the facts, the dissenting speeches could make no sense. They would repudiate a legal obligation whose scope was necessarily and conclusively determined (whatever its content) by the majority speeches. But, on the contrary, Lords Fraser and Scarman thought that the majority had given insufficient weight to the test of necessity. The test was a strict one and it was not for the court to relax that standard—'especially in a matter of this kind where there is a flavour of constitutional right of freedom of expression'.[21] The recalcitrant journalist may surely resist the court's order on the same ground, that properly applied, the law does not truly compel disclosure.

It is, no doubt, the case that a journalist minded to resist an order for disclosure of sources should reflect on his own partiality. It would be dishonest not to recognize that in the nature of things he is likely to undervalue the public interests in favour of disclosure. But this point may be pressed too far. For all the customary claims to impartiality and independence, in some contexts the court is hardly neutral either. It seems self-evident that the court is as likely in practice to overestimate the needs of the administration of justice (where that is the countervailing public interest) as the journalist to exaggerate the importance of preserving his confidence.[22]

But perhaps it is thought that the recalcitrant journalist denies the rule of law by failing to give due weight to the court's legal expertise. Should the conscientious citizen perhaps accept the court's judgment out of deference to the judges' superior access to legal knowledge? Or does the weight of the relevant public interests—if this is a different question—lie peculiarly within a lawyer's grasp?[23]

[20] *Secretary of State for Defence* v. *Guardian Newspapers* [1985] AC 339.

[21] Ibid. 359 (Lord Fraser).

[22] Cf. Lord Oliver's criticism of Lord Donaldson's interpretation of s. 10, considered above (Ch. 4).

[23] It should be noted that the court must assess the demands of public interests—

We have canvassed the distinction between rules and principles in this context, and it is clear that section 10 of the Contempt of Court Act 1981 requires an application of principle.[24] It enacts a rule against ordering disclosure of sources, but the rule is subject to exceptions whose nature and scope resist rule-governed application. Once a relevant exception applies—an obligation of disclosure may be justified in the interests of justice or national security or for the prevention of disorder or crime—the statute requires a balancing exercise, in which the public interest in non-disclosure must be weighed against the relevant opposing public interest. As Lord Bridge's speech in *Morgan-Grampian* demonstrates, there must be a discriminating value judgment in which everything depends on the facts of the case. The weight of the principle favouring the journalist's immunity, in recognition of the desirability of a strong press, cannot be stated in advance. As Lord Wilberforce explained, in a previous case: 'There is a public interest in the free flow of information, the strength of which will vary from case to case. In some cases it may be very weak; in others it may be very strong.'[25]

Now, we should not assume that the lawyer necessarily has greater insight than the layman into the true value of the relevant principles by virtue of wider knowledge of other parts of the law. If the rule of law requires the consistent enforcement of a single coherent set of principles of justice and fairness—as Dworkin's model of 'integrity' suggests—it is true that we cannot finally settle a question in one part of the law in isolation from analogous questions in others. But since the weight of a principle depends on the facts to which it is applied, we cannot determine that weight by consulting the institutional records (statute and precedent). I have argued that a statute can only enshrine a principle previously understood: its weight cannot in any sense be determined by formal enactment. And it seems unlikely that weight can be captured by precedent. Each application of a principle in a previous decision will necessarily be unique—a judgment of value dependent on the facts of that case, which will never be exactly repeated.

We know that the administration of justice must sometimes suffer because relevant information must be withheld. The House of Lords acknowledged the importance of preserving the anonymity of informants, where the Gaming Board depended on information supplied in connection with its statutory functions.[26] A similar result obtained

despite the distinction between principle and policy entailed by the separation of powers—because the litigants' rights depend on that assessment. The court is not accorded a policy-making role—in any usual sense of that expression—but must weigh the requirements of specified public interests in determining the content of legal rights (see generally Ch. 3, above).

[24] Ch. 4, above.

[25] *British Steel Corp.* v. *Granada TV* [1981] AC 1096, 1174.

[26] *Rogers* v. *Home Secretary* [1973] AC 388.

where information relating to the care and custody of children was passed to the NSPCC.[27] The courts have also accepted in previous cases that journalists' sources of information should, so far as possible, be protected in the interests of freedom of speech and freedom of the press.[28] None of these precedents, however, can provide the correct solution to a case like *Morgan-Grampian*. There is no 'legal' answer, in any technical sense, at all.

It follows that a judge has no professional expertise which insulates his judgment in the present context from the layman's critical appraisal. The lawyer, like the layman, can only weigh the relevant principles by appeal to ordinary moral or political reasons, for that is the task which the statute assigns. It follows that the legal determination involved in a case like *Morgan-Grampian* is a perfectly ordinary (though difficult) judgment of political morality. The statute demands an exercise of judgment, made on the basis of the relevant facts—one where, as Lord Griffiths noted in a similar case, 'different people may come to different conclusions on the same facts'.[29] A court's judgment obtains no preferred status in reason by virtue of being the opinion of lawyers; and the well-informed and conscientious journalist seems perfectly qualified to decide the scope of his own legal duty, subject only to the (important) proviso concerning partiality. The outcome of the balancing exercise is only as sound as the reasons on which it is grounded; and it is an essential ingredient of the rule of law that those reasons be exposed to public scrutiny and criticism—a scrutiny based on rational grounds, accessible to everyone.[30]

The rule of law is a complex ideal. It certainly demands a citizen's allegiance to the law, in the sense of requiring an honest attempt to meet his legal obligations. But it need not be taken to demand mute obedience, where those obligations are controversial. The rule of law permits and encourages moral and political argument about how a citizen's legal rights and duties are to be understood and interpreted. And the broader the standards of judgment the law requires, the wider correspondingly will be the range of argument. Even if for practical purposes all must (ultimately) submit to the court's authority, it seems unwise to condemn the citizen who is conscientious—even if misguided—in his dissent. It does no service to the rule of law to cast every dissident in the role of anarchist or traitor to that ideal. And it may do great harm. Since the journalist can weigh reasons as well as the judge, the latter should be

[27] *D.* v. *NSPCC* [1978] AC 171.
[28] See discussion of *British Steel* case above (Ch. 4).
[29] *Re an Inquiry under the Company Securities (Insider Dealing) Act 1985* [1988] AC 660, 704.
[30] Cf. J. R. Lucas, *The Principles of Politics* (Oxford, 1966), 107.
[31] *Trial by Jury*, Hamlyn Lectures, 8th series, revised edn. (London, 1966), 160–5.

slow to invoke the rule of law against the former. Their disagreement will often be about the weight of reasons, not about the vice or virtue of disobedience.

The role of the jury

These conclusions may perhaps be supported by reflection on the role of the jury in serious criminal cases. The jury has been strongly defended, particularly by Lord Devlin,[31] as an institution which not only provides for lay participation in criminal trials, but permits something akin to a lay veto on the prosecution of oppressive charges. Although the trial judge directs the jury on questions of law, he cannot formally direct a conviction.[32] There is therefore scope for the jury to take account of justice and morality in reaching its verdict, even if in doing so it departs to some extent from the judge's interpretation of the applicable law.

Devlin envisaged an opposition here between legality and equity ('*aequum et bonum*')[33]—the jury could modify the harshness of a general rule of law by taking greater account than could a judge of the merits of the particular case: 'Juries do not deliberately marshal legal considerations on one side and broader considerations of justice and mercy on the other and bring them into conflict on the field of conscience.'[34] They were more likely to 'confuse the issues'. However, the dichotomy is sometimes more accurately presented as a genuine difference between rival interpretations of what the law, properly understood, truly requires. An adequate conception of the rule of law, in other words, encompasses both legality and equity in appropriate degrees.

The trial of Clive Ponting in 1985 for an offence under section 2 of the Official Secrets Act 1911 is an apt illustration. Ponting, a senior civil servant in the Ministry of Defence, was accused of 'leaking' confidential documents to a member of the House of Commons Select Committee on Foreign Affairs. The documents related to the sinking of the Argentinian cruiser *Belgrano* during the Falklands war in 1982, and showed that ministers had decided against revealing the full circumstances of the incident, even though previous accounts given to Parliament had been inaccurate. Although the defence conceded that Ponting had not been *authorized* to make the disclosure, within the terms of section 2(1)(a), it was argued that the recipient of the documents

[32] *DPP* v. *Stonehouse* [1977] 2 All ER 909. See e.g. Lord Salmon at 928: 'If the judge is satisfied that, on the evidence, the jury would not be justified in acquitting the accused and indeed that it would be perverse of them to do so, he has no power to pre-empt the jury's verdict by directing them to convict. The jury alone has the right to decide that the accused is guilty.'

[33] *Trial by Jury*, 151–8. [34] Ibid. 160.

was a person to whom it was 'in the interest of the state his duty' to communicate the information. The trial judge, however, denied the availability of this defence on the ground that Ponting's only relevant duty was his official duty—he could not plead a higher moral or constitutional duty—and the 'interest of the state' was synonymous with government policy (including the policy of non-disclosure of information to Parliament).[35]

Ponting's acquittal in the teeth of this direction may fairly be viewed as a legitimate repudiation by the jury of the judge's account of the law. (There was little controversy about the salient facts.) By its wording section 2 plainly envisaged that someone might have a duty to communicate information although he was not authorized to communicate it; and this suggests the possibility of a moral duty distinct from the duties of office. Moreover, the judge's reliance on the speeches in *Chandler* v. *DPP*[36] for his reading of the phrase 'interest of the state' was not persuasive. Although Lord Devlin treated the 'state' as a reference to the 'organs of government of a national community', his approach was carefully grounded on the government's responsibility for the defence of the realm: 'So long as the Crown maintains armed forces for the defence of the realm it cannot be in its interest that any part of them should be immobilised.'[37] And Lord Reid actually denied that the 'state' meant government or executive, preferring 'the country or the realm' or 'the organised community'.[38]

In an instructive analysis of the *Ponting* case, Neil MacCormick has invoked Hans Kelsen's identification of the state with the legal order: the state was a 'personification' of the 'unity' of the legal order.[39] It follows that the upholding of the law and the constitution is the highest interest of the state. Ponting's defence consisted essentially in the contention that any interest in securing the implementation of government policies should yield, in the circumstances of that case, to the higher interest in upholding the constitution. His actions could be understood as intended to preserve ministerial responsibility to Parliament by frustrating executive decisions calculated to undermine it.

However, Kelsen's theory does not provide an answer to the proper construction of the statute. It merely illuminates constitutional considerations which the judge appeared to overlook. MacCormick rightly insists on closer attention to the content of the rule of law, and the true meaning of the concept of *Rechsstaat*. From that perspective, it should be obvious that the public interest in the effective implementation

35 *The Times*, 9 Feb. 1984.

36 [1964] AC 763. (The case is considered below, Ch. 9.)

37 Ibid. 807; cf. Lord Pearce at 813.

38 Ibid. 790.

39 'The Interest of the State' (citing Kelsen's *Pure Theory of Law* and *General Theory of Law and State*).

of government policy must be placed in the wider context of constitutionalism. There will always have to be some restrictions on the disclosure of government information, especially where it concerns defence and security. 'But it will always be a legitimate question whether it can be an official's duty in the interest of the state-as-constitutional-state to disclose to Parliament information which Ministers of the Crown wish to hold back from Parliament.'[40] MacCormick concludes that the jury's interpretation of the statute was sound, and the judge's reading mistaken.

Freedom of conscience and representative government

Lord Devlin drew an analogy between the relationship of the executive to Parliament, in respect of legislation, and the relationship of the judge to the jury.[41] Parliament accepted the direction of the executive, which initiates major legislation, just as the jury accepts the judge's direction. But liberty and justice depended on there being limits to each power of direction; and he thought the two institutions—Parliament and the jury—were likely to stand or fall together: 'Each jury is a little parliament.' The analogy points to a more fundamental connection with our interpretation of the rule of law, which places ultimate responsibility on each individual, taking account of political morality as he understands it, to determine finally for himself what the law requires. We would expect to find a similar—indeed even stronger—sense of individual responsibility inherent in the role of elected representatives, who make the law rather than apply it. As Devlin expresses the point: 'The judge gets his way by giving directions of law and the executive gets it by the party whip; and both sorts of command may in matters of conscience be rejected.'[42]

The primary role accorded by constitutional theory to the individual conscience is perhaps most clearly revealed in its view of the role of the Member of Parliament, and that of the local councillor. The MP is the representative of his constituents, rather than the delegate of his electors: he cannot be mandated to vote against his conscience, even in matters of acute political controversy or strong sectional interest. His representative status is intended to encourage the exercise of independent judgment, permitting him to set party policy and electoral commitments within the broader context of political principle. He can take full account of justice as well as fairness (in Dworkin's sense of those terms).[43] Despite the inevitable and pressing constraints of party discipline, in legal theory every vote in the legislature involves a 'matter of conscience'—not merely in the most sensitive cases of ethical con-

[40] Ibid. 186. [41] *Trial by Jury*, 162–4. [42] Ibid. 162–3. [43] See Ch. 4, above.

troversy, where theory and practice most nearly coincide and the party whip is temporarily suspended. The well-known speech of Edmund Burke to the electors of Bristol continues to reflect the accepted position:

> Parliament is not *a congress* of ambassadors from different and hostile interests; which interests each must maintain, as an agent and advocate, against other agents and advocates; but parliament is a *deliberative* assembly of *one* nation, with *one* interest, that of the whole; where, not local purposes, not local prejudices ought to guide, but the general good, resulting from the general reason of the whole. You choose a member indeed; but when you have chosen him, he is not a member of Bristol, but he is a member of *parliament*.[44]

It would, no doubt, be naïve to expect constitutional theory and political reality perfectly to coincide. We should not be surprised to find that the legal basis of the British polity is grounded in aspirations for justice and democracy which are often disappointed in practice. Its most fundamental doctrine, the rule of law, is as much a political ideal as a description of existing arrangements; and ordinary politics will likewise be only an imperfect reflection of its role in constitutional theory. Marshall and Moodie considered the 'fiction' that House of Commons divisions reflect Members' opinions about the merits of arguments deployed in the chamber 'not far removed from the sort of sham or falsehood with which Bentham and Dicey charged Blackstone'; but they accepted that such 'shams' might have to serve 'in place of a "Founders' conception" of constitutional purposes and proprieties set out in a formal document'.[45]

If we cannot expect the convictions and conduct of politicians to be as open to reflective deliberation as judicial decision-making, where reasoned argument must normally be offered in support of the court's conclusions, we can none the less embrace Burke's conception as an ideal worth striving for. It is the ideal commended by John Rawls as the appropriate standard for judging actual institutions. Representatives are not mere agents of their constituents, but must exercise discretion and judgment in enacting legislation: 'they must seek first to pass just and effective legislation, since this is a citizen's first interest in government, and secondly, they must further their constituents' other interests insofar as these are consistent with justice'.[46] He adds that the 'principles of justice are among the main criteria to be used in judging a representative's record and the reasons he gives in defence of it'.

Constitutional theory must not depart too far from political practice, however. If theory and practice diverge too sharply, the theory loses its

[44] 3 Nov. 1774: *Works*, new edn. (1826), iii. 19–20.

[45] Geoffrey Marshall and Graeme C. Moodie, *Some Problems of the Constitution* (London, 1959), 25.

[46] *A Theory of Justice*, 227. Rawls derives the principles of justice from his theory of 'justice as fairness'.

power to organize political development and our general conception of government becomes incoherent. The customary divorce between law and convention in legal thinking—a doctrine inherited from Dicey—is quite incompatible with a proper understanding of public law.[47] Legal theory must take account of modern party discipline and its impact on the activities of elected representatives. Accordingly, the courts have declined to interfere with the decisions of local authorities purely on the grounds that, in voting in support of Council resolutions, individual councillors have been strongly influenced by their party affiliations and the threat of party disciplinary sanctions:

> The law does not forbid pressure in general; to do so would be to ignore reality. Nor does it forbid all sanctions which may be imposed for voting contrary to the wishes of those who have power to impose them. The party whip may be withdrawn, newspapers may comment unfavourably, constituents may decline to re-elect, the local party may deselect. None of those measures is unlawful or an improper fetter on the representative's judgment.[48]

The Court of Appeal has even accepted, in acknowledgement of the political realities, that a councillor might lawfully vote in support of a resolution 'contrary to his own intellectual assessment of the merits, taken in isolation, in order to secure unanimity of vote'—provided that he retained an unfettered discretion in the sense that he acts in accordance with his own judgment.[49] He may believe that the maintenance of party unanimity is of greater importance than principled dissent, all things considered—ultimately of greater value in advancing his wider vision of justice. A council resolution could not therefore be impugned on the ground that it was supported by several councillors who had formerly opposed its adoption at a meeting of the majority party group. The threat of withdrawal of the party whip as a sanction for breach of the party group's standing orders, which required members to refrain from speaking or voting in opposition to decisions of the group, did not fetter a councillor's discretion because he could continue to sit as an independent member and vote as he saw fit. Russell LJ affirmed the general principle:

> Party loyalty, party unanimity, party policy were all relevant considerations for the individual councillor. The vote becomes unlawful only when the councillor allows these considerations or any other outside influences so to dominate as to exclude other considerations which are required for a balanced judgment.[50]

A resolution could be upset if it depended on the vote of a councillor who, by 'blindly toeing the party line', had failed to exercise any real choice or independent discretion.

[47] See Ch. 10, below.
[48] *R.* v. *Greenwich LBC, ex p. Lovelace* [1991] 3 All ER 511, 525 (Staughton LJ).
[49] *R.* v. *Waltham Forest LBC, ex p. Baxter* [1988] QB 419, 428.
[50] Ibid.

It follows from the general principle that no representative can be bound by any election promise or commitment. Burke was emphatic on the point:

But *authoritative* instructions; *mandates* issued, which the member is bound blindly and implicitly to obey, to vote, and to argue for, though contrary to the clearest conviction of his judgment and conscience,—these are things utterly unknown to the laws of this land, and which arise from a fundamental mistake of the whole order and tenour of our constitution.[51]

The legal status of the mandate and the role of the party election manifesto, in the context of local government, were considered in *Bromley LBC* v. *Greater London Council*.[52] The House of Lords held unlawful a supplementary rate precept levied by the Greater London Council on all London boroughs to finance the cost of reducing fares on public transport in London by 25 per cent in accordance with the Labour party's manifesto. The court held that the levy was made in breach of the Transport (London) Act 1969. Lord Diplock accepted that a Council member might give considerable weight to approval of the manifesto by the electorate when deciding whether the policies in question should be implemented. The majority party on the Council had erred in law, however, by regarding themselves as irrevocably committed to the fare reduction. He endorsed the traditional view that the Council member once elected was not the delegate of those who had voted in his favour, but was the representative of all the electors in his ward. Accordingly, there was no difference between those Councillors who were members of the majority party and those of a minority:

In neither case when the time comes to play their part in performing the collective duty . . . to make choices of policy or action on particular matters, must members treat themselves as irrevocably bound to carry out pre-announced policies contained in election manifestos even though, by that time, changes of circumstances have occurred that were unforeseen when those policies were announced and would add significantly to the disadvantages that would result from carrying them out.[53]

The doctrine of mandate, then, enjoys only qualified legal recognition. The party manifesto is a factor which may properly be weighed in the balance of competing considerations in settling policy; but it must not be allowed to fetter the decision-making process by imposing a binding commitment on elected representatives whose duties should be performed in the interests of the electorate as a whole. And the *Bromley* case establishes that the 'constitutional duty to govern in the

[51] *Works*, new edn. (1826), iii. 19–20.
[52] [1983] 1 AC 768.
[53] Ibid. 829; see also Lord Brandon at 853, and Oliver LJ at 789–93.

interests of all and not in the interests of party'[54] is also a legal duty: as an important element of political morality, it does not depend solely on the force of public opinion, without means of legal enforcement, as has sometimes been alleged.[55]

Admittedly, the application of these principles to Parliament remains a matter of self-regulation. Members' freedom and independence from outside groups or organizations are protected by the rules of parliamentary privilege. And the House of Commons has resolved that no Member should restrict his freedom of action by agreeing to act as the representative of any outside body—'the duty of a Member being to his constituents and to the country as a whole, rather than to any particular section thereof'.[56] However, the absolute protection accorded by Article 9 of the Bill of Rights 1689—'that the freedom of speech and debates or proceedings in Parliament ought not to be impeached or questioned in any court or place out of Parliament'—is taken to prevent judicial challenge to the nature of legislative deliberations. The separation of powers is understood to require reciprocal restraint. Judicial conduct and integrity cannot strictly be questioned in the House of Commons, under rules of order, except on a substantive motion for that purpose; and the judges refrain from adverse comment on parliamentary conduct and wisdom.[57]

Nevertheless, the legal and constitutional position of Members of Parliament is clear and exemplifies the primary role of the individual conscience in our 'protestant' conception of the rule of law.[58] Norman Marsh, in his discussion of the rule of law as a 'supra-national concept', also concluded that its basis consisted in 'trust in the moral judgment of the individual, isolated as far as possible from distracting pressures and influences'.[59] And when the rule of law is understood to permit, and to require, the participation of every citizen in the continuous process of defining legal obligations, the gulf between law and politics, as it is usually perceived, starts to diminish. Politics involves debate about the requirements of justice for the future—the rules which should be adopted to govern a society in which people have different and conflicting demands and aspirations. Law is the process of ascertaining how existing rules and principles apply to past and present events—a necessary corollary of the idea of amending the law for the future.

[54] Sir Alfred Denning, 'The Spirit of the British Constitution' (1951) 29 Can. Bar Rev. 1180, 1191.

[55] Ibid. 1190–1.

[56] HC Deb. 440, col. 365, 15 July 1947.

[57] *R. v. HM Treasury, ex p. Smedley* [1985] 1 All ER 589, 593 (Sir John Donaldson MR); cf. Slade LJ at 597. See also Lord Hailsham, *The Dilemma of Democracy*, 105–6; Denning, 'The Spirit of the British Constitution', 1194.

[58] Cf. Ronald Dworkin, *Law's Empire* (London, 1986), 190, 413.

[59] Norman S. Marsh, 'The Rule of Law as a Supra-National Concept', in A. G. Guest (ed.), *Oxford Essays in Jurisprudence* (Oxford, 1961), 223, 253 n. 1.

Adjudication is necessarily a more narrowly confined activity than legislation: it is constrained by an existing legal record (statutes and precedent). But it need not for that reason be an arcane mystery, in which only privileged initiates may participate. The requirements of justice in particular cases are often as susceptible to reasoned discussion by ordinary laymen—given full information about the relevant facts—as are the wider questions which form the substance of political debate. Unquestioning deference to judicial wisdom is no more a virtue than undiscriminating support for a political leader or a political party. The rule of law demands only that the citizen act in good conscience, in all honesty and goodwill, when he joins the debate about the content of legal rights and duties, including his own.

Legitimate resistance to official commands: the intersection of public and private law

I have sought to defend a conception of the rule of law which emphasizes the moral responsibility and independence of the ordinary citizen. The freedoms of speech and conscience, which the common law affirms, are ultimately founded on that conception; and in constitutional theory, a citizen's obedience to the law expresses his considered and deliberate *judgment* that conformity to law is justified. It is also part of this conception that a citizen is legally entitled, and morally bound, to act on the basis of his own best understanding of what the law requires. He should defer to the judgment of others—even of courts—only to the extent that their opinions about the content of his legal obligations seems likely to be correct (or at least better informed than other opinions which might be available). A conception of the rule of law based on individual moral responsibility celebrates rather than condemns a person who, on a question of principle, adheres in good faith to an interpretation of the law which the courts have (as he believes) mistakenly denied. Even such resistance to decisions of the highest court of appeal may be morally (and legally) justified—if honest and intelligent—where it contributes to a debate which may finally result in authoritative reassessment of the content of legal obligation.

That that view of the rule of law is embedded in the common law, properly understood, is confirmed by the courts' traditional attitude towards the citizen's resistance to unlawful official demands. In *Christie* v. *Leachinsky*,[60] the House of Lords held that it was a requirement of a lawful arrest without warrant that the suspect be informed of the true ground of detention. If such information was withheld, he was entitled to resist arrest, using appropriate (minimum) force. A person was,

[60] [1947] AC 573.

prima facie, entitled to his freedom and was only required to submit to restraint if told the reason for it.[61] Citizen A was not bound to submit unresistingly to arrest by citizen B in ignorance of the charge made against him, even if citizen B held the office of constable: 'Blind, unquestioning obedience is the law of tyrants and of slaves: it does not yet flourish on English soil.'[62]

Just as personal liberty entails the right to resist an unlawful arrest, the citizen's duty of obedience to every other official instruction or order is coextensive with its legality. He is entitled, in principle, to act on his own assessment of the lawfulness of the order, resisting its demands if he judges it unlawful. A public agency is therefore unable to affect a person's ordinary legal rights merely by an assertion of official authority. If that authority is improperly exercised, or lacks adequate legal foundation, the agency's order is a *brutum fulmen*: it may be ignored with impunity, as the order of a purely private agency (in the absence of any relevant contractual relationship) may be ignored.[63]

The principle that ordinary rights in private law can only be curtailed by government in the lawful exercise of acknowledged powers has sometimes been obscured in the effort to systematize administrative law. One important consequence of modern development of an independent body of public law, reflecting the special standards of conduct and accountability applicable to public authorities, has been the erection of procedural barriers to judicial review. The courts have accorded public bodies the benefit of special procedural protection in order to prevent their paralysis by unjustified or vexatious legal challenge. In *O'Reilly* v. *Mackman*,[64] the House of Lords held that an applicant who sought to protect rights in public law would not generally be allowed to proceed by way of an ordinary action for a declaration or injunction, but must promptly seek leave to apply for judicial review.[65] It was thought undesirable that the decisions of public bodies should be vulnerable to challenge beyond the limited period necessary to ensure fairness to persons directly affected.

Now, it is not possible to pursue such reasoning to its logical conclusion without undermining the principle of legality, as traditionally understood. It has long been accepted that if a person may ignore an administrative order as *ultra vires*, he may equally plead its invalidity, if necessary, in any action (civil or criminal) brought by the public

[61] Ibid. 587–8 (Viscount Simon).

[62] Ibid. 591 (Lord Simonds).

[63] The distinction between public and private agencies is not, however, always clear-cut; and judicial review may accordingly extend to non-statutory bodies exercising *de facto* powers of public importance (see *Datafin* case, n. 74 below).

[64] [1982] 3 All ER 1124.

[65] Leave to apply must be obtained under RSC, Ord. 53: the application must normally be made within three months of the decision impugned.

authority for its enforcement (or in which its validity is placed in question).[66] If it is truly *ultra vires* it is incapable of altering his existing rights. Even if he may reasonably be required to proceed by way of judicial review if he wishes actively to challenge the order, therefore, he cannot legitimately be prevented from resisting it in proceedings taken against him by the public authority (or by anyone else). The possibility of collateral challenge to official decisions or orders is a necessary concomitant of the traditional concept of *ultra vires*.[67]

Lord Diplock's reasoning in *O'Reilly* was expressly based on the distinction between public law and private law rights. That case concerned alleged breaches of natural justice by the Board of Visitors of Hull Prison, which had imposed forfeiture of remission of sentence as punishment for disciplinary offences. The prisoners concerned had no private law rights to remission of sentence: they had only legitimate expectations, based on their knowledge of the general practice, that they would be granted maximum remission for good conduct. Even if stringent procedural constraints may fairly be imposed to regulate the enforcement of public law rights, then, it does not follow that the vindication of private law rights may be similarly constrained. The effect would be to place public authorities 'above the law', in the sense of qualifying their obligation to respect the ordinary (private) law in the exercise of their powers and functions.

The distinction here between public law and private law is fundamental. Whereas public law governs the implementation of government policy and the ordinary processes of administration, private law provides the wider framework within which both government and citizen must work. The former is fashioned primarily to constrain the pursuit of public policy in the interests of fairness to those most closely affected, and the procedural conditions for its enforcement must be tailored to reflect that balance of public and private interests. Private law, however, constitutes the ground rules of ordinary social co-operation and, together with the criminal law, provides the basis of our ordinary liberties.[68] If it is a requirement of the rule of law that government and public authorities should respect the ordinary private law—except where the law has been changed to allow departures from the ordinary rules—we should not countenance the application of procedural barriers which might undermine or weaken that basic principle.

The boundary between public and private law—and its significance

[66] For an example of such 'collateral' challenge to a local authority by-law, see *Kruse* v. *Johnson* [1898] 2 QB 91. See also *R.* v. *Reading Crown Court, ex p. Hutchinson* [1988] QB 384.

[67] For recent discussion, see generally Carl Emery, 'The Vires Defence—"Ultra Vires" as a Defence to Criminal or Civil Proceedings' [1992] CLJ 308.

[68] For a helpful account of the fundamental distinction between public and private law, see F. A. Hayek, *Law, Legislation and Liberty* (London, 1982), i, ch. 6.

for the rule of law—was correctly identified in *Wandsworth London Borough Council* v. *Winder*.[69] The tenant of a council flat refused to pay the full amount of a demand for increased rent, taking the view that the increase was unreasonable and unlawful. His defence to a claim for arrears of rent and possession of the flat was initially struck out as an abuse of process on the ground that he should be required to challenge the validity of the local authority's exercise of its powers by judicial review. In the Court of Appeal, Ackner LJ pointed out that the reasons for adopting a procedural dichotomy between public and private law applied: it would defeat its purpose, in these circumstances, if a defendant could decline to apply for leave for judicial review and wait until he was sued before raising his challenge by way of defence.[70]

The other judges were none the less unwilling to affirm the ruling against the tenant. As the majority explained, in a decision confirmed by the House of Lords, the logic of *O'Reilly* v. *Mackman* had to surrender to the more fundamental principle of legality. The tenant's defence to the local authority's claim relied on his ordinary private law rights arising from his occupancy of his flat at the previously established rent.[71] If the council's decision was *ultra vires*, as the tenant alleged, it could hardly be permitted to enforce its unlawful demands for increased rent on the ground that none of the tenants affected had sought judicial review. If private law rights have not been duly varied, by a valid exercise of statutory powers, they should not be capable of being destroyed indirectly by a procedural technicality.

Lord Fraser drew attention to a further dimension of the distinction between public and private law. The remedies granted against public authorities for *ultra vires* actions or decisions are inherently discretionary, reflecting the necessity to preserve an appropriate balance between individual right and the public interest. In private law, by contrast, rights do not depend for their enforcement on judicial discretion. The tenant in *Winder* merely sought to defend proceedings brought against him by the council. In doing so he was 'seeking only to exercise the ordinary right of any individual to defend an action against him on the ground that he is not liable for the whole sum claimed by the plaintiff'. Moreover, he put forward his defence 'as a matter of right', whereas in an application for judicial review, 'success would require an exercise of the court's discretion in his favour'.[72]

The contrary view,[73] which asserts that the tenant's private law

[69] [1984] 3 All ER 83, 976. [70] Ibid. 88–9.

[71] Ibid. 96–7 (Robert Goff LJ).

[72] Ibid. 981. A plaintiff may also be able to sue to enforce 'private rights' under a statutory scheme—by extension of the analogy with ordinary rights in private law—where his entitlement is not dependent on administrative discretion: *Roy* v. *Kensington & Chelsea Family Practitioner Cttee.* [1992] 1 All ER 705.

[73] See Sir Harry Woolf, 'Public Law—Private Law: Why the Divide?' [1986] PL 220.

rights are inherently vulnerable to any rent increase, subject only to timely challenge by judicial review, entails the consequence that *ultra vires* government action can be (legally) effective to destroy private law rights unless and until it is successfully impugned. That view may appear to derive support from recent suggestions that the decisions of public bodies are to be treated as valid until judicially condemned.[74] Such suggestions, however, undermine the essential basis of the rule of law—that government may act only within the ambit of its lawful powers, properly interpreted.[75] They also deny the citizen's ordinary right—inherent in a free society—to make his own judgment about the legality of government decisions, and to act accordingly. He may be mistaken in that judgment, even when he has access to legal advice, but he should not be forced to acknowledge the binding effect of an order or decision solely on the ground that it was made by a government agency—even one apparently acting within the general sphere of its delegated powers.[76]

Admittedly, the distinction between *ultra vires* administrative action and 'wrongful' or 'mistaken' *intra vires* action is in practice narrow and sometimes elusive. But in terms of the citizen's duty of obedience, the distinction is fundamental. If public bodies are thought to have insufficient authority to pursue their legitimate functions, they should be allowed a wider discretion, including the power to determine (for purposes in hand) appropriate questions of law.[77] Where the jurisdiction of an agency is narrowly drawn, however, the private citizen enjoys a correspondingly wider discretion to dispute its interpretation of the applicable law. The point of constraining the activities of agencies by means of general principles of law is otherwise undermined. The citizen is, in principle, entitled to ignore an order he believes unlawful and oblige the public authority to justify its exercise of power. Denying that the failure of an authority to allow a proper hearing before making an order would necessarily give rise to an action in damages for negligence, Lord Diplock reasserted the traditional view: 'The effect of the failure is to render the exercise of the power void and the person complaining of the failure is in as good a position as the public authority to know that

[74] *R.* v. *Panel on Take-overs & Mergers, ex p. Datafin* [1987] 1 All ER 564, 578 (Sir John Donaldson MR); see also *R.* v. *Monopolies & Mergers Comm., ex p. Argyll* [1986] 2 All ER 257 (assertion of discretion to sustain *ultra vires* decisions).

[75] For a powerful defence of the traditional view of *ultra vires*, see M. J. Detmold, *Courts and Administrators* (London, 1989), ch. 2. See also *Davy* v. *Spelthorne BC* [1984] AC 262, 276–7 (Lord Wilberforce); *Roy* v. *Kensington & Chelsea Family Practitioner Cttee.* [1992] 1 All ER 705.

[76] It could hardly be contested that an order which, on its face, was plainly outside the jurisdiction of a public agency could be ignored as null and void. (Cf. Lord Hailsham in *London & Clydeside Estates* v. *Aberdeen DC* [1979] 3 All ER 876, 883.)

[77] See Ch. 3, above.

is so. He can ignore the purported exercise of the power. It is incapable of affecting his legal rights.'[78]

Justice, fairness, and legislative supremacy

A conception of the rule of law which resists any radical division between political morality and law—one which, on the contrary, stresses the dependence of legal obligation on questions of justice and fairness—has profound implications for the legal authority of statute. I have already argued that the rule of law imposes constraints on legislative sovereignty which are essential to preserve the separation of powers—a fundamental feature of constitutionalism. And I have rejected the suggestion that a court which struck down (or refused to apply) a statute which seriously violated fundamental rights would be dependent on the terms of a written constitution. The common law may reasonably be taken to embrace legislative sovereignty on grounds of political morality; and it follows that the legal authority of statute ultimately depends on the nature and limits of that underlying morality. It is reasonable to suppose that Parliament enjoys its sovereignty only in circumstances which reflect its commitment to the peace, welfare, and good government of the United Kingdom. Under certain (extreme) conditions that commitment might be called into question, and legal authority thereby forfeited.[79]

It is therefore always a matter of conscience, not merely how legislation should be interpreted in the context of any particular case, but ultimately whether it should be applied at all. If in most instances it seems obvious that the rule of law requires loyal application of statutes, that is because in ordinary cases we will agree that political morality supports that conclusion. Where enactment is the culmination of a democratic procedure—reflecting our egalitarian assumptions about the appropriate distribution of political power—it is usually reasonable to accept the statute. It is reasonable to accept its authority, even if we think its requirements unreasonable.[80]

However, it will not always be reasonable to acknowledge a statute's authority. A 'wicked' statute, which seriously contradicted the fundamental tenets of our political morality—which must include our commitment to basic civil rights and democratic government—could derive no force from that morality and should therefore in reason be rejected. Stephen's statute requiring the execution of blue-eyed babies would be a clear example.[81] It could be accepted as law—even in

[78] *Dunlop* v. *Woollahra MC* [1981] 1 All ER 1202, 1209.
[79] Ch. 3, above.
[80] Cf. M. J. Detmold, 'Law as Practical Reason' [1989] CLJ 436.
[81] L. Stephen, *Science of Ethics* (London, 1882), 143; cf. A. V. Dicey, *Law of the Constitution*, 10th edn. (London, 1959), 81.

principle—only at the cost of undermining the legitimacy of parliamentary law-making and denying the point and substance of the rule of law.[82]

We may perhaps obtain a clearer perception of the limits of sovereignty by pursuing the analysis of justice and fairness offered in Chapter 4. I argued that Ronald Dworkin's ideal of 'integrity' should be understood to require an accommodation between principles of justice and fairness, where 'justice' refers to moral rights, correctly ascertained, and 'fairness' means loyalty to statutes duly enacted. Anyone who accepts integrity, as an attractive account of the rule of law, is inevitably obliged to acknowledge as law many rules which justice would condemn. He will naturally strive to interpret such rules in a manner which is consonant with justice; and he will attribute to Members of Parliament a similar commitment to the pursuit of justice as a guiding virtue—even if he cannot share the conception of justice which underlies a particular statute. (He will assume that the content of the law is ultimately as much a matter of conscience for each individual legislator as it is for himself.) Fairness, however, imposes limits on permissible modes of interpretation: it demands loyal obedience to statutory injunctions, clearly expressed. Fairness will often require an adherent of integrity to defer, against his own judgment of a rule's iniquity, to the popular will as reflected in the rule's enactment.

However, no one seeking to determine the law, in accordance with the constraints of integrity, would acknowledge a principle of *absolute* legislative supremacy. He would rightly conclude that there must be limits to the power of a majority to work its political will. As Dworkin maintains, no plausible theory of (either English or American) law could deny legislative competence or supremacy altogether.[83] But it does not follow that every 'rule' enacted by the legislature must therefore be accepted. Dicey's conception of parliamentary sovereignty, which recognized only practical, non-legal limitations, was arbitrary.[84] It failed to allow for the necessary interplay between justice and fairness in any plausible account of political morality.

According to Dworkin, a judge will have different 'higher-level' opinions about the best resolution of conflicts between justice and fairness: 'No judge is likely to hold the simplistic theory that fairness is automatically to be preferred to justice or vice versa.'[85] The appropriate resolution will, of course, depend on the facts of the particular case. If, in most cases, Hercules—Dworkin's model judge—loyally enforces statutes, even when 'abstract' justice[86] would condemn them, it can

[82] I have rejected a purely formal conception of the rule of law: Ch. 2, above.

[83] *Law's Empire*, 255.

[84] *Law of the Constitution*, 70–85.

[85] *Law's Empire*, 250.

[86] 'Justice is a matter of the correct or best theory of moral and political rights, and

only be because he believes that fairness is in those cases overriding. If he decided solely in accordance with abstract justice in such circumstances, he would deny the litigants the judgment to which he thinks them morally entitled—a judgment which makes proper allowance for fairness as well as abstract justice. But he will not always think that abstract justice should defer to fairness: his political morality will be likely to condemn a statute (deny its authority) if its iniquity is grave.

Law as integrity provides a persuasive account of judicial obligation which repudiates the familiar positivist division between the judge's legal and moral duties. Admittedly, Dworkin insists on the customary distinction between the *grounds* and *force* of law. The conditions which establish the truth or soundness of a legal proposition do not themselves justify coercion: there may be special circumstances in which a judge should not enforce the law.[87] Since, however, Dworkin's theory makes the content of law closely dependent on political morality, it seems clear that Hercules will never be obliged to enforce a statute (or any rule of common law) which his political morality condemns. His official duty and his moral duty, even in the face of wicked laws, will almost invariably coincide.

If Hercules were unwilling, in conscience, to apply statutes in all or even most cases where abstract justice would condemn them, he would be unable to engage in the interpretative enterprise which law as integrity demands. He would be a sceptic.[88] If his political morality denied that fairness could ever override justice, or could do so only in exceptional cases, Hercules would be driven to reject the legal system of his jurisdiction as pervasively unjust. He would be unable to construct an interpretation which satisfied his overall standards of political morality, and which fitted legal practice—which, in Britain, includes the well-established convention whereby duly enacted statutes are normally received as binding law. From that sceptical stance, there would be no law, in the interpretative sense, to be applied.

These conclusions apply as much to ordinary citizens as to judges. Each citizen who accepts the interpretative enterprise Dworkin recommends must also construct a theory of legal decision-making, which will determine the answers to questions of law. He too, if he is not wholly sceptical, will ground his conclusions about the law in his own

anyone's conception of justice is his theory, imposed by his own personal convictions, of what these rights actually are': ibid. 97.

[87] Ibid. 108–13.

[88] An 'internal' sceptic adopts the interpretative attitude but denies the possibility of an acceptable interpretation; an 'external' sceptic rejects the interpretative enterprise altogether (ibid. 78–85).

political morality, reflecting the various requirements of justice, fairness, and integrity. Admittedly, there remains scope for conflicts to arise between legal and moral duties. No one's personal morality, of course, is exhausted by those considerations of political morality which are directly relevant to legal decision-making. It follows that he will sometimes be forced to choose between the dictates of conscience and the requirements of an admitted legal duty. (The journalist's position in *Morgan-Grampian* may arguably be better interpreted in that way.)

It is not true, however, that such conflicts will arise whenever an 'unjust law' apparently requires his obedience. For the claim of such a law on his allegiance must be tested against his political morality—his theory of justice and fairness and their appropriate interrelation. Considerations of fairness, deferring to the wishes of the majority, may be sufficiently strong to override personal convictions about justice. The grounds and force of law will therefore normally diverge only for the citizen who is sceptical—who denies that the law imposes any obligations at all because it is radically unjust, or at least too seriously unjust to permit an interpretation of law grounded in political morality.

These reflections on Ronald Dworkin's theory of law reinforce our earlier suggestion that conscientious dissent is better viewed as part of the rule of law than as a threat to its survival. That governing ideal invites dissent because it makes each person's commitment to justice and fairness directly relevant to his obligation of fidelity to law, as he understands it. The long-term health of the rule of law depends on the loyalty it engenders throughout the community, not merely among lawyers and public officials. If it does not engage the moral conscience of the ordinary citizen, by making his sense of justice relevant to the content of law, it will fail to excite his sympathy and co-operation.

Our analysis of Hercules' theory of adjudication shows that a citizen's right to defend his own account of legal duty, when that is controversial, must include the ultimate right to challenge the validity of statute. His allegiance to the legislative command, even when backed by the moral authority of a parliamentary majority, can no more be absolute or unconditional than the judge's. He is entitled, in the final analysis, to deny the legitimacy of a statute—on the ground of its iniquity—and therefore also its legality. A sceptic, who denies our connection between law and morality, may rest on the distinction between the grounds and force of law. He may say—as Dworkin suggests one might have said of Nazi law—that there is law which imposes no (moral) obligation to obey.[89] But anyone who does acknowledge that the law entails a moral duty of obedience, at least in ordinary cases, cannot consistently

[89] Ibid. 101–8.

repudiate that duty in special cases of injustice or iniquity. He must be understood to mean that there is no moral obligation to obey an unjust 'law' because, on a proper understanding of legal interpretation, there is no legal obligation either.[90]

[90] I have argued these points a little more fully in my article 'Justice and Fairness in Law's Empire' [1993] CLJ 64.

6
Constitutional Rights and Common Law

> The roots of the right to be so secure are embedded in the common law and the safeguards accorded that right are found in common law, in statutes subsequently enacted, and in decisions of the courts made as the society in which we live has evolved. The expression of the right in a constitutional document reminds us of those roots and the tradition associated with the right.
>
> *Hunter* v. *Southam* (1983) 147 DLR (3d) 420, 426 (Prowse JA).[1]

Contemporary identification of constitutionalism with enacted or entrenched bills or charters of rights makes it sound almost paradoxical to refer in the same breath to common law and constitutional rights. The dogma of parliamentary sovereignty, and the absence of a higher or fundamental law to which all legislation must conform, has tempted many commentators to deny the existence of constitutional rights in Britain. The fundamental rights of citizens enjoy only the protection of the common law, and are therefore vulnerable to statutory encroachment at the hands of a simple parliamentary majority (usually manipulated or coerced by a government with effective control of the House of Commons).

In addition, the common law concept of liberty is only residual, it is usually alleged: freedom is what remains after statutory and common law restrictions have been taken into account. Dicey's discussion of basic liberties has seemed a particularly striking illustration of our forlorn constitutional condition. He denied, for example, that English law acknowledged 'anything like that natural right to the free communication of thoughts and opinions' which was proclaimed by the French Declaration of the Rights of Man. 'Freedom of discussion is, then, in England little else than the right to write or say anything which a jury, consisting of twelve shopkeepers, think it expedient should be said or written.'[2]

It is important to see that, while this bleak picture of English liberty

[1] Alberta Court of Appeal. The judgment relates to the right, under s. 8 of the Canadian Charter, to be secure against unreasonable search and seizure; and is cited by the Supreme Court at 11 DLR (4th) 646–7.

[2] A. V. Dicey, *The Law of the Constitution*, 10th edn. (London, 1959), 246.

contains some truth, it is not the whole truth; and the health of the polity depends on our determined rejection of so pessimistic and partial a portrait. If we are not accustomed to regarding the common law as a source of fundamental rights, it is partly because our legal analysis has often been deficient. We have failed to distinguish clearly enough between liberty and liberties. It is also important not to exaggerate the difference between common law rights and enacted rights. If the latter are entrenched against ordinary legislative repeal they acquire a special constitutional status; but their content is likely to reflect conceptions of right embedded in the common law. In the absence of such entrenchment, enactment is pointless: fundamental rights are inherently resistant to formal statutory definition.

Residual liberty and basic liberties

The idea of liberty as residual reflects the fundamental principle of the rule of law that every invasion of individual liberty by the state is prima facie illegal; and everything which is not expressly forbidden the individual is permitted. No government measure or action which infringes my liberty is lawful unless it is authorized, and the burden is on government to prove authorization. This is the aspect of the rule of law illuminated by *Entick* v. *Carrington*,[3] and it provides the foundation of constitutional rights. The legality of the issue and execution of general warrants of search and seizure could not be established, and the King's Messengers were therefore liable for trespass. The judges would see if justification were provided by statute or common law: 'If no such excuse can be found or produced, the silence of the books is an authority against the defendant . . .'[4]

However, the common law is also solicitous of liberties—particular liberties recognized as having intrinsic value in a free society. It acknowledges the freedoms of speech and assembly, as well as liberty of the person and rights of property. The case-law is replete with references to the importance of freedom of expression and freedom of conscience as public interests which deserve judicial protection.[5] A constitutional right at common law is a product of these two interacting faces of the rule of law. My right (for example) to freedom of speech is the outcome, first, of my undifferentiated residual liberty—whose restriction needs lawful authority—and, secondly, of the court's

[3] (1765) 19 State Trials 1030.

[4] Ibid. 1066.

[5] See Alan Boyle, 'Freedom of Expression as a Public Interest in English Law' [1982] PL 574. For recent examples of the importance attributed to freedom of speech (and the press) see *Re W (a minor)* [1992] 1 All ER 794; *Derbyshire CC* v. *Times Newspapers* [1992] 3 All ER 65; [1993] 1 All ER 1011. See generally *Brind* v. *Home Secretary* [1991] 1 All ER 720; and cases considered below.

attachment to the value of free speech. The principle of freedom of expression, which has independent weight in the interpretation of both common law and statute, is of critical importance in determining the scope and effect of purported restrictions on my liberty.

In his dissenting judgment in the Court of Appeal in *Wheeler* v. *Leicester City Council*,[6] Browne-Wilkinson LJ recognized that freedoms of speech and conscience were fundamental—and so immune from interference without express parliamentary sanction—despite the absence of a written constitution. He noted that modern polarization of political attitudes had diminished the effectiveness of conventions which had formerly protected individuals and minorities from discrimination. But he did not suggest that, with the erosion of convention, the common law was helpless. Citing previous authority to illustrate the fundamental importance accorded to freedom of speech,[7] he concluded that it was 'undoubtedly part of the constitution of this country that, in the absence of express legislative provisions to the contrary, each individual has the right to hold and express his own views'.[8]

Browne-Wilkinson LJ's approach demonstrates the basic dynamic of constitutional rights at common law. The positive value accorded to freedoms of speech and conscience was harnessed to the general principle of residual liberty to protect the applicant from oppressive treatment by the local authority:

> Basic constitutional rights in this country such as freedom of the person and freedom of speech are based not on any express provisions conferring such a right but on freedom of an individual to do what he will save to the extent that he is prevented from so doing by the law. Thus, freedom of the person depends on the fact that no one has the right lawfully to arrest the individual save in defined circumstances. The right to freedom of speech depends on the fact that no one has the right to stop the individual expressing his own views, save to the extent that those views are libellous or seditious.[9]

The authority had required the applicant's rugby club to endorse its views on sporting links with South Africa, as a condition of permission to use a local recreation ground for practice. It had thereby unlawfully interfered with the 'fundamental right of the club and its members to freedom of speech and conscience'.[10] The intrinsic importance of the freedom justified a jealous and critical scrutiny of a claim to statutory support for encroachment on residual liberty. It could not assist the local authority that their stance in respect of apartheid was part of their policy of promoting good race relations; and that the Race Relations Act 1976, section 71 imposed a duty to ensure that their functions were

[6] [1985] 2 All ER 151, 155–9.
[7] *Verrall* v. *Great Yarmouth BC* [1981] 1 QB 202, 205, 210, 216.
[8] [1985] 2 All ER 157. [9] Ibid. 158. [10] Ibid. 159.

exercised with due regard for such an objective. Although the Act made racially discriminatory actions unlawful, it conferred no power to penalize individuals for holding particular views. General words in an Act of Parliament could not be taken as authorizing interference with such 'basic immunities' as those of freedom of the person and freedom of speech: 'Parliament (being sovereign) can legislate so as to do so; but it cannot be taken to have conferred such a right on others save by express words.'[11]

Although the House of Lords chose to frame its speeches in the more conventional language of administrative law, declining to endorse Browne-Wilkinson LJ's bolder reasoning from fundamental rights, the court agreed with his conclusion. Lord Templeman, moreover, came close to an explicit affirmation of the importance of liberties of speech and conscience in his remark: 'A private individual or a private organisation cannot be obliged to display zeal in the pursuit of an object sought by a public authority and cannot be obliged to publish views dictated by a public authority.'[12]

In the context of the criminal law, the House of Lords' decision in *Brutus* v. *Cozens*[13] rightly reflected the importance of freedom of speech as a public value. The defendant had angered spectators at Wimbledon by interrupting a tennis match, which involved a South African player, in order to protest against apartheid. He was acquitted by the magistrates of an offence under section 5 of the Public Order Act 1936; but the Divisional Court held that his conduct fell within the provision as an affront to the spectators, which evinced contempt for their rights. In allowing the defendant's appeal, and rejecting such an artificially extended definition of insulting behaviour, the House of Lords emphasized the need carefully to circumscribe the scope of the offence. As Lord Reid observed, 'It would have been going much too far to prohibit all speech or conduct likely to occasion a breach of the peace because determined opponents may not shrink from organising or at least threatening a breach of the peace in order to silence a speaker whose views they detest.'[14] Vigorous and distasteful speech was permitted as long as it could not reasonably be described as threatening, abusive, or insulting.[15]

If basic liberties may be invoked, when threatened, to justify restrictive interpretation of statutes, they also play a crucial role in the development of the common law. The right to freedom of expression,

[11] Ibid. 158. See also *Marcel* v. *Commr. of Police of Metropolis* [1991] 1 All ER 845, 851 (Browne-Wilkinson V.-C.).

[12] [1985] AC 1054, 1080. The case is considered more fully in Ch. 7, below.

[13] [1973] AC 854.

[14] Ibid. 862.

[15] See also *Jordan* v. *Burgoyne* [1963] 2 QB 744 (Parker LCJ described 'threaten, abuse or insult' as 'very strong words').

for example, cannot be only residual because in many contexts the freedom is rightly perceived as an important value entitled to independent weight in adjudication. The House of Lords' decision in *Attorney-General* v. *BBC*[16] is a fine example. The court denied that the Attorney was entitled to an injunction restraining the BBC from broadcasting a programme about the 'Exclusive Brethren', even though it raised issues which were relevant to the proceedings of a rating valuation court, in which the Brethren sought exemption for their meeting place from rates.

Lord Fraser held that the court must hold a balance between the principle of freedom of expression and the principle that the administration of justice must be protected from interference. He thought neither principle inherently more important than the other: in the context, the principle of freedom of expression was overriding. The class of inferior courts protected by the law against contempt should be limited to those which were truly courts of law, exercising the judicial power of the state. If it were illogical to exclude other tribunals from protection, logic gave way to the need for a test which could be applied with reasonable certainty and avoided too great a curtailment of the right to freedom of speech. Lord Salmon considered that the broadcast raised matters of great public importance. If its content were true, it rendered a valuable public service. And if the Brethren had sued for libel, and the BBC pleaded justification, no injunction would have been granted to prevent repetition.[17] Lord Scarman observed that a prior restraint was a drastic interference with freedom of speech, which should be ordered only when there was a substantial risk of grave injustice.

The distinction between residual liberty and specific individual liberties finds a parallel in the work of Ronald Dworkin, who has emphasized the importance of distinguishing between rights to particular liberties and the idea of a general right to liberty.[18] Residual liberty is a notion which places the burden on the state to justify restraint—there is a presumption in favour of liberty—but the strength of that justification must reflect the nature of the restraint. Dworkin expresses this point by denying the existence of any general *moral* right to 'liberty'. He insists that if someone has a right to something—in any useful sense of that expression—it must be wrong for the government to deny it to him even though it would be in the general interest to do so. In this anti-utilitarian sense of 'right', there can be no general right to liberty.

A great many laws which diminish one's liberty may be properly

[16] [1980] 3 All ER 161.
[17] See *Bonnard* v. *Perryman* [1891] 2 Ch 269.
[18] *Taking Rights Seriously* (London, 1977), ch. 12.

justified on utilitarian grounds, as being in the general interest or in the general welfare: they do not thereby infringe individual rights, merely on account of their necessary curtailment of freedom. The notion of rights implies that some special justification is needed for government action which overrides them, even if that action is taken in the general interest. It is in that sense that we generally recognize rights to specific liberties, such as freedom of speech or religion or political activity. Dworkin denies that such liberties may be derived from a more general right to liberty. There must be independent criteria of value of different sorts of liberty. He suggests that rights to specific liberties may be derived from a more fundamental concept of equality, that every citizen has a right to equal respect and concern.[19]

Admittedly, few rights can be absolute: even genuine rights must sometimes yield to countervailing requirements of public interest or private right. There is, however, an important difference between the operation of a genuine principle of freedom of speech in cases involving general public interests, on the one hand, and those involving conflicting individual rights, on the other.[20] Where, for example, speech must be curbed in deference to interests of national security, the restrictions should be justified by compelling grounds of serious national danger. The risk of some degree of danger to national security is already accepted as part of the price of the principle of freedom of speech, which acknowledges individual *rights* of speech. It is implicit in a genuine right that its exercise may work against (some facet of) the public interest: a right to speak only where its exercise advanced the public welfare or public policy (or caused no damage) would be a hollow guarantee against repression. That perception explained Browne-Wilkinson LJ's approach to statutory construction in *Wheeler*: the danger to the 'fundamental freedoms of the individual' could not be overlooked on the ground that 'the council were acting from the highest motives in seeking to promote a cause of which most people would approve'.[21] To show merely that censorship would advance the public interest is not sufficient justification: there must be public danger of a most serious and perhaps unusual kind before speech can properly be restricted.[22]

The balancing process is necessarily affected—even if only as a matter of degree—where the right of free speech must be reconciled with countervailing individual rights. In many cases, the opposing rights will be of equal or even greater strength. The right to a fair trial

[19] Ibid. Cf. H. L. A. Hart, 'Rawls on Liberty and its Priority' (1973) 40 Univ. of Chicago LR 534–55.
[20] See Frederick Schauer, *Free Speech: A Philosophical Enquiry* (Cambridge, 1982), ch. 9.
[21] [1985] 2 All ER 157.
[22] Cf. Schauer, *Free Speech*, 132–3.

provides a clear example.[23] It is inconceivable that the courts could countenance the prosecution of *unfair* trials: recourse to the courts for the determination of one's legal rights would be futile, or worse, if it carried no guarantee of a fair hearing. The right to a fair trial would therefore seem to be absolute, as a matter of English law—even if the requirements of fairness are necessarily a matter of judgment, dependent on all the circumstances of the case. In criminal cases, the judge may exclude even relevant and probative evidence of the crime charged in the interests of ensuring the defendant a fair trial. Moreover, the evidence liable to exclusion is not limited to material whose prejudicial quality is likely to exceed its probative value: evidence unfairly obtained from the defendant in the course of the police investigation may often be rejected.[24]

It does not follow that a stringent *sub judice* rule is necessarily justified. It seems unlikely, for example, that the impartiality of professional judges will be much affected by comment in the press about pending civil cases, and there will often therefore be no genuine conflict between the principles of free speech and fair trial. Although the possibility of conflict is much greater in criminal cases, where a jury may be unfairly prejudiced against the defendant by exposure to comment in the media, it is reasonable to incur some risk in the interests of press freedom. The likelihood of prejudice will depend on the nature of the comment and the interval of time between publication and trial.[25] The defendant's right to a fair trial remains intact, and may be protected, if necessary, by other means. Where his trial has actually been affected by adverse publicity (or where that seems likely) his conviction may be quashed on appeal as unsafe and unsatisfactory.[26]

Whether or not it is right to restrict freedom of expression in any particular case therefore depends on the strength of the countervailing right or interest demanding protection. Our commitment to free speech permits restriction only where it is truly necessary; but it may not be difficult to establish necessity where the right to a fair trial would otherwise be endangered. The House of Lords' refusal, in *Attorney-General* v. *English*,[27] to dismiss as trivial the danger posed to a pending

[23] See generally Eric Barendt, *Freedom of Speech* (Oxford, 1985), ch. 8; Laurence H. Tribe, *American Constitutional Law*, 2nd edn. (New York, 1988), 856–61.

[24] *Sang* [1979] 2 All ER 1222; Police & Crim. Evid. Act 1984 s. 78.

[25] Cf. *A.-G.* v. *News Group Newspapers* [1986] 2 All ER 833 (publication affecting forthcoming trial for libel). See also *A.-G.* v. *Guardian Newspapers* [1992] 3 All ER 38 (risk of prejudice must be practical, not theoretical).

[26] Despite strong criticism of the defendant's 'trial by television' in *Savundra* [1968] 1 WLR 1761, the Court of Appeal declined to quash his conviction on the grounds that there was no real risk that the jury was influenced by the pre-trial publicity, and that the Crown's case was in any event overwhelming.

[27] [1983] 1 AC 116 (for comment see e.g. Zellick [1982] PL 343; Redmond [1983] CLJ 9; cf. Barendt, *Freedom of Speech*, 226).

criminal trial by a newspaper article has been too readily condemned by legal commentators. The Contempt of Court Act 1981, section 2(2) applies to a publication which creates a 'substantial risk that the course of justice in the proceedings in question will be seriously impeded or prejudiced'. Lord Diplock's view that the statute thereby excluded only remote risks of prejudice to a forthcoming trial reflected the strength of the court's commitment to the right to a fair trial—a commitment embedded in the common law.

None the less, the court held that the publication in *English*, which might have influenced the course of a trial for murder, did not constitute a contempt: section 5 of the Act provides that a publication which forms part of a bona fide discussion of public affairs is not unlawful if the risk of prejudice to legal proceedings is merely incidental to the discussion. Where the section applies it plainly displaces the ordinary balancing process at common law. The court does not, of course, accord the fair trial principle intrinsically less weight—no statute could accomplish such a (remarkable) result: the principle is simply overridden when the conditions of section 5 are satisfied. The court defers to the statutory rule which serves to strengthen press freedom where it applies.[28] But the principle that a defendant charged with murder is entitled to a fair trial remains inviolate. If his trial is prejudiced by the press discussion, he is entitled in justice to an acquittal.

The right of access to the courts for the effective assertion and protection of legal rights is, like the associated right to a fair trial, clearly an important ingredient of the rule of law. Constitutional rights—whatever their juristic basis—are worthless guarantees of freedom unless accompanied by means of judicial enforcement. In *Attorney-General* v. *Times Newspapers*,[29] the House of Lords upheld the award of an injunction restraining the *Sunday Times* from publishing an article about the negligence action concerning the manufacture and marketing of the thalidomide drug, which had caused appalling deformities. Lord Diplock held that such public discussion of the merits of the action would amount to contempt of court as likely to inhibit the litigants' exercise of their 'constitutional right to have their legal rights and obligations ascertained and enforced in courts of law'.[30]

The strength of this constitutional right justifies a strong presumption of parliamentary intent whereby statutory provisions restricting access to the courts are to be narrowly construed: 'It is a principle not by any means to be whittled down that the subject's recourse to Her Majesty's

[28] For discussion of the relation between rules and principles, see Chs. 4 and 5, above. See also *A.-G.* v. *Guardian Newspapers* [1992] 3 All ER 38, 47, where Brooke J. states that the language of the statute is 'slightly different' from the common law, but 'the underlying philosophy is the same'.

[29] [1974] AC 273. [30] Ibid. 310.

courts for the determination of his rights is not to be excluded except by clear words.'[31] There may well be constitutional limits even to the power of 'clear words' to deny the citizen's right to seek justice in the courts. The *Anisminic* case,[32] in which the House of Lords circumvented a statutory ouster clause by bold application of the *ultra vires* doctrine, can reasonably be interpreted as an indication that the sovereignty of Parliament may be subject to limits which secure the fundamental elements of the rule of law.[33]

The principle of preserving access to independent courts of law operated in conjunction with the idea of residual liberty to protect the rights of a convicted prisoner in *Raymond* v. *Honey*.[34] The House of Lords held that a prison governor, who had prevented the forwarding of a prisoner's application to the High Court, was guilty of contempt. Lord Wilberforce invoked the general principle, deriving from the notion of residual liberty, that a convicted prisoner, despite his imprisonment, retained all civil rights which are not taken away expressly or by necessary implication. Accordingly, the governor's power to interfere with the prisoner's application could only be justified by the Prison Rules, made under the authority of the Prison Act 1952; and since the Act provided only for the regulation and management of prisons in general terms, it could not be taken to authorize 'hindrance or interference with so basic a right'[35] as that of unimpeded access to a court. If the Rules purported to allow such interference they were necessarily *ultra vires*.[36]

The enactment of fundamental rights

I have suggested that, suitably interpreted, the common law may be treated as a source of important individual rights, reflecting the moral judgments about basic values which justice seems to support. However, the common law is often considered inferior to bills or charters of rights as a vehicle for protecting fundamental liberties. It is mistakenly thought that *restatement* of individual rights in a constitutional document could transform their strength, when they have to be asserted in opposition to countervailing public interests.[37]

A charter entrenched against ordinary legislative repeal may certainly be a powerful instrument. The modern history of the American

[31] *Pyx Granite Co.* v. *Ministry of Housing and L. Govt.* [1960] AC 260, 286 (Viscount Simonds). [32] [1969] 2 AC 147.

[33] See Ch. 3, above. [34] [1982] 1 All ER 756. [35] Ibid. 760.

[36] Cf. Lord Browne-Wilkinson, 'The Infiltration of a Bill of Rights' [1992] PL 397, esp. 402–3.

[37] For various proposals to enact fundamental rights (generally without entrenchment against repeal) see S. Bailey, D. J. Harris, and B. L. Jones, *Civil Liberties: Cases and Materials*, 3rd edn. (London, 1991), ch. 1; Colin Turpin, *British Government and the Constitution*, 2nd edn. (London, 1990), 121–33.

Supreme Court illustrates the considerable power of a bill of rights which can be applied in the context of judicial review of primary legislation, enabling the courts to strike down statutes thought to encroach unacceptably on constitutional rights. In the absence of entrenchment coupled with the power of judicial review, however, a formal charter could have little impact on our constitutional landscape, as a matter of legal principle.[38] The idea that the weight or force of basic rights might be enhanced by enactment—by their assertion in statutory form—is quite confused, even if it is only intended that the statute would serve as an authoritative source for the interpretation of other statutes and of the common law.[39] The idea that there is some significant *structural* difference between common law rights and those asserted by a bill or charter—sometimes expressed by distinguishing between 'negative' and 'positive' rights—is a confusion which results from the common error of reducing common law freedoms to residual liberty alone.[40]

A charter of rights may be understood either as a set of rules or as a corpus of principle. The first possibility is distinctly unpromising. Attempts to take literally the First Amendment's injunction that 'Congress shall make no law . . . abridging the freedom of speech . . .' have not met with success in the United States. Treated as a rule, the First Amendment makes no allowance for the necessity of limiting freedom in deference to countervailing public interests, even where these are very strong. It also denies the possibility of regulation designed to protect the free speech rights of other speakers.[41]

Nor is it possible to escape the problem by adopting a narrow definition of 'speech'. A rule obtains its object by the binding force of its terms: when those terms apply, the rule must be enforced. But if a broad definition would have unacceptable results—perhaps precluding control even of harmful conduct intended to communicate ideas—too strict a definition of 'speech' would be arbitrary.[42] An unduly narrow

[38] Compare Sir Leslie Scarman, *English Law: The New Dimension*, Hamlyn Lectures, 26th series (London, 1974). Scarman proposed the establishment of a Supreme Court with power to quash legislation as unconstitutional in addition to entrenched provisions: ibid., part 7.

[39] It may, however, be possible to guard against *implied* legislative abrogation of rights by suitable language (although a charter's effectiveness in this respect would inevitably be a question of common law). See works cited at n. 37, above.

[40] Common law rights are 'negative' in the sense that they constitute freedom (within established limits) from state or governmental control. There are no positive rights against the state to ensure that liberties may be more readily exercised. Although positive rights may sometimes be granted by courts on the basis of a written constitution, it is usually the traditional civil liberties, viewed as negative rights against state interference, which are thought to be the principal beneficiaries of a bill of rights.

[41] See Barendt, *Freedom of Speech*, 32.

[42] For the arbitrary nature of the American Supreme Court's attempted distinction between speech and conduct, see Tribe, *American Constitutional Law*, 825–32.

rule—excluding 'obscenity', defamation, invasion of privacy, and other harmful forms of expression—would not respect the underlying theory or theories which justify the rule. The value of freedom of speech demands recognition even in cases where powerful reasons exist for censorship.[43] A rule against interference with speech, subject to exceptions to protect other rights or interests, would give insufficient protection. It would permit the exceptions to override the right to freedom of speech, where they applied, without any scrutiny of the *weights* of the relevant rights or interests in each particular case.

It seems clear that a bill of rights must be understood as a statement of principles, permitting important rights to be *evaluated* in the context of each claim to limit their application. Repudiating the 'absolutist' stance of those attempting a literal interpretation of the First Amendment, the Supreme Court has generally adopted a balancing of interests approach, akin to that required by the European Convention on Human Rights.[44] Application of the famous 'clear and present danger' test is one form of the balancing process.[45] In one sense, Americans are not applying their written constitution at all: they are actually weighing the principle of freedom of speech against other principles.[46]

It is true that the free speech principle has generated a series of judge-made rules, which determine the standard of justification for restrictions on the right according to categories of countervailing interests.[47] But the rules are generated in response to the overriding principle of free speech which the First Amendment asserts; and that principle determines the scope of acknowledged exceptions to the right enshrined.[48] In *Chaplinsky* v. *New Hampshire*,[49] the Court excluded from

[43] Cf. Schauer, *Free Speech*, 89–92.

[44] The approach of the European Court of Human Rights is considered below.

[45] *Schenk* v. *US* 249 US 47, 52 (1919) (Holmes J.); Tribe, *American Constitutional Law*, 841–61; Dworkin, *Taking Rights Seriously*, 27. The 'absolutists' Black and Douglass JJ. expressed their opposition to the 'clear and present danger' test in *Brandenburg* v. *Ohio* 395 US 444 (1969). See also *Cox* v. *Louisiana* 379 US 536, 581 (1965): civil rights demonstration was conduct, outside the protection of the First Amendment (Black J., dissenting).

[46] Cf. M. J. Detmold, *The Unity of Law and Morality* (London, 1984), 224–5.

[47] e.g. *Brandenburg* v. *Ohio* 395 US 444 (1969): a State could proscribe advocacy of the use of force or violation of law only where such advocacy was 'directed to inciting or producing imminent lawless action' and was 'likely to incite or produce such action'. See generally Tribe, *American Constitutional Law*, ch. 12.

[48] Laurence Tribe distinguishes between the Court's approach to direct and indirect restrictions on speech, explaining that case-by-case balancing of interests takes place only in relation to indirect restrictions. But he recognizes that 'similar judgments underlie the categorical definitions' which apply to direct restrictions: 'Any exclusion of a class of activities from first amendment safeguards represents an implicit conclusion that the governmental interests in regulating those activities are such as to justify whatever limitation is thereby placed on the free expression of ideas': *American Constitutional Law*, 792.

[49] 315 US 568, 571–2 (1942).

the ambit of the First Amendment speech which makes no contribution to the exchange of information or ideas, but whose 'very utterance inflicts injury' or 'tends to incite an immediate breach of the peace'. However, in subsequent cases the Court has held the application of the 'fighting words' doctrine to be dependent on the actual context in which provocative language was used. In a decision reminiscent of *Brutus* v. *Cozens*,[50] the Court refused to sustain the defendant's conviction for offensive conduct in wearing a jacket exhibiting the message 'Fuck the Draft'. Not only was there no evidence of any intention to provoke violence, or any likelihood of its occurrence, but there was no insult directed at any particular person.

The decisions of the English and European courts in the thalidomide case well illustrate the distinction between rule and principle in the context of constitutional rights. The House of Lords held it to be a contempt of court to prejudge the questions raised by the pending negligence action against the manufacturers of the drug.[51] The European Court of Human Rights, in *Sunday Times* v. *United Kingdom*,[52] condemned the restraint imposed as an unjustified fetter on the principle of freedom of speech guaranteed by Article 10 of the European Convention. The majority did not think the injunction *necessary* to protect the quality of justice and safeguard the authority of the judiciary—that there was a 'pressing social need' to prevent all media discussion of the strength of the case against the company.

The chief significance of the judgment of the European Court was its repudiation of the notion that one should proceed by rule. It rejected the approach of the House of Lords, which had adopted a general rule against 'prejudgment' in the press of the merits of a case awaiting judicial decision. A number of grounds had been suggested as justification for censorship: under certain conditions publicity might hinder a fair trial of the action, degenerate into trial by newspaper, intimidate other potential litigants, and even undermine respect for the whole legal process. The European Court acknowledged the validity of each of these various grounds—even condemning prejudgment, if unduly partial. It noted that the proposed *Sunday Times* article was couched in moderate terms and did not present merely one side of the evidence, or claim that the litigation could have only one possible result. What the court repudiated was the idea that such grounds could be applied in the form of rules to abridge the principle of free speech. On the facts of the case, it could not reasonably be thought that the drug company would be denied a fair trial, or that the authority of the judiciary would be unduly impaired, if the *Sunday Times* were permitted to comment.[53]

50 [1973] AC 854, considered above.
51 [1974] AC 273. 52 Series A, no. 30 (1979).
53 The court also thought it incumbent on the mass media to impart information and

The European Court's judgment is a neat illustration of the point that the weight of a principle varies according to all the circumstances of the case. In view of the importance attached to the principle of freedom of expression, it had to be given its full weight in determining the legitimacy of the House of Lords' injunction. That determination could not be foreclosed by the adoption in advance, and on the basis of some abstract comparison of conflicting principles, of any rule against prejudging the issues in pending litigation. Indeed, any such rule must inevitably be morally arbitrary, to some degree. A general rule against prejudgment simply prefers the demands of the administration of justice for censorship, and devalues in comparison the principle of freedom of expression. In many cases, inevitably, the balance is likely to lie the other way.

We should, however, be sceptical of the European Court's denial that there was a balancing of principles involved. Seeking to distinguish its analysis from the House of Lords' approach, it was suggested that the court was 'faced not with a choice between two conflicting principles but with a principle of freedom of expression that is subject to a number of exceptions which must be narrowly interpreted'.[54] Exceptions to principles may be either rules or principles, and the exceptions stated in Article 10(2) are plainly principles. Their breadth shows that the article must actually enshrine a general principle—of freedom of speech—which gives way to countervailing public interests, falling within the relevant categories, when these are of sufficient strength. The cogency of an exception, no less than the general principle, will depend on the facts of the case (as the court acknowledges). If the exceptions were treated as rules, applicable largely as a matter of *definition*, they would be likely to devour the principle of freedom of speech.[55]

Perhaps it is thought that freedom of expression must be accorded greater *weight* by virtue of its primary position in the scheme of Article 10. But that is to make the mistake of supposing that weight can be enacted. If weight depends on the facts of each case, as the European Court accepts, it cannot be asserted a priori that any of the principles relevant to Article 10 are necessarily overriding. Freedom of speech has precedence, as at common law, in the sense that any and every encroachment must be *justified*. If we are left in any genuine doubt,

ideas concerning matters before the courts; and members of the public had rights to receive such information: ibid., para. 65.

[54] Ibid.

[55] The European Court emphasized that it was not sufficient that the interference involved belonged to one of the classes of exception specified in Art. 10 (2): the court had 'to be satisfied that the interference was necessary having regard to the facts and circumstances prevailing in the specific case before it' (ibid.).

freedom of speech ought to prevail. But whether or not a contrary principle will indeed justify restraint—perhaps to safeguard the administration of justice—cannot be known in advance of the particular case arising for decision.

It follows that there is no fundamental *structural* difference between the common law protection of basic rights and that provided by the European Convention.[56] The application of general principles requires an assessment of their weight in the circumstances of particular cases; and both common law and Convention should be understood fundamentally as analogous expressions of principle. The House of Lords' prejudgment rule imposed an arbitrary constraint on freedom of expression: if it infringed Article 10, it may also be thought to have given insufficient weight to an important principle of common law.[57]

Lord Fraser was therefore mistaken, in *Attorney-General* v. *BBC*,[58] when he cited the European Court's decision in the thalidomide case to suggest that there was a difference of approach between that court and the House of Lords. He thought it could not be expected that decisions of the two courts would invariably be consistent. However, the discrepancies must reflect a difference in the intrinsic value accorded to freedom of speech: they are not the inevitable product of opposing philosophical methods. The Attorney-General could not succeed in the *BBC* case unless he could convince the court of the need for restraint—that publication should be held to be a contempt. He had to rebut the common law *presumption* of freedom of expression, which is a corollary of the principle of residual liberty. The House of Lords, as we have seen, had to balance the relevant principles, giving freedom of speech its proper weight in the circumstances of the case; and, in the event of doubt, freedom of speech would necessarily prevail.[59] It is the same process as an application of Article 10 would require.

Lord Goff reached similar conclusions in the *Spycatcher* case,[60] where the court had to balance the freedoms of speech and the press against the public interests (in so far as they could be established) in confidentiality and national security:

[56] In practice, of course, the extent to which common law *rules* are applied to restrict individual rights, even in cases where that seems unjustified, must depend on the willingness of the superior courts to modify (or abandon) the rules in response to underlying principle. Cf. *Derbyshire CC* v. *Times Newspapers* [1992] 3 All ER 65; [1993] 1 All ER 1011.

[57] Compare the decision of the Court of Appeal: [1973] 1 All ER 815.

[58] [1980] 3 All ER 161, 176.

[59] The Attorney had to satisfy the court that a rating valuation court should be regarded as an inferior court. Even if that submission had been accepted, he would have been required to show the need for restraint in the circumstances of the case: see Lord Salmon at 168–70, approving the view expressed by Lord Denning in the Court of Appeal: [1979] 3 All ER 45, 50–2, 54–5.

[60] *A.-G.* v. *Guardian (No. 2)* [1988] 3 All ER 545.

The only difference is that, whereas Article 10 of the Convention, in accordance with its avowed purpose, proceeds to state a fundamental right and then to qualify it, we in this country (where everybody is free to do anything, subject only to the provisions of the law) proceed rather upon an assumption of freedom of speech, and turn to our law to discover the established exceptions to it.[61]

The House of Lords refused to grant a final injunction restraining the *Sunday Times*, the *Guardian*, and the *Observer* newspapers from publishing extracts from a book of memoirs by a retired intelligence officer, published abroad in breach of his duty of confidentiality owed to the Crown.[62] Affirming the 'general rule' that 'anyone is entitled to communicate anything he pleases to anyone else, by speech or in writing or in any other way',[63] Lord Keith rejected the Attorney-General's submission that, whenever a Crown servant had made a wrongful disclosure, anyone to whom knowledge of the information came and who was aware of the breach of confidence came under a duty not to communicate it to anyone else. He cited the decision of the High Court of Australia in *Commonwealth of Australia* v. *John Fairfax*,[64] in which Mason J. emphasized the court's duty to determine a government claim to confidentiality in the light of the public interest in open discussion of public affairs. Confidentiality would be upheld only where disclosure would be inimical to the public interest because national security, relations with foreign countries, or the ordinary business of government would be prejudiced.

Although Lord Keith chose to ground his decision on the view that all possible damage to the interest of the Crown had already been done by publication of the book abroad—it was unnecessary to engage in a balancing of public interests—it is clear that the common law acknowledges a basic commitment to freedom of political speech (concerning matters of government and public affairs), which constitutes an important constraint on the scope of the principle protecting confidentiality. Lord Goff envisaged a balancing operation, in which the court would weigh the public interest in maintaining the confidence against a countervailing public interest favouring disclosure. It was established in the jurisprudence of the European Court that there must be a pressing social need for restrictions to be imposed on freedom of speech, and that the restrictions should be no more than is proportionate to the need. Lord Goff denied that English law led to any different conclusion.[65]

It is true that at the interlocutory stage,[66] the House of Lords majority

[61] Ibid. 660.

[62] The court held that members and former members of the security and intelligence services owed a lifelong duty of confidentiality.

[63] [1988] 3 All ER 640.

[64] [1980] 32 ALR 485, 492–3.

[65] [1988] 3 All ER 660.

[66] [1987] 3 All ER 316.

decided to sustain the injunctions restraining the newspapers from publishing material derived from the book: they held that the government would otherwise be deprived of a fair hearing in support of permanent injunctions, notwithstanding publication of the book's allegations abroad. In his forthright condemnation of the decision, Lord Bridge declared in dissent that it undermined his confidence in the capacity of the common law to safeguard the fundamental freedoms essential to a free society. The contents of *Spycatcher* had already become a matter of public knowledge.[67]

The minority view of Lords Bridge and Oliver certainly found favour with the European Court of Human Rights, as Lord Bridge had predicted. The majority judgment of the European Court accepted that since the interlocutory injunctions were designed to safeguard the Attorney-General's rights until the trial, as well as to protect national security, their purposes were legitimate under Article 10(2) of the Convention.[68] It was also accepted that until the interlocutory proceedings reached the House of Lords, the interference with freedom of expression could be regarded as 'necessary in a democratic society'. The Convention did not prohibit the imposition of prior restraints on publication; and the reasons for granting the injunctions were both 'relevant' and 'sufficient'. Once *Spycatcher* had been published abroad, however, the confidentiality of its contents was destroyed. In those circumstances, the Attorney's reasons for seeking continued restraints were insufficient.

The decision hardly demonstrates an incompatibility between the Convention and the common law, however. Lord Bridge had himself presumably been applying the common law, as he understood it. Moreover, Lord Templeman applied the principle of freedom of speech enshrined in Article 10, proceeding as if for all practical purposes it stated the applicable law. He was satisfied that restraint was justified by several of the specified exceptions to the right to freedom of expression. It was necessary in a democratic society in the interests of national security, for protecting the reputation or rights of others, for preventing the disclosure of information received in confidence, and for maintaining the authority and impartiality of the judiciary. In his view, a democracy was 'entitled to take the view that a public servant who is employed in the security service must be restrained from making any disclosures concerning the security service and that similar restraints must be imposed on anybody who receives those disclosures knowing that they are confidential'.[69]

The point is that the Convention could not determine the judges'

[67] Ibid. 346.
[68] *The Observer & The Guardian* v. *UK* (1991) 14 EHRR 153.
[69] [1987] 3 All ER 356.

perceptions of the weights of conflicting public interests. The appropriate weight of principles is something learned by experience: it cannot be decreed in the manner of enacting a rule, but must be correctly understood. It is the nature of principles to resist enactment—their force varies with the concrete facts of particular instances—and a bill of rights can only reassert established (comprehended) principles. If it were Lord Bridge's view that incorporation of the Convention into domestic law might change the courts' assessments of the weight of individual rights, it would seem to make little sense. It overlooks the point that basic rights have the value that they are *accorded* in particular cases: their value cannot be determined in advance by adopting a bill or charter. An asserted right which had no weight in particular cases would have no real existence; and weight is always a product of judgment and degree. Matters of judgment and degree elude a bill of rights as they elude a statute: the application of principles must be responsive to the myriad circumstances of political life.

Judge Martens's dissenting opinion in the European Court seems flawed on these grounds. He objected that, in deciding whether or not to grant the injunctions, Millett J. (at first instance) had approached the matter as a conflict between two legitimate public interests of equal weight. By contrast, under Article 10, the interest in freely receiving information 'clearly in principle' outweighed the protection of confidentiality. But matters of weight cannot be determined 'in principle', but only in relation to particular facts. Judge Martens also objected that application of the *American Cyanamid* principles, governing the issue of interlocutory injunctions,[70] was incompatible with Article 10. Millett J. had failed to consider whether the Attorney-General's claim for a permanent injunction would be likely to succeed, resting content with the newpapers' failure to show that he had no real prospect of success. The majority, however, wisely declined to review the *American Cyanamid* principles '*in abstracto*': it was the Court's function only to 'determine whether the interference resulting from their application was necessary having regard to the facts and circumstances prevailing in the specific case before it'.[71] In their view, the English courts had not applied those principles 'inflexibly or automatically', without a careful weighing of the relevant considerations.

It should also be stressed that the *range* or *scope* of a principle cannot be dictated in advance of particular cases, any more than its weight.[72] Range is equally a product of education and understanding, rather

[70] *American Cyanamid Co.* v. *Ethicon* [1975] AC 396.
[71] 14 EHRR 153, 193, para 63.
[72] Cf. Schauer, *Free Speech*, 82–92. Schauer distinguishes between 'coverage' and 'protection': a right 'covers' certain conduct by requiring greater persuasive force (weight) in order to restrict it than if the right did not exist.

than a matter of enactment. In *Home Office* v. *Harman*,[73] the House of Lords held that it was a contempt for a solicitor to show a journalist documents obtained on discovery in the course of civil litigation, even though they had already been read out in open court. Lord Scarman and Lord Simon acknowledged the implications of the question for freedom of expression:

> A balance has to be struck between two interests of the law, on the one hand the protection of a litigant's private right to keep his documents to himself notwithstanding his duty to disclose them to the other side in the litigation and on the other the protection of the right, which the law recognises, subject to certain exceptions, as the right of every one, to speak freely, and to impart information and ideas, on matters of public knowledge.[74]

The majority, however, circumvented the problem by treating the case as limited to an aspect of the law of discovery of documents, thereby evading the minority's challenge on basic principles. Lord Diplock framed the issue narrowly: 'It is *not* about freedom of speech, freedom of the press, openness of justice or documents coming into "the public domain".'[75]

There were signs of a similar approach in *British Steel* v. *Granada Television*,[76] where the plaintiffs sought disclosure of the identity of the defendants' informant, who had supplied copies of secret and confidential documents. The documents had been used by Granada in a television programme, broadcast during a national steel strike. Granada conceded that it had no right to publish the confidential documents in its possession, which had been wrongfully taken from British Steel, and some of the judges were therefore tempted to deny even marginal or peripheral connection with freedom of the press.[77]

Now, such evasions can sometimes be forestalled by positive enactment. There may be a rule whose application to particular cases necessarily invokes a principle. Section 10 of the Contempt of Court Act 1981 now applies the principle of press freedom to the matter of the confidentiality of journalists' sources. However, a rule is enacted and not the principle. The section prohibits the making of an order requiring disclosure of the source of a publication, except where the court is satisfied that such disclosure is necessary in the interests of justice or national security or for the prevention of disorder or crime. Freedom of speech or the press is not expressly asserted by section 10, though it must be invoked to make sense of the rule: the object is clearly to protect the anonymity of informants to ensure that they will remain willing to supply information to the press.[78]

[73] [1982] 1 All ER 532. [74] Ibid. 544. [75] Ibid. 534. [76] [1981] AC 1096.

[77] Lords Wilberforce, Dilhorne, and Russell. Lord Salmon dissented, emphasizing freedom of the press.

[78] See Ch. 4, above.

By contrast, an assertion of principle, in the manner of Article 10 of the European Convention, leaves the scope of its application entirely at large. Significantly, in *Home Office* v. *Harman*, Lord Diplock also denied the relevance of the European Convention.[79] Herein lies the paradox of the enactment of rights: the greater their force, and the broader their scope, the less they can be accorded positive definition. Their importance must be *acknowledged*: it cannot be decreed. Nor can their appropriate compass or scope be exhaustively defined. This is simply to say that a principle, which enshrines a fundamental right, cannot be reduced to a rule.

It is also the case that journalists' sources of information enjoy no special protection by virtue of the First Amendment. In *Branzburg* v. *Hayes*,[80] White J., speaking for the Supreme Court majority, adopted a perspective similar to that of the majority in *Granada*. In denying that journalists could claim any constitutional privilege against grand jury subpoenas requiring disclosure of sources, he acknowledged the importance of freedom of speech and the press: 'But these cases involve no intrusions upon speech or assembly, no prior restraint or restriction on what the press may publish, and no express or implied command that the press publish what it prefers to withhold . . . The use of confidential sources by the press is not forbidden or restricted; reporters remain free to seek news from any source by means within the law.'[81]

It is true that the Court in *Branzburg* was more willing to acknowledge the implications of the case for freedom of the press than were the House of Lords majority in *Granada*. None the less, the House accepted that the relation between journalist and source was one to be respected: there was a public interest in the free flow of information, whose strength would vary from case to case. In substance, then, the two courts reached similar conclusions by analogous reasoning. The Supreme Court majority rejected the minority's view that the First Amendment provided a special immunity, much as the House of Lords majority rejected Lord Salmon's plea, in dissent, for an immunity in English law—an immunity he considered to be the 'very basis of the freedom of the press and accordingly a bastion of the freedom of man'.[82]

It is in both countries a matter of balance and emphasis in particular cases, as Powell J.'s short judgment, concurring with the Supreme Court majority, clearly affirms: 'The asserted claim to privilege should be judged on its facts by the striking of a proper balance between freedom of the press and the obligation of all citizens to give relevant

[79] [1982] 1 All ER 532, 534. [80] 408 US 665 (1972).
[81] Ibid. 681. [82] [1981] AC 1096, 1193.

testimony with respect to criminal conduct . . . The balance of these vital constitutional and societal interests on a case-by-case basis accords with the tried and traditional way of adjudicating such questions.'[83]

I should summarize the argument. Constitutional rights, whose recognition stems from widely acknowledged judgments of value, can adequately be expressed only in terms of principle. Their force and scope cannot be captured by rule. A rule obtains its 'positive' force at the price of concrete definition; and attempts to define the ambit of a constitutional right will inevitably produce arbitrary results at the perimeter. It is the essence of fundamental rights that they have weight, and should be respected, in a wide variety of circumstances, but without necessarily prevailing against other interests in any particular case. The First Amendment can be read as a rule only at the cost of a narrow and arbitrary *definition* of 'speech'. Instead of a contradiction between constitutional rights and common law, as is sometimes suggested, there exists a different paradox—a paradox which afflicts the notion of posited (enacted) rights to fundamental freedoms. A bill of rights may, of course, have symbolic or inspirational power; but it can only affirm the value of previously accepted principles, whose weight must be adjudged—as the common law adjudges it—on the facts of the particular case. Dicey's account of the rule of law, which emphasized the dependence of constitutional principles on judicial decisions in particular cases, expressed a truth whose importance has often been overlooked.[84]

Entrenched rights and traditional values

Although a charter of rights cannot, by enactment, enhance the value of fundamental rights, or alter the intrinsic weight of principles, it may serve to frustrate rules which would otherwise restrict their application in particular cases. Where a bill of rights is accorded a 'higher' constitutional status, permitting the courts to repudiate legislation passed in violation of the rights declared, ordinary legal and moral reasoning from general principle has free rein. Constitutional rights at common law can triumph over statutory incursions on general principles, made on the grounds of other public interests. In Canada, within the spheres of the rights to life, liberty, and security of the person, no statutory rule may impose restraint 'except in accordance with the principles of fundamental justice',[85] which in turn 'are to be found in the basic tenets' of the Canadian legal system[86]—within, that is, the fundamental precepts of common law constitutionalism.

[83] 408 US 665, 710. [84] *Law of the Constitution*, 195–6.
[85] Canadian Charter of Rights and Freedoms, s. 7.
[86] *Re BC Motor Vehicle Act* [1985] 2 SCR 486.

It is the unimpeded development of common law reasoning, exploring the 'natural' compass of its basic principles and unconstrained by statutory limitation, which explains the impact of the Canadian Charter. It has been held, for example, that an Act prohibiting the transaction of business on Sunday violated the freedom of conscience and religion guaranteed by section 2(a) of the Charter.[87] The Canadian Supreme Court declined to follow an earlier decision,[88] which had taken a more restricted view of the scope of freedom of religion under the Bill of Rights, which had only 'recognised and declared' existing freedoms as they were enjoyed at the time of the Bill's enactment. The Charter permitted the court to condemn the statute in defence of a conception of the freedom based on the 'centrality of individual conscience' and the 'inappropriateness of governmental intervention to compel or to constrain its manifestation'.[89] The inherent logic of the common law supplied the natural meaning of the principle the Charter affirms: 'With the entrenchment of the Charter the definition of freedom of conscience and religion is no longer vulnerable to legislative incursion.'[90]

The principle of equality has also been strengthened against legislative incursion by the Charter's affirmation that everyone 'is equal before and under the law and has the right to the equal protection and equal benefit of the law without discrimination'.[91] Although equality rights are not infringed by every legislative distinction or differentiation—legislative rules inevitably depend on classifications—the Charter enables the courts to protect vulnerable groups and minorities from unfair discrimination at the hands of the state. Formal equality before the law must be supplemented by a wider substantive conception: 'The promotion of equality entails the promotion of a society in which all are secure in the knowledge that they are recognised at law as human beings equally deserving of concern, respect and consideration.'[92]

It is important, however, to recall the conflict between justice and fairness: the claims of democracy must be set against those of constitutional rights.[93] A charter entrenched against ordinary legislative repeal heightens the tension between Parliament's authority over classes of cases, and judicial authority in respect of particular cases.[94] The dichotomy between the general interest and individual right, which transcends distinctions between 'written' and 'unwritten' constitutions, remains to be resolved. At some point, principle must give way to rule—common law reasoning, sensitive to single cases, give way to

[87] *R.* v. *Big M Drug Mart* (1985) 18 DLR (4th) 321.
[88] *Robertson and Rosetanni* v. *R.* [1963] SCR 651.
[89] 18 DLR (4th) 361. [90] Ibid. 363. [91] S. 15.
[92] *Andrews* v. *Law Society of British Columbia* (1989) 56 DLR (4th) 1, 15 (McIntyre J.).
[93] Ch. 4, above. [94] Ch. 3, above.

statutory enactment. A charter of rights may strengthen the judicial arm of the state at the expense of the legislature and executive; but some judicial deference to the other organs of state then seems a necessary concomitant of constitutional balance. A guarantee of equality, in particular, cannot be applied to substitute judicial for parliamentary opinions about precisely how to make the 'innumerable legislative distinctions and categorizations' involved in governing the community by process of law.[95]

Whatever respect the judges accord the legislators' opinions about the content of constitutional rights, their own interpretation must clearly derive its legitimacy from its connections with pre-existing common law. The rights enacted may be developed in response to fresh perceptions of their meaning or importance, but the underlying moral values will be those embedded in previous tradition. McIntyre J. expressed this point forcefully in the Canadian Supreme Court. The Charter could not be regarded as 'an empty vessel' which simply awaited judicial discretion: its interpretation was 'constrained by the language, structure and history of the constitutional text, by constitutional tradition, and by the history, traditions, and underlying philosophies' of Canadian society.[96]

No doubt these conclusions reflect the familiar truth that constitutional adjudication may have little in common with the ordinary process of statutory interpretation. A charter of rights needs a liberal and purposive construction if it is truly to safeguard basic liberties. Constitutional adjudication under a charter of rights is inevitably closer to common law reasoning, where the common law is developed as a vehicle for protecting rights, than to the narrower, more formal process of statutory interpretation. A charter, that is to say, must be a statement of principles, inviting a balancing of conflicting interests, much as the common law is truly understood as a body of principles, awaiting refinement and development in particular cases. A statute, by contrast, applies only a body of rules.[97]

In *Hunter* v. *Southam*,[98] the Canadian Supreme Court rightly stressed that the task of expounding a constitution was 'crucially different' from that of construing a statute. Its function was to 'provide a continuing framework for the legitimate exercise of governmental power and, when joined by a bill or charter of rights, for the unremitting protection of individual rights and liberties'. But ordinary common law adjudication must fulfil a similar function, subject—to some degree—to

[95] *Andrews* 56 DLR (4th) 26 (McIntyre J.). See also *Ref. Re Public Service Employee Relations Act* [1987] 1 SCR 313 (where McIntyre J. interpreted freedom of association under the Charter in accordance with previous Canadian traditions and philosophy).

[96] *Ref. Re Public Service* [1987] 1 SCR 313, 394.

[97] Ch. 4, above.

[98] (1984) 11 DLR (4th) 641, 649 (Dickson J.).

express legislative incursion into basic rights and liberties.[99] In the absence of a written constitution, the common law must provide a continuing framework for the legitimate exercise of governmental power. The Canadian Charter of Rights and Freedoms has been called a purposive document: 'Its purpose is to guarantee and to protect, within the limits of reason, the enjoyment of the rights and freedoms it enshrines.'[100] The chief purpose of the common law must surely be to offer similar protection to those same rights and freedoms, which constitute its underlying substance.

Residual liberty and the power of the state

It is apparent that the right to equal respect and concern is a right against the state. The principle against unjust or hostile discrimination applies to the actions of government and public authorities. We do not believe that the same freedom to act upon arbitrary preferences which, in many but not all contexts, we permit the private individual should extend to government. If government could discriminate at will between persons, the rule of law would be wholly undermined: we insist on government constrained by general rules with the object of preventing arbitrary treatment at the hands of the state.

Unfortunately, Dicey's emphasis on legal equality between official and ordinary citizen has been misunderstood as proposing a fundamental equality between citizen and state.[101] His account of constitutional law as proceeding from the decisions of the courts in ordinary civil and criminal cases, involving public officials, has led many to suppose that the state has no special existence in legal doctrine—with the result that public authorities enjoy the same residual freedom of action as private individuals, subject only to explicit legal restraint.[102] However, the state is acknowledged by the common law in the form of the Crown, to which special rules apply. Those rules provide for the well-known privileges and immunities which form part of the royal prerogative; but such rules do not exhaust the Crown's recognition as a unique constitutional entity.

Dicey's emphasis on the courts' protection of private law rights was not misplaced. Such rights do constitute the foundation of liberty and security; and their infringement by public authority demands adequate legal justification. But the whole point of the rule of law would be lost if the government were treated in all respects like an ordinary citizen,

[99] The extent of permissible encroachment on basic rights and liberties is controversial: Ch. 3, above.

[100] *Hunter* v. *Southam* (1984) 11 DLR (4th) 641, 650.

[101] *Law of the Constitution*, 193–5; 202–3.

[102] See e.g. Eric Barendt, 'Dicey and Civil Liberties' [1985] PL 596 at 606.

even in private law. Dicey's object was to deny officials special exemption from the ordinary law: that was the ground of his antipathy to *droit administratif*.[103] His work should not have been treated as supporting the notion that government may sometimes act without explicit legal authority for encroachments on the citizen's liberty.

The idea that whatever is lawful for the private individual is also lawful for government underlay the court's decision in *Malone* v. *Metropolitan Police Commissioner*.[104] The plaintiff challenged the legality of the tapping of his telephone by the Post Office under the warrant of the Home Secretary and on behalf of the police, who had suspected the plaintiff of handling stolen property. Such warrants were issued as a matter of administrative practice, and statutory recognition of the practice was at best indirect and implicit. It was held that, in the absence of trespass or any cause of action for invasion of privacy or confidentiality, the plaintiff had no ground of complaint. Since tapping entailed no breach of the ordinary law, no authorization by statute or common law was needed: 'If the tapping of telephones by the Post Office at the request of the police can be carried out without any breach of the law, it does not require any statutory or common law power to justify it.'[105] It could lawfully be done because there was nothing to make it unlawful.

That conclusion, however, substitutes a formal, literalist conception of the rule of law for the deeper theory which constitutes its point. The practice of issuing a warrant acknowledged the need for proper authorization; and the absence of any lawful basis for such a practice demonstrated the illegality of tapping.[106] Although the judge thought that the common law was perhaps 'sufficiently fertile' to prohibit all telephone tapping save in suitably limited classes of case, he considered that only the legislature could prescribe detailed restrictions on the exercise of the power in those limited cases. But then the plaintiff should have succeeded on the current state of the law. In *Entick* v. *Carrington*, Lord Camden took the absence of proper safeguards, in the case of the issue of general warrants of search and seizure, as proof of their illegality: 'the want of them is an undeniable argument against the legality of the thing'.[107]

The Interception of Communications Act 1985 was subsequently enacted in response to a ruling of the European Court of Human Rights that existing practice contravened Article 8 of the European Convention: 'the minimum degree of legal protection to which citizens are entitled

[103] *Law of the Constitution*, ch. 12.
[104] [1979] 2 All ER 620.
[105] Ibid. 638 (Sir Robert Megarry V.-C.).
[106] Cf. Vaughan Bevan, 'Is Anybody There?' [1980] PL 431.
[107] (1765) 19 St. Tr. 1030, 1067.

under the rule of law in a democratic society' was lacking.[108] The judge had frankly acknowledged that 'in any civilised system of law the claims of liberty and justice would require that telephone users should have effective and independent safeguards against possible abuses';[109] but it is hard to believe that the common law was truly helpless.

The *Malone* case is weak authority for treating the state, or the Crown, as if it were a private individual. Regarded simply as an action between private litigants, there were undoubtedly some difficulties in the way of granting a remedy. But if the case is viewed, in substance, as a test of the limits of public power, it takes on a different aspect. A division between public power and private right is an integral part of the common law: the whole law of judicial review is founded on the distinction. A public official who contravenes the ordinary law, without special authority, is accountable as if he were a private citizen. It does not follow, however, that, acting as a public official, he enjoys the same rights and liberties as a private individual, without suitable qualification. No simple analogy is available between private and governmental action because the latter is inherently different from the former: it asserts the authority of the state.[110]

Dicey acknowledged as much, it may be suggested, by treating the royal prerogative as including all the non-statutory powers of the Crown: 'Every act which the executive government can lawfully do without the authority of an Act of Parliament is done in virtue of this prerogative.'[111] He has been accused of failing to distinguish here between the Crown's natural and regal capacities, in contrast to Blackstone's insistence on the 'singular and eccentrical' nature of the prerogative.[112] However, it seems quite unrealistic to compare the exercise of the 'ordinary' powers of government with those of private individuals.

In treating such matters as awards of the Criminal Injuries Compensation Board,[113] and the employment of civil servants,[114] as manifestations of the prerogative, notwithstanding their obvious counterparts in the ordinary civil law, the courts have surely acknowledged political reality. Dicey's loose definition of the prerogative, if analytically

108 *Malone* case (1984) Eur. Ct. HR, Series A, Vol. 82, para. 79.

109 [1979] 2 All ER 649.

110 Cf. George Winterton, 'The Prerogative in Novel Situations' (1983) 99 LQR 407. Winterton observes, in respect of *Malone*, that 'government surveillance is hardly the same as private eavesdropping'.

111 *Law of the Constitution*, 452.

112 Sir William Wade, *Constitutional Fundamentals*, Hamlyn Lectures, 32nd series, revised edn. (London, 1989), 58–62; 'Procedure and Prerogative in Public Law' (1985) 101 LQR 180 at 190–8.

113 *R.* v. *Criminal Injuries Compens. Bd., ex p. Lain* [1967] 2 QB 864.

114 *GCHQ* case [1984] 3 All ER 935.

imprecise, has at least the merit of recognizing that even 'ordinary' rights, when invoked in aid of the Crown, inevitably become extraordinary. In *Victoria* v. *Australian Building Construction Employees' and Builders' Labourers Federation*,[115] Brennan J. questioned the proposed analogy between a Royal Commission and a private enquiry. He rejected the view, which had previously found favour with the High Court of Australia,[116] that the Crown could necessarily make enquiry about any matter which was open to enquiry by the individual: 'what distinguishes a prerogative commission from an inquiry which any person is at liberty to make is that it is an inquiry on behalf of the Executive Government for a purpose of government'.[117]

The point is underlined by the incongruity of the *Malone* decision with a subsequent ruling, that the minister's decision to issue a warrant for tapping was subject to judicial review.[118] It was settled that where interception by the Security Service was concerned, a warrant should issue only where there was reasonable cause to believe that major subversive activity was being conducted, which was likely to injure the national interest. The relevant criteria had been repeated and accepted as binding by successive Home Secretaries; and a duty to act fairly applied, requiring the minister to issue warrants only in accordance with these criteria. It would be a strange result if the minister's decision could be impugned on the grounds of fairness, as an illegitimate exercise of public power, but the right to intercept must itself be accepted in the absence of specific authorization.

The special position of the Crown, when it seeks to rely on rights analogous to the private law rights of individuals, has been clearly acknowledged in decisions relating to breach of confidence. Private rights of confidentiality in respect of trade secrets, commercial information, or even domestic confidences are readily protected, subject only to an exception for the revelation of 'iniquity'. However, in *Attorney-General* v. *Jonathan Cape*,[119] Lord Widgery CJ refused to grant an injunction restraining publication of confidential discussions in Cabinet on the ground that no harm would be done in the circumstances by the disclosure. Although he agreed that the court could in principle restrain the publication of governmental secrets, the Attorney-General had first to satisfy the court that restraint was in the public interest: nor would the court impose restrictions 'beyond the strict requirement of public need'.[120] The correctness of Lord Widgery's approach was accepted by

[115] (1982) 41 ALR 71, 167; see also Mason J. at 114.
[116] *Clough* v. *Leahy* (1904) 2 CLR 139, 157 (Griffith CJ).
[117] 41 ALR 168.
[118] *R.* v. *Home Secretary, ex p. Ruddock* [1987] 2 All ER 518, considered further in Ch. 8, below.
[119] [1976] QB 752 (see further Ch. 10 below).
[120] Ibid. 771.

the House of Lords in the *Spycatcher* case, where Lord Keith endorsed the observations of the Australian High Court:

> The equitable principle has been fashioned to protect the personal, private and proprietary interests of the citizen, not to protect the very different interests of the executive government . . . This is not to say that Equity will not protect information in the hands of the government, but . . . when Equity protects government information it will look at the matter through different spectacles. It may be a sufficient detriment to the citizen that disclosure of information relating to his affairs will expose his actions to public discussion and criticism. But it can scarcely be a relevant detriment to the government that publication of material concerning its actions will merely expose it to public discussion and criticism.[121]

These decisions show that the government cannot take advantage of private law rights as if it were merely a private litigant. The nature of government under the rule of law necessitates a modification of the ordinary rules of private law. Government secrets will not receive automatic protection in an action for breach of confidence because there are constitutional considerations which apply: 'in a free society there is a continuing public interest that the workings of government should be open to scrutiny and criticism'.[122] In the same way, it does not follow from the freedom of the individual to act except where expressly restrained, that the government enjoys a similar freedom. The conception of government under the rule of law surely entails the opposite conclusion.

There is nothing in *Entick* v. *Carrington* which prevents recognition of the unique power of the state, or the further development of common law principles necessary to tame it. *Entick's* literal application in *Malone* to deny a remedy for unauthorized telephone tapping makes an ironic contrast with its invocation, in the United States, in support of a broad, purposive interpretation of the Fourth and Fifth Amendments. Brandeis J. observed that 'as a means of espionage, writs of assistance and general warrants are but puny instruments of tyranny and oppression when compared with wire-tapping'.[123] Every unjustifiable intrusion by government on the privacy of the individual violated 'the right to be let alone—the most comprehensive of rights and the right most valued by civilized men'. He cited *Boyd* v. *United States*,[124] where the Supreme

[121] *Commonwealth of Australia* v. *John Fairfax* (1980) 32 ALR 485, 492–3 (cited at [1988] 3 All ER 641–2).

[122] [1988] 3 All ER 660 (Lord Goff). See also *Derbyshire CC* v. *Times Newspapers* [1992] 3 All ER 65; [1993] 1 All ER 1011 (citing *New York Times* v. *Sullivan* 376 US 254 (1964)): local authority unable to sue for libel in respect of its governing or administrative reputation in view of the importance of freedom of political speech. Cf. J. A. Weir, 'Local Authority v. Critical Ratepayer—A Suit in Defamation' [1972A] CLJ 239 at 241.

[123] *Olmstead* v. *US* 277 US 438, 476 (1927).

[124] 116 US 616, 627–30 (1886).

Court denied that the principles of *Entick* v. *Carrington* were confined by 'the concrete form of the case . . . with its adventitious circumstances'; they applied to all government invasions of 'the sanctity of a man's home and the privacies of life'. It is the same principle, whether or not enshrined in formal enactment: it is simply a question of imaginative and courageous interpretation:

It is not the breaking of his doors, and the rummaging of his drawers, that constitutes the essence of the offence; but it is the invasion of his indefeasible right of personal security, personal liberty, and private property, where that right has never been forfeited by his conviction of some public offence—it is the invasion of this sacred right which underlies and constitutes the essence of Lord Camden's judgment.[125]

[125] Ibid. See generally Graham Zellick, 'Government Beyond Law' [1985] PL 283, esp. 294–8; B. V. Harris, 'The "Third Source" of Authority for Government Action' (1992) 109 LQR 626, esp. 630–7.

7
Equality

> ... I do not mean to say that there may not be cases in which it would be the duty of the court to condemn by-laws ... as invalid and unreasonable. But unreasonable in what sense? If, for instance, they were found to be partial and unequal in their operation as between different classes; if they were manifestly unjust; if they disclosed bad faith; if they involved such oppressive or gratuitous interference with the rights of those subject to them as could find no justification in the minds of reasonable men, the court might well say, 'Parliament never intended to give authority to make such rules; they are unreasonable and *ultra vires*'.
>
> *Kruse* v. *Johnson* [1898] 2 QB 91, 99 (Lord Russell of Killowen CJ).

Ronald Dworkin's defence of 'formal equality' or 'equality before the law' reveals the power of Dicey's doctrine of the rule of law, when our conception of law is expanded beyond discrete legal rules to encompass underlying commitments of political principle.[1] His notion of 'integrity' explains the importance of equality as a general constitutional requirement. The common law doctrine of precedent is itself grounded on the idea that those similarly situated should be treated alike: previous decisions must be distinguished, if at all, on grounds of principle, which *justify* the different treatment of succeeding cases. The rule of law is not limited to an abstract commitment to legislation in the form of general rules. Adjudication at common law consists in the application of a body of substantive legal principle which assumes, as a fundamental axiom, that all are to be equally treated, subject only to relevant differences of situation and circumstance.[2]

The Equal Protection Clause of the Fourteenth Amendment to the United States Constitution has been understood to guarantee the protection of *equal laws*, not merely the equal application of the laws. It has been interpreted as giving 'the same protection to all for the preservation of life, liberty and property, and the pursuit of happiness'.[3] Since laws necessarily differentiate between persons for legitimate purposes, in practice the Clause requires differences of treatment to be justified. Legislative classifications are reasonable and permissible, rather than arbitrary and unconstitutional, where they relate to a legitimate

[1] See Ch. 2, above.
[2] Cf. Ronald Dworkin, *Taking Rights Seriously* (London, 1977), 112–13.
[3] *Slaughter House Cases* 16 Wall. (83 US) 36, 127 (1873) (Swayne J.).

statutory objective. Executive and administrative acts are also subject to the Clause. Even though a statute satisfies the principle of equal protection on its face, 'unjust and illegal discriminations between persons' in its application are forbidden: it is unconstitutional 'if it is applied and administered by public authority with an evil eye and an unequal hand'.[4]

If a purely formal conception of equality before the law seems unacceptably narrow, the pursuit of substantive equality may easily endanger other values, especially those of liberty and justice. It is certainly the case that all should be subject to the law, impartially applied and administered. But it is neither realistic nor even desirable that all should be subject to equal burdens or enjoy identical benefits. The content of the law must obviously reflect the varying circumstances of different groups of people. However, the same underlying values which explain our adherence to formal equality will suggest the outlines of a wider conception. Formal equality reflects the principle that everyone should be accorded proper respect as a person of moral independence, who may not be treated less favourably by the state on account of his character or convictions or aspirations. He is not obliged to share the ideals or purposes of his government, and so may not be penalized for repudiating them. He may not be made to suffer because he is thought less worthy than others—for whatever reason, subject only to breaches of the law (which must itself satisfy the requirement of equal respect). Those ideas of moral independence and responsibility which underlie the principal civil liberties, and inform the concept of the rule of law, assist in understanding the important idea of equality.[5]

In *R.* v. *Drybones*,[6] the Canadian Supreme Court struck down a law which made it an offence for an Indian to be intoxicated when off a reserve. The guarantee of equality before the law, contained in the Bill of Rights 1960,[7] was violated by a law which created an offence applying only to members of a certain race. Ritchie J. rejected an interpretation of equality which required only that all those to whom a particular law applied should stand on an equal footing—an interpretation which would permit the 'most glaring' discriminatory legislation against a racial group provided that discrimination was uniformly applied to all members of the group.[8] An individual was denied equality before the

[4] *Yick Wo* v. *Hopkins* 118 US 356 (1886). See generally Polyvios G. Polyviou, *The Equal Protection of the Laws* (London, 1980), ch. 2.

[5] See Chs. 2–6, above.

[6] (1969) 9 DLR (3d) 473.

[7] S. 1 'recognised and declared that in Canada there have existed and shall continue to exist without discrimination by reason of race, national origin, colour, religion or sex, the following human rights and fundamental freedoms, namely, (b) the right of the individual to equality before the law and the protection of the law'.

[8] The court thereby rejected the approach in *Gonzales* (1962) 32 DLR (2d) 290, 296

law if it were made an offence punishable at law, on account of his race, for him to do something which other Canadians were at liberty to do.

Once it is accepted, however, that the Diceyan principle of equality cannot be confined to purely *formal* equality, it inevitably proves hard to resist a thoroughgoing review of the supposed justifications of a provision. The point becomes apparent from reflection on *Attorney-General of Canada* v. *Lavelle*,[9] where the Supreme Court denied that the Indian Act conflicted with the Bill of Rights by discriminating unfairly between Indian men and women, as regards loss of rights on marriage to non-Indians. Invoking Dicey's account of equality, as a feature of the rule of law, Ritchie J. attempted to confine the scope of the Bill of Rights to 'equality in the administration or application of the law by the law enforcement authorities and the ordinary courts of the land'.[10] It is not easy, however, to bring *Drybones* within quite such a narrow definition; and the court's attempt to distinguish that case in *Lavelle* is hardly successful.[11] The former decision cannot be adequately explained without attention to the nature and *grounds* of the discrimination imposed; and *Lavelle* can best be justified, if at all, on the basis that the discrimination was not wholly irrational when considered in the light of the necessity to define Indian status and the traditional role and responsibilities of the husband and father.[12]

In applying section 15 of the Charter of Rights and Freedoms, which guarantees the 'equal protection and equal benefit of the law without discrimination', the Supreme Court has now adopted a purposive approach, requiring consideration of the content, objectives, and application of a law in the context of the general principle of equality. The express prohibition against discrimination is clearly apt to challenge distinctions based solely on an individual's association with a particular group;[13] and the court has asserted the power to review the place of the group 'in the social, political and legal fabric' of Canadian society.[14]

Although there is no general power of review of legislation in Britain,

(Tysoe J.), which Hall J. compared with *Plessy* v. *Ferguson* (1896) 153 US 537, overturned by the US Supreme Court in *Brown* v. *Board of Education of Topeka* (1953) 347 US 483.

[9] (1973) 38 DLR (3d) 481.

[10] Ibid. 495.

[11] Laskin J., dissenting, held that *Drybones* could not be distinguished on the ground that the challenged provision had created a punishable offence: 'the gist of the judgment lay in the legal disability imposed upon a person by reason of his race when other persons were under no similar restraint' (ibid. 507).

[12] Laskin J. expressly declined to apply a test of reasonable classification, as applied by the US Supreme Court. But see W. S. Tarnopolsky, 'The Canadian Bill of Rights and the Supreme Court Decisions in *Lavell* and *Burnshine*: A Retreat from *Drybones* to Dicey?' 7 Ottawa LR 1, at 22–3. See generally Polyviou, *Equal Protection*, 153–60.

[13] *Andrews* v. *Law Society of British Columbia* (1989) 56 DLR (4th) 1, 18 (McIntyre J.).

[14] Ibid. 32 (Wilson J.); see also *Turpin* [1898] 1 SCR 1296, 1332.

analogous criteria may none the less be applied in supervision of administrative acts and decisions. The courts' insistence that powers should be exercised on proper grounds, and not for ulterior purposes, together with the doctrine that wholly unreasonable decisions are *ultra vires*, amounts to a constitutional requirement of respect for equality.[15] Differences of treatment at the hands of government, or other public authority, must as a general rule be justified on the basis of a lawful and legitimate governmental objective. Arbitrary treatment is unconstitutional and therefore unlawful. Lord Russell's affirmation of the principle of equality, in *Kruse* v. *Johnson*,[16] indicated the power of the common law to provide a remedy against discriminatory treatment which lacks genuine (judicially recognized) statutory authority.

Lord Russell's dictum was invoked by the South African Transvaal Provincial Division in striking down a government instruction requiring separate post office facilities for 'Europeans' and 'non-Europeans'. In *Minister of Posts and Telegraphs* v. *Rasool*,[17] Tindall J. held that discrimination based solely on race or colour could not be taken to be authorized by statute, which provided for the issue of 'necessary' instructions, because its operation was partial and unequal as between different classes. That decision was reversed by the majority of the Appellate Division, who denied that such discrimination was unreasonable where it did not entail inequality of rights and facilities. Gardiner AJA's persuasive dissenting judgment, however, insisted that an order or by-law which discriminated on the grounds of race was invalid, and that the 'fundamental principle' of equality could be overridden only by express legislative provision. Gardiner boldly applied a principle of critical morality, embedded in (English and South African) common law, to resist a measure which was plainly the product of racial prejudice and which insulted those of 'non-European' ethnic origin.[18]

Equality and rationality: the rule of law and abuse of power

In the *GCHQ* case,[19] Lord Diplock distinguished a number of grounds of judicial review of the exercise of discretion by a public authority: illegality, irrationality, and procedural impropriety (with the possible addition of proportionality). It is, however, often difficult to differentiate in practice between these various grounds. Procedural unfairness

[15] See discussion below. The nature and limits of judicial review of administrative action are further considered in Chs. 8 and 9.

[16] [1898] 2 QB 91, 99–100, cited above. [17] 1934 AD 167.

[18] For full discussion, see David Dyzenhaus, *Hard Cases in Wicked Legal Systems* (Oxford, 1991), 53–63.

[19] *Council of Civil Service Unions* v. *Minister for the Civil Service* [1984] 3 All ER 935, 950–1.

cannot be entirely divorced from questions of substance;[20] and the decisions of the courts reflect changing perceptions of the distinction between 'illegality' and 'irrationality'.[21] Lord Diplock applied the latter label to decisions which were 'outrageous' in their 'defiance of logic or of accepted moral standards'.[22] The distinction was perhaps intended to reflect the need for criteria of review drawn (in the case of statutory powers) from beyond the text of the statute itself. But since questions of logic and moral standards are relevant to the construction of statutes, questions of 'rationality' cannot be neatly divorced from those of 'illegality'. Textual interpretation cannot sensibly be distinguished from the application of common law values: the meaning of statutes cannot be derived in abstraction from the wider common law context in which they are (necessarily) placed. Acts of Parliament are rarely construed so as to permit actions which violate basic moral standards: our convictions about justice rightly, and inevitably, colour our interpretation of the statutory text.[23]

Lord Greene, in the *Wednesbury* case,[24] expounded the principles of review as overlapping ingredients of the general notion of abuse of power, which included (but was not exhausted by) deliberate bad faith. And there was much sense in Lord Donaldson's refusal, in a case involving a non-statutory body, to separate the various heads of review.[25] The different categories were difficult to apply to the decisions of a body—the Panel on Take-overs and Mergers—whose constitution, functions, and powers were '*sui generis*'. In the context of that case, he preferred to enquire, more generally, whether something had 'gone wrong of a nature and degree which required the intervention of the court'.[26]

The artificiality of attempts to distinguish sharply between 'illegality' and 'irrationality' is demonstrated by recent cases which emphasize the courts' duty to refrain from interference in matters of financial administration, requiring political judgment.[27] Lord Bridge explained that 'illegality' referred to administrative action taken in contravention of the statute, properly construed—including action in disregard of relevant matters or influenced by irrelevant matters.[28] Action which involved the 'formulation and the implementation of national economic policy', and which required House of Commons approval, could not be

[20] See Ch. 8, below.

[21] Cf. *Hammersmith & Fulham LBC* v. *Sec. of State for the Environment* [1990] 3 All ER 589, 636–7 (Lord Bridge).

[22] [1984] 3 All ER 951.

[23] See further Ch. 4, above.

[24] *Associated Provincial Picture Houses* v. *Wednesbury Corp.* [1948] 1 KB 223.

[25] *R.* v. *Panel on Take-overs & Mergers, ex p. Guinness* [1989] 1 All ER 509, 512–13.

[26] Ibid. 513, 527.

[27] *Nottinghamshire CC* v. *Sec. of State for the Environment* [1986] AC 240; *Hammersmith* case (above, n. 21).

[28] *Hammersmith* case [1990] 3 All ER 589, 637.

impugned—where it met the requirements of 'legality'—on grounds of 'irrationality' without showing 'the extremes of bad faith, improper motive or manifest absurdity'.[29] If, however, judicial review is not to be assimilated to appeal on the merits of the action concerned, it is hard to see what sort of challenge or enquiry is being excluded.[30] No special rules are needed for cases of financial affairs, no matter how politically sensitive or controversial. Lord Bridge's summary of the principle being applied merely restated the ordinary constitutional position:

> If decisions have been taken in good faith within the four corners of the Act, the merits of the policy underlying the decisions are not susceptible to review by the courts and the courts would be exceeding their proper function if they presumed to condemn the policy as unreasonable.[31]

The difficulties entailed in separating the various grounds of review for abuse of power, as well as the important underlying role of equality, are well illustrated by *Wheeler* v. *Leicester City Council*.[32] The English Rugby Football Union had accepted an invitation to take part in a tour of South Africa, and three members of the Leicester Football Club were included in the team. In pursuance of its policy to discourage sporting links with that country, the city council urged the club to press the Union and their own participants to abandon the tour. Although the club asserted its agreement in condemning apartheid, it refused to apply the pressure requested. Differences of opinion existed over the best way to oppose apartheid, and, as amateur sportsmen, the club members should enjoy individual choice about when and where to play. The council banned the club from using a public recreation ground for practice as a sanction for its failure to condemn the tour in accordance with the council's policy.

The Court of Appeal, affirming the judge at first instance, refused to grant relief against the ban. The council had a statutory duty to promote good race relations in the performance of its various functions,[33] and its view that the ban served that purpose could not be regarded as irrational or perverse. The court's decision might be defended on the basis of a narrow or formal view of the requirement of rationality, which would permit administrative action to be impugned only when no real connection could be established between the action and its pretended (legitimate) objective. The case of the red-haired school-teacher, dismissed on account of the colour of her hair, would clearly be irrational on this test.[34]

[29] Ibid.
[30] For the distinction between appeal and review, see Ch. 8, below.
[31] [1990] 3 All ER 637. [32] [1985] 2 All ER 151, 1106.
[33] Race Relations Act 1976 s. 71.
[34] Cf. *Short* v. *Poole Corp*. [1926] Ch 66 (Warrington LJ), cited by Lord Greene MR in the *Wednesbury* case.

In a powerful dissent, Browne-Wilkinson LJ agreed that the council had not acted perversely, but denounced the ban as an unacceptable constraint on freedoms of speech and conscience. Parliament had not, in the Race Relations Act, authorized the punishment of citizens who lawfully dissented from the views of a public authority. Basic constitutional rights could not be curtailed in the absence of express statutory provision.[35]

The House of Lords allowed the club's appeal, but without adopting Browne-Wilkinson LJ's approach. The court seemed unwilling or unable to specify clearly the precise ground of *ultra vires* on which it struck down the council's decision, but the speeches none the less illuminate the broader concept of abuse of power: 'The club having committed no wrong, the council could not use their statutory powers in the management of their property or any other statutory powers in order to punish the club.'[36] Lord Roskill was inclined to the view that, contrary to the judgments in the lower courts, the council's ban was unreasonable or perverse. If it were not, he thought that it was assailable on the ground of the unfair manner in which the council had sought its objective. Although Lord Roskill referred to 'procedural impropriety' in this connection, it is clear that procedure and substance were not truly distinguishable. The 'crucial question' was whether the council's action, by trying to force acceptance of their own policy on their own terms, could 'be said to be so "unreasonable" as to give rise to "*Wednesbury* unreasonableness" . . . or to be so fundamental a breach of the duty to act fairly which rests on every local authority in matters of this kind' as to justify the court's intervention.[37]

It is apparent that the court's decision was not based on the ordinary civil or political rights of the club members: Lord Roskill expressly declined to endorse Browne-Wilkinson LJ's 'somewhat wider ground' of decision. In what sense was the decision impugned as unfair? It seems clear that the House of Lords embraced a wider concept of rationality than that of the lower courts—a concept which placed constraints on the council's *objective*, as well as on the coherence of its methods. The council's action was 'irrational' in the sense that it violated the club members' *equality*—their rights not to be punished, or be subjected to adverse discrimination, on the ground of a public authority's disapproval of their characters or conduct.

The *Wheeler* decision was followed in *R.* v. *Lewisham London Borough Council, ex parte Shell*,[38] where the Divisional Court held that the council had unlawfully decided to boycott Shell products, when the company refused to give undertakings to withdraw from its commercial interests in South Africa. The council defended its policies of disinvestment and

[35] [1985] 2 All ER 158: see also Ch. 6, above.
[36] Ibid. 1113 (Lord Templeman).
[37] Ibid. 1111.
[38] [1988] 1 All ER 938.

boycott as part of its stance against apartheid, which was itself regarded as an aspect of its wider concern with race relations. Eighteen per cent of the borough was black. On a narrow view of 'unreasonableness', the council's decision could not be challenged. The council was entitled to decide from experience that it was in the interest of good race relations that trading with a particular company should cease because of its links with apartheid. The council's further objective, however, rendered its decision an abuse of power: it sought to put pressure on Shell to withdraw from South Africa, an objective amply demonstrated by the council's involvement in a national campaign by the Joint Action Against Apartheid group of local authorities, directed solely at Shell. The attempt to coerce the management of Shell was inextricably mixed up with the desire to improve race relations, and the impermissible objective had the 'effect of vitiating the decision as a whole'.[39]

In the *Lewisham* case, there were no civil or political rights at stake: Shell had no (legal or moral) right that it should continue to enjoy the economic patronage of the council. None the less, the court's decision rightly upheld the company's right to equal treatment. It had not acted unlawfully; nor was it in breach of the contract compliance scheme devised by the Commission for Racial Equality. It was therefore entitled to be protected from adverse discrimination based on the council's disapproval of its commercial policy. It is fundamental to the idea of equality, in constitutional law, that no one should suffer coercion, or be denied advantages given to others, because his lawful conduct meets with public or government disapprobation. As a legal 'person', the company would seem entitled to the same protection as a private individual in this respect.

The principle applied in these cases seems fundamental to the rule of law, which insists that governmental authority be exercised within the constraints of general rules—precisely in order to prevent discrimination against particular persons or groups. Formal equality, in the sense of the equal application of the law, must as a matter of logical consistency be accompanied by the more substantive doctrine, forbidding hostile discrimination: its rationale would otherwise be defeated by the manipulation of the powers of public authorities for extraneous purposes. Many of the cases in which the courts have struck down executive decisions made for improper purposes, or more generally as abuses of power, can therefore be understood as examples of judicial review in defence of equality—the right to be free from unfair or hostile discrimination at the hands of the state.[40]

[39] Ibid. 952 (Neill LJ).

[40] Cf. *Preston* v. *Inland Revenue Commrs.* [1985] 2 All ER 327, 339–40 (Lord Templeman). Lord Templeman cites the well-known *Padfield*, *Congreve*, and *Laker* cases as instances of 'unfairness' amounting to abuse of power where the minister acted for an ulterior purpose.

This rationale also explains the decision of the Divisional Court in *R. v. Ealing London Borough, ex parte Times Newspapers*.[41] The removal of Times Newspapers' printing operations from Fleet Street to Wapping brought about a bitter dispute with their employees' trade unions. A number of London borough councils, which exercised powers under the Public Libraries and Museums Act 1964, banned all copies of Times Newspapers' publications from their libraries as a mark of sympathy with the unions' cause. It is tempting to view such conduct as an unconstitutional interference with freedom of expression, and it was argued by counsel that the ban violated the 'right to receive information and ideas without arbitrary interference'.[42] That approach to the matter gained support from the nature of the local authorities' justification: it was suggested that they would be entitled to censor books by an author known to favour apartheid or support the IRA or to be 'an enemy of the state'.[43]

As in the *Wheeler* case, however, the court was able to avoid a determination of the legality of the ban on that ground. Its decision that the ban constituted a serious abuse of power was rested on the fact that it had been imposed for irrelevant or ulterior reasons—reasons which had no legitimate basis in the duties placed on the authorities under the 1964 Act. It could hardly be maintained that the failure to display *The Times* in itself amounted to a breach of the statutory duty to 'provide a comprehensive and efficient library service'.[44] It was, however, clear that its absence from the shelves was not the result of a bona fide assessment of the needs of the service. The ban reflected the local authorities' disapproval of the conduct of Times Newspapers. Its purpose 'was set by a political attitude to a so-called workers' struggle against a tyrannical employer with the object of punishing the employer'.[45]

We have noticed the power of Dworkin's principle of 'integrity' to illuminate features of law which resist explanation in terms of justice and fairness (as Dworkin defines those ideals).[46] It seems clear that 'integrity' derives its appeal from an underlying commitment to equality: other ideals (of justice and fairness) must be compromised—because they sometimes conflict—but the resulting accommodation of values must be universally applied. All must be governed according to the same scheme of principle, even if that scheme represents a compromise between conflicting principles of justice and fairness. Dworkin's analysis suggests that an adequate account of the legitimacy of judicial review may also need to travel beyond the requirements of justice and fairness.

[41] (1986) 85 LGR 316. [42] Ibid. 326. [43] Ibid. 324.
[44] Public Libraries and Museums Act 1964 s. 7(1).
[45] 85 LGR 326 (Watkins LJ). [46] Chs. 2 and 4, above.

If we treat 'irrationality' as an aspect of a broader concept of abuse of power, we can understand more clearly the purposes and operation of judicial review. Where an action or decision is impugned because it violates civil or political rights or established rights in private law, without adequate statutory authority, review safeguards the interests of justice. Justice requires that when public authorities seek to curtail private law rights, or to limit the 'constitutional' rights with which we associate the rule of law, they should be strictly bound by the limits of their legal powers, properly interpreted.[47] Justice also requires that rights or benefits expressly conferred by statute—for example, welfare benefits—should be duly acknowledged and honoured. 'Fairness'—the fulfilment of the popular will—may also be thought to support judicial intervention, at the instance of a party aggrieved, where a public authority is compelled to perform its statutory duty, imposed in the public interest.[48] However, such support is usually incidental: rules of standing generally limit complainants to those who have suffered injustice from the agency's failure to perform its duty.[49]

In many cases, however, neither justice nor fairness—in these senses—explain the court's intervention. The complainant can sometimes show no infringement of his private legal or 'constitutional' rights; nor does he allege that some statutory benefit is being wrongly withheld. He pleads only that an agency has injured his general interests, or thwarted his legitimate aspirations, in the course of action which exceeds its jurisdiction, properly understood. Deliberate attempts to coerce the citizen, applying unauthorized means of persuasion or pressure, represent only the clearest instances. In such cases the court may intervene, justifiably, in defence of equality.

We may suppose that the complainant has no *other* moral right against the administrative action (or decision) in question: we do not think that such action, which contributes to the general welfare, should none the less be prevented in justice to him. For example, it does not impinge (unacceptably) on his rights to freedom of conscience or freedom of speech. It may also be true that the action in question serves the interests of fairness, by advancing the general policy or purposes of a statute, or analogous purposes. If none the less it is held invalid as *ultra vires*, the legitimacy of judicial review may best be sought in some conception of equality. It may be thought that the

[47] When administrative action impinges on such important values as freedom of speech or conscience—or other liberties traditionally prized—a strict interpretation of the ambit of such powers will generally be legitimate (see further Ch. 6, above).

[48] This distinction between 'justice' and 'fairness' reflects Dworkin's analysis, considered in Ch. 4, above.

[49] Questions of *locus standi* are considered in Ch. 9, below. A complainant is, of course, entitled in justice to the benefits which a statute, duly enacted, confers on him even if he exerted any political influence he enjoyed against the statute's enactment.

community benefits unfairly at the complainant's expense. He is forced to sacrifice his interests for the benefit of others, or the general good, in circumstances where the burden seems harsh or excessive—and for that reason unlawful unless imposed by government with clear and convincing authorization.

It may be considered part of a metaphorical 'contract' between citizen and state, in the manner of Fuller's notion of reciprocity,[50] that no one shall suffer disadvantage at the hands of government except in the proper exercise of lawful authority—with the safeguards against abuse of power which that implies. The rule of law, then, through its insistence on 'formal' equality—the subjection of all to the requirements of the law—protects a more fundamental equality. It justifies and requires the practice of subjecting the exercise of public powers to judicial review, grounded on an appropriately elaborated concept of 'jurisdiction', limiting the scope of the powers conferred. And an adequate account of that idea must include a test of proportionality: the scale of the burdens imposed on individuals should reflect the real requirements of the public interest, and not be more onerous than can reasonably be justified.[51]

A conception of equality underlies the fundamental distinction between policy and law, on which our account of the separation of powers relied. In the formulation and execution of policy, government is not obliged to treat people equally: it may make reasonable distinctions between citizens in order to achieve its ambitions for the whole community.[52] As the framework within which government must be conducted, however, the law must be even-handed. That is not, of course, to deny that policies may be enshrined in statute, and discrimination thereby given legal force. But the rule of law does entail that judicial interpretation of statute, and review of executive action under statutory powers, should reflect the ideal of equality. Administrative action should discriminate between citizens for proper reasons, sufficiently related to legitimate governmental purposes, as those may be gleaned from the statute, properly—reasonably—construed. While policy-making is the province of government, and ultimately of Parliament, the manner of its execution must be subject to appropriate judicial control.

I have suggested that the common law doctrine of *stare decisis* itself reflects the ideal of equality.[53] Courts should respect the *rationes decidendi* of previous decisions so that everyone's case is judged according to the same principles. Differences in treatment must be justified by

[50] See discussion of the work of Lon Fuller and that of John Finnis in Ch. 2, above.
[51] See further Ch. 8, below.
[52] Cf. Ronald Dworkin, *Law's Empire* (London, 1986), 222–3, 243–4, 310–11.
[53] Ch. 2, above.

compelling reasons of justice or fairness—fresh perceptions of individual rights, correctly understood, or statutory alterations to the previous law. Although the execution of policy cannot be similarly constrained—government must be free to change public policy according to its perceptions of the public interest—unnecessary discrimination between persons should be inhibited by law. Moreover, the division between law and policy should not be drawn without sensitivity to the details of particular cases. A deliberate change of government policy will not always justify differences of treatment between persons who are otherwise similarly circumstanced. It seems reasonable to argue that serious or damaging distinctions between such persons should require a proportionately persuasive justification. 'Policy' should not become an excuse for the infliction of any injustice on private individuals without possibility of recourse to the courts.

It follows that the House of Lords' analysis in *Findlay* v. *Home Secretary*[54] failed to address the strength of the application for relief, even if the ultimate decision was defensible. In October 1983 the Home Secretary announced a new policy regarding use of his powers, under the Criminal Justice Act 1967, to release prisoners on licence. Prisoners convicted of the murder of police or prison officers, terrorist murder, sexual or sadistic murder of children, or murder by firearm in the course of robbery, would now generally serve at least twenty years of their life sentences before release. Prisoners serving sentences of over five years for offences of violence or drug trafficking would no longer normally be eligible for parole. The House of Lords rejected a submission that, by adopting the new policy, the minister had unlawfully fettered his discretion to examine the merits of each individual case. Such examination was not excluded by a policy which required exceptional circumstances or compelling reasons to justify early release because of the weight attached to the nature of the offence, in the light of such considerations as deterrence, retribution, and public confidence in the criminal justice system.

In the Court of Appeal, Sir John Donaldson MR had admitted to anxiety about whether the minister's policy had created so rigid a division between the specified groups of prisoners, on one hand, and other prisoners, on the other, as to be unreasonable: 'The creation of categories, based on differences of degree rather than kind, will always carry with it a risk of unfairness at the interface.'[55] A policy which denied parole to a man sentenced to six years' imprisonment for drug trafficking or violence, but not to one given twelve years for a different offence, took some justification. His conclusion that the policy was not unreasonable clearly lacked conviction. Exceptional circumstances, he

[54] [1984] 3 All ER 801. [55] Ibid. 814.

reflected, might be interpreted in practice so as to soften the stark contrast between the treatment of offenders who fell just inside or outside a particular category; and it might be that serious offenders outside the categories would also be refused parole. Treatment of this objection to the policy by the House of Lords was cursory. Lord Scarman saw nothing wrong with classifying prisoners according to the nature of their offences and the length of their sentences, provided that other relevant factors, such as prison record and personal or family circumstances, could also be taken into account.

Considerations of equality were not quite exhausted, however, by matters of arbitrary definition. In the Court of Appeal, Browne-Wilkinson LJ recognized that 'in commonsense terms' the change of policy was retrospective in operation, since existing prisoners within the specified categories had previously been considered for parole on the basis of the same criteria as other prisoners. The significance of this point is that the new policy thwarted expectations of early release which had naturally been encouraged by previous practice. Two of the applicants were life-sentence prisoners, who had been moved to open prisons as a prelude to release on licence. Their claim to be exempted from the new policy was rejected by the House of Lords on the ground that they had no expectation which the court could protect. According to Lord Scarman, 'the most that a convicted prisoner can legitimately expect is that his case will be examined individually in the light of whatever policy the Secretary of State sees fit to adopt, provided always that the adopted policy is a lawful exercise of the discretion conferred on him by the statute'.[56]

The proviso, however, rather begged the question at issue. Part, at least, of the grievance caused by a change of policy which applied to existing prisoners must have consisted in their being treated differently from other offenders, in the same categories, who had already been released. Could they not reasonably expect to be treated as favourably as other recent prisoners who had received similar sentences for similar crimes (and whose sentences may have partly overlapped with their own)? The injustice inherent in the frustration of expectations, reasonably entertained, is obviously aggravated by disparities in the treatment of similar people, according to the date of introduction of the new policy.

Browne-Wilkinson LJ offered the somewhat formalistic answer to the 'retrospectivity' objection—Forbes J. in the Divisional Court had thought it wholly semantic[57]—that since parole was discretionary, no prisoner had a *right* to earlier release. The sentence was imposed by the trial judge, without regard to parole. In Browne-Wilkinson LJ's view,

[56] Ibid. 830. [57] See ibid. 812 (Sir John Donaldson MR).

any other conclusion would block any change in parole policy which might adversely affect the expectations of existing prisoners; and Lord Scarman echoed that apprehension.[58] Other decisions, however, show that, though legitimate expectations may not be invoked to prevent changes of policy altogether, they may perfectly well limit their nature and timing. In some cases, the courts have held that changes of policy should only apply in future instances, or be permitted to defeat settled expectations only where the requirements of the public interest are of special strength.[59]

Sir John Donaldson MR suggested that a legitimate expectation could give rise to *locus standi* for judicial review, but provided no independent ground of complaint: 'Were it otherwise, any consistent exercise of discretionary powers in a particular way would soon cause the discretionary element to wither.'[60] However, the nature and effect of a person's expectation must inevitably depend on all the circumstances; and Donaldson's interpretation is quite inconsistent with the general principle of fairness which the modern law of judicial review enshrines. If in some cases an expectation may sharply curtail the government's freedom to abandon an earlier policy, in others it may only require a new policy to be applied with sensitivity to the particular facts.[61]

The minister wished to protect the public from offenders convicted of serious offences of violence, and to restore public confidence in the administration of criminal justice. He had acted in response to public disquiet at the rising level of violent crime and drug abuse. If all existing prisoners who currently harboured expectations of early release were excepted from the change of policy, it would clearly be many years before the new policy could be fully implemented. It is perhaps a reasonable conclusion that recognition of the applicants' claims to exemption would have imposed an unacceptably onerous constraint on the discretion to alter government policy. The right to be treated equally with those in similar categories, who had already been released on licence in accordance with previous practice, could not be absolute. Nor could it be as strong as the right to equality under the ordinary civil law. The distinction between law and policy reflects that difference. None the less, the right to equality—whose association with the rule of law is fundamental—deserved consideration in the general context of the case. It should not have been largely overlooked merely because the executive cannot be estopped from changing public policy.

[58] Ibid. 821 (Browne-Wilkinson LJ); 830 (Lord Scarman).
[59] e.g. *R.* v. *Home Secretary, ex p. Khan* [1985] 1 All ER 40, 48 (Parker LJ).
[60] [1984] 3 All ER 811.
[61] See further Ch. 8, below.

Equality and justice

The conclusion that the principle of equality before the law imposes important constraints on the exercise of public power explains the considerable disquiet sometimes aroused by use of central government's economic powers to achieve particular policy objectives. A White Paper issued in 1975, for example, announced that the government would have regard to firms' observance of its non-statutory incomes policy in deciding applications for financial assistance under the Industry Act 1972 and also in awarding contracts.[62] Companies which made pay settlements considered to be in breach of the government's guidelines were 'blacklisted'; and contractual conditions were imposed in other cases requiring contractors to observe the guidelines. Some aspects of the government's policy, where it involved the exercise of statutory powers, were arguably unlawful.[63] However, it was generally assumed that there were no legal restrictions on the power to award contracts, since the Crown is usually considered to enjoy a freedom of contract similar to that of the individual subject.[64]

Some commentators were tempted to argue that resort to non-statutory forms of economic management was acceptable provided that Parliament none the less exercised proper political control.[65] The Fair Wages Resolutions, approved by the House of Commons since 1891, provided respectable precedents for using the power to award contracts to achieve social policy objectives. It is also true that the government abandoned the application of sanctions against firms in breach of the guidelines after a House of Commons vote opposing their use.[66] However, the threat which such measures pose to the rule of law cannot be evaded merely by repudiating Dicey's disavowal of arbitrary or wide discretionary powers.[67] The underlying issue of principle remains even if the exercise of such powers is now a constitutional commonplace.

The point of the rule of law seems to be seriously undermined if the executive can achieve its purposes without resort to Parliament for the grant of specific powers, where those purposes entail discrimination between private citizens according to governmental perceptions of their

[62] *The Attack on Inflation*, Cmnd. 6151 (1975).

[63] Sir William Wade, *Constitutional Fundamentals*, Hamlyn Lectures, 32nd series, revised edn. (London, 1989), 70–1.

[64] Ibid. See further Terence Daintith, 'Regulation by Contract: The New Prerogative' (1979) 32 *Current Legal Problems* 41; id., 'The Executive Power Today: Bargaining and Economic Control', in Jeffrey Jowell and Dawn Oliver (eds.), *The Changing Constitution*, 2nd edn. (Oxford, 1989).

[65] e.g. G. Ganz, 'Comment' [1978] PL 333.

[66] See generally Colin Turpin, *British Government and the Constitution*, 2nd edn. (London, 1990), 490–14.

[67] Cf. Ganz, 'Comment', 346.

merits and demerits. Sir William Wade was right to condemn these procedures as unconstitutional: 'To attempt to govern without Parliament by abuse of miscellaneous powers, in the manner that the Stuart kings did by abuse of the royal prerogative, is a complete repudiation of primary constitutional principle.'[68] However, the distinction between unconstitutional conduct and illegality, on which Wade relies, seems less secure. In so far as it rests on the power of government to invoke all the ordinary rights and powers of the private citizen, in order to achieve its purposes without special authorization, it overlooks an aspect of the rule of law explored in the previous chapter. Dicey's principle of equality before the law should not be subverted by too readily accepting analogies between the 'ordinary' powers of the Crown and those of private individuals.[69]

The view that public authorities are legally entitled to employ their economic patronage in pursuit of policy objectives, while disregarding wider constitutional considerations, is no longer tenable. The *Lewisham* and *Ealing* cases establish that the contracting powers of local authorities are restricted in ways which do not apply to private individuals or organizations.[70] Moreover, an increasing awareness of the power exercised *de facto* in the 'public sphere' by 'private' bodies, which perform regulatory functions akin to those of governmental authorities, has also served to limit the scope of freedom of contract. In *Nagle* v. *Feilden*,[71] the Court of Appeal denied the power of the stewards of the Jockey Club to reject the plaintiff's application for a trainer's licence 'arbitrarily or capriciously'. Recognition of the monopolistic power of the Club combined with considerations of justice to those dependent on its decisions for their livelihood to limit the stewards' contractual freedom.

It follows that the pre-contractual powers of similar organizations may be considered susceptible to judicial review, even if the supervisory jurisdiction is excluded where contractual relations actually exist with those subject to their authority.[72] For example, a clear distinction between the pre-contractual and contractual aspects or phases of a relationship of public employment has been drawn in one of the leading cases on the scope of judicial review.[73] Admittedly, the public law

[68] *Constitutional Fundamentals* (revised edn.), 70.

[69] See Ch. 6, above. Cf. Colin Turpin, *Government Procurement and Contracts* (London, 1989), 214–16.

[70] Local and certain other public authorities are now prohibited by statute from taking account of non-commercial considerations in awarding contracts: see Local Govt. Act 1988 s. 17. See further P. P. Craig, *Administrative Law*, 2nd edn. (London, 1989), 499–502.

[71] [1966] 2 QB 633. Cf. *McInnes* v. *Onslow-Fane* [1978] 1 WLR 1520.

[72] See e.g. *Law* v. *Nat. Greyhound Racing Club* [1983] 1 WLR 1302; *R.* v. *Disciplinary Cttee. of the Jockey Club, ex p. The Aga Khan, The Times LR*, 9 Dec. 1992.

[73] *R.* v. *East Berks. Health Authy., ex p. Walsh* [1985] QB 152.

rights of the employee, supplementing his private law contractual rights, arose in that instance from statute. None the less, the *GCHQ* case provides authority for the view that judicial review of a decision-making power cannot be excluded merely because the power has a common law rather than a statutory source.[74] And in *R.* v. *Panel on Take-overs and Mergers, ex parte Datafin*[75] the court emphasized that the *nature* of the tribunal's functions, rather than the *source* of its powers, was the crucial determinant of the possibility of judicial review.

It is hard to resist the conclusion that the exercise of economic and contractual power in the 'public sphere' should no longer be considered properly analogous to its exercise in the private sphere. And if local authorities and quasi-governmental bodies are subject to public law principles of justice and fairness in the management of their commercial functions, the imposition of similar constraints on central government cannot be resisted either in logic or in principle.[76]

In Chapter 2, we noticed the connection established by F. A. Hayek's work between legality and justice. Justice was associated with a conception of (formal) equality: the consistent application of general rules of law ensured that all equally enjoyed the benefits of a spontaneous order, permitting everyone the opportunity to pursue his own private interests while respecting a similar freedom in others. Justice was secured by regular administration of the ordinary law. We have seen, however, how formal equality must be accompanied by a broader, more substantive conception in order to protect individuals and organizations from unfair discrimination by the state. The exercise of political power cannot be sufficiently controlled by the application of general rules, applied without regard to the intended objectives of particular actions. The freedom permitted the private citizen to pursue his aims within the constraints of general rules cannot be allowed in the same way to public authorities, whose only legitimate freedom is their discretion to act in furtherance of the public interest.

It is important, none the less, that the proper discretion of public officials and agencies is not usurped by the courts: the right to equality should not be invoked as a means of destroying the fundamental separation of powers between government and judicature.[77] In *Inland Revenue Commissioners* v. *Federation of Self-Employed and Small Businesses*,[78] the House of Lords held that a taxpayer would not generally be

[74] *Council of Civil Service Unions* v. *Minister for the Civil Service* [1984] 3 All ER 935, 950 (Lord Diplock).

[75] [1987] QB 815.

[76] See esp. Dawn Oliver, 'Is the *Ultra Vires* Rule the Basis of Judicial Review?' [1987] PL 543; Sue Arrowsmith, 'Judicial Review and the Contractual Powers of Public Authorities' (1990) 106 LQR 277; B. V. Harris, 'The "Third Source" of Authority for Government Action' (1992) 109 LQR 626.

[77] Ch. 3, above. [78] [1981] 2 All ER 93.

permitted to challenge an assessment of liability to tax made in respect of another taxpayer. The Commissioners' duties were owed to the Crown and the relevant legislation conferred no rights on individuals in relation to the tax payable by others. However, the court chose to dismiss the application on the ground that the Federation had not made out a sufficient prima facie case of illegality to justify further investigation. In cases of exceptional gravity, it was thought that a taxpayer might obtain relief. That conclusion may be defended, perhaps, on the basis of his right to equality; but its legitimacy is not self-evident.

It would be mistaken to extend the scope of equality rights much beyond cases of deliberate coercion or intended discrimination against particular persons. The House of Lords' decision should not be interpreted as authorizing an *actio popularis*, permitting anyone dissatisfied with public policy to impugn its legality in the courts. Where inequalities are the unintended by-product of a policy conducted in good faith in the public interest they can rarely form the basis of legitimate legal challenge. By drawing the boundaries of the principle of equality too widely, judicial review may become a means of political opposition rather than a remedy for actual injustice to ascertainable individuals. To expand the courts' supervisory jurisdiction to permit complaints of government action which does not impinge directly on the complainants would strike unacceptably at the separation of powers, drawing the courts into the arena of ordinary politics and usurping the roles of other, more democratic institutions.

Lord Diplock held that the court could intervene if the Revenue discriminated in favour of a class of taxpayers for 'ulterior reasons extraneous to good management', thereby depriving the national exchequer of large sums of money.[79] Discriminatory treatment of that kind would seem plainly contrary to the general principle of equality before the law. Lord Scarman expressed this idea by his reference to the 'principle of fairness'. He asserted the existence of a 'legal duty owed by the Revenue to the general body of the taxpayers to treat taxpayers fairly, to use their discretionary powers so that, subject to the requirements of good management, discrimination between one group of taxpayers and another does not arise, to ensure that there are no favourites and no sacrificial victims'.[80] We should normally expect 'sacrificial victims' to demonstrate identifiable personal injury, however, before acknowledging the breach of rights to equality which can be judicially enforced. Legal duties imposed on public bodies need not be coextensive with legal rights conferred on individual citizens. But persons who are clearly and directly disadvantaged by selective tax

[79] Ibid. 106. [80] Ibid. 112.

concessions (or other public financial assistance) granted to business competitors ought to be able to challenge their compatibility with the relevant legislation. Their *locus standi* would reflect their rights to equality which the 'principle of fairness' assures.[81]

It seems clear that the court's defence of equality, in the sense explained, forms part of a wider commitment to administrative justice or fairness, whose requirements are ultimately dependent on all the circumstances of the particular case.[82] It is true that Hayek, whose work illuminates many aspects of the rule of law, took pains to deny that justice involved a balancing of interests in the particular case, or aimed at producing a just result. But, of course, he was writing in the context of the ordinary rules of private law, which he rightly saw as the foundation of the relations between government and citizen, as much as between private citizens. We do not contradict his interpretation of equality or justice by acknowledging the additional and independent contribution made by modern public law.

Hayek distinguished clearly between the particular rules of organization of government, which enable officials to execute their tasks, and the general rules which serve to secure a spontaneous order of private individuals and organizations, and which are abstract in the sense that they do not serve any common purpose (other than preservation of the spontaneous order).[83] He was reluctant to accord administrative law—in the narrow sense of rules empowering agencies to act for specific purposes—the same dignity as ordinary private law, for fear that such agencies might claim the obedience of the private citizen to their objectives. In a free society, the means assigned to government agencies for particular tasks 'do not include the private citizen'.[84]

Hayek's vision of liberty under law must, however, be supplemented by suitable means of control of the executive, which is legitimately charged with a wide variety of functions in aid of the public interest. Administrative law, in the wider sense of principles of judicial supervision, must seek a form of justice appropriate to its special role. Since it is inevitably the nature of government activity—beyond the enforcement of general rules of just conduct (i.e. private law)—to interfere with the circumstances of private persons for public purposes, the application of public law must descend to comparable particularity if it is to provide adequate protection.

The meaning of justice and fairness must depend on the context. The abstract justice which Hayek defends in respect of the spontaneous order, dependent on private law, must be replaced, in the public law

[81] See further Ch. 9, below.
[82] See Ch. 8, below.
[83] *Law, Legislation and Liberty* (London, 1982), i, esp. chs. 2 and 6.
[84] Ibid. 133.

field, by a more concrete, individualized conception, apt to prevent coercion of the private citizen beyond the reasonable and legitimate requirements of the public good. We cannot enjoy the advantages of government activity in pursuit of social and economic ends, with all the necessary discriminations between individuals which that entails, without the disadvantages of uncertainty and subjectivity which mark our dependence on judicial discretion, applied in defence of the (somewhat abstract) right to fair treatment at the hands of the state. We examine the futility of resisting that discretion, or denying that right, in the following chapter.[85]

[85] Judicial 'discretion' is intended to denote the exercise of moral judgment beyond the constraints of legal rule: the reference is to the consistent application of principle, inevitably sensitive to context. Discretion to tailor the remedy of judicial review to the broader demands of public policy is firmly denied.

8

The Separation of Powers and Judicial Review

> ... judicial review is a demanding arena, as the courts cannot shrink from rulings bearing on even the most socially divisive issues of the day—political, moral, economic. Here the judicial role is not to resolve the issues but to act as a check or to keep the ring, trying to ensure that those responsible for decisions in the community do so in accordance with law, fairly and reasonably. And fairly and reasonably have their ordinary meanings and, as they ordinarily do, overlap.
>
> Sir Robin Cooke, 'The Struggle for Simplicity in Administrative Law', in Michael Taggart (ed.), *Judicial Review of Administrative Action in the 1980s* (Oxford, 1986), 16–17.

In our earlier discussion of the separation of powers,[1] we invoked Ronald Dworkin's distinction between principle and policy to assist in defining the specific character of the judicial function. Although individual rights in public law must be sharply distinguished from private law rights—as rights against the state, their content is closely related to the nature and scope of the powers and duties entrusted to public officials and agencies—we will find that the principle/policy dichotomy affords as powerful a tool for analysis of public as of private law. It illuminates the distinction drawn by constitutional theory between legality, on the one hand, and matters of policy (and efficiency),[2] on the other.

Judicial review of administrative action exists to safeguard legality. The rule of law requires that public authorities act only within the limits of their powers, properly understood. But a court may not interfere with action lawfully taken within the jurisdiction of a public authority. It is usually said that the court is concerned with the lawfulness of administrative decisions, but not with their merits, which would be relevant only to an appeal (granted expressly by statute).[3] That distinction was emphasized by Lord Greene MR, in reviewing the exercise by a local authority of its discretion under the Sunday Entertainments Act 1932.[4] The court was not a court of appeal: 'When

[1] Ch. 3, above.
[2] Cf. Ch. 3, above, n. 25.
[3] See Sir William Wade, *Administrative Law*, 6th edn. (Oxford, 1988), 36–9.
[4] *Assocd. Provincial Picture Houses* v. *Wednesbury Corp.* [1948] 1 KB 223.

discretion of this kind is granted the law recognises certain principles upon which that discretion must be exercised, but within the four corners of these principles the discretion . . . is an absolute one and cannot be questioned in any court of law.'[5] The court could intervene only where the authority had been influenced by irrelevant considerations, or had failed to take account of relevant matters; or where it had reached 'a conclusion so unreasonable that no reasonable authority could ever have come to it'.[6]

Since, however, the exercise of discretionary power is properly subject to substantive, as well as purely procedural, restraints, administrative and political choice may become closely intertwined with legal principle. In this field, therefore, the separation of powers is in practice neither straightforward nor self-evident; but it should not on that account be rejected as futile. On the contrary it forms, as we have seen, an essential pillar of the rule of law. I shall argue that the court's jurisdiction is properly defined in terms of the rights of the applicant for review: the court's primary concern with his interests—as opposed to the wider objectives of the public authority—lies at the heart of the judicial function. The legitimacy of judicial review in a democratic polity, where Parliament is the ultimate judge of the wisdom of government policy, stems from the recognition that 'the doctrine of ministerial responsibility is not in itself an adequate safeguard for the citizen whose rights are affected'.[7]

The court's perspective is rightly and inevitably different from that of the public authority under challenge. The court must determine, not what the wider public interest requires, but whether, in acting to further the public interest, the authority has treated the applicant fairly. Since the constraints of justice or fairness[8] will usually be compatible with a range of courses of action on the part of the public authority, judicial review need not eclipse or subvert the legitimate scope of administrative choice. In an interesting speech, Lord Hailsham denied that the court was substituted for the public bodies entrusted with the relevant powers and discretions. The wide range of authorities and the varied conditions under which they exercised power made it unwise to lay down rules of 'universal validity' for all cases:

> But it is important to remember in every case that the purpose of the remedies is to ensure that the individual is given fair treatment by the authority to which he has been subjected and that it is no part of that purpose to substitute the

[5] Ibid. 228.

[6] Ibid. 234.

[7] *R.* v. *Toohey; ex p. Northern Land Council* (1981) 151 CLR 170, 222 (Mason J.) Cf. *FAI Insurances* v. *Winneke* (1982) 151 CLR 342.

[8] In the present context, these terms are used synonymously: they are not intended to reflect the (Dworkinian) distinction elaborated in Ch. 4, above.

opinion of the judiciary or of individual judges for that of the authority constituted by law to decide the matters in question . . . The purpose of judicial review is to ensure that the individual receives fair treatment, and not to ensure that the authority, after according fair treatment, reaches on a matter which it is authorised or enjoined by law to decide for itself a conclusion which is correct in the eyes of the court.[9]

The preface to Lord Hailsham's dictum is of some significance. Although the court's focus of attention on the applicant's interest marks the distinctive characteristic of judicial review, the requirements of fairness cannot be precisely formulated or even exhaustively defined. They are necessarily dependent on the facts of the particular case. If the justification for judicial review is the need for independent appraisal of administrative action, inspecting its impact on the persons most closely affected, the court's approach must be sensitive to all the circumstances. The jurisdiction cannot be reduced to a series of inflexible rules. Independent moral judgment—unconstrained by rule—fastens on the facts of particular cases in all their complexity; and a jurisdiction devised to secure fairness is necessarily committed to independent moral judgment.[10]

It follows that the distinction between the legality of administrative action and its merits, though fundamental, is in practice one of degree. Although there will often be a wide range of options available to a public authority in exercise of a discretionary power, in some cases its freedom of manœuvre will be much more closely circumscribed. Inevitably, the principles of administrative law must sometimes dictate a particular course of action, when for practical purposes the distinction between legality and merits will disappear. All attempts to deny such possibilities, in expounding legal doctrine, are doomed to failure: the variety and unpredictability of relevant circumstances conspire to make them arbitrary.

It is sometimes claimed, for example, that though the identification of relevant and irrelevant considerations is ultimately a task for the court, the *weight* to be attributed to such considerations must be within the exclusive province of the tribunal or public body to determine. The court will not substitute its own view of the importance of any relevant factor.[11] However, no distinction can be drawn between relevance and weight as a matter of general principle, which can be universally applied. Since the identification of material factors, in the case of a statutory power, must depend on construction of the terms of the grant of power, it must equally be a matter of construction—and so within the legitimate province of the court—whether or not the statute

[9] *Chief Const. of NW Police* v. *Evans* [1982] 3 All ER 141, 143–4.
[10] Cf. M. J. Detmold, *The Unity of Law and Morality* (London, 1984).
[11] e.g. *Pickwell* v. *Camden LBC* [1983] QB 962, 990 (Forbes J.).

permits a range of possible outcomes dependent on varying treatment of the material factors. Logically, it must be a matter of interpreting the requirements of the statute in the context of the issue arising for decision.

If an authority enjoys autonomy to balance the relevant considerations, that must be a conclusion based on interpretation of the statute—not a proposition adopted a priori. In some cases a minister's decision has been quashed where he has attributed undue weight to a factor which was admittedly a relevant one.[12] The courts have rightly recognized that a case may arise in which a minister's policy may be impugned 'on the basis that he was attaching wholly unreasonable weight to a particular factor or, if it was not known what weight he was attaching to what factor, that the results of his policy were such that he must have done so'.[13]

Adoption by an authority of a rigid policy, in such a way as to fetter its discretion, is essentially a form of according improper weight to one factor, or one set of material factors. The extent to which an authority may be permitted to confine its exercise of discretion by adopting a policy must also depend on the circumstances of the case. There can be no general principle dictating the limits of such a policy, such that it should never be more than one relevant factor influencing a tribunal's decision: it is entirely a question of what the particular context requires.[14] Lord Reid was rightly anxious, in *British Oxygen* v. *Board of Trade*,[15] to qualify Bankes LJ's well-known dictum[16] distinguishing between a policy and a rule: 'the circumstances in which discretions are exercised vary enormously and that passage cannot be applied literally in every case . . .'. A ministry which had to deal with a multitude of similar applications for financial assistance could properly evolve a policy so precise that it might well be called a rule. There could be no objection, provided that the ministry did not refuse to listen to representations. If, however, it may sometimes be permissible to apply a policy strictly, with minimal reference to the particular case, there will be cases at the opposite end of the spectrum, where the circumstances arising are so unusual or unexpected or serious as to require that the policy itself be reviewed or, perhaps, abandoned.

Despite the constitutional importance of the division of functions

[12] e.g. *S. Oxfordshire DC* v. *Sec. of State for Environment* [1981] 1 WLR 1092: Woolf J. accepted that a time-expired planning permission might be a relevant factor in determining a fresh application, but thought that it could not plausibly be treated as a 'vitally material consideration'.

[13] *Findlay* v. *Home Secretary* [1984] 3 All ER 801, 813–14 (Sir John Donaldson MR).

[14] Cf. D. J. Galligan, 'The Nature and Function of Policies within Discretionary Power' [1976] PL 332.

[15] [1971] AC 610, 625.

[16] *R.* v. *Port of London Authy., ex p. Kynoch* [1919] 1 KB 176, 184.

between executive and judiciary, then, the distinction between the merits of administrative action and its legality cannot be captured by any simple formulas, mechanically applied. The distinction between appeal and review is necessarily one of degree—depending on the circumstances of the particular case. An exercise of discretion may be rightly held invalid for want of regard to an essential consideration, or for reliance on extraneous factors; and in some cases the weight of certain factors may determine the outcome, leaving minimal discretion to the authority or none. In the case of a statutory power, judicial delimitation of the statutory purposes may leave little or no scope for reasonable disagreement about the administrative action required in all the circumstances of a particular case.

In *Ashby* v. *Minister of Immigration*,[17] Cooke J. stressed that the court could interfere only where the statute expressly or by implication identified a factor as one which must be considered: it was not enough that the minister had ignored a consideration which could properly or reasonably be taken into account. In the context of immigration, a subject linked with foreign policy, the court would be slow to intervene. The force of the general principle, however, does not detract from the significance of the ensuing qualification:

> Nevertheless, even in statutes concerned with immigration and policy in that regard, I would not exclude the possibility that a certain factor might be of such overwhelming or manifest importance that the courts might hold that Parliament could not possibly have meant to allow it to be ignored. Such a situation would shade into the area where no reasonable minister could overlook a certain consideration or reach a certain result.[18]

Cooke J.'s qualification might be thought to apply only in exceptional cases. But it is adequate to demonstrate the dependency of the scope of review on the particular context: the boundary between executive freedom of choice and judicial control is fluid, in the sense that it cannot be drawn by reference to 'neutral' or value-free rules of administrative law. This conclusion is reinforced by reflection on Lord Greene's secondary, or residual, principle of review: 'if a decision on a competent matter is so unreasonable that no reasonable authority could ever have come to it, then the courts can interfere'.[19] Lord Greene denied that the test was what the court itself considered unreasonable; and he thought that to satisfy it would require 'something overwhelming'. Nevertheless, as stated the distinction lacks that substantive content which would enable it to be elaborated as a

[17] [1981] 1 NZLR 222, citing *CREEDNZ* v. *Governor-General* [1981] 1 NZLR 172.

[18] [1981] 1 NZLR 222, 226. Cf. *West Glamorgan CC* v. *Rafferty* [1987] 1 All ER 1005, 1021 (Ralph Gibson LJ).

[19] *Wednesbury* case [1948] 1 KB 223, 230.

matter of legal principle: it is a distinction of degree, dependent on cautious evaluation, and constituting essentially a plea for judicial self-restraint.[20]

Constitutional rights and judicial review

The virtue of judicial restraint must depend on the nature of the illegality alleged. Likewise, the distinction between appeal and review must be an elastic one, permitting more intensive scrutiny of executive action which threatens basic liberties than might be appropriate in other cases. Accordingly, in a case where the factual basis of the decision to deport an applicant for refugee status seemed insecure, the House of Lords intervened to prevent his removal.[21] Lord Bridge expressed the opinion that, within the well-known limitations on the scope of judicial review, the court was 'entitled to subject an administrative decision to the more rigorous examination . . . according to the gravity of the issue which the decision determines'.[22]

Since the individual's right to life was the most fundamental of all human rights, the basis of a decision which was alleged to put the applicant's life at risk called for special scrutiny. Lord Templeman agreed that, 'where the result of a flawed decision may imperil life or liberty a special responsibility lies on the court in the examination of the decision-making process'.[23] Judicial review should clearly reflect the weight attributed to individual rights and liberties in other parts of the common law. Consistent evaluation and protection of individual rights is demanded by our commitment to equality, and forms an important component of the rule of law.[24]

The decision of the House of Lords in *Brind* v. *Home Secretary* seems superficially to contradict such a view.[25] The Home Secretary had issued directives to the IBA and the BBC prohibiting the direct broadcasting of words spoken by representatives of proscribed organizations in Northern Ireland, and of words spoken in support of such organizations. The ban also applied to representatives and supporters of Sinn Fein, Republican Sinn Fein, and the Ulster Defence Association. The directives were issued pursuant to the Broadcasting Act 1981, section 29(3), and clause 13(4) of the BBC's licence and agreement, which permitted the Secretary of State to prohibit the broadcasting of any specified matter or class of matter.

[20] Sir Robin Cooke has called Lord Greene's test a distracting circumlocution: 'The Struggle for Simplicity', 15.

[21] *Bugdaycay* v. *Home Secretary* [1987] 1 All ER 940.

[22] Ibid. 952. [23] Ibid. 956.

[24] Chs. 2 and 7, above. Cf. Jeffrey Jowell and Anthony Lester, 'Beyond *Wednesbury*: Substantive Principles of Administrative Law' [1987] PL 368.

[25] [1991] 1 All ER 720.

The court declined to hold that the minister had acted unlawfully or unreasonably. He had explained his belief that the live appearances of terrorists and their supporters on television and radio caused outrage and fear, and gave a false impression of the strength and legitimacy of terrorism. It remained permissible for the terrorist's words to be reported verbatim; and the directives did not apply to words spoken in the course of parliamentary proceedings, or in support of a candidate at any parliamentary or local election. The House of Lords rejected an argument that the ban was disproportionate to the government's objective—a challenge equivalent to the European test of whether it corresponded to a pressing social need—on the ground that adoption of such a test would blur the distinction between appeal and review. Lord Lowry thought that there could 'be very little room for judges to operate an independent judicial review proportionality doctrine in the space which is left between the conventional judicial review doctrine and the admittedly forbidden appellate approach'.[26]

On closer scrutiny, however, there are signs that the judges were aware of the need to tailor the principles of review to the nature of the claim. Although Lord Ackner stressed the limited character of the court's supervisory jurisdiction, in the absence of a statutory right of appeal, he acknowledged the special need for vigilance: 'In a field which concerns a fundamental human right, namely that of free speech, close scrutiny must be given to the reasons provided as justification for interference with that right.'[27] Lord Bridge denied that the courts were powerless to prevent the infringement of fundamental rights even when administrative discretions were conferred in apparently unlimited terms. The court was 'entitled to start from the premise that any restriction of the right to freedom of expression requires to be justified and that nothing less than an important competing public interest will be sufficient to justify it'.[28] If it fell to the minister to make the primary judgment in the exercise of his discretion, the court could exercise a secondary judgment about the reasonableness of the minister's decision.

The court's reluctance to embrace proportionality as a ground of review seems misplaced. There must inevitably be a spectrum of legitimate judicial responses to administrative acts and decisions. At one end of the spectrum, the court should enquire only whether a measure is so disproportionate in its effect, having regard to the minister's stated purpose, as to be wholly unreasonable. At the other end, more intensive appraisal seems appropriate: the court should ask whether the measure is proportionate in the sense of being no more coercive than is truly justified (in the court's own judgment) to achieve

[26] Ibid. 739. [27] Ibid. 730. [28] Ibid. 723.

the purpose in view. The proximity of the court's approach to the latter position must depend on the nature of the decision under review: a threat to fundamental rights or liberties will justify a more rigorous standard of scrutiny. These conclusions seem implicit in the speeches of Lords Bridge and Ackner, even though not expressly acknowledged.

The House of Lords denied that the Home Secretary must exercise his discretion in accordance with the European Convention on Human Rights on the grounds that the Convention formed no part of domestic law. However, the court's refusal to treat the Convention as a constraint on the proper exercise of discretion is scarcely consistent with its acknowledged status as a guide to statutory construction.[29] If there is a presumption that Parliament has legislated consistently with the United Kingdom's treaty obligations, so that the Convention may be deployed for the purpose of resolving legislative ambiguities, it is hard to see why Parliament should not equally be presumed to intend that a minister's powers, when conferred in broad terms, should be exercised consistently with the Convention. In either case, the presumption must be the conscious product of judicial choice, the reference to parliamentary intent largely a device which pays necessary homage to the dogma of parliamentary sovereignty. In reality, the court embraces the Convention as a source of construction in view of its claims to recognition in political morality.[30] If the United Kingdom government is bound by the Convention in international law, Parliament should clearly legislate in accordance with it and therefore be taken to have done so in the event of doubt. It is open to Parliament to take a different course by the use of clear words. Much the same argument, *mutatis mutandis*, applies to the exercise of executive powers.

An approach which adjusts the degree of judicial scrutiny to the nature of the rights affected by executive action can embrace the Convention just as it can accommodate proportionality as a ground of review. Lord Templeman strikingly assimilated the supervisory jurisdiction to the role of the European Court, concluding on the facts that the interference with freedom of expression was necessary for, and proportionate to, the minister's legitimate objective. He considered the interference with freedom of expression minimal and the minister's reasons compelling. Significantly, he denied that the court was limited to asking whether the Home Secretary had acted irrationally or perversely: the *Wednesbury* principles were an inadequate basis for review.

[29] Lord Ackner, ibid. at 734, thought it 'well settled that the convention may be deployed for the purpose of the resolution of an ambiguity in English primary or subordinate legislation'; citing, *inter alia*, *Salomon* v. *Customs & Excise Commrs.* [1967] 2 QB 116, 143 (Diplock LJ) and *Garland* v. *British Rail Engineering* [1983] 2 AC 751, 771 (Lord Diplock).

[30] See further Ch. 10, below.

He thought that the courts could not 'escape from asking themselves only whether a reasonable Secretary of State, on the material before him, could reasonably conclude that the interference with freedom of expression which he determined to impose was justifiable'.[31]

Lord Templeman accepted that the courts should not substitute their own views for those of the minister, but equated that limitation with the 'margin of appreciation' which the European Court affords the minister in deciding how far a restriction on freedom of speech is justified. If, then, that margin of appreciation leaves somewhat less scope for executive discretion than an ordinary application of the English doctrine of irrationality, a more intensive judicial scrutiny seems demanded in the present context by the threat to a basic constitutional right.

The principle that the level of scrutiny must reflect the nature of the rights or interests at stake, in any particular case, is fully established in respect of the evidential basis of administrative decisions. In appropriate cases, the *Wednesbury* principles of review are displaced by judicial fact-finding on the ground that the existence of certain facts is a condition of the exercise of a discretionary power. Accordingly, in *Khawaja* v. *Home Secretary*,[32] the House of Lords held that the power to deport an 'illegal entrant' under the Immigration Act 1971 applied only to a person who, in the court's view, was truly an illegal entrant. Lord Scarman explained that the *Wednesbury* doctrine of review should not extend to interference with liberty unless Parliament has enacted 'unequivocably' that it should. Drawing an analogy with the court's power to enquire into the truth of the return to a writ of habeas corpus, he invoked the rule that, 'where the exercise of executive power depends on the precedent establishment of an objective fact, the courts will decide whether the requirement has been satisfied'.[33]

Lord Bridge justified a 'robust exercise of the judicial function in safeguarding the citizen's rights'[34] by calling attention to the draconian nature of the power asserted. A claim by the executive to imprison a person without trial, as a prelude to expulsion from the country, could be upheld only if 'clearly justified by the statutory language'. In the absence of explicit statutory provision to the contrary, the court could properly adjust the scope of review to the needs of the circumstances, as Lord Scarman's speech affirmed: 'If Parliament intends to exclude effective judicial review of the exercise of a power in restraint of liberty, it must make its meaning crystal clear.'[35]

[31] [1991] 1 All ER 726.
[32] [1983] 1 All ER 765 (rejecting the earlier decision in *Zamir* v. *Home Secretary* [1980] 2 All ER 768 which adopted a less rigorous standard of review).
[33] [1983] 1 All ER 781.
[34] Ibid. 790.
[35] Ibid. 782.

Procedure and substance

The distinction between the court's supervisory and appellate jurisdictions is sometimes equated with a parallel distinction between procedure and substance. There is some merit in this equation since it captures the nub of the difference between review and appeal; but the distinction between procedure and substance ultimately proves elusive and must therefore be sharply qualified in practice. It cannot provide a wholly convincing account of the separation of powers between government and judicature.

In *Chief Constable of the North Wales Police* v. *Evans,*[36] Lord Brightman repudiated Lord Denning's contention, in the Court of Appeal, that when a probationer police constable was dismissed (or required to resign) he should not only be given a fair hearing but was entitled to a fair and reasonable decision. It was wrong to suppose that the court sat in judgment on the correctness of the decision. Judicial review was concerned, not with the decision itself, but with the decision-making process. Judicial review was 'not an appeal from a decision, but a review of the manner in which the decision was made'.

Admittedly, Lord Brightman qualified this opinion by confining it to cases concerning the rules of natural justice: other considerations arose when a decision was impugned as being unreasonable. But the qualification seems strictly unnecessary, and weakened his assertion of general principle. Undoubtedly, review abstracts from the decision itself to focus on the decision-making process. However, we need a suitably flexible concept of process, which should be understood to include not only the procedural safeguards afforded but also the quality of the deliberation: were relevant considerations properly identified, or was the decision 'vitiated by self-misdirection'?[37] Did the decision enjoy an adequate basis in both law and fact?

Judicial review is primarily concerned with the manner in which a decision was made, rather than with its substance; but in practice the former merges by imperceptible degrees into the lattter. Lord Greene's provision, in *Wednesbury*, for the manifestly unreasonable decision was only an alternative expression, in more overtly substantive form, for the decision flawed by extraneous influences or overlooking relevant considerations. Dismissal of the red-haired teacher because she had red hair would be 'so unreasonable that it might almost be described as being done in bad faith; and, in fact, all these things run into one another'.[38]

[36] [1982] 3 All ER 141, 155.
[37] Ibid.
[38] [1948] 1 KB 223, 229. The red-haired teacher example was provided by Warrington LJ in *Short* v. *Poole Corp.* [1926] Ch 66. (See further Ch. 7, above.)

If, on review, the court finds that an administrative decision is erroneous—as Lord Denning held that Evans was wrongly dismissed—that must be the result of its examination of the deliberative process. It is the same conclusion which would be reached on an appeal but by a different route. There is no usurpation of the role of the public authority: the court will often find the decision-making process flawed, but without forming (or expressing) a view about the correctness of the decision. But where procedural errors have led to a wholly mistaken decision, as in *Evans* itself, it is right that the court should condemn it: the applicant would seem entitled to nothing less as a matter of justice. Just as there is no clear distinction between the relevance of material considerations and their weight, so that the *Wednesbury* principles sometimes dictate a particular result on the merits of a case, the distinction between procedure and substance ultimately dissolves. Whether or not a decision vitiated for breach of natural justice could lawfully be reached after proper procedure will depend on all the circumstances. If a hearing would have demonstrated that charges against a man were quite unfounded, he is entitled in justice to their dismissal.

The interrelation between natural justice and fairness, in the wider, substantive sense, is well illustrated by the decision of the Federal Court of Australia in *Minister for Immigration and Ethnic Affairs* v. *Pochi*.[39] The minister appealed against a decision of the Australian Administrative Appeals Tribunal, which had recommended that his decision to deport an alien be revoked. The respondent alien had been convicted of an offence which permitted the minister to make a deportation order, but it was accepted that, standing alone, the conviction was not sufficient to justify the order. Although there were grounds for suspicion that the respondent had also been involved in illegal drug activities, which might justify his deportation, the evidence did not prove it. The Federal Court dismissed the minister's appeal, Deane J. stating his view that the Tribunal was obliged to require any conduct alleged against the respondent, as a basis for sustaining the deportation order, to be 'established, on the balance of probabilities, to its satisfaction by some rationally probative evidence and not merely raised before it as a matter of suspicion or speculation'.[40]

Although not bound by the rules of evidence or procedure applicable in the courts, it was established that the Tribunal must observe the requirements of natural justice. Deane J. considered American jurisprudence, which stressed that, though not technically a criminal proceeding, deportation was in practice a serious penalty capable of inflicting great hardship.[41] He concluded that United States principles

[39] (1980) 44 FLR 41. [40] Ibid. 62.

[41] *Bridges* v. *Wixon* 326 US 135 (1945); *Woodby* v. *Immig. & Naturaliz. Service* 385 US 276 (1966).

of 'procedural due process' were not limited to purely procedural steps, preliminary to the decision, but extended to control the material on which the decision itself could properly be based. Similarly, natural justice required the Administrative Appeals Tribunal to act on probative evidence. Rules of procedure which governed the making of findings of material fact would otherwise give only a futile illusion of fairness: 'There would be little point in the requirements of natural justice aimed at ensuring a fair hearing by such a tribunal if, in the outcome, the decision maker remained free to make an arbitrary decision.'[42] Principles of procedural due process accordingly secured an important element of substantive fairness.

The court approved Diplock LJ's well-known analysis of natural justice. The requirement that a person exercising quasi-judicial functions should base his decision on evidence meant that it must be based on material which tended logically to show the existence or non-existence of relevant facts:

> It means that he must not spin a coin or consult an astrologer, but he may take into account any material which, as a matter of reason, has some probative value in the sense mentioned. . . . If it is capable of having any probative value, the weight to be attached to it is a matter for the person to whom Parliament has entrusted the responsibility of deciding the issue.[43]

That last sentence, however, needs qualification. We cannot exclude the possibility that, in particular circumstances, the relevant material may establish a state of facts beyond reasonable controversy. In that event, the tribunal or agency may in practice be bound to reach a particular decision. If arbitrary action is excluded by the principles of natural justice, it is also true that what is arbitrary may only be determined, in the last analysis, on the facts of a particular case. It follows that English law is logically committed to a 'substantial evidence' ground of review: a decision made on wholly inadequate evidence should be no more immune from challenge than one which lacks any evidential basis at all. In the analogous field where the court exercises a statutory power of review, the Court of Appeal has already expressed a similar view.[44] Lord Sumner's well-known conclusion that a magistrate who convicted someone of an offence without evidence none the less acted *intra vires* stemmed, it is now widely recognized, from a mistaken conception of jurisdiction.[45] A decision made entirely

[42] (1980) 44 FLR 41, 65–7.

[43] *R.* v. *Deputy Ind. Injuries Commr., ex p. Moore* [1965] 1 QB 456, 487–8. Cf. *Mahon* v. *Air New Zealand* [1984] AC 808, 821 (Lord Diplock).

[44] *Ashbridge Investments* v. *Minister of Housing & Local Govt.* [1965] 1 WLR 1320; *Coleen Properties* v. *Minister of Housing & Local Govt.* [1971] 1 WLR 433. 'Substantial evidence' means 'such relevant evidence as a reasonable mind might accept as adequate to support a conclusion': *Consolidated Edison Co.* v. *Nat. Lab. Rels. Bd.* 305 US 197, 229 (1938).

[45] *R.* v. *Nat Bell Liquors* [1922] AC 128, 151. Cf. *Sec. of State for Education* v. *Tameside*

without evidence has no validity; and decisions which lack any reasonable basis in evidence cannot (rationally) be treated differently.

The ultimate unity of procedure and substance has been explicitly acknowledged by Cooke J. in the Court of Appeal of New Zealand. In *Daganayasi* v. *Minister of Immigration*[46] the court condemned the minister's refusal to prevent the applicant's deportation, following her conviction of an offence of remaining in New Zealand after her entry permit had expired. The minister had a statutory discretion to prevent deportation, which would otherwise ensue, when satisfied that a case presented exceptional circumstances of a humanitarian nature which would render deportation unduly harsh or unjust. The applicant's child suffered from a rare metabolic disease for which he was being treated in New Zealand. Although the minister's medical referee had advised that the boy could safely be moved with his mother to Fiji, it subsequently appeared that the child's specialist clinic had not been fully consulted, and would have given different advice.

The Court of Appeal held that the substance of the medical report should have been disclosed to the applicant or her solicitor so that she was given an opportunity to contradict any unfavourable statement. Cooke J. accepted that the existence of exceptional circumstances of a humanitarian nature could not be determined without regard to the 'general run of immigration cases': to that extent, the government's immigration policy was part of the setting in which the minister was entitled to judge the individual case. The statutory context nevertheless made clear that the individual circumstances were the 'crucial consideration', and the principles of natural justice therefore applied. As an additional ground, however, Cooke J. was prepared to rest on mistake of fact: the applicant should not suffer as a consequence of the minister's failure to take account of relevant considerations which ought to have been within his knowledge. He derived support from Lord Wilberforce's expansive restatement of legal principle:

> If a judgment requires, before it can be made, the existence of some facts, then, although the evaluation of those facts is for the Secretary of State alone, the court must inquire whether those facts exist, and have been taken into account, whether the judgment has been made upon a proper self-direction as to those facts, whether the judgment has not been made upon other facts which ought not to have been taken into account.[47]

In conclusion Cooke J. combined both grounds of review, and adopted a broader perspective. Denying that fairness was confined to

MBC [1977] AC 1014, 1047 (Lord Wilberforce); and see Wade, *Administrative Law*, 6th edn. 319–29; P. P. Craig, *Administrative Law*, 2nd edn. (London, 1989), 265–8.

[46] [1980] 2 NZLR 130.

[47] *Sec. of State for Education* v. *Tameside MBC*, above, n. 45.

procedural matters, he clearly thought it relevant to note the independent merits of the applicant's case. She had 'bona fide and substantial grounds for claiming that the statutory test was fulfilled': to that extent 'she had a legitimate expectation of a favourable decision'.[48] Judging the whole case in perspective—the merits of her request, the procedure adopted, the referee's report, and the grounds of the minister's decision—she had not been fairly treated. What was done in good faith had in practice produced injustice.

The application of a principle of justice or fairness in all the circumstances inevitably circumvents, and ultimately eliminates, narrower rules which unduly circumscribe the court's jurisdiction. There is no general duty on ministers or administrative bodies to give reasons for their decisions; and a failure to give reasons in itself provides no support for a challenge on the ground of irrationality.[49] However, the requirements of justice sometimes demand that reasons be given; and the general rule is therefore subject to qualification in particular cases. In *R.* v. *Secretary of State for Foreign and Commonwealth Affairs, ex parte Everett*,[50] the Court of Appeal reviewed the application of a policy of withholding passports from persons living abroad, for whose arrest warrants had been issued in the United Kingdom. The court denied that the minister was obliged to grant an applicant a hearing in such cases, but held that the reason for refusing a passport should be given and the applicant told that any exceptional circumstances, arising perhaps on compassionate grounds, could be considered.

The case illustrates the close interaction of procedure and substance. A valid policy, prima facie applicable on the facts, must always be subject to exceptions in appropriate cases; and the applicant should therefore be afforded an opportunity to show that his case was indeed exceptional. The requirements of fair procedure were tailored to meet the circumstances of the case. If exceptions could be made to the policy in particular cases on special grounds, its fair implementation required that a passport should not be refused 'in terms which would lead a reasonable applicant to believe that no exceptions were ever made' and that his application had 'inevitably reached the end of the road'.[51]

The 'general rule' that there is no duty to give reasons was further eroded in response to perceived demands of justice by another recent decision of the Court of Appeal.[52] Natural justice required the Civil Service Appeal Board to give reasons for its assessment of compensation due to a prison officer, who had been unfairly dismissed. The board

[48] [1980] 2 NZLR 130, 145.

[49] *Padfield* v. *Minister of Agriculture* [1968] AC 997; *Lonrho* v. *Sec. of State for Trade* [1989] 2 All ER 609, 620 (Lord Keith).

[50] [1989] 1 All ER 655.

[51] Ibid. 660 (Nicholls LJ).

[52] *R.* v. *Civil Service Appeal Board* [1991] 4 All ER 310.

was a 'judicial body' which determined questions of right arising between the Crown and its employees, and no appeal lay from its decisions. In the absence of reasons for the determination, it was impossible for the applicant to judge its legality and know whether he should seek judicial review. The court rejected an argument that the absence of reasons did not involve a question of procedure: the form of the board's award was itself an aspect of procedure and accordingly subject to the requirements of natural justice.[53]

Legitimate expectations and administrative justice

The doctrine of legitimate expectations is today a primary vehicle for the implementation of the duty to act fairly. Indeed, the doctrine largely restates the general principle of justice or fairness in more technical form. It lends an air of analytical precision to what otherwise seems to lack determinacy and objectivity; but such pretensions prove to be mainly illusory on closer examination. Strictly speaking, it seems mistaken to identify the expectation with the right accorded: rather the citizen's expectation grounds a concomitant public law right, usually the right to a particular procedure but sometimes entailing substantive protection—a right to a certain action or decision, subject only to compelling contrary public interest.

In *Schmidt* v. *Home Secretary*,[54] Lord Denning, who first invoked the doctrine, stated that an alien who had been allowed to enter the United Kingdom for a limited period would have a right to make representations before being deported within that period. His expectation of being allowed to remain for the permitted time grounded a right to procedural fairness. Similarly, in *O'Reilly* v. *Mackman*,[55] a prisoner was held entitled to challenge the legality of a prison board's disciplinary award, whereby he forfeited remission of sentence, alleging a breach of natural justice. He had a legitimate expectation that he would be granted the maximum remission of sentence for good behaviour, based on his knowledge of the general practice; and he could invoke the rules of natural justice in support of that expectation.

Acknowledgement of a person's legitimate expectation largely states a conclusion about what justice requires in the circumstances of his case. His right is the converse of the public authority's duty to treat him fairly. There is no simple correspondence between right and (actual) expectation: an expectation of some substantive benefit (for example, continuing leave to reside for the permitted period) may bring only procedural safeguards against its withdrawal. The nature and strength of the expectation are therefore *reasons* for the court's

[53] Ibid. 322 (McCowan LJ). [54] [1969] 2 Ch 149. [55] [1983] 2 AC 237.

intervention to secure administrative justice; but the quality of that intervention is a function of all the circumstances of the case. Moreover, the expectation may only be notional: its recognition then states a conclusion about what justice requires, rather than asserting that anyone's subjective aspirations were truly justified. The applicants in *Schmidt* and *O'Reilly* were surely entitled to natural justice whatever expectations they actually entertained regarding their likely treatment.

It would be better to reserve the term 'legitimate expectation' for cases where the court insists that the expectation (actual or notional) be completely vindicated. The right will then mirror the expectation precisely and constitute a coherent concept within the wider entitlement to fair treatment. (Of course, recognition of the right will still depend on the requirements of justice in all the circumstances.) This will apply where the executive is held bound to honour an express undertaking as to the kind of hearing it will afford the applicant,[56] or where a person's expectation of some particular benefit is held to constitute a legal entitlement, subject only to countervailing reasons of public interest of adequate strength.[57] It will also apply where the expectation is based on settled practice, which the court enforces as a rule unless cogent reasons are given for changes in the practice. In the *GCHQ* case,[58] Lord Fraser held that the civil servants at GCHQ enjoyed a legitimate expectation that they would be consulted before their trade union membership rights were withdrawn—subject to overriding requirements of national security—because prior consultation had been the invariable practice when conditions of service were to be altered significantly. In Lord Diplock's analysis, by contrast, the expectation is merely a ground for invoking natural justice: the civil servants had a legitimate expectation that they would continue to enjoy the benefits of trade union membership. The right accorded is a right to consultation, the expectation of continued trade union membership merely a (strong) reason for imposing the duty to apply a fair procedure.[59]

The content of the duty to act fairly always depends on the circumstances of the particular case, and the scope of the doctrine of legitimate expectation is therefore largely a matter of semantic convenience. Nevertheless, in its narrower guise the doctrine highlights the importance of settled practices and expectations in determining standards of just treatment. By deferring to existing or customary arrangements the court permits those subject to its jurisdiction to determine their own rules. In its appeal to the standards and values shared by litigants—

[56] Cf. *A.-G. of Hong Kong* v. *Ng Yuen Shiu* [1983] 2 AC 629.
[57] Cf. *ex p. Khan*, below.
[58] *Council of Civil Service Unions* v. *Minister for Civil Service* [1984] 3 All ER 935, 944.
[59] Ibid. 952; see Patrick Elias, 'Legitimate Expectation and Judicial Review', in J. L. Jowell and D. Oliver (eds.) *New Directions in Judicial Review* (London, 1988).

citizen and public authority—the law can reflect the practice of government, and share responsibility for shaping the constraints which justice or fairness recommends. Although, therefore, the requirements of justice are ultimately a matter of personal moral judgment, and cannot be entirely reduced to clear-cut rules or even collective agreement, the court can often appeal to settled practices and established expectations as a basis for decision.[60]

If no sharp distinction can ultimately be drawn between procedure and substance, legitimate expectations may fall anywhere within a wide spectrum. The strongest may require a decision of the public body in the applicant's favour, subject only to countervailing considerations of public interest of especial weight. Accordingly, in *R.* v. *Home Secretary, ex parte Kahn*,[61] the Court of Appeal held that the minister had acted unfairly in refusing to permit the entry of a child from Pakistan, whom a Pakistani couple settled in England wished to adopt. A Home Office circular, issued to interested parties, had specified the conditions which must be satisfied before such permission would be granted; and it could not then be refused on other grounds. The couple appeared to satisfy the conditions specified. The minister was entitled to change his policy in respect of future cases, but he could not resile from his stated criteria in the present case without at least giving the applicant an appropriate hearing. Parker LJ attributed a strength to the procedural constraints which gives them a substantive dimension: a new policy could only be implemented *vis-à-vis* a recipient of such a circular after a 'full and serious consideration' whether there was 'some overriding public interest' which justified a 'departure from the procedures stated'.[62] It is clear from the context that the judge included the minister's stated criteria within the term 'procedures'; and procedure and substance cannot readily be distinguished.

The *Kahn* decision was followed in a subsequent case,[63] where Taylor J. observed that while the doctrine of legitimate expectation imposed a duty to act fairly, it was not confined to the right to be heard. No such right could be claimed because the case concerned (necessarily secret) interception of the applicant's telephone calls. The minister was nevertheless held bound to comply with published criteria governing the issue of warrants for such interception: 'in a case where *ex hypothesi* there is no right to be heard, it may be thought the more important to fair dealing that a promise or undertaking given by a minister as to how he will proceed should be kept'.[64]

Sometimes the strength of a prima facie case for favourable treatment

[60] Cf. F. A. Hayek, *Law, Legislation and Liberty* (London, 1982), i, ch. 4, esp. 85–8.
[61] [1985] 1 All ER 40. [62] Ibid. 48.
[63] *R.* v. *Home Secretary, ex p. Ruddock* [1987] 2 All ER 518.
[64] Ibid. 531.

will permit an adverse decision by the public body only after careful review of the circumstances, and only in the light of any representations made by the party most closely affected. A presumption operates in his favour. The *Daganayasi* case provides a good example, where the strength of the expectation warranting judicial protection was grounded in the importance of the private interest in question.[65] At the other end of a spectrum which encompasses both procedure and substance, there will be cases which merit only minimal procedural safeguards, or none. The obligation to act fairly will not necessarily entail any duty to grant a hearing.

In *ex parte Madden*,[66] the court held that the Police Complaints Board had unlawfully fettered its statutory discretion by regarding itself as bound to comply with the minister's guidance—to which it was only required to 'have regard'—and had wrongly refused to recommend the institution of disciplinary proceedings against police officers on the sole grounds that the Director of Public Prosecutions had decided that there was insufficient evidence to bring criminal charges. McNeill J. considered that, as complainants disappointed by the Board's failure properly to consider their complaints, the applicants had *locus standi* even though they had no right to make representations: 'they clearly came within the ambit of the statutory duty'.[67] The case further illustrates the interconnection between procedure and substance. McNeill J. held that the 'fettered discretion' rule was 'strictly only a label for one aspect of natural justice'. That rule applied even if the complainants had no right to be heard by the Board: the 'great web' of natural justice could not be artificially 'canalised', but was 'infinite in its capacity to cater for infinitely varying factual situations and decision-making procedures'.[68]

In some cases, the context may deny the legitimacy of any relevant private expectation. The most significant individual interest, standing alone, cannot normally override or qualify a general policy, which is otherwise lawful, if the result would be to render the policy wholly ineffectual by defeating its fundamental objectives. That view seemed to be the basis of the decision in *Findlay* v. *Home Secretary*,[69] where the House of Lords upheld the minister's power to introduce a change of policy concerning the grant of parole to prisoners in specified categories. The new policy, which was intended to ensure that prisoners convicted of serious offences served the greater part of their sentences, dashed the applicants' hopes of early release from prison.

[65] [1980] 2 NZLR 130 (considered above).
[66] *R.* v. *Police Complaints Board, ex p. Madden* [1983] 2 All ER 353.
[67] Ibid. 372, citing *IRC* v. *Nat. Fed. of Self-Employed* [1982] AC 617, 630–2 (considered below, Ch. 9).
[68] Ibid. 373. [69] [1985] AC 318.

Two of the applicants were serving life sentences, and had anticipated the grant of parole much earlier than would now be likely. Lord Scarman none the less rejected a submission that they should be excepted from the new policy. In the context of the relevant legislative provisions, the most that a convicted prisoner could expect was that his case would be examined individually in the light of whatever policy the Secretary of State saw fit to adopt. Any other view would entail the conclusion that the statutory discretion could 'in some cases be restricted so as to hamper, or even to prevent changes of policy'.[70] Although the court's reasoning is open to serious criticism, the decision may perhaps be defended on the ground that public confidence could only be restored if the new policy were applied at once to all prisoners falling within the relevant categories.[71]

That is the only realistic ground of distinction from *Khan*,[72] where the applicant was entitled to be excepted from the change of policy. It was unlikely that any favourable treatment accorded to Khan, as a result of the government's previous assurances, would have had any deleterious consequences for public policy; and there remained the proviso that his aspirations could be thwarted if a public interest of overriding importance so demanded. The recognition or denial of legitimate expectations—the determination of what justice requires—inevitably expresses an accommodation between private and public interest. The greater the danger that changes of policy will be seriously impeded, the weaker will be the claim to be exempted from those changes. The contest between the two relevant principles—that government promises should be honoured but that changes of policy in the public interest should not be prevented—can only be satisfactorily resolved in the circumstances of individual cases. Any other solution would necessarily be arbitrary: the respective weights of those principles will obviously vary greatly from case to case.

A similar balancing of claims, or weighing of principles, was evidently envisaged by Lord Denning in another well-known decision concerned with the duty to act fairly. In the *Liverpool Taxi Fleet Operators* case,[73] the Liverpool Corporation sought to renege on an undertaking, given to the Operators' Association, that it would not increase the number of taxi cab licences above three hundred until proposed legislation had been enacted. The Court of Appeal held that the Corporation was obliged to afford the Association a proper hearing before it could lawfully repudiate its promise. Lord Denning considered that the authority was bound to honour the undertaking so long as that was

70 Ibid. 388.
71 See further Ch. 7, above.
72 [1985] 1 All ER 40 (considered above).
73 *R.* v. *Liverpool Corp., ex p. Liverpool Taxi Fleet Op. Assoc.* [1972] 2 QB 299.

compatible with its public duty: the new policy could be justified only by an overriding public interest.[74]

It follows that there is no necessary clash between the principles of administrative justice—or duty to act fairly—and the rule that a public authority cannot be prevented by estoppel from the exercise of its discretionary powers in the public interest.[75] Quite apart from the importance of using public powers for the public good, it is generally thought that a public body should not be permitted to enlarge its powers, in violation of the *ultra vires* principle, by making binding representations about their scope. At least within the ambit of the agency's lawful authority, however, good reasons of pressing public policy should be demonstrated before undertakings or assurances are repudiated. Action taken in disregard of such assurances, unless properly justified, constitutes an abuse of power. And any justification must reflect the weights of the public and private interests involved. As Lord Denning explained in the *Laker Airways* case,[76] the Crown could not be estopped from using its powers in the proper exercise of its duty to act for the public good:

> It can, however, be estopped when it is not properly exercising its powers, but is misusing them; and it does misuse them if it exercises them in circumstances which work injustice or unfairness to the individual without any countervailing benefit to the public.[77]

The interdependence of procedure and substance does not imply that the court's view of the merits should weaken its insistence on fair procedure. It is dangerous to assume that a failure to hear representations, or grant a hearing, could have made no difference to the outcome. A seemingly undeserving case may turn out, on closer inspection, to possess merits not readily apparent.[78] Nevertheless, there may be exceptional cases where it can be safely concluded that a hearing would have served no useful purpose;[79] or where a breach of natural justice may be thought sufficiently repaired by a properly conducted appeal.[80] The inadequacy of an 'instrumentalist' theory of

[74] Ibid. 308. Cf. C. F. Forsyth, 'The Provenance and Protection of Legitimate Expectations' [1988] (L) 238.

[75] See e.g. *Howell* v. *Falmouth Boat Construction Co.* [1951] AC 837; and generally Craig, *Administrative Law*, ch. 16.

[76] *Laker Airways* v. *Dept. of Trade* [1977] QB 643 (see further Chs. 9 and 10, below).

[77] Ibid. 707. See also *HYV* v. *Price Commission* [1976] ICR 170, 185 (dictum by Lord Denning approved in *Preston* v. *IRC* [1985] 1 AC 835, 865 (Lord Templeman)).

[78] [Cf. *John* v. *Rees* [1970] Ch. 345, 402 (Megarry J.).]

[79] Cf. *Malloch* v. *Aberdeen Corp.* [1971] 1 WLR 1578, 1595 (Lord Wilberforce), 1600 (Lord Simon). See further D.H. Clark, 'Natural Justice: Substance and Shadow' [1975] PL 27.

[80] *Calvin* v. *Carr* [1980] AC 574; *Reid* v. *Rowley* [1977] 2 NZLR 472.

natural justice was noticed in Chapter 2. Procedural fairness is not required solely in the interests of efficient administration: it acknowledges a person's autonomy and dignity. But the ingredients of fair procedure cannot be determined wholly in isolation from the circumstances of the particular case.[81]

A public authority must normally be free to determine the balance of public and private interests; but within a range of decisions which could properly be made if the private interest affected is given adequate weight. And that means adequate weight in view of the nature of the case as a whole—including its general merits, in the sense of whether, all things considered, the applicant has been fairly treated. In *Daganayasi*, then, it was the fundamental importance to the whole life of the applicant, and the health of her child, together with the strength of the prima facie case in her favour—when the facts were properly elicited—which required (at minimum) a rigorous standard of procedure before rejecting her claim.

In striking contrast, the English Court of Appeal dismissed the claim of an Italian national, convicted of serious offences, that the minister had acted in breach of natural justice in ordering his deportation without disclosing to him all the information on which the order was based.[82] The court accepted that the minister should normally disclose information of which the criminal was unaware and which was thought to be persuasive; but the strength of the case for deportation made any such disclosure unnecessary in all the circumstances. Lord Denning explained that whether the offender should be given an opportunity to comment on any new material depended on its likely impact: if an adverse factor might turn the scale against him, he should be invited to deal with it. In all the circumstances, however, such material could have made no difference to the outcome.

Templeman LJ even considered that the minister would have failed in his duty if he had *not* ordered deportation. None the less, he rightly repudiated the idea that a convicted criminal, against whom a recommendation had been made for deportation, was at the Home Secretary's mercy, who might perform an act of grace in declining to make an order. The applicant had rights and the minister had responsibilities. The applicant was entitled to make representations and to be fairly treated: the minister was obliged to treat the applicant fairly in determining whether the public interest required his deportation.[83]

[81] For an analogy, see *R.* v. *Central Criminal Court, ex p. Randle* [1992] 1 All ER 370, 393: suspicion that no good defence existed to a criminal prosecution relevant to . . . process.

[82] *R.* v. *Home Secretary, ex p. Santillo* [1981] 2 All ER 897.

[83] Ibid. 922.

It follows from the present discussion that English law cannot deny the principle of proportionality, whether or not it is regarded primarily as an aspect of *Wednesbury* unreasonableness. Although the rigour of the court's scrutiny should vary according to the nature of the administrative action in question, there can be no escape from the need to review the balance between public and private interests. The extension of legitimate expectations from procedure to substance involves the court in examining the *justifiability* of administrative action in all the circumstances of particular cases, even if there is often room for legitimate (and lawful) differences of view between court and agency.

Parker LJ's strictures in *Khan* would provide little comfort to a disappointed applicant if the existence of an 'overriding public interest', sufficient to justify departure from published criteria for decision, were a matter entirely for the executive. It is a reasonable inference that such an overriding interest must be established by government to the court's satisfaction before an expectation, otherwise entitled to protection, may lawfully be overridden. The requirement of proportionality is clearly part of the governing principle of fairness. In *Daganayasi*, the court's assessment of the applicant's case, against the background of the government's immigration policy, involved the conclusion that the harshness of her treatment was wholly disproportionate to any benefits which might accrue to the public interest.

Judicial discretion and the rule of law

I have argued that the principle of fairness resists familiar modes of classification. It cannot be confined to procedural matters because in practice procedure ultimately merges with substance. Legitimate expectations may place a wide range of constraints on administrative action—of varying degrees of strength—depending on the nature of particular cases. And we have rejected any straightforward division between the merits of executive decisions and their legality: an important distinction in legal theory, its practical application must be sensitive to context. In some circumstances, where rights of constitutional importance are affected, or where legitimate expectations have special strength, an appraisal of administrative action may properly have an intensity which sharply reduces the gulf between appeal and review.

The challenge which judicial review seems (superficially) to pose to the division of powers between government and the courts can now be clearly identified. The distinction between principle and policy, which we suggested lay at the root of the separation of powers,[84] may appear

[84] Ch. 3, above.

to be threatened by a jurisdiction whose inherently elastic nature can hardly be denied. If the right to fair treatment is necessarily sensitive to context and circumstance, how can the court be understood to determine rights as opposed to policies? The principle of fairness might be thought sufficiently flexible to encompass considerations of general policy, and to carry the danger of converting administrative discretion into judicial discretion, allowing the courts to usurp the role of other public agencies in deciding how public policy should be applied in particular instances.

It would be a mistake to belittle the nature of this challenge since it strikes at the core of a liberal conception of the rule of law. It questions the extent to which a democratic polity, incorporating the basic elements of the separation of powers, can consistently permit considerations of justice and fairness—inevitably sensitive to particular circumstances—to govern the exercise of political power. It has been doubted whether contemporary developments in administrative law are truly compatible with the distinction between law and government, on which the idea of the rule of law depends.[85] The extension of natural justice to a broader sphere of administrative action, through the very flexible concept of procedural fairness, has been thought inconsistent with the independent application of rules of law, unaffected by considerations of policy. Application of a general principle whose content depends on context has been alleged to undermine the autonomy and generality of the legal order.[86]

Moreover, Herbert Wechsler emphasized the dangers of *ad hoc* adjudication in his well-known critique of judicial review in the American Supreme Court.[87] He rightly denied that review could be withheld on grounds of expediency—the Court could not abdicate its constitutional functions because government actions entailed value choices. But he identified principled reasoning with legal analysis of general application: 'A principled decision . . . is one that rests on reasons with respect to all the issues in the case, reasons that in their generality and their neutrality transcend any immediate result that is involved.'[88]

Although it is true that untutored judicial discretion must present as great a threat to freedom and autonomy as uncontrolled executive discretion, we should not confuse the rule of law, properly elaborated, with its positivist interpretation. The danger of judicial discretion is

[85] Ibid.
[86] Martin Loughlin, 'Procedural Fairness: A Study of the Crisis in Administrative Law Theory' (1978) 28 U. of Toronto LJ 215.
[87] 'Toward Neutral Principles of Constitutional Law' (1959) 73 Harv. LR 1.
[88] Ibid. 19.

easily exaggerated if we overlook the role of legal principles, which underlie and justify more concrete rules, or forget the dependence of legal principle on ordinary moral reasoning.[89] Judicial discretion is not reduced to arbitrary will merely because it is governed by principles rather than rules; and judicial review does not become indistinguishable from appeal merely because the application of principles is inherently subject to the nuances of fact and circumstance. Nor is the principle of fairness an invitation to judicial policy-making. It affords a court no choice with respect to the general distribution of resources or the overall objectives of the exercise of power. The fairness principle focuses on a particular instance of the *application* of policy and its impact on the individual applicant before the court. It both permits and requires the court to strike down an administrative act or decision where, after according proper deference to the general purposes of the public agency, it finds none the less that the particular applicant has been unjustly treated.

Perhaps the distinction between deciding public policy in general and its application in particular cases is sometimes elusive. Where, in accordance with the separation of powers, administration is conducted within the scope of general rules, as opposed to legislation directed at particular persons, the distinction should normally serve well enough for practical purposes. But where public policy is deliberately formulated so as to place special burdens on identifiable persons, legality itself may require an intensified judicial response—in defence of the individual freedom and autonomy which we understand the rule of law to serve. The scope of judicial review should be related to the evident risk of abuse of power.

It was the legitimacy of bringing policy considerations directly to bear on a matter involving an individual's liberty which lay at the heart of the difference of opinion in *South Australia* v. *O'Shea*.[90] After conviction of offences of indecent assault, O'Shea had been declared to be incapable of exercising proper control over his sexual instincts and ordered to be detained during Her Majesty's pleasure. Although the Parole Board had recommended O'Shea's release on licence, after two medical practitioners had duly reported him fit to be released, the Governor in Council declined to act on the recommendation. A majority of the Australian High Court held that the requirements of natural justice were satisfied by the offender's opportunity to address the Board: he was not entitled to a further hearing before the Governor in

[89] See generally Chs. 1–6, above.

[90] (1987) 163 CLR 378. For discussion of the case, in relation to questions of justiciability, see M. C. Harris, 'The Courts and the Cabinet: "Unfastening the Buckle"?' [1989] PL 251. (See further Ch. 9, below.)

Council made the final decision. The High Court had previously held that the rules of natural justice were applicable to decisions of the Governor in Council, in appropriate cases.[91] In the present case, however, the Governor in Council had confirmed a political decision made by the cabinet, and it was not shown that that decision had been influenced by fresh material relating to the offender personally on which he had had no opportunity to comment.

Wilson and Toohey JJ. attached some importance to the fact that in South Australia all matters on which advice was to be tendered to the Governor by the Executive Council were submitted to the cabinet for decision. An earlier decision which applied the rules of natural justice to the Governor in Council could be distinguished on that ground.[92] Mason CJ, however, observed that while the cabinet was primarily concerned with 'political, economic and social concerns', it was sometimes required to decide questions which were 'much more closely related to justice to the individual'.[93] There was no reason to deny the existence of a duty to act fairly in a matter which turned 'on considerations peculiar to the individual'.

The court none the less accepted the view that the cabinet could in this instance take account of matters of public interest: it could advise against releasing an offender even where all the medical opinions supported a recommendation by the Board for release. The likely reaction of the community to the offender's release might be a relevant consideration. The legislative scheme therefore reflected the duality which Lord Scarman had identified in his analysis of the English system of parole in *Re Findlay*.[94] The operative decision was reserved to a political body, which would accept responsibility for an assessment of the public interest. It did not follow that the requirements of natural justice were therefore inappropriate: Mason CJ thought that the offender should be heard in relation to those aspects of policy which were 'closely related to the circumstances of the particular case', even if he could not address 'matters of high level general policy'.[95] It was not, however, contended that O'Shea had been deprived of a suitably unrestricted hearing before the Parole Board.

Deane J.'s dissenting judgment, asserting a breach of natural justice, reflected his reluctance to accept the relevance of general policy considerations. Rejecting any analogy with the *Findlay* case, Deane J.

[91] *FAI Insurances* v. *Winneke* (1982) 151 CLR 342.

[92] *Winneke* (previous note): no question of cabinet consideration had been involved in that case, which was analogous to one where a minister was the recipient of the statutory power: 163 CLR 404.

[93] (1987) 163 CLR 378, 387.

[94] [1985] AC 318 (considered above).

[95] 163 CLR 389.

observed that any appropriate punitive sentence which might have been imposed on the offender would have expired, and the nature of his continued detention therefore gave rise to grave concern: it was 'manifest that a discretionary power to reject, on "political" grounds such as the state of public opinion, independent medical advice and the recommendation of a specialist board for the release on licence of a person detained under such an order lies ill with acceptable minimum safeguards of human liberty and dignity'.[96]

The cabinet was not entitled, in Deane J.'s view, to reject the Board's recommendation without giving the offender an opportunity to be heard. O'Shea had a legitimate expectation of release on licence once the appropriate tribunal, acting on independent medical advice, had recommended it. The rules of procedural fairness applied whenever an administrative decision directly affected the 'rights, interests, status, or legitimate expectations of another in his individual capacity'. In cases where there was room for doubt about whether a person was sufficiently affected in his individual capacity to invoke their protection, the path to decision lay 'essentially in the ordinary processes of legal reasoning by analogy and deduction, enlightened, in an appropriate case, by considerations of public policy and common sense'.[97]

It was, of course, a reasonable conclusion to draw from the statutory scheme that the Parliament had intended the operative decision concerning release to be governed ultimately by general considerations of policy. However, it is always a question of judgment how far such an apparent intention should be respected. Talk of 'intention' here is in any case largely a metaphor: we are interested in making good sense of the statute, but always within the wider context of *constitutional* democracy.[98] Where, for example, a decision was entrusted to the Governor in Council which depended principally on considerations relating to the individual rather than issues of general policy, the court would not readily discern an intention to exclude any duty of fairness: the principle of fairness would be implied (or imported) to protect the individual concerned.[99]

The Chief Justice adverted to the 'obvious tension between protection of individual liberty, which is deeply rooted in common law tradition and democratic ideals, and the need to protect the community from offenders . . . likely to constitute a menace or risk to society'.[100] He noted that the statutory regime represented a 'marked departure' from the 'basic principle' of the common law that the severity of an

[96] Ibid. 414. [97] Ibid. 417–18. [98] See Chs. 2–4, above.

[99] Cf. Mason CJ at 163 CLR 386, citing *Winneke*: in that situation it was 'not to be supposed that Parliament intended to exclude a duty to act fairly by vesting authority . . . in the Governor in Council'. (Cf. Gibbs CJ at 151 CLR 349.)

[100] Ibid. 385.

offender's sentence should match the gravity of his crime. He thought that provision for subsequent judicial review of the offender's capacity to control his sexual instincts would afford greater protection, but was willing to assume that Parliament considered that 'political assessment of the public interest' was to be preferred to judicial decision.[101]

The real question is whether that assumption was legitimate. Deane J.'s analysis proceeded from his view of the 'extraordinary' power conferred on the South Australian cabinet. If the Parliament chose to entrust such a power to a political body, that body must make the adjustments to its proceedings necessary to ensure procedural fairness. A legislative provision would need to be 'quite unambiguous' before it should be construed as removing the right to a hearing. The difference of view in the High Court was not, then, the product of any inherent conceptual difficulty in distinguishing considerations of legal principle from those of public policy. It reflected a division of opinion about the weight to be attributed in the circumstances to the value of individual liberty. Deane J.'s approach was a rational attempt to counteract (or moderate) what he viewed as the 'tyranny of arbitrary detention'.[102]

Brennan J.'s scepticism, by contrast, betrayed a readier acceptance of preventive detention. He complained that the notion of 'legitimate expectation' was misleading: it tended to direct attention to the merits of the particular decision rather than to the 'character of the interests which any exercise of power' was apt to affect.[103] But that distinction—by denying the importance of the Board's recommendation in favour of release—simply assumed the narrow conception of the offender's right which Brennan J. wished to advance. Recognition of a prima facie right to release, based on that recommendation and grounded in a stronger commitment to personal freedom, would make it harder to distinguish the nature of the offender's interest from the merits of his case.

The objection, then, that contemporary developments in administrative law have undermined the rule of law must be rejected. The increasing dependence of judicial decisions on general principles, broadly expressed and tailored to the demands of individual cases, has on the contrary strengthened the rule of law by acknowledging the importance of rights—an anti-utilitarian notion, whose force as a brake on public policy necessarily depends on all the circumstances.[104] Evidence of disagreement about the scope or weight of individual rights reveals no theoretical weakness in the structure of judicial review: it is a familiar feature of ordinary legal and moral reasoning.

[101] Ibid. 390. [102] Ibid. 420. [103] Ibid. 411.

[104] For the anti-utilitarian sense of rights, see Ronald Dworkin, *Taking Rights Seriously* (London, 1977), chs. 4 and 7; *A Matter of Principle* (Oxford, 1985), ch. 17. For a comparable analysis, which emphasizes the court's role in protecting fundamental liberties, see P. W. Hogg, 'Judicial Review: How Much Do We Need?' (1974) 20 McGill LJ 157.

Finally, we should note that the test of justice or fairness—though inherently value-laden—is none the less mainly negative in application. The court does not primarily determine what justice demands, but whether instead an administrative decision has been *unfairly* applied, or caused *injustice*. The separation of functions between courts and government thereby generates distinct approaches to particular instances. The court's perspective is rightly different from that of the agency responsible for public policy; and its review jurisdiction imposes constraints on the exercise of power, in the interests of parties adversely affected, without directing its overall objectives.

We have noticed F. A. Hayek's defence of abstract general rules as the proper interpretation of justice, an account based on the role of private law. If we now embrace the idea of rights against the state, as a suitable counterweight to the necessary deployment of public power in the general interest, we can apply his insights in a different context. Hayek argued, in respect of the rules of just conduct which he took to be the primary content of law, that in the absence of positive criteria of justice, we could fall back on negative criteria which show what is unjust.[105] Rules of just conduct were determined by a persistent effort to bring consistency into the system of rules inherited by each generation.

Hayek drew an analogy with scientific progress: we could approach truth, or justice, by persistently eliminating the false or unjust, though never certain of achieving ultimate truth or justice. If legal positivism had succeeded in demonstrating that there were no 'objective' criteria of justice, it did not follow that justice was solely a matter of will or emotion. If it were, the whole basis of liberalism would indeed have disappeared. Hayek argued, as Dworkin has argued, that, working within a body of existing rules, solutions to problems of justice may be discovered, not arbitrarily decreed. We were 'bound by justice to develop the existing system in a particular way' and could demonstrate that we 'must alter particular rules in a certain way to eliminate injustice'.[106] It should equally be possible to reject unfair administrative decisions without stipulating precisely what fairness requires; and the risk of arbitrariness may be reduced by judicial deference to standards of fairness widely shared, and reflected in settled practices and reasonable expectations. Hayek's discussion amounts to a defence of the common law method of decision; and the general principles of judicial review are today an integral part of the common law.

[105] *Law, Legislation and Liberty*, ii. 38–44.
[106] Ibid. 44.

9
The Limits of Public Law

> The judiciary cannot, as the legislature may, avoid a measure because it approaches the confines of the constitution. We cannot pass it by because it is doubtful. With whatever doubts, with whatever difficulties, a case may be attended, we must decide it, if it be brought before us. We have no more right to decline the exercise of jurisdiction which is given, than to usurp that which is not given. The one or the other would be a treason to the constitution.
>
> *Cohens* v. *Virginia* 19 US (6 Wheat.) 264, 404 (1821), *per* Marshall CJ.

The House of Lords' attempt, in the *GCHQ* case,[1] to mark out areas of government as inherently unsuitable for legal control threatened to deprive that decision of significant content. Having recognized that judicial review could not in principle be limited to statutory powers, but should extend to control the exercise of 'prerogative' powers, the court proceeded to deny jurisdiction in the case of almost all the established prerogatives. It is only if the royal prerogative is deemed to encompass all the non-statutory powers of central government—abandoning the traditional feature that they be unique to the Crown—that anything remains on which the newly extended jurisdiction can fasten.[2]

According to Lord Roskill, large areas of central government activity were not subject to supervision. Prerogative powers which related to the making of treaties, the defence of the realm, the prerogative of mercy, the grant of honours, the dissolution of Parliament, the appointment of ministers, and other unspecified matters were not susceptible to judicial review because 'their nature and subject-matter' was such as 'not to be amenable to the judicial process'. The courts were not the place 'wherein to determine whether a treaty should be concluded or the armed forces disposed in a particular manner or Parliament dissolved on one date rather than another'.[3]

It is, however, a fundamental part of the theory of the rule of law that, at least within the realm, all aspects of government are conducted within the law; and it follows that the possibility of judicial review, in

[1] *Council of Civil Service Unions* v. *Minister for the Civil Service* [1984] 3 All ER 935.

[2] Cf. H. W. R. Wade, 'Procedure and Prerogative in Public Law' (1985) 101 LQR 180, at 197–8.

[3] [1984] 3 All ER 935, 956.

appropriate cases, should not lightly be excluded. Though the doctrine of 'act of state' raises a legitimate issue of justiciability—amounting to a denial of the court's jurisdiction—it is confined to government action taken abroad (and perhaps even then inapplicable to a British citizen).[4] It is fundamental to the rule of law that no such plea exists in respect of executive action within the United Kingdom, as Lord Camden affirmed in 1765: 'With respect to the argument of state necessity . . . the common law does not understand that kind of reasoning . . .'[5]

The mark of justiciability in public law is provided by what we have defined as the essential characteristic of judicial review—the court's concern with the rights and interests of the applicant, as opposed to the merits of the relevant action or decision as a matter of public policy. Justiciability should in principle be the correlative of jurisdiction, and determined by the ordinary principles of administrative law. An applicant is entitled to invoke the remedy of judicial review whenever his rights in public law are threatened or infringed by a public authority. And these rights include not only 'constitutional' rights—his rights to the basic liberties, such as freedom of speech—but the general right to fair treatment at the hands of the state. I have suggested that the latter right cannot be entirely reduced to a series of narrower rights, in the sense that someone is the beneficiary only of a set of particular rules, but that fairness—or justice—is ultimately a matter of moral judgment in all the circumstances.[6]

It does not follow that the court's jurisdiction is infinitely elastic, so that the frontier between law and policy can be manipulated at will, according to judicial inclination. If there is a plausible, well-grounded complaint of injustice, alleging that the applicant's interests have not been fairly taken into account by a public authority—where his interests are specially affected—judicial review should normally be available. When the court rejects a claim because it concerns a field of public responsibility, or department of government, which is inherently immune from legal control, it acts arbitrarily—failing to apply ordinary legal principles to the circumstances of the particular case.

It is an important corollary of the idea that administrative justice must be tailored to the circumstances of individual cases, that the legitimacy of judicial review can only be determined in the light of particular facts. Notions of justiciability—if they introduce abstract or formal restrictions on legal control—overlook this point, seeking to isolate areas of public power for special treatment on the basis of their general characteristics. It is not possible to segregate governmental functions, making some wholly impervious to judicial supervision,

[4] *Walker* v. *Baird* [1892] AC 491; *Nissan* v. *A.-G.* [1970] AC 179.
[5] *Entick* v. *Carrington* (1765) 19 State Trials 1029, 107J.
[6] Ch. 8, above.

without causing injustice in particular cases. Theories of justiciability which fasten on broad categories of executive powers, according to their general character or function, therefore undermine the rule of law by challenging the *raison d'être* of judicial review.

If judicial review is to serve its purpose as a safeguard for the rights and interests of those most directly affected by government action, it cannot be accepted that certain powers should be wholly immune from scrutiny. In *Laker Airways* v. *Department of Trade*,[7] the Court of Appeal rejected an argument that exercise of the treaty-making power could not be reviewed. If it could be shown that the power had been abused, invoking the 'prerogative' to circumvent the statutory scheme for the grant and revocation of licences by the Civil Aviation Authority, the court could intervene. If the minister wished to prevent Laker's *Skytrain* service from operating, as a result of a change of aviation policy, he could only invoke the limited powers granted by the Civil Aviation Act. The Act was held to govern the rights and duties of British citizens in all aspects of civil aviation, and the minister could not be allowed to render Laker's licence useless by withdrawing their designation under the Bermuda Agreement between the United Kingdom and the USA, on which Laker's right to fly into New York depended.

Although Roskill and Lawton LJJ held that the prerogative power had been curtailed by statute, Lord Denning was willing to review its exercise more directly. He asserted that, 'when discretionary powers are entrusted to the executive by the prerogative—in pursuance of the treaty-making power—the courts can examine the exercise of them so as to see that they are not used improperly or mistakenly'.[8] On either analysis, exercise of the prerogative was subject to supervision to forestall an abuse of power and in defence of the applicant's right to fair treatment.

The court's approach in *GCHQ* overlooks the essential nature of judicial review as a remedy for the protection of an applicant's rights or interests. It is only if he alleges that executive action constitutes an abuse of power in relation to him—that his personal interests were insufficiently respected in the balance of decision—that there is any warrant for judicial intervention. The executive is subject to the supervisory jurisdiction on grounds of legal principle, which fasten on the applicant's right to fair treatment, rather than political policy; and there is no need to distinguish in this respect between prerogative and statutory powers.

Dumbutshena CJ, in the Zimbabwe Supreme Court, appeared to recognize this point.[9] He thought that there were few executive

[7] [1977] 2 All ER 182.

[8] Ibid. 193. Cf. *Preston* v. *IRC* [1985] 2 All ER 327, 339–40 (Lord Templeman).

[9] *Patriotic Front—ZAPU* v. *Minister of Justice* 1986(1) SA 532.

prerogatives—in Zimbabwe the creatures of constitutional conventions and practices—which ousted the jurisdiction of the court, which was properly invoked 'whenever the exercise of executive prerogatives affects the private rights, interests and legitimate expectations of the subjects or citizens'.[10] Admittedly, the Chief Justice mentioned a number of prerogative powers which would not be subject to review, on the ground that they were 'not matters in which the court is qualified to substitute its own judgment for the judgment and opinion of those responsible for the conduct of foreign affairs'.[11] But that qualification only restated the ordinary grounds of review. The substitution of judicial for ministerial judgment on questions of government policy would subvert the court's jurisdiction, whatever the nature of the power under review. When substitution of judgment occurs—when review most closely resembles an appeal—it must be in defence of important individual rights or interests, in the context of the government's legitimate pursuit of its own ambitions for public policy.[12]

In the *Everett* case,[13] considered above, the Court of Appeal firmly repudiated a submission that the court should not review the withdrawal of a passport, or the refusal to grant or renew one. Literal adherence to the *GCHQ* doctrine of justiciability would preclude judicial scrutiny of an aspect of foreign affairs; and the grant of a passport involves a request in the name of the Queen to a foreign power to afford its holder free passage and protection. Taylor LJ's robust reply to that contention demonstrated the proper basis of judicial review. The grant or refusal of a passport did not involve matters of high policy: 'It is a matter of administrative decision, affecting the rights of individuals and their freedom of travel . . . The ready issue of a passport is a normal expectation of every citizen, unless there is good reason for making him an exception.'[14]

If, then, public law is understood primarily as protecting individual rights—including the right to fair treatment—against excess or abuse of power, there is little room for any independent theory of justiciability: the only question is whether the applicant can establish the violation of right which he alleges. If the requirement of justiciability means only that the court should not appraise the wisdom of matters of 'high policy'—the major part of the doctrine of 'act of state'—there can be no objection: that much is already implicit in the basic theory of judicial review. In many instances, no doubt, the exercise of a non-statutory power will be invulnerable to review because its operation threatens no rights. In practice, a statutory discretion will often be more readily susceptible to review:

[10] Ibid. 539. [11] Ibid. 541. [12] See Ch. 8, above.
[13] [1989] 1 All ER 655; Ch. 8 above. [14] Ibid. 660.

Its exercise very often affects the right of the citizen; there may be a duty to exercise the discretion one way or another, the discretion may be precisely limited in scope; it may be conferred for a specific or an ascertainable purpose; and it will be exercisable by reference to criteria or considerations express or implied. The prerogative powers lack some or all of these characteristics.[15]

Justiciability and national security

The courts are not normally the place to question the conclusion of treaties or the disposition of the armed forces because usually these activities do not place special burdens on particular citizens. But there can be no principle against judicial review where executive action, even in the sphere of 'high policy', violates an applicant's right to fair treatment, where his interests are unjustly sacrificed (given wholly inadequate weight) to the general welfare. Wilson J.'s judgment in the Canadian Supreme Court, in *Operation Dismantle* v. *The Queen*,[16] provides a helpful analogy. The plaintiffs alleged that a government decision to permit the United States government to test cruise missiles in Canada violated their rights to life, liberty, and security of the person under section 7 of the Charter of Rights and Freedoms. They argued that the decision made Canada more likely to be a target for nuclear attack, but the court unanimously affirmed the decision of the Federal Court of Appeal that the statement of claim disclosed no reasonable cause of action. Wilson J., with whom the other judges agreed in this respect, thought that if asked, the court was obliged to decide whether the rights of citizens had been violated: it could not relinquish its jurisdiction on the ground that the issue was non-justiciable or raised a 'political question'.[17]

Wilson J. held that the government's decision did not give rise to any violation or threatened violation of the plaintiffs' rights. The government could properly take steps to protect the community against external threats to its collective well-being, even if such steps incidentally increased the risk to the lives or security of some or all of its citizens. The Charter dealt with direct impingement by government on the life, liberty, and personal security of the individual citizen: it had no application to matters of foreign relations where the actions of government were not directed at any member of the political community. A declaration of war, for example, would increase the risk to citizens of death or injury but would not thereby violate the Charter. If, however, government action taken in the interests of national defence posed a special threat to some specific segment of the population (for example,

[15] *R.* v. *Toohey, ex p. Northern Land Council* (1981) 151 CLR 170, 219 (Mason J., who also thought, however, that prerogative powers were 'in some instances by reason of their very nature not susceptible to judicial review').

[16] [1985] 1 SCR 441.

[17] Ibid. 464–74.

if the cruise missiles were tested using live warheads), Charter rights might then be infringed.

The judgment usefully illustrates the distributive character of individual rights in public law: they ground claims by citizens to fair treatment or to particular benefits, which are enforceable against the government or the state. They will usually constrain pursuit of the collective welfare in the interests of specified classes of citizen—or, in the case of constitutional rights, in order to protect fundamental interests of every citizen. A well-reasoned approach to judicial review of executive action, based on recognition of rights in public law, can dispense with any independent requirement of justiciability. Wilson J. denied that the Canadian Supreme Court sat in judgment on the wisdom of the government's defence policy: it was occupied with the 'totally different question' of whether the policy violated the appellants' rights under section 7 of the Charter.

In *Chandler* v. *DPP*,[18] the House of Lords held that the court could not receive evidence, at the trial of an offence under the Official Secrets Act 1911, section 1, that it would be in the national interest to abandon nuclear weapons. The defendants, who had sought to immobilize an airfield used by nuclear bombers, were in practice unable to deny that they had acted for a 'purpose prejudicial to the safety or interests of the state'. The disposition of the armed forces was a matter committed to the authority of the Crown, and the 'state' meant the 'organised community' or the 'organs of government of a national community'.[19] However, Lord Devlin acknowledged the court's jurisdiction to correct any abuse of a prerogative power, even in the context of national defence. The existence of a prejudicial purpose was ultimately a question of fact, to be proved beyond reasonable doubt, and was not simply a matter of ministerial stipulation. It could be presumed that government policy in relation to defence reflected the 'interests of the state'; but the presumption was not irrefutable:

> The servants of the Crown, like other men animated by the highest motives, are capable of formulating a policy *ad hoc* so as to prevent the citizen from doing something that the Crown does not want him to do. It is the duty of the courts to be alert now as they have always been to prevent abuse of the prerogative.[20]

While, therefore, the court could not make its own determination of what public policy required, it could nevertheless examine a charge of bad faith which would undermine a government determination. That conclusion was surely entailed by the defendant's right to an acquittal in the absence of adequate proof of his guilt. If the court refrained from enquiry into the merits of government policy, it did so, not because a

[18] [1964] AC 763. [19] Ibid. 790, 807. [20] Ibid. 811.

minister's assertion was conclusive, but because that was not the question which it had to decide.[21]

Lord Devlin's analysis was approved and adopted by Lord Scarman in the *GCHQ* case.[22] He explained that national security was a matter to be considered by the court in the context of the case before it; and that, though it must observe 'limits dictated by law and common sense', the court did 'not abdicate its judicial function'. Lord Parker's famous dictum, in *The Zamora*,[23] that 'those who are responsible for the national security must be the sole judges of what the national security requires', should not be understood to deny the court's duty to act on evidence. Lord Parker had meant only that the court could not substitute its own opinion for that of the responsible minister. The Crown's claim to requisition a cargo of copper, then in the custody of the Prize Court, was in fact rejected: no sufficient evidence had been presented to support the right to requisition. Lord Devlin's analysis did not, of course, receive unanimous acclaim in *GCHQ*: having committed themselves to an independent doctrine of justiciability, Lords Diplock and Roskill were naturally unable (or unwilling) to appreciate its merits.

The House of Lords decided, in *GCHQ*, that the demands of national security, supported by affidavit, justified the government's failure to consult the civil service trade unions before the union membership rights of GCHQ employees were withdrawn. The civil servants' rights to fair treatment were therefore overridden in the wider public interest. Although the respective weights to be accorded the public and private interests were—primarily—for the government, and not the courts, to determine, it was necessary for the Crown to establish by evidence that the decision had truly been based on grounds of national security. Despite Lord Diplock's claim that the requirements of national security were '*par excellence* a non-justiciable question',[24] the court actually decided that a plausible justification for the course of action taken had been presented. And in principle even the balance of interests—between the requirements of fairness and the demands of security—must ultimately be open to judicial review. Lord Scarman surely stated the general principle correctly:

> Once the factual basis is established by evidence so that the court is satisfied that the interest of national security is a relevant factor to be considered in the determination of the case, the court will accept the opinion of the Crown or its responsible officer as to what is required to meet it, unless it is possible to show that the opinion was one which no reasonable minister advising the Crown could in the circumstances reasonably have held.[25]

[21] Ibid. 810. [22] [1984] 3 All ER 935, 947–8. [23] [1916] 2 AC 77, 107.

[24] [1984] 3 All ER 952. Lord Roskill reached 'clear conclusions' about the requirements of national security in the circumstances of the case: ibid. 960.

[25] Ibid. 948.

Lord Scarman here assimilates the position to the treatment of claims of public interest immunity, which affords a helpful parallel. There must be appropriate deference to the government's view of the public interest; but what is appropriate will depend on the context: the court does not abdicate its responsibility to protect legal rights. In *Burmah Oil* v. *Bank of England*,[26] Lord Scarman acknowledged that a court would be 'slow to question' a minister's judgment, where he averred that disclosure of the contents of a document might cause 'the nation or the public service a grave injury'. The court would not even inspect the document unless some indication existed of a lack of good faith or error of judgment or error of law on the part of the minister. In that sense, the minister's claim could be said to be conclusive. 'It is, however, for the judge to determine whether the minister's opinion is to be treated as conclusive.' In all cases, the court retained 'its power to inspect or to balance the injury to the public service against the risk of injustice, before reaching its decision'.[27]

The High Court of Australia has reached similar conclusions.[28] Stephen J. considered that in 'cases of defence secrets, matters of diplomacy or affairs of government at the highest level, it will often appear readily enough that the balance of public interest is against disclosure'.[29] He denied, however, that an immunity claim was ever conclusive, even if in some areas the court's acceptance 'may often be no more than a matter of form'. A claim had 'no automatic operation': it always remained the court's function to determine its outcome. The reasons for secrecy—however cogent—must always be balanced against the requirements of justice. Documents concerned with national security or defence are, in principle, treated only as constituents of a wider class of government documents—'state papers' in Gibbs ACJ's formulation—which enjoys only qualified protection, depending *inter alia* on the contents of particular documents:

> It is in all cases the duty of the court, and not the privilege of the executive government, to decide whether a document will be produced or may be withheld. The court must decide which aspect of the public interest predominates, or in other words whether the public interest which requires that the document should not be produced outweighs the public interest that a court of justice in performing its functions should not be denied access to relevant evidence.[30]

The necessity for judicial assessment of immunity claims, however grounded, is particularly plain in the context of criminal proceedings. It is inconceivable that a plea of public interest immunity, based on considerations of national security, could properly serve to deprive a

[26] [1979] 3 All ER 700. [27] Ibid. 732–3.
[28] *Sankey* v. *Whitlam* (1978) 142 CLR 1.
[29] Ibid. 58–9. [30] Ibid. 38–9 (Gibbs ACJ); see also ibid. 43.

defendant of documents needed for his defence in the absence of judicial scrutiny—even if ministers were obliged to resist disclosure in the national interest.[31] If the withholding of documents would seriously undermine the defendant's ability to establish his innocence, a plea of immunity could be accepted only at the price of repudiating the accused's fundamental right to a fair trial. The Court of Appeal has rightly insisted on the necessity for judicial determination of any immunity asserted by the prosecution: if the Crown were unwilling to submit to the court's power of review, the prosecution would have to be abandoned.[32]

Lord Diplock's view that matters of national security were non-justiciable was prayed in aid of the decision in *ex parte Cheblak*,[33] in which the Court of Appeal affirmed the legality of decisions during the Gulf war to detain and deport a Lebanese citizen, who enjoyed indefinite leave to remain in the United Kingdom, on the ground that his deportation would be 'conducive to the public good for reasons of national security'.[34] A bare recital of the statutory grounds for deportation was later amplified by a statement that the man was known to have links with an (unspecified) organization which the Home Secretary believed might take terrorist action against Western targets. The court rejected a complaint, on grounds of natural justice, that more detailed reasons were needed to enable the man to answer the allegation that his presence posed a threat to national security. An affidavit sworn on behalf of the Home Secretary stated that no further details could be disclosed without unacceptable risk to security; and the court therefore acted without evidence of the real nature or strength of the case for deportation.

It is sometimes necessary to deny a litigant access to the information he needs in support of his case. It is not inconsistent with the rule of law to acknowledge that the administration of justice must sometimes defer to other weighty public interests, as the doctrine of public interest immunity attests.[35] Nevertheless, it is hard to justify the refusal to provide adequate information on which the court depends to review

[31] Public interest immunity cannot be waived: see *Air Canada* v. *Secretary of State for Trade* [1983] 1 All ER 910, 925 (Lord Scarman). The application of the immunity to criminal proceedings was affirmed in *R.* v. *Governor of Brixton Prison, ex p. Osman (No. 1)* [1992] 1 All ER 108.

[32] *Ward* [1993] 2 A11 ER 577. It is settled law that the privilege protecting sources of information which lead to the detection of crime cannot prevail if production of the evidence is necessary to the defence case: *Marks* v. *Beyfus* (1890) 25 QBD 494; *Rogers* v. *Home Secretary* [1973] AC 388, 407 (Lord Simon); *ex p. Osman (No.1)* [1992] 1 All ER 108, 118.

[33] [1991] 2 All ER 319.

[34] See Immigration Act 1971, ss. 3(5), 15(3).

[35] The analogy is made by Lord Denning MR and Geoffrey Lane LJ in *R.* v. *Home Secretary, ex p. Hosenball* [1977] 3 All ER 452, 460, 462, 463–4.

the grounds of a man's detention and deportation. The decision can only be defended, if at all, on the basis that an alternative safeguard existed which could be more suitably invoked in all the circumstances than judicial review. The applicant was entitled to make representations to a non-statutory panel of advisers; and the Home Secretary would be accountable to Parliament in the event of his failure to accept their advice. The advisers would be possessed of the information and evidence which the court had been denied.[36]

Moreover, the court's jurisdiction was not excluded in principle, even if in practice there would be no intervention unless the applicant could provide evidence that the minister had acted in bad faith. And the court's jurisdiction extended to decisions of the advisory panel, if it acted unfairly within the inevitable constraints of its sensitive task. The requirements of natural justice or fairness necessarily depend on the context. As Geoffrey Lane LJ expressed the point, in a similar case: 'What is fair cannot be decided in a vacuum: it has to be determined against the whole background of any particular case.'[37]

Public law rights and remedial discretion

Theories of justiciability have an obvious affinity with the American 'political question' doctrine, whose credentials have been questioned by a number of writers. Louis Henkin, for example, urged the need to distinguish between the courts' ordinary respect for the 'political' domain, where the political branches of government act within their constitutional powers, and a 'pure theory' of justiciability, under which the courts would forgo their ordinary function of judicial review of constitutionality.[38] He argued that the considerations distilled from older cases by Brennan J. in *Baker* v. *Carr*[39] were elements of the ordinary respect which the courts showed to the substantive decisions of the political branches. In deciding that the recognition of a foreign government, or of the sovereignty of a foreign country over a particular territory, were matters within the President's constitutional authority, the court did not decline jurisdiction, but exercised it.

Henkin interpreted Frankfurter J.'s well-known dissent in *Baker* v. *Carr*, in which he rejected the plaintiffs' complaint against 'legislative

[36] Lord Donaldson MR described the panel's approach as an 'independent quasi-judicial scrutiny'—an inquisitorial rather than adversarial procedure. For comparison with Canadian provisions, see Ian Leigh, 'The Gulf War Deportations and the Courts' [1991] PL 331.

[37] *Ex p. Hosenball* (n. 35 above), 464.

[38] 'Is there a "Political Question" Doctrine?' (1976) 85 Yale LJ 597. Cf. Michael E. Tigar, 'Judicial Power, the Political Question Doctrine, and Foreign Relations' (1970) 17 UCLA LR 1135.

[39] 369 US 186, 217 (1962).

malapportionment', as a denial that the Constitution accorded the right alleged: the equal protection clause did not require 'one man—one vote'. That was certainly Harlan J.'s spproach:

> Once one cuts through the thicket of discussion devoted to 'jurisdiction', 'standing', 'justiciability' and 'political question', there emerges a straightforward issue which . . . is determinative of this case. Does the complaint disclose a violation of a federal constitutional right . . . ?'[40]

He held that the plaintiffs' allegations failed to show an infringement by Tennessee of any rights assured by the Fourteenth Amendment. It was fundamentally a question of the relation between legislative policy and constitutional rights: as long as there existed a possible rational legislative policy for retaining an existing apportionment, such a decision could not be said to 'breach the bulwark against arbitrariness and caprice that the Fourteenth Amendment affords'.[41]

Henkin argued that the considerations of judicial prudence and wisdom, stressed by Alexander Bickel as grounds for restricting judicial review,[42] played a legitimate role in the form of established principles permitting a court to withhold relief for 'want of equity'. Any theory of public law rights must accommodate some flexibility in the grant of remedies. The analogy with private law rights is here at its weakest, since administrative law remedies, whose effect may reach far beyond the individual applicant, cannot be easily assimilated to those afforded by private law.

The basic principle in English law was affirmed by Lord Diplock, rejecting an argument that an employer, who had chosen not to co-operate with the Advisory, Conciliation, and Arbitration Service, should be denied a remedy in respect of unlawful action by the Service: 'where a statutory authority has acted *ultra vires* any person who would be affected by its act if it were valid is normally entitled *ex debito justiciae* to have it set aside . . . '.[43] The court might, however, refuse a remedy on grounds of laches or of acquiescence, or possibly where the *ultra vires* act had been induced by unlawful acts of the complainant himself.

In exceptional cases, the demands of public administration may even deny an applicant a remedy for unlawful action without any fault on his part. In *R.* v. *Monopolies and Mergers Commission, ex parte Argyll Group,*[44] the need for finality and certainty in the financial markets, and the nature of the applicant's own interest in the proceedings, were

[40] Ibid. 330–1.
[41] Ibid. 337.
[42] 'The Supreme Court, 1960 Term—Foreword: The Passive Virtues' (1961) 75 Harv. LR 40.
[43] *Grunwick Processing* v. *ACAS* [1978] 1 All ER 338, 364.
[44] [1986] 2 All ER 257. See also *R* v. *Panel on Take-overs & Mergers, ex p.Datafin* [1987] QB 815.

invoked to justify the court's decision to refuse relief against an *ultra vires* decision by the Commission. The interests of the applicant in intervening in the reference to the Commission of a rival company's takeover bid, though legitimate, had to be evaluated in the light of the purpose of the administrative process under the Fair Trading Act 1973.

Recognition of the need for remedial discretion, however, does not import a doctrine of justiciability under a different name. The withholding of a remedy should be an exceptional course, in which the nature and strength of the applicant's interest is fully taken into account. There is no denial of the court's jurisdiction. A flexible law of remedies offers a legitimate means of reconciling the applicant's grievance with the necessary demands of administration. Unlike a 'pure' doctrine of justiciability, it does not forestall judicial scrutiny on the dubious grounds of the class or category of action or decision impugned.[45]

It is unnecessary, and illegitimate, for the courts to decline jurisdiction on grounds of public policy, or even because there may be alternative remedies which apply. In a judgment subsequently approved by the House of Lords, Shaw LJ argued forcefully that a prisoner was entitled to seek review of an unjust decision by a prison board of visitors, even if he could also petition the Secretary of State in respect of a grievance, under the Prison Rules.[46] He firmly repudiated the view of the Divisional Court that a board of visitors should be immune from judicial supervision. The court should not close its doors against those alleging unfair treatment, even if prison discipline might be undermined by prisoners advancing capricious complaints. The nature of any relief accorded would inevitably be a matter of judicial discretion: 'Public policy or expediency as well as merits may well be factors to consider and they may influence the answer to any application for relief; but to deny jurisdiction on the ground of expediency seems . . . to be tantamount to abdicating a primary function of the judiciary.'[47] He thought that there could be no external fetters on the exercise of the court's jurisdiction to control the proceedings of bodies with the power to affect the rights or liberties or status of the citizen: the only necessary restraint was internal—the court's discretion in respect of remedy.

In *Leech* v. *Parkhurst Prison Deputy Governor*,[48] the House of Lords applied Shaw LJ's reasoning to the decisions of prison governors, adjudicating on charges of disciplinary offences. The exercise of such powers affected the rights and legitimate expectations of prisoners, and a governor was obliged to comply with the rules of natural justice. The minister's statutory duty to ensure compliance with prison legislation

[45] Cf. Henkin, 'Is there a "Political Question" Doctrine', 622.
[46] *R.* v. *Hull Prison Bd. of Visitors, ex p. St Germain* [1979] 1 All ER 701, 713–19.
[47] Ibid. 717.
[48] [1988] 1 All ER 485.

did not remove the possibility of judicial review by rendering it unnecessary:

Just as the allegation of a wrong of a kind recognised as remedial by private law is sufficient to found the court's ordinary jurisdiction, so the allegation of a wrong of a kind recognised as remediable by public law is sufficient to found jurisdiction in judicial review. In either case jurisdiction is only ousted by clear express statutory provision.[49]

It could not be predicted with confidence what the effects of enlarging the scope of judicial review would be: the possibility that the governor's authority would be undermined, and the task of maintaining discipline seriously aggravated, could not be excluded. None the less, the court could not properly refuse jurisdiction on these general grounds of public policy: legal principle supported the prisoner's right of recourse to the courts. If the consequences for prison discipline were truly deleterious, it was for Parliament, not the courts, to deny judicial review.[50] Parliament had not taken that course, when enacting the Prison Act 1952, and it could not be right for the court, 'in the name of pragmatism or of public policy', to usurp the legislative function and, 'by denying in practice a jurisdiction which cannot be denied in logic . . . impose in the case of a particular class of decision-maker an administrative substitute for the supervision of the court'.[51]

Legality of administration and individual rights

The legitimacy of judicial review derives, we have argued, from the desirability of protecting individual interests and expectations which, though supported by considerations of political principle, are vulnerable to abuse in the ordinary course of politics and administration. However, the coherence of a rights-based view of public law naturally depends on the nature and integrity of the rights enforced. Matters of right must be distinguishable from public policy or public interest. If the whole field of government is reduced, by specious reasoning, to questions of individual right, the distinction between principle and policy collapses, and adjudication cannot be distinguished from ordinary politics. Every public authority has the duty of observing the law in the conduct of its activities, and in determining the scope of its own jurisdiction; but it hardly follows that every official action or decision is appropriately subject to judicial review.

Nor will it necessarily involve any question of right. No one has a general *right* that public bodies observe the law, because such an assertion of right is meaningless. A citizen naturally expects a public authority conscientiously to perform its duties; but his *right* is a right to

49 Ibid. 496 (Lord Bridge). 50 Ibid. 501 (Lord Bridge). 51 Ibid. 511 (Lord Oliver).

fair treatment in its dealings with him. If he thinks that its policies or practices are contrary to the public interest, or contradict the intentions of Parliament—as he conceives them—he must have recourse to the political process. The courts can provide a substitute for political control only at the price of destroying the legitimacy and coherence of judicial review.

The limits of the judicial function in the field of public law were properly reflected in the House of Lords' decision in *Gouriet* v. *Union of Post Office Workers*.[52] Gouriet was denied relief against a threatened boycott of mail to and from South Africa because, merely as a member of the public, he had no *locus standi*. Gouriet did not allege the infringement of any private right; and a 'public right'—really a misnomer for the public interest[53]—could only be asserted by the Attorney-General, intervening as an officer of the Crown. The Post Office Act 1953 made it a criminal offence to delay a postal packet in the course of transmission; but the notion that Gouriet could proceed on the basis of his interest in the law being enforced was firmly rejected. As Lord Wilberforce explained, the statement that the plaintiff had a 'right' to the services of the Post Office could be accepted only if the term were 'given a reduced meaning not extending to a right capable of direct enforcement by the civil law'.[54]

Much of the court's reasoning, however, must be treated with reserve. The Attorney-General had refused his consent to a relator action, and a comparison was made with his various powers in relation to criminal proceedings. His discretion to stop a prosecution by entering a *nolle prosequi*, or to direct the institution of a prosecution, was held to be invulnerable to review; and to permit review of his refusal of consent to a relator action—as Lord Denning had been willing to do in the Court of Appeal[55]—would be to countenance an illegitimate exception to the general rule.[56] However, the 'general rule' against review now appears anachronistic in the light of *GCHQ*, and the abandonment of previous restrictions on supervision of the prerogative. The existence of unreviewable discretions is in obvious conflict with the principle of the rule of law.[57]

If exercise of the discretion with regard to relator actions is not

[52] [1977] 3 All ER 70.

[53] The term 'public right', though commonly used in this context, is a misnomer in the sense that a right, if genuine, is essentially an individual interest protected even at the cost of the public interest: it acknowledges a claim *against* the majority or the general welfare based on the special importance of the individual interest it asserts. (See generally Ronald Dworkin, *Taking Rights Seriously*, London, 1977).

[54] [1977] 3 All ER 70, 79. [55] [1977] 1 All ER 715–16.

[56] See [1977] 3 All ER 70, 88–9 (Viscount Dilhorne).

[57] Cf. Barry Hough, 'Judicial Review where the Attorney-General Refuses to Act: Time for a Change' (1988) 8 *Legal Studies* 189.

susceptible to review, it must be because there is, *ex hypothesi*, no one whose rights entitle him to complain. The court's denial of jurisdiction in *Gouriet*, superficially asserting a principle of non-justiciability, should be interpreted as an analysis of legal rights. Lord Wilberforce denied the court's competence to act on its own judgment, in the absence of the Attorney-General's request:

> The decisions to be made as to the public interest are not such as courts are fitted or equipped to make. The very fact that . . . decisions are of the type to attract political criticism and controversy, shows that they are outside the range of discretionary problems which the courts can resolve.[58]

But political controversy cannot always be avoided; and its undesirability cannot provide a reliable indication of the limits of the judicial function.

In the absence of any threat to Gouriet's rights, however, the court had no jurisdiction to intervene. As in general the Attorney-General had no power to interfere with the assertion of private rights, so in general no private individual could represent the public 'in the assertion of public rights'.[59] A plaintiff who alleges that an abuse of power has inflicted special damage on himself enjoys *locus standi*: he seeks to enforce his rights in public law, rather than vindicate his personal view of the public interest. Questions of public interest or public policy are not properly the subject of judicial concern, except in so far as they impinge on the rights of the parties before the court. As Lord Wilberforce added, in explanation of his doctrine of restraint: 'Judges are equipped to find legal rights and administer, on well-known principles, discretionary remedies. These matters are widely outside those areas.'[60]

It may be doubted whether denial of review of the decision to prosecute, as a matter of administrative law, is consistent in principle with the inherent jurisdiction of a criminal court to prevent an abuse of process.[61] The court's intervention would have a similar justification in each case: it is hard to defend the legality of a decision to prosecute if the proceedings, once commenced, would constitute an abuse of the process of the court. Even if the institution of proceedings is generally beyond judicial control, in deference to the strict separation of functions between judge and prosecutor, the defendant's right to a fair trial demands a power to stop a prosecution which is oppressive or vexatious or undertaken for illegitimate reasons.

In the context of a truly oppressive prosecution, which the judge considered an abuse of the process of criminal justice, the right to a fair trial would be rendered meaningless. *Ex hypothesi*, the judge could not discharge his duty to ensure, by appropriate rulings on law, procedure, and evidence, that he presided over what he believed to be a fair trial.

[58] [1977] 3 All ER 84. [59] [1977] 3 All ER 80 (Lord Wilberforce).
[60] Ibid. 84. [61] See Ch. 10, below.

He cannot say that it is legally fair, if morally unfair. A judgment of fairness is necessarily a moral judgment, to which all relevant circumstances (including those concerning the initiation of the proceedings) are inevitably pertinent. In *Connelly* v. *DPP*, Lord Devlin acknowledged the inherent jurisdiction as a concomitant of the overriding principle of fairness, affirming the 'inescapable duty to secure fair treatment for those who come or are brought before' the courts.[62] To turn a blind eye to the decision to prosecute, whatever the circumstances, would be to abdicate both legal and moral responsibility. 'The courts cannot contemplate for a moment the transference to the executive of the responsibility for seeing that the process of law is not abused.'[63]

In *Atkinson* v. *United States Government*,[64] the House of Lords attempted to sever legal from moral responsibility by denying the power of a magistrate to refuse to commit a prisoner, under the Extradition Act 1870, on the ground that a committal would be oppressive or contrary to natural justice. Though there were cases in which it would be clearly contrary to natural justice to surrender a man, where a conviction of an extradition crime had been obtained abroad by improper means, the only remedy lay in the ultimate discretion of the secretary of state. *Atkinson* was bravely distinguished, however, in a judgment of the Divisional Court, which affirmed a magistrate's power to halt committal proceedings on the ground of abuse of process.[65] Although the power should be only rarely exercised, it was not confined to instances of improper conduct on the part of the prosecuting authorities. An elapse of time for which they were not to blame might be sufficient to deny the accused a fair trial, so that any proceedings would constitute an abuse of process. It is the defendant's right to a fair trial which compels the court's supervision.[66]

The inherent jurisdiction to dismiss a charge for abuse of process affords a powerful and persuasive analogy in the present context. The prospect of forming a judgment about the fairness of a prosecution in all the circumstances led Lord Hodson, in *Connelly*, to repudiate the inherent jurisdiction altogether. He was disconcerted by the inevitably subjective quality of a judgment of fairness: different judges would take different views about what was unfair in the context of each case.[67] The likelihood of conflicting judgments cannot, however, be a legitimate reason for denying the court's jurisdiction. The judge is not

[62] [1964] AC 1254, 1354. [63] Ibid. [64] [1971] AC 197.

[65] *R.* v. *Telford JJ., ex p. Badhan* [1991] 2 All ER 854.

[66] In *Attorney General's Reference (No. 1 of 1990)* [1992] 3 All ER 169 the Court of Appeal accepted 'reluctantly' that proceedings might be stayed on the grounds of prejudice resulting from delay, even without fault on the part of the prosecution, as it was 'not possible to anticipate in advance all the infinitely variable circumstances' which might arise in the future.

[67] See also *DPP* v. *Humphrys* [1977] AC 1, 26 (Viscount Dilhorne).

enabled to intervene merely because he thinks that, as a matter of policy, the prosecution should not have been brought.[68] It must be a case of real injustice, sufficiently gross and exceptional to justify the court's interference. If that is a difficult, necessarily personal judgment, it is nevertheless one which cannot ultimately be shirked.

Lord Devlin's remarks were approved by the New Zealand Court of Appeal in *Moevao* v. *Department of Labour*.[69] Richardson J. acknowledged the need for judicial circumspection in view of the 'twin problems of an absence of objectively ascertainable standards and the relative unfamiliarity of the courts with the weighing of all the considerations which may bear on the exercise of prosecutorial responsibility'.[70] The sensitivity, complexity, and subjectivity of the judicial task did not, then, justify a blanket refusal of jurisdiction on grounds of non-justiciability. The court instead rightly appreciated the need for wise judgment, in which the accused's right to a fair trial would be interpreted in the light of all the circumstances. Woodhouse J. also noticed Lord Hodson's anxiety, but rejected his conclusions. The question of whether or not a prosecution was oppressive had to be answered, 'like any serious issue for the courts, by some kind of judicial evaluation'; and the fact that all the relevant tests could not readily be supplied with absolute assurance or that their practical application seemed difficult 'could be no reason for ignoring the important need' for that evaluation.[71]

Moevao contrasts strikingly with Richardson J.'s approach in *Ashby* v. *Minister of Immigration*.[72] The minister's decision to issue temporary entry permits to members of the Springbok rugby team, which planned to tour New Zealand, was challenged for failure to take account of the 1965 International Convention on the Elimination of All Forms of Racial Discrimination. In an affidavit the minister deposed that he did not give specific consideration to the Convention, but was aware of the opposition of the United Nations and the New Zealand government to apartheid. Richardson J. held that the identification of considerations relevant to the minister's exercise of discretion was not a justiciable issue. He noted that the Immigration Act conferred a wide discretion, permitting great weight to be given to government perceptions of the national interest. All analysis of the national interest was simply beyond legitimate judicial review: immigration policy was a sensitive and often controversial political issue; and the court could not easily distinguish

[68] Ibid. 45 (Lord Salmon). [69] [1980] 1 NZLR 464. [70] Ibid. 482.

[71] Ibid. 474. Cf. *Jago* v. *District Court of NSW* (1989) 87 ALR 577, 580–4 (Mason CJ); 600–3 (Deane J.). Brennan J.'s more restrictive view of the scope of 'abuse of process', which entailed a narrower (and less persuasive) conception of the right to a fair trial, is more consistent with denial of jurisdiction to review the decision to prosecute: ibid. 591–9.

[72] [1981] 1 NZLR 222. (Cooke J.'s judgment is considered above, Ch. 8.)

particular factors which must be taken into account to arrive at a valid decision.

Richardson J.'s reliance on the notion of justiciability stemmed from an inadequately structured account of judicial discretion. He apparently envisaged a freedom to accept or decline intervention according to the general nature of the discretion impugned:

> The willingness of the courts to interfere . . . must be affected by the nature and subject-matter of the decision in question and by consideration of the constitutional role of the body entrusted by statute with the exercise of the power. Thus the larger the policy content and the more the decision-making is within the customary sphere of elected representatives the less well-equipped the courts are to weigh the considerations involved and the less inclined they must be to intervene.[73]

These remarks suggest legitimate reasons for caution, but highlight the need for a systematic approach, grounded in principle. The possibility of review in appropriate circumstances cannot be denied for the reasons explained in *Moevao*: the court may be obliged to intervene in justice to the applicant. Neither Cooke J. nor Somers J. was prepared to abdicate his judicial function. Though unwilling to hold the minister bound to take account of the Convention, whose bearing on the subject was in any case doubtful, both judges recognized that certain factors might be identified as requiring consideration. Somers J. was at least content to assume that in the exercise of his discretion there might be 'some matters so obviously or manifestly necessary to be taken into account that a minister acting reasonably would be bound to take them into account'.[74]

Unspecific notions of 'pure' justiciability should not, then, be allowed to frustrate the court's duty to determine the existence and content of legal rights in the context of particular cases. The rigour of the court's scrutiny may properly reflect the importance of the interests likely to be affected by a public authority's action or decision. Where basic civil rights may be at risk, the court's appraisal should be suitably intensive; in other cases it may be reasonable to pay greater deference to the judgments of public officials. Such discriminations, however, are properly a part of the identification of those public law rights which may be enforced by judicial review: they do not permit wholesale judicial abstention on the grounds of the 'political' or discretionary nature of the administrative process. Richardson J.'s caution in *Ashby* may best be defended on the ground that, despite the reluctance of Cooke and Somers JJ. to relinquish jurisdiction, the minister's decision

[73] Ibid. 230, citing his own remarks in *CREEDNZ* v. *Governor-General* [1981] 1 NZLR 172, 197–8.
[74] 1 NZLR 233–4.

threatened no rights. Richardson J.'s instinct against review of an issue of public policy was, to that extent, well founded.[75]

The principle that the character of an applicant's interest must determine the rigour of the court's appraisal extends to both law and fact. Judicial control of the factual basis of an agency's actions must inevitably be sensitive to context and circumstance. The strict standard of scrutiny applied to the power to expel an 'illegal entrant', in *Khawaja*,[76] may not be appropriate to the power to admit a 'refugee' who claims political asylum. But that distinction cannot be made on the ground, suggested by Lord Templeman, that applications for leave to enter and remain in the United Kingdom 'do not in general raise justiciable issues'.[77] He observed that the necessary decisions might involve the immigration authorities in the pursuit of enquiries abroad, in consulting official and unofficial organizations, and in making value judgments: such decisions were 'administrative and discretionary rather than judicial and imperative'.

In *Khawaja*, however, Lord Wilberforce drew attention to the inevitable dependence of decisions about illegal entry on extensive fact-finding operations by the immigration authorities which could not be repeated by the court. The true ground of distinction must lie in the protected status acquired by a resident who enjoys the benefit of an express grant of leave to enter, and who may even have lived in Britain for many years.[78] It is not a question of 'justiciability'; nor is the answer fully determined by the statutory language.[79] It is a matter of defining—with the assistance of statute—the nature and scope of the applicant's rights in public law, and of according them appropriate protection.

Justiciability and standing

In challenging the legality of a government circular on the ground that it encouraged doctors to commit criminal offences, the plaintiff in *Gillick* v. *West Norfolk Area Health Authority*[80] would seem to have had no more right to be heard than Gouriet. The House of Lords held in that case that the courts could determine the legality of a circular, issued by the Department of Health and Social Security to area health

[75] Significantly, the applicants' *locus standi* was not discussed. (On standing, see further below.)

[76] [1983] 1 All ER 765 (see Ch. 8, above).

[77] *Bugdaycay* v. *Home Secretary* [1987] 1 All ER 940, 955.

[78] Cf. *Khawaja* [1983] 1 All ER 790 (Lord Bridge).

[79] *Pace* Lord Bridge in *Bugdaycay* at 945. Cf. Herbert Wechsler, 'Toward Neutral Principles of Constitutional Law' (1959) 73 Harv. LR 1, 9: 'the only proper judgment that may lead to an abstention from decision is that the Constitution has committed the determination of the issue to another agency of government than the courts . . . That . . . is *toto caelo* different from a broad discretion to abstain or intervene.'

[80] [1985] 3 All ER 402.

authorities, giving advice on the circumstances in which a doctor might lawfully prescribe contraceptives for a girl under 16. The plaintiff had failed to obtain an assurance that none of her five daughters, below that age, would receive such treatment without her prior knowledge and consent. The House of Lords set aside a declaration in the plaintiff's favour, which had been granted by the Court of Appeal, concluding that a doctor had a discretion to give contraceptive advice and treatment when the girl showed sufficient intelligence and understanding. A majority of the judges decided that he would not be committing an offence of causing or encouraging unlawful sexual intercourse with a girl under 16, contrary to the Sexual Offences Act 1956.

However, Gillick would seem to have had no *locus standi*, unless she could plausibly allege the violation of her rights in public law. Lord Bridge acknowledged that Gillick had no private right which she could assert against the Department, and thought it difficult to formulate the basis of the court's jurisdiction to intervene as a matter of public law. He was apparently troubled by the fact that the circular did not purport to be issued in the exercise of any statutory power or in the performance of any statutory function.

It is difficult to see, however, why the absence of a statutory jurisdiction should be a barrier to judicial review. Lord Bridge observed that judicial review could not be invoked to question the wisdom or reasonableness of the innumerable circulars issued by government departments; but it is not the function of the courts in any case to judge the wisdom of governmental acts and decisions. The absence of a statutory background has not been thought an insuperable impediment to review of the exercise of prerogative powers, or indeed of *de facto* powers wielded by 'self-regulatory' agencies in the (loosely defined) 'public sphere'.[81] It is true that, as Lord Bridge observed, the memorandum was purely advisory in character and did not bind medical practitioners; but if an 'official' government document is none the less likely to have great influence on medical practice, that seems something of a quibble as a ground for denying judicial review.[82]

Nevertheless, there were surely good reasons for judicial caution. Since it was accepted as unlikely that any of the plaintiff's daughters would seek contraceptive treatment, her rights were neither violated nor threatened by the government circular. When Lord Bridge admitted that the issue in the plaintiff's proceedings against the health authority

[81] See *R.* v. *Panel on Take-overs & Mergers, ex p. Datafin* [1987] 1 All ER 564.

[82] The concept of 'jurisdiction' (of an executive body) is perhaps today only a metaphor. Abuse of power seems a better foundation for judicial review than *ultra vires*, strictly understood: see Dawn Oliver, 'Is the *Ultra Vires* Rule the Basis of Judicial Review?' [1987] PL 543. But compare H. W. R. Wade, 'Judicial Review of Ministerial Guidance' (1986) 102 LQR 173. Lords Scarman and Fraser treated the case as involving the exercise of a statutory discretion.

was 'purely academic', and that Gillick was engaged in a moral crusade against the 'ethos expressed'[83] in the Department's circular, he implicitly denied the legitimacy of judicial review. The court's analysis of Gillick's rights as a parent—which were held to be derived from, and coterminous with, parental duty—was necessarily an abstract one. In consequence, the judges were drawn into a general discussion of wide-ranging moral and social considerations, a discussion whose connection with Gillick's own circumstances was inevitably remote.

Lord Bridge was unduly optimistic in asserting that 'the occasions of a departmental non-statutory publication raising . . . a clearly defined issue of law, unclouded by political, social or moral overtones, will be rare'.[84] They will be non-existent. All questions of law have political, social, and moral implications, even if these are often veiled and sometimes uncontroversial. In denying his instinct against review, Lord Bridge was obliged to fall back on something akin to a doctrine of justiciability which, conscientiously applied, would actually have barred consideration of Gillick's claim:

> In cases where any proposition of law implicit in a departmental advisory document is interwoven with questions of social and ethical controversy, the court should . . . exercise its jurisdiction with the utmost restraint, confine itself to deciding whether the proposition of law is erroneous and avoid either expressing *ex cathedra* opinions in areas of social and ethical controversy in which it has no claim to speak with authority, or proffering answers to hypothetical questions of law which do not strictly arise for decision.[85]

But law cannot be divorced from ethics, controversial or otherwise. The court lacked authority because it did not decide a matter of (legal) right.

The division between politics and adjudication cannot survive a jurisdiction which encompasses the decision of abstract moral and social questions. Such questions are not, strictly speaking, questions of legal right at all. Admittedly, legal rights are essentially moral rights, sensitive to the moral and political context in which they are asserted or acknowledged; and there is therefore no division of subject-matter between law and politics, objectively ascertainable. Gillick's case raised interesting issues about abstract rights—the moral rights of parents to resist governmental intrusion into the province of child-rearing. The

83 [1985] 3 All ER 402, 425–6.

84 Ibid. 427. Lord Bridge thought that *Royal College of Nursing* v. *DHSS* [1981] AC 800, which involved construction of the Abortion Act 1967, provided an example. The moral overtones were obvious, and judicial opinion almost equally divided. The case none the less raised directly the contractual rights and duties of nurses, required to assist with a novel procedure for terminating pregnancy, as well as their insurance position and possible criminal liability. Despite the form of the proceedings, the issues were not hypothetical.

85 [1985] 3 All ER 427. Cf. Lord Templeman at 436–7.

function of the courts, however, is to decide the scope and content of concrete rights—to determine what the litigants' rights require in all the circumstances of particular cases. Abstract rights have no weight: their weight is a function of their application to specific cases, when they must be evaluated in the light of countervailing rights or relevant aspects of public policy (as embodied in legislation or government decisions).[86]

The analysis made by Lords Scarman and Fraser was perhaps persuasive as a matter of moral philosophy: the court could not exclude the possibility that a doctor should sometimes prescribe contraceptives without the girl's parents' knowledge or consent. But since the analysis lacked any specific context—in the absence of any tangible threat to Gillick's abstract parental rights—it exerted no claim to legal authority. Moral philosophy, debated in abstraction from particular instances, acquires no binding quality because it is written by judges. As Lord Diplock had remarked in *Gouriet*: 'the jurisdiction of the court is not to declare the law generally or to give advisory opinions: it is confined to declaring contested legal rights, subsisting or future, of the parties represented in the litigation before it and not those of anyone else'.[87]

It follows from this approach that the question of standing cannot be separated from the substance of an application for judicial review, as the House of Lords acknowledged in *Inland Revenue Commissioners* v. *Federation of Self-Employed and Small Businesses*.[88] In that case, the Federation's challenge to an arrangement regarding payment of arrears of tax, made between the Revenue and Fleet Street employers and unions, was rightly dismissed. No rights of the Federation or its members were violated by the arrangement even if, as was claimed, the Revenue had given preferential treatment to the Fleet Street print workers. Lord Wilberforce distinguished the position of taxpayers from that of ratepayers:

> The produce of rates goes into a common fund applicable for the benefit of the ratepayers. Thus any ratepayer has an interest, direct and sufficient, in the rates levied on other ratepayers . . . The structure of the legislation relating to income tax, on the other hand, makes clear that no corresponding right is intended to be conferred on taxpayers.[89]

To acknowledge such rights would subvert the whole system, whereby the commissioners' duties were owed to the Crown, and matters relating to income tax were 'between the commissioners and the taxpayer concerned'.

[86] See Chs. 4–6, above. Ronald Dworkin distinguishes between 'abstract' and 'concrete' rights in *Taking Rights Seriously*, ch. 4.

[87] [1977] 3 All ER 70, 100. For a similar view of *Gillick's* case, see Carol Harlow, '*Gillick*: A Comedy of Errors?' (1986) 49 MLR 768.

[88] [1981] 2 All ER 93.

[89] Ibid. 98–9.

It is none the less hard to quarrel with Lord Scarman's view that the Revenue owed a duty to the general body of taxpayers to treat all taxpayers fairly—a duty to ensure that there were 'no favourites and no sacrificial victims'.[90] He was surely correct to insist that the duty of fairness was a legal as well as moral one, and not merely a matter of 'policy', entirely beyond legitimate judicial concern. But it does not necessarily follow that one taxpayer enjoyed rights in respect of another's assessment. I have suggested that, in some circumstances, judicial review might be justified in defence of the complainant's right to equality.[91] But that right should not be interpreted as a barrier to any kind of unequal treatment: it cannot be permitted to frustrate the implementation of reasonable policy, which will inevitably involve some discrimination between different persons. Provided that such discrimination is made, in good faith, for the proper purpose of efficiently collecting revenue, the fair treatment of taxpayers *inter se* is ordinarily a matter of distributive justice, in which the Revenue must be finally accountable to Parliament for its conduct of its statutory functions.[92]

Lord Scarman affirmed the general principle that it was 'wrong in law . . . for the court to attempt an assessment of the sufficiency of an applicant's interest without regard to the matter of his complaint'.[93] It is wrong because his interest depends on his establishing a claim of right which the court can protect; and a complaint about the justice of arrangements for collecting taxes from other taxpayers generally raises no claim of right. The courts cannot undertake to review the fairness of such arrangements from the perspective of no citizen in particular: that is precisely the concern of ordinary politics, or of practical administration. The distinction between taxpayers and ratepayers could only be justified if the latter were regarded as having a continuing property interest in the common fund, so that local authorities acted as trustees in their management of the rates collected.[94] A similar approach to the product of income tax, or all payments to the exchequer, would be quite unrealistic: it would undermine the concept of rights and improperly extend the scope of judicial review.

The court considered, however, that a taxpayer might be permitted to challenge assessments on other taxpayers in cases of exceptional

[90] Ibid. 112; see Ch. 7, above.

[91] Ch. 7, above.

[92] Lord Wilberforce held that the court's intervention 'would involve permitting a taxpayer or a group of taxpayers to call in question the exercise of management powers and involve the court itself in a management exercise: [1981] 2 All ER 100; cf. Lord Roskill at 119–20.

[93] Ibid. 113.

[94] See *Bromley LBC* v. *GLC* [1983] AC 768. It has been argued that the fiduciary approach was unrealistic even in the case of rates: see John Griffith, 'Fares Fair or Fiduciary Foul' [1982] CLJ 216; Patrick McAuslan, 'Administrative Law, Collective Consumption and Judicial Policy' (1983) 46 MLR 1.

gravity;[95] and Lord Diplock apparently endorsed the liberal approach to standing previously advocated by Lord Denning. The Master of the Rolls had considered it a 'matter of high constitutional principle that if there is good ground for supposing that a government department or a public authority is transgressing the law . . . in a way which offends or injures thousands of Her Majesty's subjects, then any one of those offended or injured can draw it to the attention of the courts of law and seek to have the law enforced, and the courts in their discretion can grant whatever remedy is appropriate'.[96]

The danger is obvious here that an essentially arbitrary judicial discretion may be substituted for legal principle. Administrative law should be primarily concerned with the protection of individual interests and eschew evaluation of the public interest more generally. Everything depends on the meaning in practice of 'those offended or injured'. In the absence of any violation of individual right, the court's intervention seems illegitimate. References to 'transgressing the law' merely beg the question. Everyone is entitled to take a (considered) view of the requirements of law—including the public authority under challenge; and there is no reason, where matters of legal right cannot be distinguished from public policy, to accord the court's view any special authority.[97]

A rigorous view of the appropriate ambit of judicial review, limited to deciding questions of individual right, would largely dispense with separate requirements of standing, just as it does with independent doctrines of justiciability.[98] The justification for traditional analysis lies in the assumption that standing is a preliminary or jurisdictional issue which is independent of the merits of the claim for relief.[99] This assumption was bolstered by decisions which identified standing with the assertion of rights in private law: in such cases there appeared to be little connection between the question of standing and the grounds of *ultra vires*. The development of the doctrine of legitimate expectation, however, has permitted administrative law to be largely restated in terms of rights in public law; and it can readily be seen that such rights provide both entitlement to invoke the court's jurisdiction and also the

95 [1981] 2 All ER 99 (Wilberforce); 104 (Diplock); 108 (Fraser); 120 (Roskill).

96 *R.* v. *GLC, ex p. Blackburn* [1976] 3 All ER 184, 192.

97 Cf. *R.* v. *Sec. of State for the Environment, ex p. Rose Theatre Trust Co.* [1990] 1 All ER 754, 768 (Schiemann J.): '. . . the law does not see it as the function of the courts to be there for every individual who is interested in having the legality of an administrative action litigated'.

98 Not entirely: it may sometimes be legitimate to permit representative bodies to assert the rights of others, who may not themselves be parties. See e.g. *R.* v. *Sec. of State for Employment, ex p. Equal Opportunities Commission* [1992] 1 All ER 545.

99 Cf. Peter Cane, 'The Function of Standing Rules in Administrative Law' [1980] PL 303.

perimeter of the public authority's powers. A claim of right in public law founds the supervisory jurisdiction just as a claim of right in private law founds the court's ordinary jurisdiction.[100]

When, for example, the court reviews the manner of exercise of a statutory discretion, its examination is properly concentrated on the applicant's own position: did the authority treat him unfairly? It is not suggested that the appropriate criteria would necessarily differ in respect of each complainant. Many people may be affected by a decision whose validity depends largely on considerations which can be stated, and evaluated, independently of any particular case. None the less, it is only the applicant's particular challenge which justifies the court's intervention at all.[101] And there is always the possibility—which reflects the main strength and rationale of common law adjudication—that the impact of a decision on the applicant is in fact unique, or sufficiently unusual to require its adaptation fairly to meet his circumstances.

In a powerful critique of American proposals for extending the range of plaintiffs permitted to challenge the validity of government action, R. L. Brilmayer argued that traditional rules for standing and 'ripeness' served to protect the integrity of judicial review.[102] Widening the jurisdiction to receive the complaints of the ideological, or non-Hohfeldian, plaintiff[103] undermined the important sensitivity of courts to the impact of challenged laws or decisions on affected individuals. Brilmayer rightly stressed that the court's power to elaborate legal principle lay only in the course of its application to parties whose rights would be directly affected. The development of binding precedent, governing future cases, was a by-product of necessary adjustments to pre-existing rules—adjustments compelled by considerations of fairness in the particular case. There was no warrant for any wider judicial function: it was the limited, incremental development of precedent which justified departure from existing rules and distinguished adjudication from legislation and the formulation of policy. If the doctrine of 'ripeness' was invoked to forestall judicial review in hypothetical cases—allowing the court to refuse declaratory relief in the absence of objective evidence of a threat of harm—the rules of standing performed a similar function: they ensured 'the legitimacy of a judicial process that applies principles

[100] Cf. Lord Bridge in *Leech* v. *Parkhurst Prison Deputy Governor* [1988] 1 All ER 485, 496 (cited above).

[101] Cf. Cane, 'The Function of Standing Rules', 321–2.

[102] 'Judicial Review, Justiciability and the Limits of the Common Law Method' (1977) 57 Boston ULR 807. Brilmayer considers judicial review in the American context, encompassing review of legislation on grounds of constitutionality.

[103] Ibid. 827. The non-Hohfeldian plaintiff 'does not have traditional legally protected rights at stake, nor do such plaintiffs have a concrete interest in the outcome of disputes in which they assert the legal rights of parties not before the court'.

from previous cases to decide the claims of future litigants by requiring that such principles by derived only as an incident of determining the rights of the parties before the court'.[104]

It is true that the court's order will often have wide-ranging consequences: a decision may be quashed which affects a large number of people. The analogy between private and public law rights can be pressed too far. However, the impact of the challenged decision on the wider public, and its contribution to the public interest (as determined by the public authority) are already accounted for: they form the context in which the applicant's complaint of unfair treatment is evaluated, and in which the court exercises its own discretion in respect of remedies. The right to fair treatment at the hands of the state is not an absolute right to thwart the public interest or frustrate the implementation of public policy. It is a right to equality of consideration and respect in the exercise of powers which necessarily encroach to some degree on private interests for the greater benefit of all.

[104] Brilmayer further argues that a plaintiff whose only interest in a case is his dislike of government practices, rather than any particular wrong done to himself, may be a poor representative of future plaintiffs more directly injured by such practices. Future plaintiffs may none the less be affected by abstract determinations of legal principle made in the previous case.

10
Law, Convention, and Prerogative

> In order . . . that conventions may be regarded in this way, as being of the same nature as law, it is necessary that conventions should be distinguished from mere practices. In any organisation a pattern of activity develops and is continued out of habit or simply for the sake of convenience. Such patterns exist in constitutional matters . . . On the other hand there are patterns which persist because a constitutional principle extending beyond mere practical convenience underlies them.
>
> J. D. B. Mitchell, *Constitutional Law*, 2nd edn. (Edinburgh, 1968), 39.

The royal prerogative remains an important legal source of governmental power in the modern constitution. In legal theory, ministers and judges are appointed under the prerogative. Civil servants owe their appointments and their conditions of service to the prerogative: they hold office at the pleasure of the Crown. Offenders may be pardoned, or their sentences reduced or remitted, under the prerogative of mercy. Parliament is summoned, prorogued, and dissolved by virtue of the prerogative. It is in reliance on prerogative powers that the government conducts foreign affairs, and directs the disposition of the armed forces. As inherent powers of the executive government, originating in those of the medieval kings, their definition remains unsettled. There are residual powers to act in defence of the realm against both external aggression and internal strife.[1]

As a 'residue of discretionary or arbitrary authority, which at any given time is legally left in the hands of the Crown',[2] the existence of the royal prerogative seemed to contradict Dicey's conception of the rule of law. He attempted to overcome the contradiction by resort to an account of 'constitutional morality': 'rules for determining the mode in which the discretionary powers of the Crown (or of the Ministers as servants of the Crown) ought to be exercised'.[3] Accordingly, the

[1] The prerogative power to preserve the Queen's peace has recently been held to include the power to supply equipment required by police forces for the more efficient discharge of their duties: *R.* v. *Home Secretary, ex p. Northumbria Police Authority* [1988] 1 All ER 556.

[2] A. V. Dicey, *The Law of the Constitution*, 10th edn. (London, 1959), 424.

[3] Ibid. 422–3.

prerogatives of appointment and dismissal must be exercised, in practice, in accordance with the wishes of Parliament: a government which had lost a vote of confidence was required to resign. The government should not conclude treaties in opposition to the will of Parliament. In general, though the survival of the prerogative placed large powers in the hands of the Prime Minister and cabinet, constitutional convention ensured that they were exercised according to the wishes of the House of Commons. Dicey insisted, however, that convention must be distinguished from law: the maxims of constitutional morality or 'political ethics' could not be enforced by the courts, and hence had 'no claim to be considered laws'.[4]

These conclusions are surely somewhat remarkable. For all his emphasis on the 'absolute supremacy or predominance of regular law as opposed to the influence of arbitrary power'—his insistence that 'Englishmen are ruled by the law, and by the law alone'[5]—Dicey had apparently abandoned all legal restraint on the exercise of prerogative power in favour of a simple faith in practical politics. As an essay in constitutionalism, his position indeed represented no advance on Blackstone's account: 'In the exertion . . . of those prerogatives, which the law has given him, the king is irresistible and absolute, according to the forms of the constitution. And yet, if the consequence of that exertion be manifestly to the grievance or dishonour of the kingdom, the parliament will call his advisers to a just and severe account.'[6]

If Dicey perhaps cannot be blamed for failing to predict the modern weakness of Parliament in the face of the executive, especially where the government enjoys the support of a large majority in the lower House, his theory clearly fails to provide a satisfactory account of constitutional government, founded on law. Could we really accept that the common law knows nothing of the rules governing the appointment and dismissal of ministers, or even of the nature of cabinet government? That no legal limits exist to many of the powers of the executive government, which may manipulate this 'absolute' discretion in its own interests? That view lent plausibility, perhaps, to the notion that the appropriate sanction for unconstitutional action was an exercise of personal monarchical power—that the personal responsibility of the Sovereign was the ultimate, and sometimes only, legal safeguard against the abuse of prerogative power on the part of ministers. The rights of the Sovereign to refuse a request for a dissolution or dismiss a ministry continue to enjoy qualified academic support; but the qualifications eclipse the powers for all practical purposes. It is inevitably an almost worthless guarantee. J. D. B. Mitchell wrote of the power of dismissal that 'its exercise would be so dangerous to the monarchy that its use

[4] Ibid. [5] Ibid. 202. [6] *Commentaries*, i, ch. 7, p. 251.

could only be justified in . . . extreme circumstances, and history alone would decide the appropriateness of the decision'.[7]

Dicey's insistence on a strict separation between law and convention retains a hold on orthodox constitutional theory similar to his doctrine of unlimited parliamentary sovereignty—a doctrine qualified only in practice, as a matter of benign convention and political prudence. The two views are plainly closely connected: each reflects its proponent's narrow, implausible Austinian jurisprudence. Rules of law, properly speaking, must be promulgated or at least declared, by courts if not by the legislature; and they must, it was thought, provide for the application of a sanction in the event of their breach.[8] Conventions must be sharply distinguished (on this view) because they are constituted by political *practice*, albeit sometimes sanctified by long usage or general approval: they cannot be regarded as laws in the absence of judicial enforcement.

The Supreme Court of Canada appears to have lent its authority to Dicey's thesis.[9] According to a majority of the court, the nature of a convention, as political in inception and depending on a consistent course of political recognition, was incompatible with its legal enforcement. The absence of any legal sanction was evidently crucial:

> The conventional rules of the Constitution present one striking peculiarity. In contradistinction to the laws of the Constitution, they are not enforced by the courts. One reason for this situation is that, unlike common law rules, conventions are not judge-made rules. They are not based on judicial precedents but on precedents established by the institutions of government themselves. Nor are they in the nature of statutory commands which it is the function and duty of the courts to obey and enforce. Furthermore, to enforce them would mean to administer some formal sanction when they are breached. But the legal system from which they are distinct does not contemplate formal sanctions for their breach.[10]

In defence of this view, a distinction is sometimes drawn between 'enforcement' and 'recognition'. There are numerous occasions on which the courts have considered constitutional conventions, but though their existence is recognized as a matter of 'political fact', they are never accorded legal force. Dicey's denial that conventions were 'enforced or recognised by the courts' has been explained in a similar manner: far from advocating a strange legal myopia in respect of political reality, he asserted only that conventions were not *recognized as legal rules*.[11]

[7] *Constitutional Law*, 2nd edn. (Edinburgh, 1968), 177. See also Geoffrey Marshall, *Constitutional Conventions* (Oxford, 1984), ch. 2.

[8] Dicey considers Austin's views on sovereignty in *Law of the Constitution*, 70–6. See generally John Austin, *The Province of Jurisprudence Determined*, ed. Hart (London, 1954).

[9] *Reference re Amendment of the Constitution of Canada (Nos. 1, 2 & 3)* (1982) 125 DLR (3d) 1.

[10] Ibid. 84.

[11] Colin Munro, 'Laws and Conventions Distinguished' (1975) 91 LQR 218, at 229–31.

This explanation, however, overlooks the importance of legal principle. It has been claimed in defence of Dicey's thesis that, whereas legal rules form part of a *system*, conventions possess no such unifying feature: 'an inference has to be made according to the strength and purpose of the particular political practice involved'.[12] But legal systems contain principles as well as rules, and their identification may depend, in the constitutional sphere, on the strength and purpose of the practices they justify. Lord Simon, for example, described the freedom of the House of Lords to depart from its previous decisions as 'one of those conventions which are so significant a feature of the British Constitution';[13] and Sir John Donaldson MR has referred in a similar way to the principle of the separation and independence of the courts from Parliament.[14] The Canadian Supreme Court accepted that the 'main purpose of constitutional conventions is to ensure that the legal framework of the Constitution will be operated in accordance with the prevailing constitutional values or principles of the period'.[15] If the prevailing constitutional value in that context was the principle of Canadian federalism, it is only an impoverished sort of legal theory which could deny it the dignity of law.

Constitutional practice and legal principle

It was perhaps a sense of the inadequacy of a theory which severed law from constitutional principle which led Dicey to search for legal consequences of breaches of convention, which would operate indirectly. He was, after all, well aware of the important role of legal principle in the development of the common law.[16] It is only by convention that a government must resign or advise a dissolution after defeat on a vote of confidence, but a breach of convention would have legal implications. Military and financial embarrassment would soon arise from the refusal of the House of Commons to pass the annual Army Act (as was then required) or the Appropriation Act. The maintenance of military discipline, and the collection and expenditure of taxes, would alike become illegal: 'The breach, therefore, of a purely conventional rule, of a maxim utterly unknown and indeed opposed to the theory of English

[12] Ibid. 233.

[13] *R.* v. *Knuller* [1973] AC 435, 484.

[14] *R.* v. *HM Treasury, ex p. Smedley* [1985] QB 657, 666 ('a constitutional convention of the highest importance').

[15] (1982) 125 DLR (3d) 1, 84. The Canadian patriation affair is considered below.

[16] Dicey's discussion of the rule of law consists largely of an analysis of legal principles.

[17] *Law of the Constitution*, 450. Sir Ivor Jennings observed that a substantial time might elapse in practice before such consequences ensued: *The Law and the Constitution*, 5th edn. (London, 1959), 128–9.

[18] Dicey, *Law of the Constitution*, 450–1.

law, ultimately entails upon those who break it direct conflict with the undoubted law of the land.'[17] It is, however, only the modern development of a 'constitutional' jurisprudence, beyond the 'principles of private law' which Dicey stressed, which could today justify the 'right to assert that the force which in the last resort compels obedience to constitutional morality is nothing else than the power of the law itself'.[18]

Taken seriously, the law–convention dichotomy, for all its popularity with constitutional lawyers, would deny the possibility of a genuine public law—or at least of public law principles fashioned in response to the growth and evolution of political power. But its intellectual stranglehold has been severely weakened by recent developments in administrative law. The most important, in the present context, has been a gradual recognition that the exercise of prerogative power might be subject to judicial review. The traditional doctrine was that the courts could determine the existence and extent of a prerogative power, but could not review its exercise: the power remained, in that sense, 'irresistible and absolute'.

However, Lord Denning asserted it as a fundamental principle of the constitution that, though the law did not interfere with the proper exercise of executive discretion, it could impose limits on the scope of the prerogative; and it could intervene if the discretion were 'exercised improperly or mistakenly'.[19] His views have been vindicated by the House of Lords. In the *GCHQ* case,[20] Lord Diplock stated that a decision-making power could derive no immunity from review simply by virtue of its common law, as opposed to statutory, foundation. Lord Scarman considered that previous limitations had been 'overwhelmed by the developing modern law of judicial review'.[21]

There is some risk of exaggerating the significance of the House of Lords' decision. The court was anxious to stress that the possibility of judicial review depended, in each case, on the nature of the power in issue: a number of prerogative powers would remain inviolate since their manner of exercise would not be 'justiciable'.[22] If, however, the exercise of prerogative power has been acknowledged, in principle, as subject to judicial review, we may reasonably ask about the source of appropriate criteria. We should recur to Dicey's instructive text:

[19] *Laker Airways* v. *Department of Trade* [1977] QB 643, 705.

[20] *Council of Civil Service Unions* v. *Minister for the Civil Service* [1984] 3 All ER 935.

[21] Ibid. 948.

[22] See Ch. 9 above, where 'justiciability' is equated with the existence of legal rights. The court's recent refusal to review the Home Secretary's decision to provide equipment to chief constables is best explained as a case where executive action under prerogative powers was 'directed towards the benefit or protection of the individual'. There was no 'violation of property or other rights of the individual' inconsistent with statutory provisions: *R.* v. *Home Secretary, ex p. Northumbria Police Authy.* [1988] 1 All ER 556, 571 (Purchas LJ).

... we may use the term 'prerogative' as equivalent to the discretionary authority of the executive, and then lay down that the conventions of the constitution are in the main precepts for determining the mode and spirit in which the prerogative is to be exercised, or ... for fixing the manner in which any transaction which can legally be done in virtue of the royal prerogative ... ought to be carried out.[23]

Dicey here instances the making of war and declaration of peace, which might not be thought justiciable, but adds that the statement 'holds good ... of all the discretionary powers exercised by the executive, otherwise than under statutory authority'.

It is fair to conclude that constitutional convention will today provide a primary source of legal principle to regulate the prerogative. Indeed, the *GCHQ* case itself might qualify as such an instance. The Prime Minister (and Minister for the Civil Service) had issued an instruction under the Civil Service Order in Council 1982, a prerogative instrument, withdrawing from civil servants working at the Government Communications Headquarters the right of belonging to a trade union. There had been no previous consultation with the civil service unions. The court held that, though the employees had no legal right to such consultation as a matter of private law—they held their appointments only at the pleasure of the Crown—they had a legitimate expectation of prior consultation which, in principle, the court would protect.

That expectation arose from past practice, as Lord Fraser explained: 'the evidence shows that, ever since G.C.H.Q. began in 1947, prior consultation has been the invariable rule when conditions of service were to be significantly altered'.[24] In the circumstances, the duty to consult was overridden by the demands of national security since consultation had involved a risk of precipitating disruptive action, taken in protest. If the danger to national security had not been established, the minister's instruction would have been declared invalid because unfair. The court's application of natural justice, based on legitimate expectations, appeared to constrain the exercise of prerogative on the basis of constitutional convention—a well-established governmental practice of union consultation, in respect of civil servants who had no rights to insist on the practice as a matter of (private) law.[25]

In theory, like civil servants, ministers are appointed and dismissed under the prerogative, holding office at the pleasure of the Crown. Some reflections on law and prerogative, at this higher constitutional level, are prompted by the decision of the Judicial Committee of the

[23] *Law of the Constitution*, 426.

[24] [1984] 3 All ER 935, 944.

[25] According to O. Hood Phillips, the internal regulation of the civil service does not fall within the category of constitutional conventions 'except perhaps for such a broad principle as the negotiation of pay and conditions of service ...' [1964] JSPTL 60, at 68.

Privy Council in *Adegbenro* v. *Akintola*,[26] where proceedings were brought for a declaration by the former Premier of Western Nigeria against the Governor. The former Premier challenged the validity of his dismissal from office, which had occurred after receipt by the Governor of a letter, signed by a majority of the members of the House of Assembly, stating that they no longer supported the Premier.

Section 33(10) of the Constitution provided that the Governor should not remove the Premier from office 'unless it appears to him that the Premier no longer commands the support of a majority of the members of the House of Assembly'. However, the court rejected a submission that that 'support' could only be judged by a record of votes given on the floor of the House. Viscount Radcliffe acknowledged the weight of 'considerations of policy and propriety', relevant to exercise of the Governor's power, but refused to accord them the force of legal restrictions which the court could 'import into the written document'. It is mistaken, however, to treat the decision as confirmation of Dicey's attempt to divorce law from convention. There were many good reasons to dissuade a Governor from exercising his power of removal except on indisputable evidence of actual voting in the House, but it would be wrong, as a matter of legal principle, to fetter the Governor's freedom of action. It was impossible to say that situations could not arise in which these reasons would be 'outweighed by considerations which afforded to the Governor the evidence he is to look for, even without the testimony of recorded votes . . .'.[27] The Constitution would not be construed as imposing a limitation incompatible with the discretion granted to the Governor for the exercise of 'delicate political judgment'.

A proper interpretation of the Constitution—and the extent to which it envisaged the observance of convention deriving from British political practice—depended on the constitutional scheme as a whole, viewed as a matter of principle. The court did 'not find that the scheme or provisions of the Constitution of Western Nigeria' required a restriction of the Governor's power of removal of the kind proposed. Nor did it think that its preferred construction was 'contrary to the basic assumption of such democratic constitutions that the Government of the territory cannot in the end be conducted without the support of a majority of members of the elected House'.[28] The Judicial Committee's advice was a fine illustration of the interaction of law and convention, in the context of a written constitution, and of the dependence of the legal result, in the last analysis, on political principle. It is a reasonable inference that an answer which *was* contrary to that basic democratic assumption would have been rejected as a matter of law. Although the scope for drawing analogies between written and 'unwritten' con-

[26] [1963] AC 614. [27] Ibid. 630–1. [28] Ibid. 633.

stitutions is controversial, the significance of convention for the content of legal principle applies equally to both.

It is sometimes assumed that appeal to convention simply asserts a practice of certain behaviour in particular circumstances and reports a general belief that the practice is binding. O. Hood Phillips, for example, offered the following working definition: 'rules of political practice which are *regarded as binding* by those to whom they apply, but which are not laws as they are not enforced by the courts or by the Houses of Parliament'.[29] Sir Ivor Jennings, on the other hand, suggested a further criterion for the existence of a convention: whether there was a reason for the rule.[30] Mere belief on the part of the political actors is insufficient: they may be mistaken in thinking themselves bound.

The question relates to the identification of a social or political rule. A detached observer need take no view about the merits of a supposed obligation, content to describe only the mental attitude of others. But neither a 'political actor' nor a constitutional theorist can enjoy a comparable detachment. When *he* asserts the existence of a rule, and signifies his acceptance of its demands, he implicitly recognizes that the rule is *justified*. He is not simply reporting a general practice of obedience, but indicating approval. If he thinks that the rule is pernicious, and its adherents misguided, he does not recognize it as binding—he rejects it as wrong.[31]

What is true of the politician and the constitutional theorist, however, is equally true of the judge. It follows that the recognition of convention by a court in the course of adjudication generally entails its acceptance as a rule which is legitimate. It is acknowledged as a rule of practice which is grounded in political principle. Curial 'recognition' implies judicial approval. In the result, the distinction between recognition and enforcement—that last refuge of orthodox theory—plainly dissolves. To recognize a convention is necessarily to endorse the principle which justifies it; and, in a context where legal doctrine is developed to reflect that principle, recognition means enforcement. Indeed, in the absence of a willingness to *act* on the basis of convention—to acknowledge its significance for legal rights and obligations—a court's 'recognition' would be empty and futile. The positivist distinction between recognition and enforcement is grounded in an implausibly theoretical view of the judicial function: it overlooks the moral and political responsibility inherent in the practical activity of adjudication.[32]

[29] *Constitutional and Administrative Law*, 7th edn. (London, 1987), 113, emphasis added.

[30] *The Law and the Constitution*, 5th edn. (London, 1959), 136.

[31] For discussion of social rules, see H. L. A. Hart, *The Concept of Law* (Oxford, 1961), 79–88; Ronald Dworkin, *Taking Rights Seriously* (London, 1977), 48–58.

[32] Cf. M. J. Detmold, *The Australian Commonwealth* (Sydney, 1985), ch. 14: positivism expresses a purely theoretical conception of law, overlooking its practical nature.

Attorney-General v. *Jonathan Cape*[33] provides a helpful example. The judgment was, in form, an application of the equitable principle restraining a breach of confidence. In substance, the case provides for the enforcement of a rule which serves the convention of collective responsibility. Lord Widgery considered that a doctrine which had been developed to restrain the unfair use of commercial secrets, and been extended to protect domestic secrets, could be further applied to protect governmental secrets. The expression of opinions by cabinet ministers in the course of cabinet discussion was a matter of confidence, and the publication of a former minister's diaries could therefore be restrained, in a proper case, to protect that confidence.

The decision both acknowledged the importance of collective responsibility, as a constitutional convention, and indicated a legal remedy for conduct tending to undermine it. Recognition of convention entailed judicial evaluation. It was not simply a question of what politicians and statesmen happened to believe: '*The maintenance of the doctrine of joint responsibility within the cabinet is in the public interest*, and the application of that doctrine might be prejudiced by premature disclosure of the views of individual ministers.'[34] Lord Widgery's judgment not only acknowledged the virtues of collective responsibility, but took them into account—accorded them weight—as a necessary part of the practical matter of deciding whether or not to grant relief. The judge ultimately refused the injunction sought because he considered that, on a balance of public interest, the case for suppression had not, in all the circumstances, been made out. The doctrine of joint responsibility would not be endangered by the publication of ministers' views ten years (and three general elections) after they were expressed.

No better illustration of judicial endorsement of collective responsibility, together with assessment of its weight in particular cases, could be found than the doctrine of public interest immunity. Since no automatic exemption is granted from the ordinary duty to disclose relevant documents in the course of litigation—even for cabinet documents—the court is compelled to determine the content and cogency of constitutional convention.[35] In the High Court of Australia, Mason J. accepted the view of the Radcliffe Committee on ministerial memoirs that collective responsibility could not survive unless ministers were willing to observe the confidentiality of their deliberations.[36] He identified this reason as the basis of the public interest against disclosure of cabinet proceedings—the element which had to be weighed

33 [1976] QB 752.

34 Ibid. 771 (emphasis added).

35 See *Conway* v. *Rimmer* [1968] AC 910; *Burmah Oil* v. *Bank of England* [1980] AC 1090.

36 *Sankey* v. *Whitlam* (1978) 142 CLR 1, 97–8, citing Committee of Privy Councillors on Ministerial Memoirs, Cmnd. 6386 (1976), paras. 33–4.

in the balance with the needs of the administration of justice in deciding whether to require disclosure. It was the 'inherent difficulty of decision-making if the decision-making processes of cabinet' were at risk of premature publication which would justify immunity: 'the efficiency of government would be seriously compromised if cabinet decisions and papers were disclosed whilst they or the topics to which they relate are still current or controversial'.[37]

Reviewing the legal status of the cabinet, and its relation to the Federal Executive Council, the Full Federal Court of Australia recently acknowledged the force of constitutional practice in a similar context: 'Given . . . the significance of the cabinet as the repository of *de facto* decision-making power, it is hard to deny the constitutional significance of the conventions that regulate its operations.'[38] Public interest immunity should not be based on the secrecy demanded by Executive Councillors' oaths, or on the confidentiality historically attached to advice tendered to the Crown by its advisers. It was the impact of disclosure of cabinet papers on the convention of collective responsibility which was the 'principal consideration': 'In this way, the law and political science meet.'[39]

It follows that when a court upholds a claim for public interest immunity on these grounds, it affirms the legal status of convention; and Dicey's division between law and convention is thereby broken down. The court cannot stand aloof, recognizing but not enforcing: it is committed by the demands of adjudication to take action, either ordering discovery or commanding secrecy.[40] The Federal Court cited Blackburn J.'s uncompromising defence of confidentiality in support of joint responsibility. In such cases the court was concerned with the machinery of government, not with 'the rules or customs of a private society': 'Cabinet secrecy is an essential part of the structure of government which centuries of political experience have created. To impair it without a very strong reason would be vandalism, the wanton rejection of the fruits of civilisation.'[41]

Law and convention in the Supreme Court of Canada

We should pause to consider the influential opinions of the Canadian Supreme Court with regard to law and convention. An examination of

[37] 142 CLR 97.

[38] *Commonwealth of Australia* v. *Northern Land Council* (1991) 103 ALR 267, 286.

[39] Ibid. 288. For general discussion of the cabinet and its legal status, see M. C. Harris, 'The Courts and the Cabinet: "Unfastening the Buckle"?' [1989] PL 251.

[40] Unlike legal privilege, public interest immunity cannot generally be waived: if applicable, it must be enforced: *Sankey* v. *Whitlam* (1978) 142 CLR 1, 44 (Gibbs ACJ); *Air Canada* v. *Sec. of State for Trade* [1983] 1 All ER 910, 925 (Lord Scarman).

[41] *Whitlam* v. *Australian Consolidated Press* (1985) 73 FLR 414, 422.

the juristic nature of the law–convention dichotomy, in constitutional matters, was necessitated by litigation arising from the final patriation of the Canadian Constitution.[42] The federal government wished to terminate the residual British role in Canada's constitutional arrangements, enact a Charter of Rights binding on both the federal government and the provinces, and provide for future constitutional amendment to be effected in Canada. A joint resolution would be adopted by each of the two Houses of the Canadian Parliament in the form of an address to the Queen, requesting enactment of the new Constitution by Parliament at Westminster.

The question was whether this procedure could properly be adopted in the face of opposition to the new arrangements on the part of most of the provinces. It was argued that federal action to amend the Constitution, in such a way as to affect the legislative competence of the provinces, without the provinces' consent, was both illegal and unconstitutional as a breach of convention. The governments of Manitoba, Newfoundland, and Quebec had referred to their respective Courts of Appeal the question whether or not any relevant convention existed,[43] and the judgments of the Supreme Court, on the consolidated appeals, provide an important consideration of the relevant law and convention, and the nature of the connection between them.

A majority of six out of nine judges in the Supreme Court accepted the contention of the provinces that the passing of the resolution without provincial assent would be 'unconstitutional in the conventional sense'. Canada was a federal union, and the federal principle could not be reconciled with a state of affairs in which provincial legislative powers could be modified by the unilateral action of the federal authorities. The power of the Canadian Senate and House of Commons to pass resolutions or petition the Crown was, however, unlimited as a matter of law. What might be desirable as a limitation on the power of the federal authorities as a matter of political principle could not 'translate into a legal limitation, without expression in imperative constitutional text or statute'.[44]

A majority of the court thereby endorsed the familiar distinction between legal rule and political principle. In the absence of any provision of the British North America Act 1867 expressly limiting the authority of the federal Parliament to request amendments to the Constitution by resolution, the court was powerless to intervene. Theories about

[42] For a convenient general account, see Marshall, *Constitutional Conventions*, ch. 11.

[43] The governing provincial statutes were widely drawn: e.g. under the Newfoundland Judicature Act 1979, the Lieutenant-Governor in Council could refer to the Court of Appeal any matter which he thought fit to refer.

[44] *Reference re Amendment of the Constitution of Canada (Nos. 1, 2 & 3)* (1982) 125 DLR (3d) 1, 29.

Canadian federalism were matters of political significance alone: 'They do not engage the law, save as they might have some peripheral relevance to actual provisions of the British North America Act 1867 and its interpretation and application.'[45] However desirable was federal–provincial accord, it was irrelevant in law: it was not possible to 'qualify the issue of legality by considerations of fairness or equity or political acceptability or even judicial desirability'.[46]

The result of this view, however, was that the Canadian House of Commons and Senate could secure by simple resolution what the 1867 Act denied them authority to achieve by statute. Indeed, no constitutional safeguard existed—as a matter of law—to prevent the federal authorities from unilaterally procuring, by resolution, an amendment to the British North America Act designed to turn Canada into a unitary state (as the Attorney-General of Canada conceded in argument). The effect would be wholly to undermine the legislative scheme established by the Statute of Westminster 1931. Section 7(1) excluded repeal or amendment of the British North America Acts from the general power to repeal or amend United Kingdom statutes conferred by section 2: its purpose was precisely to protect provincial legislative powers from encroachment by the federal Parliament. Section 7(3) expressly restricted the legislative powers conferred by the Act on the Canadian Parliament and the provincial legislatures 'to the enactment of laws in relation to matters within the competence of the Parliament of Canada or of any of the legislatures of the provinces respectively'.

In these circumstances, the dissenting view seems more persuasive. A minority of judges held that the two Houses of Parliament could not accomplish, through the intervention of the Imperial Parliament, what the Parliament of Canada was itself unable to do. It was the court's duty to preserve the federal basis of the Constitution from such collateral attack. This was 'an attempt by the federal Parliament to accomplish indirectly' what it was 'legally precluded from doing directly' by 'perverting the recognised resolution method of obtaining constitutional amendments by the Imperial Parliament for an improper purpose'.[47] Since it was beyond the power of the federal Parliament to enact such an amendment, it was equally beyond the power of its two Houses to effect such an amendment through the agency of the Imperial Parliament.

The minority derived strong support for their approach from the advice of the Privy Council in the *Labour Conventions* case.[48] That case held that the federal Government was unable to secure enactment of legislation, for the purpose of giving effect to treaty obligations, which

[45] Ibid. [46] Ibid. 32. [47] Ibid. 77.
[48] *A.-G. for Canada* v. *A.-G. for Ontario* [1937] AC 326.

would trespass upon the exclusive legislative competence of the provinces. Lord Atkin had stated:

> It would be remarkable that while the Dominion could not initiate legislation, however desirable, which affected civil rights in the Provinces, yet its Government not responsible to the Provinces nor controlled by Provincial Parliaments need only agree with a foreign country to enact such legislation, and its Parliament would be forthwith clothed with authority to affect Provincial rights to the full extent of such agreement. Such a result would appear to undermine the constitutional safeguards of Provincial constitutional autonomy.[49]

The analogy with the present case was plain. The federal government's authority to ratify international treaties might be accepted; but 'what was held unconstitutional by the Privy Council was the use of that lawful procedure to legislate indirectly beyond the powers invested in the federal Parliament by . . . the British North America Act'.[50]

The Canadian Supreme Court unanimously endorsed Sir Ivor Jennings's test for the recognition of conventions: 'first, what are the precedents; secondly, did the actors in the precedents believe that they were bound by a rule; and thirdly, is there a reason for the rule?'[51] The court agreed that precedents and usage did not themselves establish the existence of convention: 'They must be normative.'[52] The convention that provincial consent should be obtained before amendments were sought to the Constitution which would change the balance of legislative powers was clearly normative. Its function was to preserve the federal character of the Canadian Constitution. The majority considered, none the less, that it could not be enforced because breach of convention gave rise to political remedies alone.

The main reason for the absence of a legal sanction was stated to be that conventional rules were 'generally in conflict with the legal rules which they postulate and the courts are bound to enforce the legal rules'. Such conflict would not entail the commission of illegality: 'It results from the fact that legal rules create wide powers, discretions, and rights which conventions prescribe should be exercised only in a certain limited manner, if at all.'[53] Accordingly, although as a matter of law the Queen could refuse her assent to legislation, by convention the power was severely curtailed. The legal rule created an absolute discretion and the conventional rule completely neutralized it.

I have suggested, however, that the House of Lords has accorded legal force to a convention circumscribing the exercise of otherwise unfettered prerogative power. In the *GCHQ* case, Lord Fraser observed that expectations protected in public law may conflict with the claimant's

[49] Ibid. 352. [50] (1982) 125 DLR (3d) 1, 60.
[51] *The Law and the Constitution*, 136.
[52] 125 DLR (3d) 90. [53] Ibid. 84.

rights in private law.[54] Moreover, a juxtaposition of opposites is a familiar feature of other parts of the law. Equitable principles often contradict, and may sometimes neutralize, rules of common law. The equitable doctrines of promissory estoppel and mistake (for example) heavily qualify the operation of common law rules in the field of contract.

An analogy with the dichotomy between law and equity was in fact drawn, in the present context, at an earlier stage of these proceedings. The Newfoundland Court of Appeal had adopted a suggestion by Justice Rand that the Statute of Westminster 1931 had made the British Parliament in effect a 'bare legislative trustee' for the Dominion.[55] The Court of Appeal considered the British Parliament a trustee for both federal and provincial legislatures: 'Any amendment enacted by the Parliament of Great Britain affecting the legislative competence of either of the parties, without that party's consent, would not only be contrary to the intendment of the Statute of Westminster, 1931 but it could defeat the whole scheme of the Canadian federal Constitution.'[56] Such an enactment would therefore be ineffective to alter the Canadian Constitution: it would be *ultra vires* as a matter of Canadian law.

A majority of the Supreme Court, however, shortly rejected a submission that, by enacting the Statute of Westminster, the United Kingdom Parliament had relinquished or yielded its previous omnipotent legal authority in relation to the British North America Act 1867. There had been no legal diminution of United Kingdom legislative supremacy. The legal competence of the Imperial Parliament remained unimpaired; and, moreover, the argument which appealed to the dissenting judges confused 'the issue of process . . . with the legal competence of the British Parliament'. The effect of section 7(1) of the Statute of Westminster, reinforced by section 7(3), was to preserve the authority of the United Kingdom Parliament in relation to future amendment of the British North America Act affecting federal–provincial relations.

But it seems that the court failed to distinguish between the legislative sovereignty of the Westminster Parliament as a matter of English law, on the one hand, and Canadian law, on the other. It was, no doubt, correct to assume that, in English law, the authority of Parliament at Westminster to legislate for Canada was unaffected by the aspirations of the Canadian provinces. In subsequent litigation over the validity of the final version of the Canada Act, the English courts declined to investigate the political realities of Dominion consent.[57] It was argued (for the plaintiff Indian chiefs) that the effect of the Statute of Westminster

[54] [1984] 3 All ER 935, 944.
[55] 'Some Aspects of Canadian Constitutionalism' (1960) 38 Can. Bar Rev. 135.
[56] (1981) 118 DLR (3d) 1, 17.
[57] *Manuel* v. *A.-G.* [1982] 3 All ER 786.

was to deprive the British Parliament of power to legislate for Canada except as reserved by section 7; and that section 4, requiring a declaration of Dominion consent, was declaratory of existing law whereby Dominion consent must actually be given to legislation affecting Canada. Dominion consent, which should be understood to mean the agreement of all the constituent constitutional fractions, including the Indians, had plainly not been given. Sir Robert Megarry V.-C. considered an English court bound by the 'simple rule that the duty of the court is to obey and apply every Act of Parliament, and that the court cannot hold any such Act to be *ultra vires*'. There may be questions about what the Act means, but 'once an instrument is recognised as being an Act of Parliament, no English court can refuse to obey it or question its validity'.[58]

It is, however, necessary to distinguish the question whether any given United Kingdom statute is valid as a matter of Canadian law. The point may easily be tested. Could the Westminster Parliament now repeal the Canada Act 1982 and substitute a new constitution for Canada of its own devising? It seems plain that no Canadian court would acknowledge any such remaining legislative power. For the transferee of legislative sovereignty, if not for the transferor, it is as true of legal principle as of political fact that 'freedom once conferred cannot be revoked'.[59] It follows that the scope of United Kingdom legislative authority in respect of Canada was not settled, as a matter of Canadian law, by English legal opinion of the effect of the Statute of Westminster. Sir Robert Megarry recognized that a statute purporting to repeal a grant of independence, or an Act applying to a foreign country, would be ignored in the country concerned. His own duty of full obedience to the Canada Act 1982 applied by virtue of his 'sitting as a judge in an English court'.

The Supreme Court's rejection of the argument based on abuse of the resolution procedure was therefore too quick. By failing to distinguish between the validity of the resulting United Kingdom statute as a matter of English law, on the one hand, and Canadian law, on the other, the court evaded the crucial issue. The Statute of Westminster was framed to protect the federal character of Canada by preventing changes being made in the constitutional balance of powers by unilateral action of the federal authorities. It is reasonable to conclude that use of the resolution procedure to procure amendment against the wishes of the provinces was rendered unlawful by necessary implication from

58 Ibid. 793.

59 *Ndlwana* v. *Hofmeyr* (1937) AD 229, 237. South African courts considered that the UK Parliament could not legislate to repeal the Status of the Union Act or the Statute of Westminster. See also similar remarks by Lord Denning: *Blackburn* v. *A.-G.* [1971] 2 All ER 1380, 1382–3.

the terms of the Statute of Westminster, and further that a United Kingdom statute enacted in compliance would be *ultra vires* and invalid as a matter of Canadian law.

We should prefer the view of the Newfoundland Court of Appeal, that the Imperial Parliament had surrendered to the provinces its legislative sovereignty over matters declared by the British North America Act 1867 to be within their exclusive legislative competence. The modification of the constitutional status of the provinces of Canada as autonomous communities was 'thereby withdrawn from future British parliamentary competence except with the consent of the provinces'.[60] There should be no surprise that parliamentary sovereignty turns out, on analysis, to be less than absolute—at least as a matter of Canadian law. I shall argue that similar conclusions may be drawn even in Britain, suggesting that the distinction between application and interpretation of statutes is ultimately one of degree. For practical purposes, at least, a statute held to be inapplicable to the circumstances arising has no more force—for those circumstances—than a statute rejected as void.[61]

From this perspective, the conclusions of the Newfoundland court are consistent with the well-known decision of the High Court of Australia in *Copyright Owners Reproduction Society* v. *EMI (Australia)*.[62] The court declined to apply a United Kingdom Act of 1928, increasing the rate of royalties payable in respect of musical recordings, because of the constitutional practice governing relations between the United Kingdom and the Commonwealth, at the time of enactment, whereby United Kingdom legislation would not extend to a Dominion unless expressly adopted. It was 'contrary to general conceptions and understanding of relations between the United Kingdom and the self-governing Dominions to interpret such legislation . . . as an exercise of the residual legislative power of the Parliament at Westminster to impose its will upon a Dominion'.[63] The court treated the convention as giving rise to a rule of statutory construction. The effect, however, was to deny the statute any application in Australia. In this instance, constitutional convention had triumphed over legislative supremacy: it had been embraced as a superior source of law. The point emerges clearly enough from the short judgment of McTiernan J.:

[60] (1981) 118 DLR (3d) 1, 18. See further Eric Colvin (1982) 4 Sup. Ct. Law Rev. 3, who argues (adopting H. L. A. Hart's terminology) that 'the central issue in the . . . Reference was surely the circumstances under which the rules of recognition of the Canadian legal system accept enactments of the UK Parliament as law for Canada'. It is important to note that the role of the UK Parliament in Canada's amendment process was exercised at the instance of Canada: s. 7 of the Statute of Westminster had been inserted to satisfy the Canadian desire to entrench the federal division of powers. See also First Report of the Foreign Affairs Committee (Kershaw Report), vol. 11, HC 42 of 1980–1: Memo. by Prof. H. W. R. Wade (at 103).

[61] See Ch. 11, below.

[62] (1958) 100 CLR 597.

[63] Ibid. 611 (Dixon CJ).

There was, of course, at that time, nothing to impose any constitutional limitations upon the legislative power of the Parliament of the United Kingdom in relation to the Dominions, but a long course of constitutional practice and convention had an operation growing out of the acceptance of constitutional principles that did not depend upon enacted law . . . The rule of construction which found its source in the political and constitutional relations between the United Kingdom and the Commonwealth of Australia before the Statute of Westminster would raise a presumption that the Act of 1928 was not intended to operate of its own force in this country.[64]

Convention as a source of constitutional law

We should now review the results of our reflections on law and convention, distinguishing between the positive and critical morality of the constitution.[65] Conventions are those rules which are rightly thought to govern political practice, binding the political actors on genuine constitutional grounds, whatever their actual beliefs on the matters in issue. Their major purpose is 'to give effect to the principles of governmental accountability that constitute the structure of responsible government'.[66] They express, in other words, conclusions of political principle, and so cannot, in the last analysis, be distinguished from the law. In matters of constitutional significance, legal doctrine and political principle are inevitably interdependent and intertwined.

Sir Ivor Jennings denied that there was any 'distinction of substance or nature' between law and convention.[67] J. D. B. Mitchell came to similar conclusions, noting that in the context of constitutional law there were necessarily limits to the possibility of 'enforcing' conventional rules.[68] There seems no reason, however, why legal remedies should not sometimes be granted in support of convention, where a firm foundation exists in political principle. In substance, the *Crossman Diaries* case[69] acknowledged that possibility. According to Mitchell, however, conventions occupied a position of 'inferiority' within a hierarchy of legal norms: they could modify the working of legal institutions provided that that modification was 'not in direct contradiction to any other rule of law'.[70] The Canadian Supreme Court thought the possibility of such contradiction must deny convention the character of law entirely. But further reflection suggests that convention may in some cases contradict a rule of law and none the less prevail—as a matter of legal principle.

As a source of law, a constitutional convention could rarely, no doubt, prevail over the explicit terms of an Act of Parliament: legislative supremacy is itself, after all, a primary component of our constitutional morality. If, however, legislative supremacy is but one constituent of a

[64] Ibid. 612–13. [65] Marshall, *Constitutional Conventions*, 10–12.
[66] Ibid. 18. [67] *The Law and the Constitution*, 117. [68] *Constitutional Law*, 34–9.
[69] *A.-G.* v. *Jonathan Cape*, above. [70] *Constitutional Law*, 29.

more complex political morality founded on the rule of law, and ultimately subject to considerations of legitimacy, it is mistaken to attribute to convention an intrinsic inferiority. Ultimately, even the validity of statute must be subject to fundamental questions of political principle; and political principle is sometimes enshrined in established constitutional convention.[71]

The importance of convention, as a reflection of accepted principle, was plainly recognized by the Canadian Supreme Court, which rejected a submission that the question concerning the existence of convention was non-justiciable. In that case the nature of the question demanded an answer: it was concerned with 'a fundamental issue of constitutionality and legitimacy'. In such circumstances there can be no assurance that convention will always bow to statute. It could reasonably be argued—as the Newfoundland Court of Appeal actually held— that whatever the legality of the resolution procedure for constitutional amendment, a resulting British statute, enacted in the teeth of provincial opposition, would be void as a matter of Canadian law.

Lord Reid's well-known repudiation of convention as a source of law, in *Madzimbamuto* v. *Lardner-Burke*,[72] must therefore be viewed in context. He denied that the validity of the Southern Rhodesia Act 1965 could be impugned on the basis of any convention against legislating for Southern Rhodesia without its consent. Parliament's sovereign power remained unimpaired. But that conclusion depended on a finding that the continued exercise of legislative power in respect of Rhodesia was legitimate. Sitting as a court of Southern Rhodesia, the Privy Council was seised of an issue of legitimacy as well as legality.[73] The court had necessarily to take sides between the British authorities and the Rhodesian rebels, whatever its natural loyalty to Britain. It accepted the decisions of the courts of Uganda and Pakistan recognizing the legitimacy of their new regimes, but rejected the analogy with Rhodesia. It could not be predicted with certainty whether or not the British government would succeed in its attempts to regain control. Whatever the merits of the court's analysis, the decision cannot be taken to affirm a doctrinal separation between law and politics: legality and political morality were inextricably interlinked.[74]

These conclusions about the interconnection and assimilation of law and convention, and interdependence of legal and political principle, suggest intriguing possibilities for the subjection of executive power to legal control. In particular, once the propriety of judicial review of the

[71] For the limits of legislative supremacy, see Chs. 3 and 11.
[72] [1969] 1 AC 645, 723.
[73] Cf. Detmold, *The Australian Commonwealth*, 50, 93–5.
[74] *Madzimbamuto* is further considered in Ch. 11, below.

prerogative has been established in principle, accepted constitutional usage becomes a genuine feature of public law. Supposed illustrations of the divorce between law and convention may largely reflect outmoded (though sometimes inevitable) limitations on judicial remedies.[75] Dicey gave the example of the Queen withholding her assent from an important bill which had been passed by both Houses of Parliament: 'Here there would be a gross violation of usage, but the matter could not by any proceeding known to English law be brought before the judge.'[76] Although offered as evidence of the divide between convention and law, the point may as well be taken to illustrate the ancient constitutional rule that the Sovereign cannot be sued in her own courts.

In *The Queen* v. *Toohey, ex parte Northern Land Council*,[77] Mason J. observed, in the High Court of Australia, that if it were appropriate for the principle of immunity from suit to apply to personal acts of the Sovereign, it was 'questionable whether it should now apply to acts affecting the rights of the citizen which, though undertaken in the name of the Sovereign or his representative, are in reality decisions of the executive government'. Procedural reforms had overcome the immunity and undermined the associated doctrine that the King can do no wrong.[78] He considered it anomalous that immunity attached to the exercise of prerogative power, since it was an important constitutional development that the Sovereign acted in accordance with the advice of her ministers.

The court's decision is itself a good illustration of the modern harmony of law and convention. It rejected an argument that the exercise of statutory power by a representative of the Crown enjoyed immunity from review. Even if, as Aickin and Wilson JJ. held, the Administrator of the Northern Territory was properly viewed as the representative of the Crown, the court must none the less ensure that his statutory powers were exercised for an authorized purpose. Aickin J. stressed that the case did not involve the personal decision of the Queen or Governor-General or other representative, who were bound by ministerial advice: 'Her Majesty or her representative acts or decides in the sense that she acts or decides as she is advised by the Privy Council or an Executive Council.'[79] He was evidently unwilling to permit a legal fiction to impede the development of public law:

[75] Neither injunctions nor the prerogative remedies lie against the Crown: the latter are in theory sought at the suit of the Crown.

[76] *Law of the Constitution*, 440. See Colin Munro, 'Dicey on Constitutional Conventions' [1985] PL 637, at 645.

[77] (1981) 151 CLR 170, 220.

[78] See Crown Proceedings Act 1947.

[79] (1981) 151 CLR 170, 260, citing Kitto J. in the *Communist Party* case (1951) 83 CLR 1, 280. Gibbs CJ did not think that the Administrator represented the Crown, but in any case agreed that the Crown enjoyed no special immunity from judicial review.

If an act done by a minister pursuant to power vested in him by statute may be examined by the court in order to determine whether he has acted for purposes or with intentions which are irrelevant to the proper exercise of power, or contrary to the purposes of the grant of the power, it would seem anomalous and irrational to say that it is impossible to examine a decision made by more than one minister to advise the Governor-General to do an act which in constitutional reality he is obliged to do once advised so to do.[80]

We may pursue these speculations into other fields of prerogative power. We should not, for example, accept uncritically the view that the Attorney-General, in instituting or withdrawing legal proceedings, is necessarily free from judicial control. Despite its uncertain origins, it now seems to be a well-established convention that the Attorney-General's decision to prosecute must be taken independently of ministerial or cabinet opinion. A decision to instigate legal proceedings taken for reasons of party advantage, or even of ideological conviction, would today be widely considered improper. If the uncertainty of conventional requirements—or their limits—be thought a barrier to legal enforcement (as is often suggested), the speech of Sir Hartley Shawcross to the House of Commons in 1951 serves as sufficient response.

In his 'classic pronouncement',[81] Shawcross explained that the Attorney was entitled to consult his government colleagues for their views on relevant aspects of public policy which might influence his decision to prosecute, but the decision itself must be taken by the Attorney alone 'applying his judicial mind'. The statement had been approved by Viscount Simon, Viscount Jowitt, and Lord Kilmuir, each a former Law Officer who subsequently became Lord Chancellor. Even if the proper limits of ministerial influence are not always perfectly clear, the essential principle of independent judgment is firmly established and understood.[82] It might be concluded that one convention has ousted another: the Attorney-General's independence overrides the ordinary rule of collective responsibility; and there seems no reason why such an arrangement should not be acknowledged as a matter of law.

In practice, of course, it is likely to be difficult to prove that a decision to authorize prosecution was taken for improper or ulterior reasons; but that is a standard feature of cases of suspected bad faith or abuse of executive power.[83] It is also true that the issue may sometimes

80 151 CLR 264–5. Cf. *FAI Insurances* v. *Winneke* (1982) 151 CLR 342, esp. 349 (Gibbs CJ); 396–7 (Wilson J.).

81 J. Ll. J. Edwards, *The Attorney-General, Politics and the Public Interest* (London, 1984), 318; *The Law Officers of the Crown* (London, 1964), 223.

82 Cf. Edwards, *The Attorney-General*, 324. See also Marshall, *Constitutional Conventions*, ch. 7. A similar principle applies to grant of the A.-G.'s fiat in respect of relator proceedings (where refusal of judicial review may none the less be justified: Ch. 9, above).

83 See e.g. *R.* v. *Govnr. of Brixton Prison, ex p. Soblen* [1963] 2 QB 243.

provoke fierce public controversy.[84] It is none the less wrong to deny the possibility, in principle, of a judicial remedy—as in other cases where statutory or prerogative power affects the interests of individuals. It is hard to accept, without qualification, the view expressed by Wilson J. in the High Court of Australia, that 'the courts and the community must rely heavily upon the integrity of the Attorney-General for the faithful discharge of the prerogatives and privileges of his high office, leaving his actions to be questioned, if at all, in Parliament'.[85]

In *Barton* v. *The Queen*,[86] the High Court of Australia denied that the Attorney-General's decision to file an *ex officio* indictment was subject to judicial review, refusing to examine a claim that the Attorney had acted at the direction of the State Premier. The court could grant a stay of proceedings, once commenced, in order to prevent an abuse of process and to ensure a fair trial; but the statutory discretion to file an information could not be examined. However, the decision proceeded from an analogy between the statutory discretion, under the Australian Courts Act 1828 (UK), section 5, and the common law power of the Attorney-General in England, and was based on 'the general principle that a prerogative power was not examinable by the courts'.[87] The court's reasoning cannot, therefore, survive modern rejection of that 'general principle'. Moreover, the court was unwilling to countenance the use of *ex officio* indictments to deny the accused the advantages of committal proceedings merely 'because in the distant past the courts proceeded to hear trials on *ex officio* indictments without benefit of a preliminary examination'. It was accepted, at least, that the courts could not abdicate their responsibility in that respect to the Attorney-General.[88]

Wilson J. was impressed by the importance of the separation of functions between judges and prosecutors as a ground for denying judicial review. As Lord Dilhorne had insisted, a judge should 'keep out of the arena'. He should not have or appear to have any responsibility for the institution of a prosecution: 'If a judge has power to decline to hear a case because he does not think it should be brought, then it may soon be thought that the cases he allows to proceed are cases brought with his consent or approval.'[89] Contrary, however, to Wilson J.'s

[84] e.g. *Ponting's* case, where it was alleged that ministers had improperly influenced the decision to authorize prosecution under Official Secrets Act, s. 2: see Gavin Drewry [1985] PL 203 at 205.

[85] *Barton* v. *R.* (1980) 32 ALR 449, 476. See also *Gouriet* v. *Union of Post Office Workers* [1977] 3 All ER 70, 88 (Viscount Dilhorne).

[86] (1980) 32 ALR 449.

[87] Ibid. 455: Gibbs and Mason JJ. (Aickin J. agreeing), citing *Prosser* (1848) 11 Beav. 306; 50 ER 834.

[88] 32 ALR 463.

[89] *DPP* v. *Humphrys* [1977] AC 1, 26: cited at 32 ALR 471.

assertion, such dicta are as pertinent to the jurisdiction to prevent an abuse of process as to the question of review of the decision to prosecute. Both forms of control should be confined to exceptional cases, but neither can be abdicated—for the reasons given by Lord Devlin in *Connolly*. The court cannot escape its responsibility to ensure fair treatment of the accused.[90]

A decision to prosecute for improper reasons, or at government's dictation, would pervert the fairness of a subsequent trial as much as (for example) the defendant's exposure to double jeopardy by successive charges based on a single incident. The fairness of the trial cannot be insulated from the events which precede it—a truth acknowledged by the trial judge's discretion to exclude relevant and admissible evidence against the defendant which has been obtained by unfair means.[91] In the present case, the majority recognized that to treat the courts as 'concerned only with the conduct of the trial itself, considered quite independently of the committal proceedings' would be to overlook 'the development of the criminal process and to ignore the function of the preliminary examination and its relation to the trial'.[92]

The logic of Wilson J.'s position would entrust responsibility for deciding whether a trial should proceed wholly to the Attorney-General—the conclusion reached in an earlier case,[93] which Wilson J. expressly rejected. Acceptance of the abuse of process jurisdiction logically commits the court to the possibility of review of the decision to prosecute; and, in practice, the former inevitably assumes something of the character of the latter. The Attorney-General could file an indictment either after discharge by a committing magistrate or else in the absence of committal proceedings. Stephen J. recognized that the presumption of the majority in *Barton*—that a trial which took place without previous committal proceedings would generally be unfair—placed a 'significant practical qualification' on the Attorney-General's supposedly unexaminable power.[94]

[90] [1964] AC 1254, 1354; see Ch. 9, above. It has been recognized that, in some circumstances, the discretion of the Crown Prosecution Service to continue or abandon criminal proceedings may be subject to review: *R.* v. *Chief Const. of Kent & CPS, ex p. GL* [1991] Crim. LR 841. See also *Salvarajan* v. *Race Relations Bd.* [1976] 1 All ER 12, 21 (Lawton LJ); *R.* v. *Gen. Council of the Bar, ex p. Percival* [1990] 3 All ER 137, 149–52.

[91] See *Sang* [1980] AC 402; Police & Crim. Evid. Act 1984 s. 78; T. R. S. Allan, 'Fairness, Truth and Silence: The Criminal Trial and the Judge's Exclusionary Discretion', in Hyman Gross and Ross Harrison (eds.) *Jurisprudence: Cambridge Essays* (Oxford, 1992).

[92] 32 ALR 449, 463.

[93] *Re Forrester and R.* (1977) 73 DLR (3d) 736, 740 (Quigley J.).

[94] 32 ALR 466. See also the Div. Ct.'s decision that an application to stay proceedings on the ground of abuse of process is in 'an altogether different category' from an ordinary application to quash the indictment: 'It is an application based on principles of fairness and justice, and the contention is that it would be unjust that there should be a trial at all. It is not . . . part of the trial process.' *R.* v. *Central Criminal Court, ex p. Randle* [1992] 1 All ER 370, 386: followed in *R.* v. *Crown Court at Norwich, ex p. Belsham* [1992] 1 All ER 394.

In some circumstances, then, convention may constitute a legitimate ground for confining and controlling the exercise of executive power. It may sometimes assist in securing legal as well as political responsibility. It is now widely recognized that ministerial responsibility to Parliament is an inadequate substitute for legal control. Though (for example) the Attorney-General may in theory be answerable in the Commons for the way in which he exercises his various discretions, there are inevitably serious limitations to political accountability for individual decisions.[95] A similar point may be made with regard to the Home Secretary's exercise (by convention) of the prerogative power to pardon offenders. Since it is established convention that exercise of the prerogative of mercy is a matter of individual rather than collective responsibility, a departure from precedent may fairly be thought a breach of legal as well as political principle. It is a familiar feature of legal development that standards of reasonableness, fairness, and good faith are supplied by investigation of the norms and practices which have become established in response to widely perceived requirements of justice.[96]

Settled convention may, of course, derive from political accommodation or practical convenience, as opposed to constitutional principle. But, once established, legitimate expectations may arise on the basis of it, and such expectations may sometimes justify enforcement of convention as a matter of law. Taylor J.'s decision in *ex parte Ruddock*[97] may be thought a good example, holding that the publication and adoption, by successive Home Secretaries, of criteria governing the issue of warrants for telephone tapping had created expectations which would be judicially enforced. There is an analogy perhaps with the Attorney-General's discretion to prosecute suspected offenders: it was settled that tapping must not be authorized for party political purposes or for the ulterior purposes of any particular section of the community. The exercise of what was taken to be a prerogative power could be constrained in defence of public law rights, arising on the basis of existing practice, as explained and affirmed by repeated government statements.

A similar recognition of the interaction between principle and practice may assist in assimilating the standards stipulated by the European Convention on Human Rights. The conformity of government action to those standards may be presumed to be a matter of recognized practice—even if it is not a requirement of law, narrowly understood; and any divergence between practice and principle would seem to need justification. Some years ago, Scarman LJ thought that the courts

[95] Cf. Marshall, *Constitutional Conventions*, 118–19; Edwards, *The Attorney-General*, 119.

[96] Cf. Hugh Collins, 'Democracy and Adjudication', in Neil MacCormick and Peter Birks (eds.), *The Legal Mind: Essays for Tony Honoré* (Oxford, 1986), 78. Exercise of the prerogative of mercy was considered to be unreviewable in *Hanratty* v. *Lord Butler*, *The Times*, 12 May 1971.

[97] [1987] 2 All ER 518 (considered above, Ch. 8).

would 'interpret statutory language and apply common law principles, wherever possible, so as to reach a conclusion consistent with our international obligations'.[98] And Lord Denning MR considered the executive bound by the Convention on the ground that 'the principles stated in the Convention are only a statement of the principles of fair dealing: and it is their duty to act fairly'.[99] If settled practice may constitute a basis for the protection of interests and expectations, ensuring fair treatment at the hands of the state, its effect is strengthened by ministerial pronouncement or explicit adoption. Ratification of the European Convention, and public acknowledgement of the rights and liberties proclaimed, would seem the strongest affirmation of a code of political morality to which British government may be taken to be committed.

Comparison with the Imperial Conferences held between 1911 and 1937 seems apt. In the *Labour Conventions* case,[100] Sir Lyman Duff, Chief Justice of Canada, considered a claim that the Governor-General, acting on the advice of the Canadian government, lacked authority to conclude a treaty with a foreign state. The Report of the Imperial Conference of 1926, which declared the equality of status of Great Britain and the Dominions, had described the Governor-General of a Dominion as the representative of the Crown 'holding in all essential respects the same position in relation to the administration of public affairs in the Dominion as is held by His Majesty the King in Great Britain'. Founding an argument on the distinction between law and convention, it was urged that, whatever the conventional understanding, in point of law the power to exercise the prerogative had not been delegated by the Crown to the Governor-General of Canada. Observing that there could hardly be more authoritative evidence as to constitutional usage than the declarations of an Imperial Conference, the Chief Justice dismissed the argument, rejecting the law–convention dichotomy:

> As a rule, the crystallization of constitutional usage into a rule of constitutional law to which the Courts will give effect is a slow process extending over a long period of time; but the Great War accelerated the pace of development in the region with which we are concerned, and it would seem that the usages to which I have referred, the practice, that is to say, under which Great Britain and the Dominions enter into agreements with foreign countries in the form of agreements between Governments and of a still more informal character, must be recognised by the Courts as having the force of law.[101]

[98] *Ahmad* v. *ILEA* [1978] QB 36, 48. See now *Spycatcher* case [1990] AC 109 (Ch. 6, above).

[99] R. v. *Home Secretary, ex p. Bhajan Singh* [1976] QB 198, 207. (But compare R. v. *Chief Immig. Officer, ex p. Salamat Bibi* [1976] 1 WLR 979.)

[100] *Ref. re Weekly Rest in Industrial Undertakings Act* [1936] 3 DLR 673.

[101] Ibid. 679.

The Governor-General derived the prerogative power of making treaties on behalf of Canada from the convention which acknowledged the equal status of the Dominions, and the practice of the Dominion in concluding agreements with foreign countries. The judgment has been recently dismissed, in the Canadian Supreme Court, as an account of an 'evolution which is characteristic of customary international law', and as irrelevant to the position in domestic law.[102] This explanation overlooks the point, however, that the authority of the Governor-General in Council remained a vital matter of internal constitutional law: the case concerned precisely the powers of the federal executive in respect of matters which fell within the exclusive legislative competence of the Canadian provinces.[103]

I have counselled against the assumption that formal charters of rights are necessarily superior to common law methods of protection.[104] If, however, the declarations of an Imperial Conference provided the authoritative evidence requisite for the crystallization of constitutional usage into law, it would follow in any event that the European Convention might be fully assimilated without formal enactment. The Convention could reasonably be viewed as a declaration of the political principles which the practice of British government acknowledges, along with that of other members of the Council of Europe. Constitutional convention, in respect of human rights, would thereby receive authoritative definition, similar to that provided for developing conventions within the Commonwealth by the declarations of the Imperial Conferences. Ministers could no more lawfully neglect the requirements of the Convention, in exercise of their discretionary powers, than other duties of fairness towards the individual affected.

The role that the European Convention might play in support of the development of a humanitarian constitutional practice—as an adjunct to English principles of administrative law—is revealed by the decision in *R.* v. *Home Secretary, ex parte Kirkwood*.[105] The applicant, who faced extradition to California to stand trial for murder, sought judicial review of the minister's warrant ordering his surrender, which was issued while his application under the European Convention was still pending. He had argued that infliction of the death penalty, involving inordinate delay, if he were convicted in California, would amount to inhuman and degrading treatment. The court refused to intervene on the ground that, when exercising his powers under the Extradition Act 1870, the Home Secretary was not obliged to consider the requirements

[102] *Ref. re Amendment of the Constitution of Canada (Nos. 1, 2 & 3)* (1982) 125 DLR (3d) 1, 24–5.
[103] See discussion of the Privy Council decision in the *Labour Conventions* case, above.
[104] Ch. 6.
[105] [1984] 2 All ER 390.

of the Convention since it formed no part of municipal law. His decision to order extradition could not therefore he impugned on *Wednesbury* principles governing the exercise of executive discretion. Such a result might be thought the outcome of a somewhat implausible severance of legal duty from constitutional and political principle.

The European Convention on Human Rights should be openly accorded the force of law within the United Kingdom, subject only to clearly inconsistent statutory enactment. The present position that, though forming no part of municipal law, the Convention can nevertheless be treated as providing guidance in its application and development, seems intellectually confused. The Convention cannot afford authoritative guidance and at the same time be denied legal status.[106] This confusion in the English cases has not been duplicated in Scotland. In *Kaur* v. *Lord Advocate*,[107] the Lord Ordinary (Lord Ross) denied that the court could have regard to the Convention even as an aid to construction. He was unwilling to permit the executive to achieve legal changes which he considered could be made only by Parliament. This view seems unduly rigid in view of what is arguably the special 'constitutional' nature of the Convention, acknowledged by the grant to United Kingdom citizens of the right of individual petition to the Commission.[108] But in any event, Lord Ross exposed the contradiction which the English compromise entails: 'If the Convention does not form part of the municipal law, I do not see why the court should have regard to it at all.'[109]

Judicial recognition of the European Convention may even be compared with the Supreme Court's approach to established practice in the *Canadian Constitutional Amendment Reference*. That decision plainly demonstrated the futility of seeking to divorce law and practice in constitutional matters. The idea that the federal government could have proceeded in defiance of the court's ruling on convention, relying on its power in 'law', seems both philosophically muddled and practically quite unrealistic. The court's decision not only demonstrated that conventions were justiciable, but inevitably determined, by its pronouncement on constitutionality, what was practical politics thereafter—at least for any administration committed to constitutional government.

Finally, Sir Lyman Duff's opinion may perhaps be supported by reference to the judgment of another famous Chief Justice. It would be hard to find a better example of the crystallization of convention into

[106] See the discussion of *Brind* v. *Home Office* [1991] 1 All ER 720 in Ch. 8, above.

[107] 1981 SLT 322. For analysis, see J. L. Murdoch, 'The European Convention on Human Rights in Scots Law' [1991] PL 40.

[108] Cf. F. A. Mann, 'Britain's Bill of Rights' (1978) 94 LQR 512 at 523–4.

[109] 1981 SLT 329.

law than Coke's denial of the right of James I to administer justice in person: 'the King in his own person cannot adjudge any case, either criminal, as treason, felony, etc., or betwixt party and party, concerning his inheritance, chattels, or goods, etc., but this ought to be determined and adjudged in some Court of Justice, according to the law and custom of England'.[110] Sir Ivor Jennings doubted Duff CJ's reasoning on the ground that the constitutional usages incorporated into the common law were those of the seventeenth century.[111] But why is the common law thought incapable of accommodating modern constitutional usage? Commercial custom is enforced today where it supplies the background to contractual agreement. Despite its treatment in the Canadian Supreme Court, therefore, and notwithstanding Jennings's disapproval, we may think that Duff CJ's judgment correctly stated the position that 'constitutional law consists very largely of established constitutional usages recognised by the Courts as embodying a rule of law'.[112]

110 *Prohibitions del Roy* (1607) 12 Co. Rep. 63, 64.
111 *The Law and the Constitution*, 126–7.
112 [1936] 3 DLR 673, 678.

11
Legislative Supremacy

> Though the legislative, whether placed in one or more, whether it be always in being or only by intervals, though it be the supreme power in every commonwealth, yet, first, it is not, nor can possibly be, absolutely arbitrary over the lives and fortunes of the people . . . Their power in the utmost bounds of it is limited to the public good of the society.
>
> John Locke, *Two Treatises of Government*, ii, para. 135.

It was suggested in Chapter 3 that legislative supremacy must ultimately be limited by the principle of separation of powers—citing in support Lord Diplock's description of the 'Westminster model' of constitutions, containing a division of legislative, executive, and judicial power.[1] I sought to contest the assumption of the New South Wales Court of Appeal, that any limits on Parliament's power to make laws for the 'peace, welfare and good government' of its jurisdiction could derive only from statute, insisting that such constraints were part of the common law.[2] The Australian court had accepted uncritically the arbitrary distinction between legal doctrine and political principle, on which Dicey's rule of parliamentary omnipotence finally rests.

Although the *legitimacy* of the sovereignty doctrine, as a constitutional principle worthy of judicial respect, derives from Parliament's representative composition—or that of the House of Commons—its juridical status, in traditional treatments of the subject, was somehow grounded independently. The political notion of the ultimate sovereignty of the electorate must be distinguished (on this approach) from the legal doctrine of legislative supremacy: the courts owed their allegiance to the latter and recognized no 'trust' between Parliament and people. Dicey was clear on the point, observing that the courts would take no notice of the will of the electors: 'The judges know nothing about any will of the people except in so far as that will is expressed by an Act of Parliament, and would never suffer the validity of a statute to be questioned on the ground of its having been passed or kept alive in opposition to the wishes of the electors.'[3] The extent of judicial loyalty to statute enjoined by the doctrine of parliamentary sovereignty therefore depended on the correct interpretation of the

[1] *Hinds* v. *R.* [1977] AC 195, 212–13.
[2] See *Builders' Labourers Federation* case (1986) 7 NSWLR 372.
[3] A. V. Dicey, *The Law of the Constitution*, 10th edn. (London, 1959), 74.

legal principle alone. It was a matter of accurately formulating the fundamental rule of the legal order. Its *existence* might ultimately be a matter of political fact, but its normative content was a matter of law. The courts were required to enforce the terms of the most recent statement of Parliament's will, expressed in the proper form: *lex posterior derogat priori.*[4]

Within this tradition, two opposing conceptions have fought for recognition. On one view, Parliament's legislative supremacy is limited in only one respect: it cannot control the manner and form of future legislation.[5] From an alternative perspective, the rule should be understood to require judicial obedience to statutes expressed in the manner and form currently stipulated for—either by preceding Parliaments or by common law. Parliament can legislate effectively about the manner and form of future legislation. On the former view, though not the latter, any attempt to limit the legislative freedom of future Parliaments, in order to entrench provisions of special importance against future amendment or repeal, must fail. If such an attempt succeeded, the judges would have engineered a revolution by signalling their allegiance to a new legal order. This, however, would be a political development, and not (in any ordinary sense) a legal one.[6]

Reflection on the manner of traditional argument about the nature of sovereignty must cast serious doubt on the premisses of that debate. Disagreement about what the fundamental rule of the legal order requires in particular cases cannot be resolved by appeals to opposing conceptions of the rule. The disagreement, by its nature, poses questions about the character of the legal order itself. It raises issues of political theory concerning the justifications for, and consequences of, competing conceptions of the legal doctrine. No case raising genuine doubt about the boundaries of legislative supremacy can be settled by reference to general assertions in previous cases, or by simply reporting a practice of unquestioning judicial allegiance.

A case in which competent constitutional lawyers can take different views of what the doctrine requires necessarily raises questions about the adequacy and authority of previous formulations of the rule, and about what the limits of the practice of judicial obedience to statute should be. In short, the fundamental rule that accords legal validity to Acts of Parliament is not itself the foundation of the legal order, beyond which the lawyer is forbidden to look. That fundamental rule

[4] See e.g. J. W. Salmond, *Jurisprudence*, 10th edn. (London, 1947), s. 50; and, for comment, M. J. Detmold, *The Australian Constitution* (Sydney, 1985), 228–30.

[5] Cf. *Ellen Street Estates* v. *Minister of Health* [1934] 1 KB 590, 597 (Maugham LJ).

[6] See H. W. R. Wade, 'The Legal Basis of Sovereignty' [1955] CLJ 172. Compare R. F. V. Heuston, *Essays in Constitution Law*, 2nd edn. (London, 1964), ch. 1; Sir Ivor Jennings, *The Law and the Constitution*, 5th edn. (London, 1959), ch. 4.

derives its legal authority from the underlying moral or political theory to which it belongs. The sterility and inconclusiveness of much of the debate about the nature of sovereignty stems largely from the attempt to divorce legal doctrine from political principle. Legal questions which challenge the nature of our constitutional order can only be answered in terms of the political morality on which that order is based.[7]

The positivist orthodoxy in constitutional theory, predicated on a division between political morality and legal principle, is forced to maintain an equally sharp conceptual distinction between the application and interpretation of statutes. The duty of the courts to apply a statute is absolute: the legal doctrine of sovereignty admits of no exceptions, however strong the affront to judicial notions of justice or however extreme the consequences in a particular case. In *Madzimbamuto* v. *Lardner-Burke*,[8] Lord Reid stated:

> It is often said that it would be unconstitutional for the United Kingdom Parliament to do certain things, meaning that the moral, political and other reasons against doing them are so strong that most people would regard it as highly improper if Parliament did these things. But that does not mean that it is beyond the power of Parliament to do such things. If Parliament chose to do any of them the courts could not hold the Act of Parliament invalid.

A statute may, however, legitimately be *interpreted* so as to accord, as far as possible, with fundamental concepts of justice. A statute will be presumed to conform to the international obligations of the United Kingdom in the absence of terms which are clearly inconsistent with that result.[9] The principle *nulla poena sine lege* is expressed in the presumption against according retrospective force to statutory provisions which extend the scope of the criminal law; and the injustice of imposing punishment in the absence of fault is met by a presumption in favour of requiring *mens rea*.[10] It is assumed that Parliament does not intend a person to be deprived of his property without compensation unless such an intention has been expressed in unequivocal terms.[11] But these constituent principles of the rule of law take second place to parliamentary supremacy: presumptions of legislative intent always give way to the explicit terms of the statute. This approach was firmly insisted on by Dicey in response to Blackstone's conception of natural law:

[7] Cf. Ronald Dworkin, *Taking Rights Seriously* (London, 1977), ch. 4. Dworkin argues that an adequate theory of adjudication must identify 'a particular conception of community morality as decisive of legal issues; that conception holds that community morality is the political morality presupposed by the laws and institutions of the community' (ibid. 126). See also *Law's Empire* (London, 1986) (considered below).

[8] [1969] 1 AC 645, 723.

[9] *Bloxam* v. *Favre* (1883) 8 PD 101, 107 (Sir James Hannen P.).

[10] See Ch. 2, above.

[11] *Central Control Bd. (Liquor Traffic)* v. *Cannon Brewery Co.* [1919] AC 744, 752 (Lord Atkinson).

There is no legal basis for the theory that judges, as exponents of morality, may overrule Acts of Parliament. Language which might seem to imply this amounts in reality to nothing more than the assertion that the judges, when attempting to ascertain what is the meaning to be affixed to an Act of Parliament, will presume that Parliament did not intend to violate the ordinary rules of morality, or the principles of international law, and will therefore, whenever possible, give such an interpretation to a statutory enactment as may be consistent with the doctrines both of private and of international morality.[12]

This distinction, between the rule requiring the *application* of a statute and the principles governing its *interpretation*, seeks to reconcile the orthodox lawyer's insistence on a strict separation of law from moral or political principle, on the one hand, with his expectation that the administration of law will reflect political morality, on the other. Its plausibility, however, stems largely from linguistic considerations: a statute which was rejected (or 'disapplied') could not properly be described as one which had been applied, subject to a strict interpretation. It would not, according to ordinary linguistic usage, have been applied at all. The linguistic point, however, obscures the sense in which, at a practical level, the distinction between interpretation and application is essentially one of degree. An interpretation which limits the scope of statutory words in deference to an important principle of political morality excludes their application in those situations governed by the principle. The strict construction of an ambiguous penal provision denies its application in doubtful cases. The more important the principle of political morality, or the stronger the presumption of legislative intent which gives it expression, the narrower the range of circumstances in which the statute will be applied. The strongest presumption of legislative intent would be one which denied the statute any application at all.

The famous passage in Coke's report of *Bonham's Case*[13] is surely a fine illustration: 'it appears in our books, that in many cases, the common law will controul Acts of Parliament and sometimes adjudge them to be utterly void: for when an Act of Parliament is against common right and reason, or repugnant, or impossible to be performed, the common law will controul it, and adjudge such Act to be void'. Debate over Coke's real meaning must be conducted in the light of the unsettled relationship then existing between statute and common law, and the absence of any sharp dichotomy between legislation and adjudication.[14] In that context, it is almost meaningless to argue about whether Coke was asserting the supremacy of fundamental law

[12] *Law of the Constitution*, 62–3.

[13] (1609) 8 Co. Rep. 107, 118.

[14] Charles Howard McIlwain, *The High Court of Parliament and its Supremacy* (New Haven, Conn., 1910) 147–8; 286 ff.

over statute law, or whether the case is merely an instance of bold interpretation.[15]

The strength of the *nemo iudex* principle supported a presumption whose force eclipsed the distinction. The idea that the Royal College of Physicians should be granted the right to try offences against its own regulations, imposing fines and retaining half of the moneys resulting, was so offensive to ordinary notions of justice that it was rejected as a mistake, and in that sense contrary to Parliament's true intention. The statute was analogous to contradictory—'repugnant'—laws or laws which required the impossible, and hence 'against common right and reason'. Parliament's authority and dignity could be saved with the reflection that 'some statutes are made against law and right, which those who made them perceiving, would not put them in execution'.[16]

Considerations of fairness—in the sense of the distribution of political power—would today dictate a more cautious judicial attitude in the face of apparent legislative injustice.[17] As *Ridge* v. *Baldwin* affirmed,[18] common law requirements of natural justice may be imposed to supplement a statutory procedure. But common law rights must not be permitted, at least in ordinary circumstances, to undermine the legislative objective: 'it must be clear that the statutory procedure is insufficient to achieve justice and that to require additional steps would not frustrate the apparent purpose of the legislation'.[19] At some point, however, the rupture of shared convictions about the elements of procedural justice would entail a breakdown of communication between Parliament and courts—a breakdown evident, perhaps, in the courts' characteristic treatment of privative clauses, purporting to oust the courts' jurisdiction.[20]

Lon Fuller noted the close association of ideas made by Coke between repugnant statutes and the impropriety of a man's acting as judge in his own cause: the statute contradicted the fundamentals of common law notions of justice.[21] Just as the distinction between procedure and substance is hard to preserve, in the context of judicial review, so Fuller emphasized the connection between procedures and institutional practices and the concept of law itself, as an enterprise in the governance of human conduct. Today, Coke CJ's judgment finds

[15] Cf. Philip Allott, 'The Courts and Parliament: Who Whom?' [1979] CLJ 79.

[16] (1609) 8 Co. Rep. 118. A modern example of the same robust style of construction is *Re Sigsworth* [1935] Ch 89 (the Administration of Estates Act 1925 could not be applied to enable a murderer to benefit from his victim's estate).

[17] For this distinction between justice and fairness, see Dworkin, *Law's Empire*, and Ch. 4, above.

[18] [1964] AC 40.

[19] *Wiseman* v. *Borneman* [1971] AC 297, 308 (Lord Reid).

[20] Ch. 3, above.

[21] *The Morality of Law* (New Haven, Conn. and London, 1969), 99–101.

an echo in the New Zealand Court of Appeal, which reaffirmed the principle in *Ridge* v. *Baldwin* that an office-holder could not lawfully be dismissed without an opportunity to be heard in his defence.[22] The judgments drew attention to Lord Hailsham's description of the rule as 'fundamental', Cooke J. adding: 'This is perhaps a reminder that it is arguable that some common law rights go so deep that even Parliament cannot be accepted by the courts to have destroyed them.'[23]

Reconsideration of *Bonham's Case* suggests that modern assertions of unlimited sovereignty rest on a misunderstanding of constitutional history. Charles Howard McIlwain explained that Coke's conception of legislative supremacy did not entail the total absence of limits, as in the usual modern sense of that expression: the supremacy of the High Court of Parliament was akin to that of the United States Supreme Court.[24] It was a superior court, but one with both legislative and judicial functions, which were not clearly distinguished. It is in that context that we should understand Coke's well-known statement that 'the power and *jurisdiction* of the Parliament, for making of Laws in proceeding by Bill . . . is so transcendent and absolute, as it cannot be confined either *for causes* or *persons* within any bounds'.[25]

Blackstone, in his turn, accepted that 'Acts of Parliament that are impossible to be performed are of no validity; and if there arise out of them collaterally any absurd consequences, manifestly contradictory to common reason, they are, with regard to those collateral consequences, void'.[26] If he also cited Coke in support of Parliament's 'sovereign and uncontrolable authority', he did so in deference to those contemporary theories which insisted on an 'absolute despotic power, which must in all governments reside somewhere'. Coke clearly provided doubtful support, and the idea contradicted Blackstone's own emphasis on the separation of powers and the fundamental rights and liberties of Englishmen. Dicey simply perpetuated Blackstone's confusion.

We should therefore concede to Parliament its law-making supremacy, but within the overall constraints of the constitutional scheme as a whole.[27] Statutes, properly enacted, are entitled to great respect, but not unlimited deference: the warmth of their judicial reception may legitimately vary with the gravity of their assault, if such it be, on settled rights and expectations. And the point at which restrictive interpretation in particular cases should be described as 'disapplication'

[22] *Fraser* v. *State Services Commission* [1984] 1 NZLR 116.

[23] Ibid. 121. For Lord Hailsham's remark, see *Chief Constable of North Wales Police* v. *Evans* [1982] 3 All ER 141, 144.

[24] *The High Court of Parliament and its Supremacy*, 140.

[25] 4 *Institutes*, 36.

[26] *Commentaries*, i. 91.

[27] Cf. Sir Owen Dixon, 'The Common Law as an Ultimate Constitutional Foundation' (1957) 31 ALJ 240 at 245.

cannot be given philosophic precision. Above all, however, the extent of legislative supremacy cannot be settled in abstraction from the broader compass of political theory. Since future events are unknown, the constitutional limits to legislative power cannot be definitively stated. They remain to be refined and tested in future instances.[28]

Legislative supremacy and national sovereignty

Although there is, of course, no necessary connection between parliamentary and national sovereignty, in practice the two concepts are closely related. If Parliament were truly sovereign, in Dicey's sense, the legal systems of Scotland and England would retain their independence only at Parliament's pleasure. Scotland's separate identity as a nation would, to that extent, be a contingent one—dependent on the will of the contemporary Parliament, dominated by English members. Moreover, Britain's membership of the European Communities, and adherence to the Treaty of Rome, would be similarly vulnerable to shifts of political opinion within the House of Commons. Neither consequence of Dicey's doctrine can be accepted without analysis; and neither can be established or refuted by resort to conceptual argument alone.

In *MacCormick* v. *Lord Advocate*,[29] Lord President Cooper observed that 'the principle of unlimited sovereignty of Parliament is a distinctively English principle which has no counterpart in Scottish constitutional law'. Since the Parliament of Great Britain was created by the Union legislation of 1707, which extinguished the Parliaments of Scotland and England, it was not clear why the new Parliament should be assumed to succeed to the English conception of sovereignty. Indeed, the specific declaration that certain conditions were fundamental and unalterable—including the preservation of the Church of Scotland and the status of the Scottish superior courts—plainly indicated the contrary. Lord Cooper denied that the court had jurisdiction to determine whether the governmental act impugned—the proclamation of the Queen as 'Elizabeth the Second of the United Kingdom of Great Britain'—was inconsistent with the Treaty and Acts of Union. However, he expressly reserved the question of the court's jurisdiction in respect of the provisions relating to the Scottish courts and the 'laws which concern private right'—declared by Article XVIII to be unalterable 'except for evident utility of the subjects within Scotland'.

In a subsequent case,[30] Lord Keith dismissed a similar challenge to European Community rules, relating to access for fishing to Scottish

[28] For the position in relation to European Community law, see following section.
[29] 1953 SC 396, 411.
[30] *Gibson* v. *Lord Advocate* 1975 SLT 134.

waters, on the ground that Scottish private law was unaffected: the waters belonged to the Sovereign as trustee for *public* rights of navigation and fishing. Following Lord Cooper, he preferred to reserve his opinion 'on what the question would be if the United Kingdom Parliament passed an Act purporting to abolish the Court of Session or the Church of Scotland or to substitute English law for the whole body of Scots private law'.[31]

Admittedly, the provision obliging professors of Scottish universities to make a formal submission to Presbyterianism was repealed, without serious opposition, by the Universities (Scotland) Acts 1853 and 1932. But government proposals to replace the appellate jurisdiction of the House of Lords and the Privy Council by a court composed mainly of English judges, but with jurisdiction over Scottish and Irish appeals, were abandoned in 1873 on constitutional grounds.[32] History therefore seems to deny the familiar English interpretation of sovereignty as absolute. The extent of legislative supremacy cannot be precisely stated for all purposes, or for all conditions: it can only be determined, on grounds of constitutional principle, in cases sufficiently novel, or sufficiently grave, to probe the limits of the general rule. Neil MacCormick has concluded that 'there are no good reasons of legal theory or of political morality for insisting on the proposition that Parliament has in principle power to sweep away the Scots courts or Scots law or the Church of Scotland'.[33]

It is true that Lord Keith denied that the question, whether an Act of Parliament altering an aspect of Scots private law was 'for the evident utility' of Scottish subjects, was a justiciable issue. The judge's caution here was clearly justified. Too ready recourse to the 'evident utility' condition would undermine the separation of powers, casting the court in the role of a second legislature. Broad matters of public interest are generally not the court's direct concern:

> The making of decisions upon what must essentially be a political matter is no part of the function of the court, and it is highly undesirable that it should be. The function of the court is to adjudicate upon the particular rights and obligations of individual persons, natural or corporate, in relation to other persons or, in certain instances, to the state.[34]

The determination of questions of individual right or duty will naturally assume, quite reasonably, that relevant statutes are valid and binding as satisfying the test of 'evident utility'. But it is hard to accept that that assumption is beyond all challenge, even in the most flagrant case of breach of constitutional principle. In some circumstances, the ordinary

[31] Ibid. 137.
[32] See Neil MacCormick, 'Does the United Kingdom have a Constitution? Reflections on *MacCormick* v. *Lord Advocate*' (1978) 29 NILQ 1 at 11–15.
[33] Ibid. 19–20.
[34] 1975 SLT 137–8.

judicial deference to Parliament's judgment of the public interest, and the related requirements of justice, might surely be misplaced.

It is hardly surprising that Lord Cooper had held, in *MacCormick*, that there was no title to sue. He could not see how the court could admit the title of the petitioners to raise the point in issue before the Court of Session 'without conceding a similar right to almost any opponent of almost any political action to which public opposition has arisen'.[35] Lord Keith was careful to tie the question of *locus standi* to the admissibility of the cause of action; and it seems clear that where the scope of legislative power had sufficient relevance to a claim of private right, standing would be granted. He thought the question 'not to be purely one of title to sue, but to be bound up with the relevancy of the pursuer's averments, and the power of the court to undertake a review of that character'. If judicial review of statute were competent, it could be invoked by anyone with sufficient interest in an Act's validity.[36]

In principle, matters of standing and justiciability always depend (as we have argued[37]) on the relevant legal issues; and there must normally be some individual right or private interest to raise the court's jurisdiction, even if its exercise must also reflect an understanding of the public good. There cannot be any general rule against adjudication on 'political' matters. In the present instance, such a rule would ultimately contradict the limitations on legislative competence previously indicated.[38] How could the court overlook what it takes to be an illegal abuse of (legislative) power? No doubt a law affecting individual rights and interests could be condemned on the ground of failing the 'evident utility' test only in the most exceptional case. In principle, however, it seems hard to distinguish the limitation of legislative power effected in New South Wales by the requirement that laws respect 'the peace, welfare, and good government' of the State: 'The limit may well be wide and extensive. Ultimately, however, it is a binding limit.'[39]

The relation between legislative supremacy and national sovereignty is acutely tested by United Kingdom membership of the European Communities, which presents the most immediate and practical threat to orthodox notions of Parliament's powers. J. D. B. Mitchell argued persuasively that parliamentary sovereignty was extinguished, for the purposes of matters governed by Community law, when the United

[35] 1953 SC 413. [36] 1975 SLT 138. [37] Ch. 9.

[38] Cf. Sir Owen Dixon's observation that the Australian Constitution was a political instrument: 'It deals with government and governmental powers . . . It is not a question whether . . . considerations are political, for nearly every consideration arising from the Constitution can be so described, but whether they are compelling' (*Melbourne Corp.* v. *The Commonwealth* (1947) 74 CLR 31, 82).

[39] *Builders' Labourers Federation* case (1986) 7 NSWLR 372, 384 (see Ch. 3). See also *Pringle, Petitioner* 1991 SLT 330; Denis J. Edwards, 'The Treaty of Union: More Hints of Constitutionalism' (1992) 12 *Legal Studies* 34.

Kingdom acceded to the Communities on 1 January 1973.[40] The United Kingdom then joined what had become a new polity, based on a European legal order, so that previous rules denying Parliament the power to inhibit its successors were inapplicable. Mitchell insisted that by voluntarily entering the new order, the United Kingdom deliberately accepted an important change in national sovereignty. Although the Communities were not themselves created sovereign, the member states had agreed to a fundamental rearrangement: 'What was involved in the creation of the Communities was a rearrangement or pooling of the modes of exercising national sovereignties.'[41]

This interpretation is plainly supported, so far as concerns Community law, by the jurisprudence of the European Court, which asserts the supremacy over domestic provisions of law stemming from the Treaty of Rome on the basis of its 'special and original nature':

> The transfer by the states from their domestic legal systems to the Community legal system of the rights and obligations arising under the Treaty carries with it a permanent limitation of their sovereign rights, against which a subsequent unilateral act incompatible with the concept of the Community cannot prevail.[42]

It follows, on this reasoning, that the European Communities Act 1972, providing for the reception of Community law, was only derivative, being merely consequential to the Treaty and a preliminary to ratification. It did not create legal consequences, but derived them from the fact of accession; and it could now be repealed without legal effect. The rights created by or under the Treaty would subsist so long as the United Kingdom remained a member state. The Treaty has not been incorporated into United Kingdom law by statute, as is the customary method of giving legal effect to treaties: the specific character of Community law makes such a procedure inappropriate. It does not become national law, but retains its Community character, while being applicable within each member state. In Mitchell's view, the Treaty and Act of Accession, together with the parliamentary votes preceding the European Communities Act and the subsequent referendum vote, together amounted to a 'revolution', comparable with those revolutions marked by the Acts of Union in 1707, the Statute of Westminster 1931, and the eventual recognition of the legal independence of former Dominions. Traditional debate over the nature of parliamentary sovereignty could thus be bypassed completely:

> The doctrine of the sovereignty of Parliament, if ever it had validity, had it only within a confined system, the system created in 1707 (from which Parliament

[40] 'What Happened to the Constitution on 1st January 1973?' (1980) 11 *Cambrian Law Review* 69.
[41] Ibid. 82.
[42] *Costa* v. *ENEL* [1964] ECR 585, 593–4. See also *Van Gend en Loos* case [1963] ECR 1.

derived its being) and then only within the domestic order. The change, which resulted from the exercise of a larger sovereignty and in which Parliament played its appropriate (but not legislative) role was an exercise of residual constituent power. The limitations upon Parliament result not from any exercise of self-limitation on its part, but from a constitutional rearrangement among the member states.[43]

Mitchell's analysis, however, may well be premature. Its validity will depend on future progress towards greater economic and political unity. Most British constitutional lawyers presently seem content with a more untidy, pragmatic solution to the problem of sovereignty. It is to be expected that government and Parliament will loyally defer to the requirements of Community law, careful to avoid any conflict arising between the rules of Community law and those of English or Scottish law; and the courts will strive to interpret domestic law in conformity with that of the Community. In a number of fields, such as customs law and agriculture, Community law simply displaces previous domestic rules. Moreover, as a member of the Council of the European Communities, the United Kingdom government participates directly in the adoption of Community legislation. It is therefore well placed to ensure that compatibility between the two legal orders is maintained.[44]

The possibility of an irreconcilable clash between the competing notions of parliamentary sovereignty and the supremacy of Community law may therefore be safely viewed as of little *practical* importance, however potentially embarrassing as a matter of legal theory. For present purposes, we should acknowledge that, as regards the overriding quality of European Community law, parliamentary sovereignty is effectively 'in abeyance'.[45] The courts have not yet signalled their unqualified allegiance to the new legal order, but continue to recognize Parliament's power to repeal the European Communities Act with legal effect as a matter of constitutional law: 'Parliament's recognition of European Community law and of the jurisdiction of the European Court of Justice by one enactment can be withdrawn by another.'[46]

None the less, the process of assimilating Community law has demonstrated the inadequacies of earlier attempts to formulate an authoritative 'rule of recognition' of statutes, clearly revealing the dependence of matters of 'validity' on broader considerations of political

[43] 'What Happened to the Constitution', 83. See also id., 'The Sovereignty of Parliament and Community Law: The Stumbling-Block That Isn't There' (1979) *International Affairs* 33.

[44] See J. W. Bridge, 'Abstract Law and Political Reality in the Post-European-Accession British Constitution' [1987] *Denning LJ* 23.

[45] Colin Turpin, *British Government and the Constitution*, 2nd edn. (London, 1990), 346.

[46] *Macarthys* v. *Smith* [1979] 3 All ER 325, 334 (Lawton LJ). See also *Duke* v. *GEC Reliance* [1988] 1 All ER 626 (House of Lords refusing to construe a statute in accordance with a Directive which had no direct effect between private individuals).

principle.[47] It has turned out, as suggested above, that the 'validity' (or binding quality) of statutes is ultimately a question of degree, in the sense that their application to particular cases depends on the outcome of a striking mode of judicial interpretation. The European Communities Act 1972 has, it seems, been partially entrenched—notwithstanding the traditional view that entrenchment is incompatible with continuing sovereignty—by the courts' literal adherence to the assertion in section 2(4) that 'any enactment passed or to be passed . . . shall be construed and have effect subject to' Community law.

In *Garland* v. *British Rail Engineering*,[48] the House of Lords was able to reconcile a provision of the Sex Discrimination Act 1975 with Article 119 of the Treaty of Rome, by adopting the principle that the words of a statute were to be construed consistently with any relevant international treaty obligation of the United Kingdom if they were 'reasonably capable of bearing such a meaning'.[49] In the case of obligations arising under the Treaty of Rome the principle applied *a fortiori*. The domestic provision was capable of bearing either of two possible meanings, one of which was happily consistent with the Treaty, 'without any undue straining of the ordinary meaning of the language used'. Although Lord Diplock declined to decide whether, as a consequence of faulty drafting or legislative oversight, it might ever be necessary to deny the primacy of Community law, he indicated an answer which may now be treated as established principle:

> The instant appeal does not present an appropriate occasion to consider whether, having regard to the express direction as to the construction of enactments 'to be passed' which is contained in section 2(4) . . . anything short of an express positive statement in an Act of Parliament passed after January 1, 1973, that a particular provision is intended to be made in breach of an obligation assumed by the United Kingdom under a Community treaty, would justify an English court in construing that provision in a manner inconsistent with a Community treaty obligation of the United Kingdom, however wide a departure from the prima facie meaning of the language of the provision might be needed in order to achieve consistency.[50]

The widest departure from the prima facie meaning of the language would be a decision that an (irretrievably) inconsistent statutory provision should not be applied in the absence of such an 'express positive statement' that Parliament intended to legislate in conflict with Community law.

Lord Denning had previously reached a similar conclusion in a case

[47] For the 'rule of recognition', see H. L. A. Hart, *The Concept of Law* (Oxford, 1961), esp. 145.
[48] [1983] 2 AC 751.
[49] Ibid. 771 (Lord Diplock).
[50] Ibid. Cf. Joseph Jaconelli, 'Constitutional Review and Section 2(4) of the European Communities Act 1972' (1979) 28 *Internat. & Comparative Law Q.* 65.

where he proclaimed the priority of Article 119 over the Equal Pay Act 1970: 'That priority is given by our own law. It is given by the European Communities Act 1972 itself. Community law is now part of our law and, whenever there is any inconsistency, Community law has priority.'[51] That case was an impressive illustration of constitutional change because a majority of the Court of Appeal adopted a construction of the Equal Pay Act which conflicted with Article 119, as subsequently interpreted by the European Court.[52] Since the English statute had been re-enacted, in amended form, in 1975, it might have been expected to override any inconsistent provisions deriving legal authority from the European Communities Act 1972. The doctrine of implied repeal, under which the courts obey the most recent expression of parliamentary intent, duly enacted, would seem to inhibit the faithful application of Article 119. Admittedly, section 3 of the European Communities Act provides for the recognition of European Court rulings on Community law; but as a matter of British constitutional law, a subsequent inconsistent statute would prevail over section 3 as well as over section 2 of the European Communities Act.[53]

The Court of Appeal's ultimate decision, in accordance with the ruling of the European Court, therefore demonstrated the novel constitutional precedence now accorded to Community law.[54] That precedence has been achieved, for all practical purposes, by adoption of a principle of construction of unusual force, reflecting the courts' perception of the contemporary demands of political morality. In these circumstances, interpretation and application (or disapplication) of statutes cannot easily be distinguished. If the majority of the Court of Appeal were content simply to allow Article 119 to prevail over the inconsistent English provision, Lord Denning preferred to construe the latter so as to achieve conformity with the Treaty of Rome. The two approaches run into one another:

> In construing our statute, we are entitled to look to the Treaty as an aid to its construction; but not only as an aid but as an overriding force. If on close investigation it should appear that our legislation is deficient or is inconsistent with Community law by some oversight of our draftsmen then it is our bounden duty to give priority to Community law.[55]

[51] *Macarthys* v. *Smith* [1981] QB 180, 200.

[52] [1979] 3 All ER 325.

[53] Cf. O. Hood Phillips, 'Has the "Incoming Tide" Reached the Palace of Westminster?' (1979) 95 LQR 167, at 169. See also Lord Diplock, 'The Common Market and the Common Law' (1972) 6 *Law Teacher* 3 at 8. Lord Denning had previously stated that a UK Act would prevail over the Treaty of Rome in the event of inconsistency: *Felixstowe Docks & Ry. Co.* v. *British Transport Docks Bd.* [1976] 2 CMLR 655.

[54] For full discussion, see T. R. S. Allan, 'Parliamentary Sovereignty: Lord Denning's Dexterous Revolution' (1983) 3 OJLS 22.

[55] [1979] 3 All ER 325, 329 (Lord Denning MR).

Lord Denning's position may be regarded as lying at the borderline between creative interpretation and (notional) disobedience. Directly applicable Community law would override an inconsistent Act of Parliament except where Parliament had expressly stipulated for the opposite result. He naturally assumed Parliament's continuing, underlying intention to fulfil its obligations under the Treaty: 'If the time should come when our Parliament deliberately passes an Act with the intention of repudiating the Treaty or any provision in it or . . . of acting inconsistently with it *and says so in express terms* then . . . it would be the duty of our courts to follow the statute of our Parliament.'[56] The result is to establish a presumption of legislative intent which can be defeated only by the adoption of explicit statutory language in rebuttal. This is in effect to impose a special requirement of form—if not of 'manner and form'—for a particular purpose; and the distinction between the application of statute and its interpretation has all but disappeared.

These conclusions are confirmed by the House of Lords' ready acceptance, in *Factortame* v. *Secretary of State for Transport*, that the Merchant Shipping Act 1988, and the Merchant Shipping (Registration of Fishing Vessels) Regulations made thereunder, would take effect subject to any conflicting rights of nationals of EC member states arising under Community law.[57] The applicants were the owners and managers of fishing vessels, previously registered as British, who as Spanish nationals no longer qualified for registration under the new regulations. The Divisional Court had ordered that the Act and regulations be disapplied, and the minister restrained from enforcing them against the applicants, while a preliminary ruling on the relevant questions of Community law was sought from the European Court. Applying a presumption that an Act was compatible with Community law until declared to be incompatible, however, the House of Lords denied the court's power to grant such interim relief as a matter of English law. The court none the less acknowledged that Community rights, once established, would 'prevail over' the restrictions on registration imposed by the Act. The effect of section 2(4) of the European Communities Act was precisely 'as if a section were incorporated in . . . the 1988 Act which in terms enacted that the provisions with respect to registration of British fishing vessels were to be without prejudice to the directly enforceable Community rights of nationals of any member state of the E.E.C.'.[58]

[56] Ibid. (emphasis added). [57] [1989] 2 All ER 692.

[58] Ibid. 701. The nationality restrictions were subsequently suspended in accordance with a ruling of the Court of Justice; and interim relief was granted by the House of Lords against application of domicile and residence requirements: *Factortame* v. *Secretary of State for Transport (No. 2)* [1991] 1 All ER 70 (see esp. Lord Bridge at 107–8).

For practical purposes, however, it will usually be possible to achieve adequate harmony between Community law and national law with less strain on the ordinary perception of the courts as interpreters of parliamentary intent, engaged in the familiar task of statutory construction. In *Pickstone* v. *Freemans*, the House of Lords rejected an argument that the terms of section 1(2)(c) of the Equal Pay Act 1970 were inadequate to protect an employee's right under Article 119 to equal pay for work of equal value.[59] The provision had been inserted in the Act by the Equal Pay (Amendment) Regulations 1983, made under section 2(2) of the European Communities Act, in consequence of a decision of the European Court, which held that the United Kingdom had failed to comply with a relevant Council Directive.[60] Unwilling to find that the regulations had failed to achieve their undoubted objective of giving full effect to the decision of the European Court, the judges adopted a broad, purposive construction.

Unusually, Lord Templeman quoted part of the minister's speech in the House of Commons as evidence of government and parliamentary intention. Lord Oliver accepted that a 'strict and literal construction' of the section involved the conclusion that the regulations had failed to fulfil their purpose in the circumstances of the case; but he was prepared to introduce an additional, parenthetic phrase to achieve a more satisfactory result. Lord Keith declined even to formulate the necessary implication on the ground that its precise terms were immaterial: 'It is sufficient to say that the words must be construed purposively in order to give effect to the manifest broad intention of the maker of the regulations and of Parliament.'[61]

The significance of the court's approach for any contemporary appraisal of the scope and effect of the sovereignty doctrine emerges most clearly from Lord Oliver's speech. He acknowledged the court's departure from well-established rules of construction. The decision did not respect the principle that Parliament's intention must be ascertained from the words enacted, construed according to their plain and ordinary meaning. Nor was it normally permissible to refer to an international treaty in order to construe the words used in a subsequent statute in other than their plain and unambiguous sense. Even in the case of ambiguity, the parliamentary proceedings could not ordinarily be invoked as a source of construction. A statute which was passed to give effect to the United Kingdom's obligations under the Treaty of Rome, however, fell into a 'special category' because, unlike other treaty obligations, those obligations had been fully received into English law. A novel, purposive mode of interpretation was therefore justified

[59] [1988] 2 All ER 803.
[60] Council Directive 75/117 clarified the meaning and effect of Article 119 of the Treaty.
[61] [1988] 2 All ER 807.

by 'the manifest purpose of the legislation, by its history, and by the compulsive provision of section 2(4) of the 1972 Act'.[62]

The special moral force accorded the 'prima facie presumption that Parliament does not intend to act in breach of international law',[63] in the context of obligations arising under the Treaty of Rome, stems from the important political role which United Kingdom membership of the Community has come to assume. The strength and force of the principle of statutory construction reflects changing judicial perception of the political community which the constitutional order exists to serve. Legal doctrine must mirror political principle, which must itself respond to the realities of practical politics. If the courts are presently careful to preserve the authority of Parliament to legislate (by appropriate language) in contravention of Community law and, indeed, to secede from the Community altogether, the sovereignty doctrine may be expected to change as secession recedes as a practical option. Even before accession, Lord Denning had declined to consider whether or not Parliament could repudiate the Treaty of Rome: 'We must wait to see what happens before we pronounce on sovereignty in the Common Market.'[64]

The point at which the courts have sufficiently abandoned the traditional limits of statutory construction to justify talk of 'revolution' is largely a matter of taste. Even if a change of legal order may be identified with hindsight, the process of transition is inevitably gradual. The positivist's conception of validity—an all or nothing conception, dependent on a sharp distinction between applicability and interpretation—obscures more than it reveals.[65] *Factortame* shows that an Act may be 'valid' for some purposes and not for others. Whatever its formal validity, as a matter of domestic law, it will not be *applied* in breach of rights which are directly effective in Community law. The position is perhaps analogous to the narrow reading of an ambiguous penal provision, which renders it inapplicable to the case in hand. The result is reminiscent of the Canadian Supreme Court's treatment of statutes which violated the Bill of Rights 1960. Ritchie J. denied that the court's declaration 'repealed' the offending provision. It was confined to the circumstances of the case in which the declaration was made: 'The situation appears . . . to be somewhat analogous to a case where valid provincial legislation in an otherwise unoccupied field ceases to be operative by reason of conflicting federal legislation.'[66]

62 Ibid. 817–19.

63 *Salomon* v. *Customs and Excise Commrs.* [1967] 2 QB 116, 143 (Diplock LJ).

64 *Blackburn* v. *A.-G.* [1971] 1 WLR 1037, 1040.

65 On the awkwardness of the theories of H. L. A. Hart and Hans Kelsen in relation to the United Kingdom, see also MacCormick, 'Does the UK have a Constitution?', at 15–19.

66 *R.* v. *Drybones* [1970] SCR 282, 294–5.

In *Amministrazione delle Finanze dello Stato* v. *Simmenthal*,[67] the European Court held that provisions of the Treaty and directly applicable legislation must not only take precedence over any conflicting provision of national law, but also preclude the valid adoption of new national legislative measures to the extent to which they would be incompatible with the Community provisions. Moreover, a national court should refuse to apply incompatible provisions of national legislation, even if adopted later than the relevant Community rules, without waiting for such provisions to be set aside by further legislation or by a constitutional court. While the priority of Community law is considered to derive, as a matter of British constitutional law, from the European Communities Act, it is possible to insist that 'the expression "supremacy of Community law" . . . must refer to construction, not legislative power; to judicial interpretation, not review of validity'.[68] The distinction is, however, little more than a convenient device to preserve a fading conception of national legislative sovereignty.

There is no real need to resort to notions of 'revolution' or 'shifts of *grundnorm*' to explain the result of the *Factortame* litigation.[69] It is simply the legitimate consequence of the interpretation of sovereignty which best reflects new conceptions of the political community. There is a continuous progression from creative interpretation to a mode of application of statutes sensitive to political change. Ideas of revolution and legal discontinuity, in the present context, largely reflect mistaken attempts to sever legal validity from political principle, and the (ultimately) artificial division between interpretation and application which such mistaken attempts require.

The sovereignty doctrine, then, must be understood in the light of a moral or political theory of the polity—a conception of the national or international community implicit in political morality at any particular time.[70] The relevant polity is, of course, the one which the (British) courts exist to serve and in respect of which they were established. Their reluctance to acknowledge any irrevocable surrender of legislative sovereignty over former United Kingdom colonies, or over the

[67] [1978] ECR 629. See David Freestone, 'The Supremacy of Community Law in National Courts' (1979) 42 MLR 220.

[68] Phillips, 'Has the "Incoming Tide" Reached the Palace of Westminster?', 168.

[69] The regulations were disapplied in accordance with a ruling of the European Court, which required interim relief to be available, where necessary, for the protection of Community law rights: *Factortame (No. 2)* [1991] 1 All ER 70. For shifts of *grundnorm* as an explanation of legal revolution—corresponding to traditional accounts of parliamentary sovereignty (e.g. H. W. R. Wade, 'The Legal Basis of Sovereignty')—see Hans Kelsen, *General Theory of Law and the State* (trans. Wedberg, 1945); id., *Pure Theory of Law* (trans. Knight, 1967), esp. 208–11; J. W. Harris, 'When and Why Does the Grundnorm Change' [1971] CLJ 103.

[70] Cf. Dworkin, *Taking Rights Seriously*, ch. 4; id., *Law's Empire*.

Dominions, therefore presents no impediment to the idea of sovereignty as an evolving doctrine, whose boundaries cannot be exhaustively defined.

The courts have declined to hold that compliance with the requirement of section 4 of the Statute of Westminster 1931, that an Act extending to a Dominion must declare the request and consent of the Dominion, is a condition of its validity as a matter of English law. In *Manuel* v. *Attorney-General*,[71] Sir Robert Megarry V.-C. held that, since the Canada Act had been passed by both Houses of Parliament and had received the Royal Assent, it was an Act of Parliament which the court could not hold invalid. It would be no objection to the validity of an Act purporting to extend to a foreign state, whether a former colony or not, that it would be ignored by the state concerned. It was hard to distinguish an English statute making it an offence to smoke in the streets of Paris or Vienna from one which imposed similar constraints on Bombay or Sydney.[72] Legal validity could not be confused with enforceability.

In that case, however, there had been no change in the nature of the political community to which the English courts owed continuing allegiance. While legal principle and political reality may diverge as regards the position of the foreign state, there was no divorce between law and politics in respect of British constitutional theory.[73] 'Sitting as a judge in an English court', Sir Robert naturally asserted his 'full and dutiful obedience' to the Act of Parliament.[74] The function of the British courts is to apply the constitutional law of the United Kingdom, in accordance with the political morality on which that law is based. The altered status of a former colony reflects no change in the political allegiance of British citizens. The Vice-Chancellor's conclusion in *Manuel* must be taken in context, with appropriate weight accorded his significant proviso: 'If I leave on one side the European Communities Act 1972 and all that flows from it . . . I am bound to say that from first to last I have heard nothing in this case to make me doubt the simple rule that the duty of the court is to obey and apply every Act of Parliament.'[75]

[71] [1982] 3 All ER 786.

[72] Ibid. 792, adapting Sir Ivor Jennings's example (see *The Law and the Constitution*, 5th edn. (London, 1959), 170–1).

[73] Cf. *British Coal Corporation* v. *R.* [1935] AC 500, 520 (Viscount Sankey LC): 'Parliament could, as a matter of abstract law, repeal or disregard s. 4 of the Statute. But that is theory and has no relation to realities.'

[74] [1982] 3 All ER 794.

[75] Ibid. 793. It is, of course, necessary to distinguish the position of courts sitting in a former colony or Dominion: see the discussion of *Madzimbamuto* v. *Lardner-Burke* [1969] 1 AC 645 below.

The limits of parliamentary sovereignty

The legal doctrine of legislative supremacy expresses the courts' commitment to British parliamentary democracy. It provides for the exercise of the political will of the electorate through the medium of its parliamentary representatives. If an appropriate conception of the boundaries of the political community provides the framework for the doctrine's application, some conception of democracy must provide its substantive political content. In other words, the courts' continuing adherence to the legal doctrine of sovereignty must entail commitment to some irreducible, minimum concept of the democratic principle. In almost all likely circumstances, that political commitment will demand respect for the legislative measures adopted by Parliament as the representative assembly.

That respect, however, clearly cannot be a limitless one. A parliamentary enactment whose effect would be the destruction of any recognizable form of democracy—for example, a measure purporting to deprive a substantial section of the population of the vote on the grounds of their hostility to government policies[76]—could not consistently be applied by the courts as law. Judicial obedience to the statute in such (unlikely) circumstances could not coherently be justified in terms of the doctrine of parliamentary sovereignty, since the statute would violate the political principle which the doctrine itself enshrines. The practice of judicial obedience to statute obviously cannot itself be based on the authority of statute: it can only reflect judicial understanding of what (in contemporary conditions) political morality demands. The limits of that practice of obedience must therefore be constituted by the boundaries of that morality. An enactment which threatened the essential elements of any plausible conception of democratic government would lie beyond those boundaries. It would forfeit, by the same token, any claim to be recognized as law.

Although, therefore, the familiar distinction between the application and interpretation of statute suffices for most practical purposes, it ultimately breaks down in the face of changing views of the contours of the political community—Britain or Europe?—or serious threats to the central tenets of liberal democracy. Presumptions of legislative intent, which draw their strength from the requirements of justice, as these are presently understood, cannot in normal circumstances override the explicit terms of an Act of Parliament. This is because a commitment to representative government and loyalty to democratic institutions are themselves basic constituents of political morality. Judicial percep-

[76] Dicey regarded such a case as illustrating the 'external limit' on sovereignty: such a measure would be legally valid, but incur widespread resistance: *Law of the Constitution*, 79.

tions of justice must generally give way to the results of Parliament's deliberations, where they are plainly inconsistent. The legal authority of statute depends in the final analysis, however, on its compatibility with the central core of that morality which constitutes the rule of law.

If Parliament ceased to be a representative assembly, in any genuine sense of that idea, or if it proceeded to enact legislation undermining the democratic basis of our institutions, political morality might direct judicial resistance rather than obedience. No comfortable distinction between legal doctrine and political principle can ultimately be sustained. Such questions about the proper relationship between the courts and Parliament cannot be settled by resort to competing formulations of some supposed pre-existing legal rule: it is the scope and content of that rule—its meaning and application—which are themselves in issue. Answers can only be supplied as a matter of political theory—in terms of the values which we regard as fundamental to the constitutional order.

Dicey's insistence on distinguishing legal from political sovereignty entailed an equivalent separation of law and convention. Neither distinction can be maintained when we try to determine the limits of parliamentary sovereignty. The nature and limits of that sovereignty are constituted, just as conventions are constituted, by the political morality which underlies the legal order. In this sense, the legal doctrine of sovereignty is perhaps the most fundamental of our constitutional conventions. Dicey observed that 'if Parliament be in the eye of the law a supreme legislature, the essence of representative government is, that the legislature should represent or give effect to the will of the political sovereign, i.e. of the electoral body, or of the nation'.[77]

His examination of a number of important constitutional conventions led him to the conclusion that they were united in character by possession of a single purpose—to secure that Parliament and government were ultimately subject to the wishes of the electorate. The right to demand a dissolution was the most striking example, since it represented an appeal from the legal to the political sovereign:

> The conventions of the constitution now consist of customs which (whatever their historical origin) are at the present day maintained for the sake of ensuring the supremacy of the House of Commons, and ultimately, through the elective House of Commons, of the nation. Our modern code of constitutional morality secures, though in a roundabout way, what is called abroad the 'sovereignty of the people'.[78]

Dicey presented conventions as a means of harmonizing legal and political sovereignty, which remained conceptually distinct. A view of legal sovereignty as a component of political morality, however, locates

[77] Ibid. 429–30. [78] Ibid. 430–1.

its authority in the source from which the 'validity of constitutional maxims' is itself derived: it is equally 'subordinate and subservient to the fundamental principle of popular sovereignty'.[79]

McIlwain came to similar conclusions.[80] He found it hard to see what advantage the distinction between legal and political sovereignty had to offer to political science, since its plausibility depended on that of the doctrine of parliamentary sovereignty itself. It also seemed to have very odd results. James Bryce had argued, in defence of the distinction, that neither the people nor the Crown could issue legally binding directions to Members of Parliament or peers. In reply, McIlwain asked what, if matters of 'non-legal convention' were put aside, could prevent the Crown from proroguing or dissolving an existing Parliament whenever so inclined. And what *legal*, as opposed to conventional, requirement, existed to ensure that the Crown summoned another Parliament?

> If we adhere to the strictness of this legality, we find a rather peculiar sovereign resulting. One, in fact, whose very precarious existence is dependent upon the whim of a power outside itself. It is no answer to this to say that it is the 'King in Parliament' who does these things. Where is the 'King in Parliament' during the interval between the dissolution of one Parliament and his issuing writs for a new one?[81]

In *Hampden's Case*,[82] Berkeley J., resisting an argument that the King could not impose a tax without the consent of Parliament, accepted that Parliament was '*commune concilium regis et regni*, that is the greatest the most honourable and supreme court in the kingdom'. It was nevertheless but a *Concilium*: 'the King may call it, prorogue it, dissolve it, at his pleasure'. If, then, Parliament today is sovereign it is as much in virtue of conventions as of positive law; and it follows that the limits of sovereignty must themselves be partly settled by convention. Dicey's division between legal and political sovereignty is no more plausible than his distinction between law and convention. Each manifests the impossibility of insulating legal theory from either political practice or constitutional principle.

The political morality which underlies the legal order is not exhausted by our attachment to democratic government. If the doctrine of legislative supremacy obtains its legitimacy from the virtues of representative democracy, that must be chiefly because democracy is thought to contribute to a broader vision of the polity, affirming certain fundamental standards of civilized government. If such standards authorize a restrictive approach to the interpretation of statutes which, more broadly construed, would threaten fundamental values, they might equally justify rejection of statutes whose injustice was especially grave.

[79] Ibid. 437.
[80] *The High Court of Parliament and its Supremacy*.
[81] Ibid. 380–1.
[82] (1637) 3 *State Trials* 1090, 1101.

If an ambiguous penal provision should, as a matter of principle, be narrowly construed in the interests of fairness and liberty, a criminal statute which lacked all precision—authorizing the punishment of whatever conduct officials deemed it expedient to punish—should, on the same principle, be denied any application at all.[83] There would be no more need for a constitutional court, with extended powers of judicial review, in this context than to ensure the primacy of European Community law. It would be sufficient for the court to deny the statute's application to the particular circumstances of the case: there would be no need to make a declaration of invalidity. The result, however, would be much the same, the style of interpretation reflecting the scale of the affront to constitutional values accepted as fundamental.

The limits of the principle which requires recognition of foreign penal or confiscatory legislation provide a good illustration. Legislation by a foreign sovereign state in respect of its own nationals, or assets situated within its own territories, will normally be accorded recognition in British courts even when considered immoral or unjust. Refusal to accord such legislation validity as part of the relevant foreign law would be considered a serious breach of international comity.[84] In *Oppenheimer* v. *Cattermole (Inspector of Taxes)*,[85] however, a majority of the House of Lords refused to recognize a Nazi decree of 1941, depriving expatriate German Jews of their citizenship and providing for the confiscation of their property. Respect for the claims of international comity gave way in the face of grave iniquity. The court was confronted with 'legislation which takes away without compensation from a section of the citizen body singled out on racial grounds all their property on which the state passing the legislation can lay its hands and, in addition, deprives them of their citizenship'.[86] In the view of Lord Cross, a law of that sort constituted 'so grave an infringement of human rights' that British courts should refuse to recognize it as a law at all.[87]

Both the rule according legal validity to Acts of Parliament, and the rule requiring the recognition of foreign penal legislation, are alike important components, or products, of the political morality which necessarily informs judicial decision. Neither rule has absolute force,

[83] Cf. e.g. the Nazi law of 28 June 1935, authorizing the punishment of acts 'deserving of penalty according to the fundamental conceptions of a penal law and sound popular feeling': see Jerome Hall, 'Nulla Poena Sine Lege' (1937) 47 Yale LJ 165 at 175. A law in such terms would be unconstitutional in the United States as violating the guarantee of due process of law: see e.g. *Connally* v. *General Construction Co.* 269 US 385, 391 (1926).

[84] *Aksionairnoye Obschestro A. M. Luther* v. *James Sagor* [1921] 3 KB 532.

[85] [1976] AC 249.

[86] Ibid. 278 (Lord Cross).

[87] Ibid. See also Lord Hodson at 265 and Lord Salmon at 283–4. Lord Pearson dissented on this point and Lord Hailsham expressed no concluded opinion.

but is inevitably subject to certain ultimate constraints imposed by that morality. As F. A. Mann expressed the point:

> Suppose Parliament enacts a statute depriving Jews of their British nationality, prohibiting marriages between Christians and non-Christians, dissolving marriages between blacks and whites or vesting the property of all red-haired women in the State. Is it really suggested that English judges would have to apply and would in fact apply such a law?[88]

Contemporary analysis of parliamentary sovereignty has generally made the error of seeking to provide a single determinate solution which can be applied, in advance, to every question concerning the limits of the doctrine which may arise. Once the real nature of the ultimate rule of the constitution has been properly ascertained, it is supposed, or its correct formulation authoritatively settled, the limits of sovereignty can be clearly stated as a matter of law. We are thus required to elect between competing conceptions of 'continuing' or 'self-embracing' sovereignty.[89] If, however, the limits of the doctrine are embedded in a more fundamental constitutional morality, such attempts at formal legal definition are bound to fail. The doctrine expresses a conclusion of political principle which sufficiently captures the (legal and political) duty of the courts for most practical purposes. Whether or not judicial allegiance to statute would be justified in extreme or unusual situations must depend on the strength in those circumstances of conflicting demands of political morality.

In Chapter 4 we examined Ronald Dworkin's theory of law as integrity, which requires a resolution of the conflicting ideals of justice and fairness in the circumstances of practical politics.[90] In the following chapter, we saw that Hercules—Dworkin's model judge—may often be obliged by integrity to acknowledge as law a rule which justice would condemn. Fairness may require him to defer, against his own judgment of the rule's iniquity, to the popular will as manifested by a statute duly enacted. Hercules would accept the principle of legislative supremacy in deference to the requirements of fairness: the principle protects the power of the majority to work its political will. But he clearly would not suppose that legislative supremacy was absolute: when the threatened iniquity is sufficiently grave, it is likely that fairness would give way to justice.

If Hercules repudiates a statutory rule as unjust, he accepts the resulting defect of 'fit'—the discrepancy between the text and the

88 'Britain's Bill of Rights' (1978) 94 LQR 512 at 513.

89 See H. L. A. Hart, *The Concept of Law* 146; cf. George Winterton, 'The British Grundnorm: Parliamentary Supremacy Re-examined' (1976) 92 LQR 591.

90 In this context, 'fairness' concerns the distribution of political power (see Chs. 4 and 5).

law he declares—as the price of a superior interpretation overall.[91] His loyal acceptance of the majority of statutes meets the necessary 'threshold' requirement, which distinguishes interpretation from invention; but he is not thereby committed to accepting them all:

> When an interpretation meets the threshold, remaining defects of fit may be compensated, in his overall judgment, if the principles of that interpretation are particularly attractive, because then he sets off the community's infrequent lapses in respecting these principles against its virtue in generally observing them.[92]

Sir Ivor Jennings observed that there was no recent precedent for declaring an Act of Parliament to be *ultra vires* because it offended against the powers of Parliament conferred by the common law.[93] There were dicta on both sides: 'but the modern trend is towards admitting the supremacy of Parliament over the common law, perhaps because we have never had to face an incipient dictatorship, whether fascist or communist'. In accepting that principle for the time being, however, we 'should be grateful for Coke's dictum that if the occasion arose, a judge would do what a judge should do'.[94] If legislative sovereignty is one strand, albeit of fundamental importance, within a wider canvas of political morality or constitutional principle, traditional dispute over the merits of rival versions of the 'ultimate rule' is largely beside the point.

Arthur Goodhart drew a parallel between the British and American constitutions in respect of principles protecting judicial independence and fundamental civil liberties: 'To deny that they are obligatory under the British constitution, while recognising their legal nature under the American one, is to place all the emphasis on form and none on substance.'[95] He thought that the legislative powers of Parliament were limited by 'certain fundamental principles', which were 'universally accepted', even though he denied that any other constitutional body could prevent Parliament exceeding these limits. Goodhart also rejected Jennings's suggestion that, if Parliament were truly supreme, there was strictly speaking no constitutional law in Britain at all. Parliament enjoyed no 'absolute sovereignty' because there were fixed rules of procedure to be followed before its expression of will could claim authority, and such rules formed part of the fundamental law of the state:

91 *Law's Empire*, 257.
92 Ibid.
93 *The Law and the Constitution*, 160.
94 Ibid.
95 Arthur L. Goodhart, 'The Rule of Law and Absolute Sovereignty' (1958) 196 U. of Penn. LR 943 at 954.

> It is true, of course, that . . . it would be possible for the three elements which constitute the Queen-in-Parliament to alter the constitution by setting up a dictator, but they would have to follow the present constitutional procedure if their act were to have validity.[96]

Goodhart's dubious admission that the rules could be manipulated for such a purpose, however, was scarcely consistent with his denial that Parliament exercised 'arbitrary power'.[97]

The problems presented by an illegal seizure of power by a revolutionary government are analogous to those which arise when the lawful apparatus of government is used for ends which threaten to subvert fundamental democratic principles. On a positivist view, the revolution or *coup d'état* presents a mainly empirical problem: the question is whether the new regime is sufficiently successful, and its decrees sufficiently effective in practice, to justify the jurist in postulating a new *grundnorm*, or the court in according validity to its enacted rules.[98] A less 'scientific' or mechanical approach, however, would make allowance for a wider range of relevant considerations.

In Southern Rhodesia, after the Unilateral Declaration of Independence in November 1965, the courts were forced to choose between recognizing the decrees of the Smith regime, illegally established in defiance of the 1961 Constitution, and accepting the continued authority of the United Kingdom Parliament, which provided for the removal from the Rhodesian legislature of all further legislative power by enacting the Southern Rhodesia Act 1965.[99] The simple solution adopted by the majority of the Privy Council in *Madzimbamuto* v. *Lardner-Burke*[100]—that by virtue of the legislation enacted at Westminster the relevant regulations made by the Smith regime were unlawful and invalid—arguably failed to reflect the moral complexity of the position. Lord Pearce, who dissented, followed both the High Court of Southern Rhodesia at first instance and Fieldsend AJA on appeal,[101] in accepting a principle of necessity which might justify recognizing the validity of acts of those in control of the government where they were reasonably required for the orderly running of the state. The courts could not ignore the practical reality of the political situation. An 'uneasy compromise' had been achieved, in which the judges lawfully appointed under the 1961 Constitution had been entrusted with the duty of

[96] Ibid. 951.
[97] Ibid. 952; cf. Jennings, *The Law and the Constitution*, 65.
[98] See Hans Kelsen, *General Theory of Law and the State* (trans. Wedberg, 1945). Cf. J. W. Harris, 'When and Why Does the Grundnorm Change?' [1971] CLJ 103.
[99] The Rhodesian legislature was deprived of its powers under the Southern Rhodesia Constitution Order 1965, made under the authority of the Southern Rhodesia Act 1965, s. 2(1).
[100] [1969] 1 AC 645.
[101] 1968 (2) SA 284.

continuing to sit by a government which no longer acknowledged that Constitution:

The primary reason, one presumes, is the reasonable and humane desire of preserving law and order and avoiding chaos which would work great hardship on the citizens of all races and which would incidentally damage that part of the realm to the detriment of whoever is ultimately successful . . . For this reason it is clearly desirable to keep the courts out of the main area of dispute, so that, whatever be the political battle, and whatever be the sanctions or other pressures employed to end the rebellion, the courts can carry on their peaceful tasks of protecting the fabric of society and maintaining law and order.[102]

The principle of necessity was not thought to demand recognition of every act of the illegal regime: such acts must not impair the rights of citizens under the lawful (1961) Constitution or directly assist the usurpation. The limits of the doctrine of parliamentary sovereignty, however, should be settled in the light of all relevant moral factors—the desirability of preserving order and civil government as well as that of ending the usurpation. The authority of the United Kingdom Parliament to legislate for Rhodesia in the prevailing circumstances should reflect the dictates of 'common sense and fairness to the citizen'.[103]

A seizure of power in breach of the constitution is morally akin to manipulation of the constitution, by technically legitimate means, in breach of fundamental principles of democracy or justice. In neither case can an adequate legal response be automatically derived from a pre-ordained fundamental rule, or by abandoning such a rule in favour of a new one. In each case, the indeterminacy of the fundamental rule necessitates a thoroughgoing examination of the moral and political imperatives of the situation. The jurist cannot escape his moral responsibilities by invoking a formal doctrine of legal sovereignty, as if it afforded genuine political neutrality. In such circumstances, the 'fundamental rule' provides no answer.[104]

The limits of sovereignty clearly cannot be stated with any precision. The scope of the legal doctrine, and its implications for constitutional change, cannot be settled except by analysis of the political morality from which it derives its authority. Controversial questions of constitutional authority are moral questions requiring attention to the political traditions and values which constitute the polity. No single characterization or particular formulation of the rule enjoining judicial obedience to statute can supply answers in advance.

102 [1969] 1 AC 737.
103 Ibid.
104 Cf. R. W. M. Dias, 'Legal Politics: Norms Behind the Grundnorm' [1968] CLJ 233. Dias observes that the Rhodesian case raised the moral question of whether a constitution which perpetuated an inequality for the benefit of a minority could properly be accepted by the judges.

These conclusions suggest how the apparent conflict between Dicey's 'guiding principles' of legislative sovereignty and the rule of law might finally be resolved. I have suggested that a statute which threatened fundamentally the central tenets of our democracy could derive no authority from the doctrine of sovereignty, properly understood. Implicit in Dicey's conception of the rule of law is a view of the rights of the individual as basic to the political order. The protection of the individual in civil society is guaranteed by his freedom from arbitrary rule, uncontrolled by law. Government officials are answerable to the courts for their treatment of him—the equal subjection of all classes to the ordinary law.[105]

Dicey's principle of 'equality before the law' is surely the consequence of a deeper conception of the equality of citizens—an equality which forms the basis of our commitment to democracy itself. An Act of Parliament which sought, without reasonable justification, to destroy the citizen's right to participate in the political process would offend that deeper conception. It may also be that a fundamental idea of equality can account most plausibly for our commitment to the other important civil and political liberties.[106] We can clearly improve on Dicey's account by elaborating those principles of constitutionalism which give his whole endeavour sense and purpose. The limits of legislative supremacy are to be discovered, then, in that deeper constitutional morality from which the rule of law derives its strength and virtue.

[105] *Law of the Constitution*, 202.

[106] See Dworkin, *Taking Rights Seriously*, ch. 12; id., *A Matter of Principle* (Oxford, 1985), chs. 8 and 17.

Index